A VEDIC READER FOR STUDENTS

orthoepische
diaskeuase

śarkala?

A Vedic Reader for Students

by

Arthur Anthony Macdonell
M.A., Ph.D.
Boden Professor of Sanskrit
Fellow of Balliol College; Fellow of the British Academy
Fellow of The Royal Danish Academy

CONTAINING THIRTY HYMNS OF THE RIGVEDA IN THE ORIGINAL SAṂHITĀ AND PADA TEXTS, WITH TRANSLITERATION, TRANSLATION, EXPLANATORY NOTES, INTRODUCTION, VOCABULARY

Low Price Publications
2012

Arthur Anthony Macdonell (1854-1930)

First Published 1917
Reprinted in **LPP** 1990, 1996, 1997, 2012

ISBN 10: 81-7536-280-4
ISBN 13: 978-81-7536-280-2

Published by
Low Price Publications
A-6, Second Floor, Nimri Commercial Centre,
Ashok Vihar Phase-IV, Delhi 110052 (INDIA)
tel.: +91.11.27302453 fax.: +91.11.47061936
url: www.Lppindia.com e-mail: info@Lppindia.com

Printed at
Salasar Imaging Systems
Delhi

PRINTED IN INDIA

PREFACE

THIS *Reader* is meant to be a companion volume to my *Vedic Grammar for Students.* It contains thirty hymns comprising just under 300 stanzas. These hymns have been taken exclusively from the Rigveda, not only because that Veda represents the earliest and most important phase of the sacred language and literature of India, but because the addition of specimens from the later Vedic literature with their divergences in speech and thought would tend to confuse the learner beginning the study of the oldest period. All the books of the Rigveda have been drawn upon except the ninth. The reason of this exception is that, though the whole of the ninth book practically consists of hymns addressed to Soma only, the hymn which in my opinion represents that deity best occurs in another (the eighth) book. All the most important metres are represented, though no specimens of the rare and complex strophic measures could be given because none of the hymns composed in them seemed to be suitable for the *Reader*. I have also considered literary merit as far as possible in making the selection. As regards subject-matter, each of the more important deities is represented by one hymn, Agni alone by two. There are besides a few hymns of a different type. One is concerned with social life (x. 34), one with magical ideas (vii. 103), two with cosmogony (x. 90. 129), and three with eschatology (x. 14. 15. 135). The selection thus forms a brief epitome of the Rigveda, the earliest monument of Indian thought. The arrangement of the hymns follows their order in the text of the Rigveda as shown, together with their respective deities and subjects, in the table of contents (p. ix). As the latter list is so short, the name of the deity addressed in any selected hymn can be found at once, but it also appears in its alphabetical order in the General Index.

Unlike all Sanskrit and Vedic chrestomathies known to me, the present work is intended primarily for students who, while acquainted with Classical Sanskrit, are beginners of Vedic lacking the aid of a teacher with an adequate knowledge of the earliest period of the language and literature of India. It will moreover, I think, be found to contain much detailed information useful even to more advanced students. Hence difficult and obscure stanzas have never been omitted from any of the selected hymns, because the notes here afford an opportunity of illustrating the methods of critical interpretation (see, for instance, pages 36, 47, 139–40, 152, 166, 175).

In conjunction with my *Vedic Grammar for Students*, the *Reader* aims at supplying all that is required for the complete understanding of the selections without reference to any other book. Each hymn is preceded by a special introduction describing briefly the deity or the subject with which it deals. The text of every stanza is printed in three different forms. The first is the Saṃhitā text, in Devanāgarī characters, exactly as handed down by tradition, without change or emendation. But each Pāda or metrical line is printed separately so as to exhibit to the eye the versification of the stanza. Then comes on the right half of the page the traditional Pada text in which each word of the Saṃhitā text is given separately without Sandhi, and in which compounds and certain derivatives and case-forms are analysed. This is an important addition because the Pada text, as nearly contemporary in origin with the Saṃhitā text, furnishes us with the earliest interpretations, within the sphere of phonetics and word-formation, of the Ṛigveda. Next follows the transliterated Saṃhitā text, in which by the removal of vowel-contractions, the resolution of semivowels, and the replacement of a, the original metre of the Ṛigveda is restored and, by the use of punctuation, the sense is made clearer. The translation, which follows, is close, accounting for every word of the original, and is based on the critical method of interpretation. The notes furnish minute explanations of all matters concerned with grammar, metre, accent, syntax, and exegesis. The general introduction gives a concise account of the form and matter of the Rigveda, describing in outline its arrangement, its language and metre, its religion and mythology, besides the critical method here applied to the interpretation of its hymns. The vocabulary supplements the translation and notes by giving the derivation of every word and adding in brackets the most obvious cognates from the other Indo-European languages allied to Sanskrit, especially Avestic, Greek, Latin, and English. I have added a copious general Index for the purpose of enabling the student to utilize to the full the summary of Vedic philology which this book contains. Any one who has worked his way carefully through the pages of the *Reader* ought thus to have laid a solid foundation in Vedic scholarship, and to be prepared for further studies on independent lines.

Freedom from serious misprints is a matter of great importance in a book like this. Such freedom has, I trust, been achieved by the aid of my two friends, Dr. James Morison, Librarian of the Indian Institute, and my former pupil, Dr. A. Berriedale Keith, Regius Professor of Sanskrit and Comparative Philology in the University of Edinburgh. In the course of this obliging task Prof. Keith has supplied me with a number of suggestions, the adoption of which has undoubtedly improved the notes in many points of detail.

BALLIOL COLLEGE, OXFORD.
October 22, 1917.

CONTENTS

INTRODUCTION

1. Age of the Rigveda.

The Rigveda is undoubtedly the oldest literary monument of the Indo-European languages. But the exact period when the hymns were composed is a matter of conjecture. All that we can say with any approach to certainty is that the oldest of them cannot date from later than the thirteenth century B.C. This assertion is based on the following grounds. Buddhism, which began to spread in India about 500 B.C., presupposes the existence not only of the Vedas, but also of the intervening literature of the Brāhmaṇas and Upanishads. The development of language and religious thought apparent in the extensive literature of the successive phases of these two Vedic periods renders it necessary to postulate the lapse of seven or eight centuries to account for the gradual changes, linguistic, religious, social, and political, that this literature displays. On astronomical grounds, one Sanskrit scholar has (cf. p. 146) concluded that the oldest Vedic hymns date from 3000 B.C., while another puts them as far back as 6000 B.C. These calculations are based on the assumption that the early Indians possessed an exact astronomical knowledge of the sun's course such as there is no evidence, or even probability, that they actually possessed. On the other hand, the possibility of such extreme antiquity seems to be disproved by the relationship of the hymns of the Rigveda to the oldest part of the Avesta, which can hardly date earlier than from about 800 B.C. That relationship is so close that the language of the Avesta, if it were known at a stage some five centuries earlier, could scarcely have differed at all from that of the Rigveda. Hence the Indians could not have separated from the Iranians much sooner than 1300 B.C. But, according to Prof. Jacobi, the separation took place before 4500 B.C. In that case we must assume that the Iranian and the

Indian languages remained practically unchanged for the truly immense period of over 3000 years. We must thus rest content with the moderate estimate of the thirteenth century B.C. as the approximate date for the beginning of the Rigvedic period. This estimate has not been invalidated by the discovery in 1907 of the names of the Indian deities Mitra, Varuṇa, Indra, Nāsatya, in an inscription of about 1400 B.C. found in Asia Minor. For the phonetic form in which these names there appear may quite well belong to the Indo-Iranian period when the Indians and the Persians were still one people. The date of the inscription leaves two centuries for the separation of the Indians, their migration to India, and the commencement of the Vedic hymn literature in the north-west of Hindustan.

2. Origin and Growth of the Collection.

When the Indo-Aryans entered India, they brought with them a religion in which the gods were chiefly personified powers of Nature, a few of them, such as Dyaus, going back to the Indo-European, others, such as Mitra, Varuṇa, Indra, to the Indo-Iranian period. They also brought with them the cult of fire and of Soma, besides a knowledge of the art of composing religious poems in several metres, as a comparison of the Rigveda and the Avesta shows. The purpose of these ancient hymns was to propitiate the gods by praises accompanying the offering of melted butter poured on the fire and of the juice of the Soma plant placed on the sacrificial grass. The hymns which have survived in the Rigveda from the early period of the Indo-Aryan invasion were almost exclusively composed by a hereditary priesthood. They were handed down in different families by memory, not by writing, which could hardly have been introduced into India before about 700 B. C. These family groups of hymns were gradually brought together till, with successive additions, they assumed the earliest collected form of the Rigveda. Then followed the constitution of the Saṃhitā text, which appears to have taken place about 600 B.C., at the end of the period of the Brāhmaṇas, but before the Upanishads, which form appendages to those works, came into existence. The creators of the Samhitā did not in any way alter the diction of the hymns here collected together, but only applied to the text certain rules of Sandhi which prevailed in their time, and by which, in particular, vowels are either contracted or changed into semi-vowels, and a is often dropped after e and o, in such a way as constantly to obscure the metre. Soon after this work was concluded, extraordinary precautions were taken to preserve from loss or corruption the sacred text thus fixed. The earliest expedient of this kind was the formation of the Pada or 'word' text, in which all the words of the Saṃhitā text are separated and given in their original form as unaffected by the rules of Sandhi, and in which most compounds and some derivatives and inflected forms are analysed. This text, which is virtually the earliest commentary on the Rigveda, was followed by other and more complicated methods of reciting the text, and by various works called Anukramaṇīs or 'Indexes', which enumerate from the beginning to the end of the Rigveda the number of stanzas contained in each hymn, the deities, and the metres of all the stanzas of the Rigveda. Thanks to these various precautions the text of the Rigveda has been handed down for 2,500 years with a fidelity that finds no parallel in any other literature.

3. Extent and Divisions of the Rigveda.

The Rigveda consists of 1,017 or, counting eleven others of the eighth Book which are recognized as later additions, 1,028 hymns. These contain a total of about 10,600 stanzas, which give an average of ten stanzas to each hymn. The shortest hymn has only one stanza, while the longest has fifty-eight. If printed continuously like prose in Roman characters, the Saṃhitā text would fill an octavo volume of about 600 pages of thirty-three lines each. It has been calculated that in bulk the RV. is equivalent to the extant poems of Homer.

There is a twofold division of the RV. into parts. One, which is purely mechanical, is into Aṣṭakas or 'eighths' of about equal length, each of which is subdivided into eight Adhyāyas or 'lessons', while each of the latter consists of Vargas or 'groups' of five or six stanzas. The other division is into ten Maṇḍalas or 'books' (lit. 'cycles') and Sūktas or 'hymns'. The latter method is an historical one, indicating the manner in which the collection came into being. This system is now invariably followed by Western Scholars in referring to or quoting from the Rigveda.

4. Arrangement of the Rigveda.

Six of the ten books, ii to vii, are homogeneous in character. The hymns contained in each of them were, according to native Indian tradition, composed or 'seen' by poets of the same family, which handed them down as its own collection. The tradition is borne out by the internal evidence of the seers' names mentioned in the hymns, and by that of the refrains occurring in each of these books. The method of arrangement followed in the 'family books' is uniform, for each of them is similarly divided into groups addressed to different gods. On the other hand, Books i, viii, and x were not composed each by a distinct family of seers, while the groups of which they consist are constituted by being the hymns composed by different individual seers. Book ix is distinguished from the rest by all its hymns being addressed to one and the same deity, Soma, and by its groups being based not on identity of authorship, but of metre.

Family books.—In these the first group of hymns is invariably addressed to Agni, the second to Indra, and those that follow to gods of less importance. The hymns within these deity groups are arranged according to the diminishing number of stanzas contained in them. Thus in the second Book the Agni group of ten hymns begins with one of sixteen stanzas and ends with one of only six. The first hymn of the next group in the same book has twenty-one, the last only four stanzas. The entire group of the family books is, moreover, arranged according to the increasing number of the hymns in each of those books, if allowance is made for later additions. Thus the second Book has forty-three, the third sixty-two, the sixth seventy-five, and the seventh one hundred and four hymns. The homogeneity of the family books renders it highly probable that they formed the nucleus of the RV., which gradually assumed its final shape by successive additions to these books.

The earliest of these additions appears to be the second half of Book i, which, consisting of nine groups, each by a different author, was prefixed to the family books, the internal arrangement of which it follows. The eighth is like the family books as being in the main composed by members of one family, the Kaṇvas; but it differs from them in not beginning with hymns to Agni and in the prevalence of the strophic metre called Pragātha. The fact of its containing fewer hymns than the seventh book shows that it did not form a unit of the family books; but its partial resemblance to them caused it to be the first addition at the end of that collection. The first part of Book i (1–50) is in several respects like Book viii: Kaṇvas seem to have been the authors of the majority of these hymns; their favourite strophic metre is again found here; and both collections contain many similar or identical passages. There must have been some difference between the two groups, but the reason why they should have been separated by being added at the beginning and the end of an older collection has not yet been shown.

The *ninth book* was added as a consequence of the first eight being formed into a unit. It consists entirely of hymns addressed to Soma while the juice was 'clarifying' (pavamāna); on the other hand, the family books contain not a single Soma hymn, and Books i and viii together only three hymns invoking Soma in his general character. Now the hymns of Book ix were composed by authors of the same families as those of Books ii to vii, as is shown, for instance, by the appearance here of refrains peculiar to those families. Hence it is to be assumed that all the hymns to Soma Pavamāna were removed from Books i to viii, in order to form a single collection belonging to the sphere of the Udgātṛ or chanting priest, and added after Books i–viii, which were the sphere of the Hotṛ or reciting priest. The diction and recondite allusions in the hymns of this book suggest that they are later than those of the preceding books; but some of them may be early, as accompanying the Soma ritual which goes back to the Indo-Iranian period. The hymns of the first part of this book (1–60) are arranged according to the decreasing number of their stanzas, beginning with ten and ending with four. In the second part (61–114), which contains some very long hymns (one of forty-eight and another of fifty-eight stanzas), this arrangement is not followed.

The two parts also differ in metre: the hymns of the first are, excepting four stanzas, composed in Gāyatrī, while the second consists mainly of groups in other metres; thus 68–84 form a Jagatī and 87–97 a Triṣṭubh group.

The *tenth book* was the final addition. Its language and subject-matter show that it is later in origin than the other books; its authors were, moreover, clearly familiar with them. Both its position at the end of the RV. and the fact that the number of its hymns (191) is made up to that of the first book indicate its supplementary character. Its hymns were composed by a large number of seers of different families, some of which appear in other books; but the traditional attribution of authorship is of little or no value in the case of a great many hymns. In spite of its generally more modern character, it contains some hymns quite as old and poetic as the average of those in other books. These perhaps found a place here because for some reason they had been overlooked while the other collections were being formed. As regards language, we find in the tenth book earlier grammatical forms and words growing obsolete, while new words and meanings begin to emerge. As to matter, a tendency to abstract ideas and philosophical speculation, as well as the introduction of magical conceptions, such as belong to the sphere of the Atharvaveda, is here found to prevail.

5. Language.

The hymns of the RV. are composed in the earliest stage of that literary language of which the latest, or Classical Sanskrit, was stereotyped by the grammar of Pāṇini at the end of the fourth century B.C. It differs from the latter about as much as Homeric from Attic Greek. It exhibits a much greater variety of forms than Sanskrit does. Its case-forms both in nominal and pronominal inflexion are more numerous. It has more participles and gerunds. It is, however, in verbal forms that its comparative richness is most apparent. Thus the RV. very frequently uses the subjunctive, which as such has entirely died out in Sanskrit; it has twelve forms of the infinitive, while only a single one of these has survived in Sanskrit. The language of the RV. also differs from Sanskrit in its accent, which, like that of ancient Greek, is of a musical nature, depending on the pitch of the voice, and is marked throughout the hymns. This accent has in Sanskrit been changed not only to a stress accent, but has shifted its position as depending on quantity, and is no longer marked. The Vedic accent occupies a very important position in Comparative Philology, while the Sanskrit accent, being secondary, has no value of this kind.

The Sandhi of the RV. represents an earlier and a less conventional stage than that of Sanskrit. Thus the insertion of a sibilant between final n and a hard palatal or dental is in the RV. restricted to cases where it is historically justified; in Sanskrit it has become universal, being extended to cases where it has no justification. After e and o in the RV. ă is nearly always pronounced, while in Sanskrit it is invariably dropped. It may thus be affirmed with certainty that no student can understand Sanskrit historically without knowing the language of the RV.

6. Metre.

The hymns of the RV. are without exception metrical. They contain on the average ten stanzas, generally of four verses or lines, but also of three and sometimes five. The line, which is called Pāda ('quarter') and forms the metrical unit, usually consists of eight, eleven, or twelve syllables. A stanza is, as a rule, made up of lines of the same type; but some of the rarer kinds of stanza are formed by combining lines of different length. There are about fifteen metres, but only about seven of these are at all common. By far the most common are the Triṣṭubh (4 × 11 syllables), the Gāyatrī (3 × 8), and the Jagatī (4 × 12), which together furnish two-thirds of the total number of stanzas in the RV. The Vedic metres, which are the foundation of the Classical Sanskrit metres except two, have a quantitative rhythm in which short and long syllables alternate and which is of a generally iambic type. It is only the rhythm of the last four or five syllables (called the cadence) of the line that is rigidly determined, and the lines of eleven and twelve syllables have a caesura as well. In their structure the Vedic metres thus come half way between the metres of the Indo-Iranian period, in which, as the Avesta shows, the principle is the number of syllables only, and those of Classical Sanskrit, in which (except the śloka) the quantity of every single syllable in the line is fixed. Usually a hymn of the Rigveda consists of stanzas in the same metre throughout; a typical divergence from this rule is to mark the conclusion of a hymn with a stanza in a different metre. Some hymns are strophic in their construction. The strophes in them consist either of three stanzas (called tṛca) in the same simple metre, generally Gāyatrī, or of two stanzas in different mixed metres. The latter type of strophe is called Pragātha and is found chiefly in the eighth book.

7. Religion of the Rigveda.

This is concerned with the worship of gods that are largely personifications of the powers of nature. The hymns are mainly invocations of these gods, and are meant to accompany the oblation of Soma juice and the fire sacrifice of melted butter. It is thus essentially a polytheistic religion, which assumes a pantheistic colouring only in a few of its latest hymns. The gods are usually stated in the RV. to be thirty-three in number, being divided into three groups of eleven distributed in earth, air, and heaven, the three divisions of the Universe. Troops of deities, such as the Maruts, are of course not included in this number. The gods were believed to have had a beginning. But they were not thought to have all come into being at the same time; for the RV. occasionally refers to earlier gods, and certain deities are described as the offspring of others. That they were considered to have been originally mortal is implied in the statement that they acquired immortality by drinking Soma or by receiving it as a gift from Agni and Savitṛ.

The *gods* were conceived as human in appearance. Their bodily parts, which are frequently mentioned, are in many instances simply figurative illustrations of the phenomena of nature represented by them. Thus the arms of the Sun are nothing more than his rays; and the tongue and limbs of Agni merely denote his flames. Some of the gods appear equipped as warriors, especially Indra, others are described as priests, especially Agni and Bṛhaspati. All of them drive through the air in cars, drawn chiefly by steeds, but sometimes by other animals. The favourite food of men is also that of the gods.

consisting in milk, butter, grain, and the flesh of sheep, goats, and cattle. It is offered to them in the sacrifice, which is either conveyed to them in heaven by the god of fire, or which they come in their cars to partake of on the strew of grass prepared for their reception. Their favourite drink is the exhilarating juice of the Soma plant. The home of the gods is heaven, the third heaven, or the highest step of Viṣṇu, where cheered by draughts of Soma they live a life of bliss.

Attributes of the gods.—Among these the most prominent is power, for they are constantly described as great and mighty. They regulate the order of nature and vanquish the potent powers of evil. They hold sway over all creatures; no one can thwart their ordinances or live beyond the time they appoint; and the fulfilment of desires is dependent on them. They are benevolent beings who bestow prosperity on mankind; the only one in whom injurious traits appear being Rudra. They are described as 'true' and 'not deceitful', being friends and protectors of the honest and righteous, but punishing sin and guilt. Since in most cases the gods of the RV. have not yet become dissociated from the physical phenomena which they represent, their figures are indefinite in outline and deficient in individuality. Having many features, such as power, brilliance, benevolence, and wisdom in common with others, each god exhibits but very few distinctive attributes. This vagueness is further increased by the practice of invoking deities in pairs—a practice making both gods share characteristics properly belonging to one alone. When nearly every power can thus be ascribed to every god, the identification of one deity with another becomes easy. There are in fact several such identifications in the RV. The idea is even found in more than one late passage that various deities are but different forms of a single divine being. This idea, however, never developed into monotheism, for none of the regular sacrifices in the Vedic period were offered to a single god. Finally, in other late hymns of the RV. we find the deities Aditi and Prajāpati identified not only with all the gods, but with nature as well. This brings us to that pantheism which became characteristic of later Indian thought in the form of the Vedānta philosophy.

The *Vedic gods* may most conveniently be *classified* as deities of heaven, air, and earth, according to the threefold division suggested by the RV. itself. The celestial gods are Dyaus, Varuṇa, Mitra, Sūrya, Savitṛ, Pūṣan, the Aśvins, and the goddesses Uṣas, Dawn, and Rātrī, Night. The atmospheric gods are Indra, Apāṃ napāt, Rudra, the Maruts, Vāyu, Parjanya, and Āpas, the Waters. The terrestrial deities are Pṛthivī, Agni, and Soma. This *Reader* contains hymns addressed to all these gods, with detailed introductions describing their characters in the words, as far as is possible, of the RV. itself. A few quite subordinate deities are not included, partly because no entire hymn is addressed to them. Two such belong to the celestial sphere. Trita, a somewhat obscure god, who is mentioned only in detached stanzas of the RV., comes down from the Indo-Iranian period. He seems to represent the 'third' or lightning form of fire. Similar in origin to Indra, he was ousted by the latter at an early period. Mātariśvan is a divine being also referred to only in scattered stanzas of the RV. He is described as having brought down the hidden fire from heaven to men on earth, like the Prometheus of Greek mythology. Among the terrestrial deities are certain rivers that are personified and invoked in the RV. Thus the Sindhu (Indus) s celebrated as a goddess in one hymn (x. 75, 2. 4. 6), and the Vipāś (Bīas) and the Śutudrī (Sutlej), sister streams of the Panjāb, in another (iii. 33). The most important and oftenest lauded is, however, the Sarasvatī (vi. 61; vii. 95). Though the personification goes much further here than in the case of other streams, the connexion of the goddess with the river is never lost sight of in the RV.

Abstract deities.—One result of the advance of thougnt during the period of the RV. from the concrete towards the abstract was the rise of abstract deities. The earlier and more numerous class of these seems to have started from epithets which were applicable to one or more older deities, but which came to acquire an independent value as the want of a god exercising the particular activity in question began to be felt. We find here names denoting either an agent (formed with the suffix tṛ or tar), such as Dhātṛ 'Creator', or an attribute, such as Prajāpati, 'Lord of Creatures'. Thus Dhātṛ, otherwise an epithet of Indra, appears also as an independent deity who creates heaven and earth, sun and moon. More rarely occur Vidhātṛ, the 'Disposer', Dhartṛ, the 'Supporter', Trātṛ, the

'Protector', and Netṛ, the 'Leader'. The only agent god mentioned at all frequently in the RV. is Tvaṣṭṛ, the 'Artificer', though no entire hymn is addressed to him. He is the most skilful of workmen, having among other things fashioned the bolt of Indra and a new drinking-cup for the gods. He is a guardian of Soma, which is called the 'food of Tvaṣṭṛ', and which Indra drinks in Tvaṣṭṛ's house. He is the father of Saraṇyū, wife of Vivasvant and mother of the primaeval twins Yama and Yamī. The name of the solar deity Savitṛ, the 'Stimulator', belongs to this class of agent gods (cf. p. 11).

There are a few other abstract deities whose names were originally epithets of older gods, but now become epithets of the supreme god who was being evolved at the end of the Rigvedic period. These appellations, compound in form, are of rare and late occurrence. The most important is Prajāpati, 'Lord of Creatures'. Originally an epithet of such gods as Savitṛ and Soma, this name is employed in a late verse of the tenth book to designate a distinct deity in the character of a Creator. Similarly, the epithet Viśvakarman, 'all-creating', appears as the name of an independent deity to whom two hymns (x. 81. 82) are addressed. Hiraṇyagarbha, the 'Golden Germ', once occurs as the name of the supreme god described as the 'one lord of all that exists'. In one curious instance it is possible to watch the rise of an abstract deity of this type. The refrain of a late hymn of the RV. (x. 121) is **kásmai devā́ya havíṣā vidhema**? 'to what god should we pay worship with oblation?' This led to the word **ká**, 'who?' being used in the later Vedic literature as an independent name, Ka, of the supreme god. The only abstract deity of this type occurring in the oldest as well as the latest parts of the RV. is Bṛhaspati (p. 83).

The second and smaller class of abstract deities comprises personifications of abstract nouns. There are seven or eight of these occurring in the tenth book. Two hymns (83. 84) are addressed to Manyu, 'Wrath', and one (x. 151) to Śraddhā, 'Faith'. Anumati, 'Favour (of the gods)', Aramati, 'Devotion', Sūnṛtā, 'Bounty', Asunīti, 'Spirit-life', and Nirṛti, 'Decease', occur only in a few isolated passages.

A purely abstract deity, often incidentally celebrated throughout the RV. is A-diti, 'Liberation', 'Freedom' (lit. 'un-binding'), whose main characteristic is the power of delivering from the bonds of physical suffering and moral guilt. She, however, occupies a unique position among the abstract deities, owing to the peculiar way in which the personification seems to have arisen. She is the mother of the small group of deities called Ādityas, often styled 'sons of Aditi'. This expression at first most probably meant nothing more than 'sons of liberation', according to an idiom common in the RV. and elsewhere. The word was then personified, with the curious result that the mother is mythologically younger than some at least of her sons, who (for instance Mitra) date from the Indo-Iranian period. The goddess Diti, named only three times in the RV., probably came into being as an antithesis to Aditi, with whom she is twice mentioned.

Goddesses play an insignificant part in the RV. The only one of importance is Uṣas (p. 92). Next come Sarasvatī, celebrated in two whole hymns (vi. 61 ; vii. 95) as well as parts of others, and Vāc, 'Speech' (x. 71. 125). With one hymn each are addressed Pṛthivī, 'Earth' (v. 84), Rātrī, 'Night' (x. 127, p. 203), and Araṇyānī, 'Goddess of the Forest' (x. 146). Others are only sporadically mentioned. The wives of the great gods are still more insignificant, being mere names formed from those of their consorts, and altogether lacking in individuality: such are Agnāyī, Indrāṇī, Varuṇānī, spouses of Agni, Indra, and Varuṇa respectively.

Dual Divinities.—A peculiar feature of the religion of the RV. is the invocation of pairs of deities whose names are combined as compounds, each member of which is in the dual. About a dozen such pairs are celebrated in entire hymns, and about a dozen more in detached stanzas. By far the largest number of hymns is addressed to the couple Mitrā-Varuṇā, though the names most frequently found as dual compounds are those of Dyāvā-pṛthivī, 'Heaven and Earth' (p. 36). The latter pair, having been associated as universal parents from the Indo-European period onwards, in all probability furnished the analogy for this dual type.

Groups of Deities.—There are also a few more or less definite groups of deities, generally associated with some particular god. The Maruts (p. 21), who attend on Indra, are the most numerous group. The smaller group of the Ādityas, of whom Varuṇa is the chief, is constantly mentioned in company with their mother Aditi. Their number is stated in the RV. to be seven or, with the addition of Mārtāṇḍa, eight. One passage (ii. 27, 1) enumerates six of them, Mitra, Aryaman, Bhaga, Varuṇa, Dakṣa, Aṃśa: Sūrya was probably regarded as the seventh. A much less important group, without individual names or definite number, is that of the Vasus, whose leader is generally Indra. There are, finally, the Viśve devās (p. 147), who, invoked in many hymns, form a comprehensive group, which in spite of its name is, strange to say, sometimes conceived as a narrower group associated with others like the Vasus and Ādityas.

Lesser Divinities.—Besides the higher gods, a number of lesser divine powers are known to the RV. The most prominent of these are the Ṛbhus, who are celebrated in eleven hymns. They are a deft-handed trio, who by their marvellous skill acquired the rank of deities. Among their five main feats of dexterity the greatest consisted in transforming the bowl of Tvaṣṭṛ into four shining cups. The bowl and the cups have been variously interpreted as the moon with its four phases or the year with its seasons. The Ṛbhus further exhibited their skill in renewing the youth of their parents, by whom Heaven and Earth seem to have been meant.

Occasional mention is made in the RV. of an Apsaras, a celestial water-nymph, the spouse of a corresponding genius named Gandharva. In a few passages more Apsarases than one are spoken of; but the only one mentioned by name is Urvaśī. Gandharva is in the RV. a single being (like the Gandarewa of the Avesta), who dwells in the aerial sphere, guards the celestial Soma, and is (as in the Avesta) connected with the waters.

There are, lastly, a few divinities of the tutelary order, guardians watching over the welfare of house or field. Such is the rarely mentioned Vāstoṣpati, 'Lord of the Dwelling', who is invoked to grant a favourable entry, to remove disease, and to bestow protection and prosperity. Kṣetrasya pati, 'Lord of the Field', is besought to grant cattle and horses and to confer welfare. Sītā, the 'Furrow', is once invoked to dispense crops and rich blessings.

In addition to the great phenomena of nature, various features of the earth's surface as well as artificial objects are to be found deified in the RV. Thus besides Rivers and Waters (p. 115), already mentioned as terrestrial goddesses, mountains are often addressed as divinities, but only along with other natural objects, or in association with gods. Plants are regarded as divine powers, one entire hymn (x. 97) being devoted to their praise, chiefly with reference to their healing properties. Sacrificial implements, moreover, are deified. The most important of these is the sacrificial post which is praised and invoked in a whole hymn (iii. 8). The sacrificial grass (**barhis**) and the Divine Doors (**dvāro devīḥ**), which lead to the place of sacrifice, are addressed as goddesses. The pressing stones (**grāvāṇas**) are invoked as deities in three hymns (x. 76. 94. 175): spoken of as immortal, unaging, mightier than heaven, they are besought to drive away demons and destruction. The Mortar and Pestle used in pounding the Soma plant are also invoked in the RV. (i. 28, 5. 6). Weapons, finally, are sometimes deified: armour, bow, quiver, arrows, and drum being addressed in one of the hymns (vi. 75).

The Demons often mentioned in the hymns are of two kinds. The higher and more powerful class are the aerial foes of the gods. These are seldom called **asura** in the RV., where in the older parts that word means a divine being, like *ahura* in the Avesta (cf. p. 134). The term **dāsa** or **dasyu**, properly the name of the dark aborigines, is frequently used in the sense of fiend to designate the aerial demons. The conflict is regularly one between a single god and a single demon, as exemplified by Indra and Vṛtra. The latter is by far the most frequently mentioned. His mother being called Dānu, he is sometimes alluded to by the metronymic term Dānava. Another powerful demon is Vala, the personified cave of the cows, which he guards, and which are set free by Indra and his allies, notably the Aṅgirases. Other demon adversaries of Indra are Arbuda, described as a wily beast, whose cows Indra drove out; Viśvarūpa, son of Tvaṣṭṛ, a three-headed demon slain by both Trita and Indra, who seize his cows; and Svarbhānu, who eclipses the sun. There are several other individual demons, generally described as Dāsas and slain by Indra. A group of demons are the Paṇis ('niggards'), primarily foes of Indra, who, with the aid of the dog Saramā, tracks and releases the cows hidden by them.

The second or lower class of demons are terrestrial goblins, enemies of men. By far the most common generic name for them is Rakṣas. They are nearly always mentioned in connexion with some god who destroys them. The much less common term Yātu or Yātudhāna (primarily 'sorcerer') alternates with Rakṣas, and perhaps expresses a species. A class of demons scarcely referred to in the RV., but often mentioned in the later Vedas, are the Piśācas, eaters of raw flesh or of corpses.

Not more than thirty hymns are concerned with subjects other than the worship of gods or deified objects. About a dozen of these, almost entirely confined to the tenth book, deal with magical practices, which properly belong to the sphere of the Atharvaveda. Their contents are augury (ii. 42. 43) or spells directed against poisonous vermin (i. 191) or disease (x. 163), against a demon destructive of children (x. 162), or enemies (x. 166), or rival wives (x. 145). A few are incantations to preserve life (x. 58. 60), or to induce sleep (v. 55), or to procure offspring (x. 183); while one is a panegyric of frogs as magical bringers of rain (vii. 103, p. 141).

8. Secular Matter in the Rigveda.

Secular hymns.—Hardly a score of the hymns are secular poems. These are especially valuable as throwing direct light on the earliest thought and civilization of India. One of the most noteworthy of them is the long wedding hymn (x. 85). There are also five funeral hymns (x. 14–18). Four of these are addressed to deities concerned with the future life; the last, however, is quite secular in tone, and gives more information than any of the rest about the funeral customs of early Vedic India (cf. p. 164).

Mythological dialogues.—Besides several mythological dialogues in which the speakers are divine beings (iv. 62; x. 51. 52. 86. 108), there are two in which both agents are human. One is a somewhat obscure colloquy (x. 95) between a mortal lover Purūravas and the celestial nymph Urvaśī, who is on the point of forsaking him. It is the earliest form of the story which much more than a thousand years later formed the subject of Kālidāsa's drama Vikramorvaśī. The other (x. 10) is a dialogue between Yama and Yamī, the twin parents of the human race. This group of hymns has a special literary interest as foreshadowing the dramatic works of a later age.

Didactic hymns.—Four hymns are of a didactic character. One of these (x. 34) is a striking poem, being a monologue in which a gambler laments the misery he has brought on himself and his home by his inability to resist the attraction of the dice. The rest which describe the various ways in which men follow gain (ix. 112), or praise wise speech (x. 71), or the value of good deeds (x. 117), anticipate the sententious poetry for which post-Vedic literature is noted.

Riddles.—Two of the hymns consist of riddles. One of these (viii. 29, p. 147) describes various gods without mentioning their names. More elaborate and obscure is a long poem of fifty-two stanzas (i. 164), in which a number of enigmas, largely connected with the sun, are propounded in mystical and symbolic language. Thus the wheel of order with twelve spokes, revolving round the heavens, and containing within it in couples 720 sons, means the year with its twelve months and 360 days and 360 nights.

Cosmogonic hymns.—About half a dozen hymns consist of speculations on the origin of the world through the agency of a Creator (called by various names) as distinct from any of the ordinary gods. One of them (x. 129, p. 207), which describes the world as due to the development of the existent (sat) from the non-existent (a-sat), is particularly interesting as the starting-point of the evolutional philosophy which in later times assumed shape in the Sāṅkhya system.

A semi-historical character attaches to one complete hymn (i. 126) and to appendages of 3 to 5 stanzas attached to over thirty others, which are called Dānastutis, or 'praises of gifts'. These are panegyrics of liberal patrons on behalf of whom the seers composed their hymns. They yield incidental genealogical information about the poets and their employers, as well as about the names and the habitat of the Vedic tribes. They are late in date, appearing chiefly in the first and tenth, as well as among the supplementary hymns of the eighth book.

Geographical data.—From the geographical data of the RV., especially the numerous rivers there mentioned, it is to be inferred that the Indo-Aryan tribes when the hymns were composed occupied the territory roughly corresponding to the north-west Frontier Province, and the Panjāb of to-day. The references to flora and fauna bear out this conclusion.

The *historical data* of the hymns show that the Indo-Aryans were still engaged in war with the aborigines, many victories over these foes being mentioned. That they were still moving forward as conquerors is indicated by references to rivers as obstacles to advance. Though divided into many tribes, they were conscious of religious and racial unity, contrasting the aborigines with themselves by calling them non-sacrificers and unbelievers, as well as 'black-skins' and the 'Dāsa colour' as opposed to the 'Āryan colour'.

Incidental references scattered throughout the hymns supply a good deal of information about the social conditions of the time. Thus it is clear that the family, with the father at its head, was the basis of society, and that women held a freer and more honoured position than in later times. Various crimes are mentioned, robbery, especially of cattle, apparently being the commonest. Debt, chiefly as a result of gambling, was known. Clothing consisted usually of an upper and a lower garment, which were made of sheep's wool. Bracelets, anklets, necklaces, and earrings were worn as ornaments. Men usually grew beards, but sometimes shaved. Food mainly consisted of milk, clarified butter, grain, vegetables, and fruit. Meat was eaten only when animals were sacrificed. The commonest kind appears to have been beef, as bulls were the chief offerings to the gods. Two kinds of spirituous liquor were made: Soma was drunk at religious ceremonies only, while Surā, extracted from some kind of grain, was used on ordinary occasions.

Occupations.—One of the chief occupations of the Indo-Aryan was warfare. He fought either on foot or from a chariot, but there is no evidence to show that he ever did so on horseback. The ordinary weapons were bows and arrows, but spears and axes were also used. Cattle-breeding appears to have been the main source of livelihood, cows being the chief objects of desire in prayers to the gods. But agriculture was also practised to some extent: fields were furrowed with a plough drawn by bulls; corn was cut with sickles, being then threshed and winnowed. Wild animals were trapped and snared, or hunted with bows and arrows, occasionally with the aid of dogs. Boats propelled by paddles were employed, as it seems mainly for the purpose of crossing rivers. Trade was known only in the form of barter, the cow representing the unit of value in exchange. Certain trades and crafts already existed, though doubtless in a rudimentary stage. The occupations of the wheelwright and the carpenter were combined. The smith melted ore in a forge, and made kettles and other vessels of metal. The tanner prepared the skins of animals. Women plaited mats of grass or reeds, sewed, and especially wove, but whether they ever did so professionally is uncertain.

Amusements.—Among these chariot-racing was the favourite. The most popular social recreation was playing with dice (cp. p. 186). Dancing was also practised, chiefly by women. The people were fond of music, the instruments used being the drum (dundubhi), the flute (vāṇa), and the lute (vīṇā). Singing is also mentioned.

9. Literary merit of the Rigveda.

The diction of the hymns is on the whole natural and simple, free from the use of compounds of more than two members. Considering their great antiquity, the hymns are composed with a remarkable degree of metrical skill and command of language. But as they were produced by a sacerdotal class and were generally intended to accompany a ritual no longer primitive, their poetry is often impaired by constant sacrificial allusions. This is especially noticeable in the hymns addressed to the two ritual deities Agni and Soma, where the thought becomes affected by conceits and obscured by mysticism. Nevertheless the RV. contains much genuine poetry. As the gods are mostly connected with natural phenomena, the praises addressed to them give rise to much beautiful and even noble imagery. The degree of literary merit in different hymns naturally varies a good deal, but the average is remarkably high. The most poetical hymns are those addressed to Dawn, equal if not superior in beauty to the religious lyrics of any other literature. Some of the hymns to Indra show much graphic power in describing his conflict with the demon Vṛtra. The hymns to the Maruts, or Storm gods, often depict with vigorous imagery the phenomena of thunder and lightning, and the mighty onset of the wind. One hymn to Parjanya (v. 83) paints the devastating effects of the rain-storm with great vividness. The hymns in praise of Varuṇa describe the various aspects of his sway as moral ruler of the world in an exalted strain of poetry. Some of the mythological dialogues set forth the situation with much beauty of language; for example, the colloquy between Indra's messenger Saramā and the demons who stole the cows (x. 108), and that between the primaeval twins Yama and Yamī (x. 10). The Gambler's lament (x. 34) is a fine specimen of pathetic poetry. One of the funeral hymns (x. 18) expresses ideas connected with death in language of impressive and solemn beauty. One of the cosmogonic hymns (x. 129) illustrates how philosophical speculation can be clothed in poetry of no mean order.

10. Interpretation.

In dealing with the hymns of the RV. the important question arises, to what extent are we able to understand their real sense, considering that they have come down to us as an isolated relic from the remotest period of Indian literature? The reply, stated generally, is that, as a result of the labours of Vedic scholars, the meaning of a considerable proportion of the RV. is clear, but of the remainder many hymns and a great many single stanzas or passages are still obscure or unintelligible. This was already the case in the time of Yāska, the author of the Nirukta, the oldest extant commentary (*c.* 500 B.C.) on about 600 detached stanzas of the RV.; for he quotes one of his predecessors, Kautsa, as saying that the Vedic hymns were obscure, unmeaning, and mutually contradictory.

In the earlier period of Vedic studies, commencing about the middle of the nineteenth century, the traditional method, which follows the great commentary of Sāyaṇa (fourteenth century A.C.), and is represented by the translation of the RV., begun by H. H. Wilson in 1850, was considered adequate. It has since been proved that, though the native Indian commentators are invaluable guides in explaining the theological and ritual texts of the Brāhmaṇas and Sūtras, with the atmosphere of which they were familiar, they did not possess a continuous tradition from the time when the Vedic hymns were composed. That the gap between the poets and the interpreters even earlier than Yāska must have been considerable, is shown by the divergences of opinion among his predecessors as quoted by him. Thus one of these, Aurṇavābha, interprets nāsatyau, an epithet of the Aśvins, as 'true, not false', another Āgrāyaṇa, as 'leaders of truth' (**satyasya praṇetārau**), while Yāska himself thinks it may mean 'nose-born' (**nāsikā-prabhavau**)! Yāska, moreover, mentions several different schools of interpretation, each of which explained difficulties in accordance with its own particular theory. Yāska's own interpretations, which in all cases of doubt are based on etymology, are evidently often merely conjectural, for he frequently gives several alternative explanations of a word. Thus he explains the epithet **jātá-vedas** in as many as five different ways. Yet he must have had more and better means of ascertaining the sense of various obscure words than Sāyaṇa who lived nearly 2,000 years later. Sāyaṇa's interpretations, however, sometimes differ from those of Yāska. Hence either Yāska is wrong or Sāyaṇa does not follow the tradition. Again, Sāyaṇa often gives several inconsistent explanations of a word in interpreting the same passage or in commenting on the same word in different passages. Thus **ásura**, 'divine being', is variously rendered by him as 'expeller of foes', 'giver of strength', 'giver of life', 'hurler away of what is undesired', 'giver of breath or water', 'thrower of oblations, priest', 'taker away of breath', 'expeller of water, Parjanya', 'impeller', 'strong', 'wise', and 'rain-water' or 'a water-discharging cloud'! In short it is clear from a careful examination of their comments that neither Yāska nor Sāyaṇa possessed any certain knowledge about a large number of words in the RV. Hence their interpretations can be treated as decisive only if they are borne out by probability, by the context, and by parallel passages.

For the traditional method Roth, the founder of Vedic philology, substituted the critical method of interpreting the difficult parts of the RV. from internal evidence by the minute comparison of all words parallel in form and matter, while taking into consideration context, grammar, and etymology, without ignoring either the help supplied by the historical study of the Vedic language in its connexion with Sanskrit or the outside evidence derived from the Avesta and from Comparative Philology. In the application of his method Roth attached too much weight to etymological considerations, while he undervalued the evidence of native tradition. On the other hand, a reaction arose which, in emphasizing the purely Indian character of the Vedic hymns, connects the interpretation of them too closely with the literature of the post-Vedic period and the much more advanced civilization there described. It is important to note that the critical scholar has at his disposal not only all the material that was open to the traditional interpreters, and to which he is moreover able to apply the comparative and historical methods of research, but also possesses over and above many valuable aids that were unknown to the traditional school—the Avesta, Comparative Philology, Comparative Religion and Mythology, and Ethnology. The student will find in the notes of the *Reader* many exemplifications of the usefulness of these aids to interpretation. There is good reason to hope from the results already achieved that steady adherence to the critical method, by admitting all available evidence and by avoiding onesidedness in its application, will eventually clear up a large proportion of the obscurities and difficulties that still confront the interpreter of the Rigveda.

ERRATA

P. 14, line 27, for śitipádo read śitipādŏ.
P. 28, line 1, read नर्यपांसि.
P. 31, line 29, and p. 46, l. 29, for yó read yŏ́.
P. 48, head-line, for i. 12, 4 read ii. 12, 4.
P. 51, line 31, for yó read yŏ́.
P. 60, line 13, for no read nŏ.
P. 69, line 2, for ṭáṃ read ṭaṃ.
Pp. 68, 70, 71, 75, head-lines, for APAṂ read APAṂ.
P. 118, head-line, for APAS read ĀPAS.
P. 125, line 12, for ṿíśvácakṣās read viśvácakṣās.
P. 128, line 3, for nū̃ read nū̃́.
P. 139, line 14, for vibhídako read vibhídakŏ.
P. 142, last line, and p. 143, line 11, for anyó read anyŏ́.
P. 144, head-line, for MAṆḌŪKAS read MAṆḌŪKAS.
P. 179, line 26, for té read tĕ́.
P. 184, line 17, for tĕ read tĕ́.
P. 224, head-line and line 1, for abhīti read abhītí.

AGNI

As the personification of the sacrificial fire, Agni is second in importance to Indra (ii. 12) only, being addressed in at least 200 hymns. The anthropomorphism of his physical appearance is only rudimentary, and is connected chiefly with the sacrificial aspect of fire. Thus he is butter-backed, flame-haired, and has a tawny beard, sharp jaws, and golden teeth. Mention is often made of his tongue, with which the gods eat the oblation. With a burning head he faces in all directions.

He is compared with various animals: he resembles a bull that bellows, and has horns which he sharpens; when born he is often called a calf; he is kindled like a horse that brings the gods, and is yoked to convey the sacrifice to them. He is also a divine bird; he is the eagle of the sky; as dwelling in the waters he is like a goose; he is winged, and he takes possession of the wood as a bird perches on a tree.

Wood or ghee is his food, melted butter his beverage; and he is nourished three times a day. He is the mouth by which the gods eat the sacrifice; and his flames are spoons with which he besprinkles the gods; but he is also asked to consume the offerings himself. He is sometimes, though then nearly always with other gods, invited to drink the Soma juice.

His brightness is much dwelt upon: he shines like the sun; his lustre is like the rays of the dawn and the sun, and like the lightnings of the rain-cloud. He shines even at night, and dispels the darkness with his beams. On the other hand, his path is black when he invades the forests and shaves the earth as a barber a beard. His flames are like roaring waves, and his sound is like the thunder of heaven. His red smoke rises up to the firmament; like the erector of a post he supports the sky with his smoke. 'Smoke-bannered' (dhūmá-ketu) is his frequent and exclusive epithet.

He has a shining, golden, lightning car, drawn by two or more ruddy and tawny steeds. He is a charioteer of the sacrifice, and with his steeds he brings the gods on his car.

He is the child of Heaven (Dyáus), and is often called the son of Heaven and Earth (i. 160). He is also the offspring of the waters. The gods generated him as a light for the Āryan or for man, and placed him among men. Indra is called Agni's twin brother, and is more closely associated with him than any other god.

The mythology of Agni, apart from his sacrificial activity, is mainly concerned with his various births, forms, and abodes. Mention is often made of his daily production from the two kindling sticks (aráṇīs), which are his parents or his mothers. From the dry wood Agni is born living; as soon as born the child devours his parents. By the ten maidens that produce him are meant the ten fingers of the kindler. Owing to the force required to kindle Agni he is often called 'son of strength' (sáhasaḥ sūnúḥ). Being produced every morning he is young; at the same time no sacrificer is older than Agni, for he conducted the first sacrifice. Again, Agni's origin in the aerial waters is often referred to: he is an embryo of the waters; he is kindled in the waters; he is a bull that has grown in the lap of the waters. As the 'son of Waters' (ii. 35) he has become a separate deity. He is also sometimes conceived as latent in terrestrial waters. This notion of Agni in the waters is a prominent one in the RV. Thirdly, a celestial origin of Agni is often mentioned: he is born in the highest heaven, and was brought down from heaven by Mātariśvan, the Indian Prometheus; and the acquisition of fire by man is regarded as a gift of the gods as well as a production of Mātariśvan. The Sun (vii. 63) is further regarded as a form of Agni. Thus Agni is the light of heaven in the bright sky; he was born on the other side of the air and sees all things; he is born as the sun rising in the morning. Hence Agni comes to have a triple character. His births are three or threefold; the gods made him threefold; he is threefold light; he has three heads, three bodies, three stations. This threefold nature of Agni is clearly recognized in the RV., and represents the earliest Indian trinity.

The universe being also regarded as divided into the two divisions of heaven and earth, Agni is sometimes said to have two origins, and indeed exclusively bears the epithet dvi-jánman *having two births*. As being kindled in numerous dwellings Agni is also said to have many births.

Agni is more closely associated with human life than any other deity. He is the only god called gṛhá-pati *lord of the house*, and is constantly spoken of as a guest (átithi) in human dwellings. He is an immortal who has taken up his abode among mortals. Thus he comes to be termed the nearest kinsman of men. He is oftenest described as a father, sometimes also as a brother or even as a son of his worshippers. He both takes the offerings of men to the gods and brings the gods to the sacrifice. He is thus characteristically a messenger (dūtá) appointed by gods and by men to be an 'oblation-bearer'.

As the centre of the sacrifice he comes to be celebrated as the divine counterpart of the earthly priesthood. Hence he is often called priest (ṛtvíj, vípra), domestic priest (puróhita), and more often than by any other name invoking priest (hótṛ), also officiating priest (adhvaryú) and praying priest (brahmán). His priesthood is the most salient feature of his character; he is in fact the great priest, as Indra is the great warrior.

Agni's wisdom is often dwelt upon. As knowing all the details of sacrifice he is wise and all-knowing, and is exclusively called **jātá-vedas** *he who knows all created beings*.

He is a great benefactor of his worshippers, protecting and delivering them, and bestowing on them all kinds of boons, but pre-eminently domestic welfare, offspring, and prosperity.

His greatness is often lauded, and is once even said to surpass that of the other gods. His cosmic and creative powers are also frequently praised.

From the ordinary sacrificial Agni who conveys the offering (**havya-váhana**) is distinguished his corpse-devouring (**kravyád**) form that burns the body on the funeral pyre (x. 14). Another function of Agni is to burn and dispel evil spirits and hostile magic.

The sacrificial fire was already in the Indo-Iranian period the centre of a developed ritual, and was personified and worshipped as a mighty, wise, and beneficent god. It seems to have been an Indo-European institution also, since the Italians and Greeks, as well as the Indians and Iranians, had the custom of offering gifts to the gods in fire. But whether it was already personified in that remote period is a matter of conjecture.

The name of Agni (Lat. *igni-s*, Slavonic *ogni*) is Indo-European, and may originally have meant the 'agile' as derived from the root **ag** *to drive* (Lat. *ago*, Gk. ἄγω, Skt. **ájāmi**).

Rigveda i. 1.

The metre of this hymn is **Gāyatrī** (p. 438) in which nearly one-fourth of the RV. is composed. It consists of three octosyllabic verses identical in construction, each of which, when normal, ends with two iambics (⏑ – ⏑ ⏓). The first two verses are in the Saṃhitā treated as a hemistich; but there is no reason to suppose that in the original text the second verse was more sharply divided from the third than from the first.

१ अग्निमीळे पुरोहितं यज्ञस्य देवमृत्विजम् । होतारं रत्नधातमम् ॥	अग्निम् । ईळे । पुरःऽहितम् । यज्ञस्य । देवम् । ऋत्विजम् । होतारम् । रत्नऽधातमम् ॥
1 **Agním īḷe puróhitam,** **yajñásya devám ṛtvíjam,** **hotāram ratnadhátamam.**	*I magnify Agni the domestic priest,* *the divine ministrant of the sacrifice,* *the invoker, best bestower of treasure*

On the marking of the accent in the RV. see p. 448, 2. The verb **īḷe** (1. s. pr. Ā. of **īḍ**: **ḷ** for **ḍ** between vowels, p. 3, f. n. 2) has no Udātta because it is in a principal sentence and does not begin a sentence or Pada (p. 466, 19 A.); its first syllable bears the dependent Svarita which follows the Udātta of the preceding syllable (p. 448, 1). **puró-hitam** has the accent of a Karmadhāraya when the last member is a pp. (p. 456, top). **yajñásya** is to be taken with **ṛtvíjam** (not with **puróhitam** according to Sāyaṇa), both because the genitive normally precedes the noun that governs it (p. 285 *e*), and because it is in the same Pāda; cp. RV. viii. 38, 1; **yajñásya hí sthá ṛtvíjā** *ye two* (Indra-Agni) *are ministrants of the sacrifice.* The dependent Svarita which the first syllable of **ṛtvíjam** would otherwise bear (like **īḷe**), disappears because this syllable must be marked with the Anudātta that precedes an Udātta. **ṛtv-íj** though etymologically a compound (**ṛtu + ij = yaj**) is not analysed in the Pada text, because the second member does not occur as an independent word; cp. x. 2, 5: **agnír devā́m̐ ṛtuśó yajāti** *may Agni sacrifice to the gods according to the seasons.* **ratna-dhā́-tama** (with the ordinary Tp. accent: p. 456, 2): the Pada text never divides a cd. into more than two members. The suffix **tama**, which the Pada treats as equivalent to a final member of a cd., is here regarded as forming a unit with **dhā**; cp. on the other hand **virá-vat + tama** in 3 c and **citrá-śravas + tama** in 5 b. **rátna** never means *jewel* in the RV.

२ अग्निः पूर्वेभिर्ऋषिभिर्	अग्निः । पूर्वेभिः । ऋषिऽभिः ।
ईड्यो नूतनैरुत ।	ईड्यः । नूतनैः । उत ।
स देवाँ एह वक्षति ॥	सः । देवान् । आ । इह । वक्षति ॥

2 **Agníḥ pū́rvebhir ṛ́ṣibhir**	*Agni to be magnified by past and*
īḷio nū́tanair utá,	*present seers, may he conduct the gods*
sá devā́m̐ éhá vakṣati.	*here.*

ṛ́ṣibhis: The declensional endings **bhyām, bhis, bhyas, su** are in the Pada text treated like final members of compounds and separated, but not when the pure stem, as in the **a** dec., is modified in the preceding member; hence **pū́rvebhis** (p. 77, note 9) is not analysed. **ī́ḍyas**: to be read as **ī́ḷias** (p. 16, 2 *d*). **nū́tanais**: note that the two forms of the inst. pl. of the a dec. in **ais** and **ebhis** constantly occur in the same stanza. **sá** (49) being unmarked at the beginning of a Pāda, has the Udātta; the dependent Svarita of the following syllable disappears before the Anudātta required to indicate the following Udātta of **vā́m̐** (Sandhi, see 39). This Anudātta and the Svarita of **vàkṣati** show that all the intervening unmarked syllables **vā́m̐ éhá** have the Udātta. All the unaccented syllables following a Svarita (till the Anudātta preceding an Udātta) remain unmarked; hence the last two syllables of **vàkṣati** are unmarked; but in the Pada text every syllable of a word which has no Udātta is marked with the Anudātta; thus **vakṣati**. The latter word is the s ao. sb. of **vah** *carry* for **vah-s-a-ti** (143, 2; 69 *a*). In **á ihá vakṣati**, the prp. because it is in a principal sentence is uncompounded and accented (p. 463, 20), besides as very often being separated from the verb by another word. The verb **vah** is constantly connected with Agni, who conveys the sacrifice and brings the gods. Syntactically the first hemistich is equivalent to a rel. clause, **sá** being the correlative (cp. p. 294 *a*). The gerundive **ī́ḍyas** strictly speaking belongs in sense to **nū́tanais**, but is loosely construed with **pū́rvebhis** also, meaning 'is to be magnified by present seers and (was) to be magnified by past seers'. The pcl. **utá** *and* (p. 222) is always significant in the RV.

३ अ॒ग्निना॑ र॒यिम॑श्नव॒त्
पोष॑मे॒व दि॒वेदि॑वे ।
य॒शसं॑ वी॒रव॑त्तमम् ॥

अ॒ग्निना॑ । र॒यिम् । अ॒श्न॒व॒त् ।
पोष॑म् । ए॒व । दि॒वेऽदि॑वे ।
य॒शस॑म् । वी॒रव॑त्ऽतमम् ॥

3 **Agnínā rayím aśnavat**
póṣam evá divé-dive,
yaśásam vīrávattamam.

Through Agni may one obtain wealth day by day (and) *prosperity, glorious* (and) *most abounding in heroes.*

aśnav-a-t: sb. pr. of **amś** *attain*, 3. s. ind. pr. **aśnóti** (cp. p. 134); the prn. 'he' inherent in the 3. s. of the vb. is here used in the indefinite sense of 'one', as so often in the 3. s. op. in classical Sanskrit. **rayím, póṣam:** co-ordinate nouns are constantly used in the RV. without the conjunction **ca**. **divé-dive:** this is one of the numerous itv. compounds found in the RV., which are always accented on the first member only, and are analysed in the Pada text like other compounds (189 C *a*). **yaśásam**: this is one of the few adjectives ending in **-ás** that occur in the RV.; the corresponding n. substantives are accented on the first syllable, as **yáś-as** *fame* (83, 2 *a*; 182, p. 256). **vīrá-vat-tamam**: both the suffix **vant** (p. 264, cp. 185 *a*) and the superlative suffix **tama** are treated in the Pada text like final members of a cd.; **vīrávant** being here regarded as a unit, it is treated as the first member in the analysis (cp. note on **ratna-dhā́tama** in 1 c). In these two adjectives we again have co-ordination without the connecting pcl. **ca**. Their exact meaning is 'causing fame' and 'produced by many heroic sons', fame and brave fighters being constantly prayed for in the hymns.

४ अग्ने॒ यं य॒ज्ञम॑ध्व॒रं	अग्ने॑ । यम् । य॒ज्ञम् । अ॒ध्व॒रम् ।
वि॒श्वतः॑ परि॒भूरसि॑ ।	वि॒श्वतः॑ । प॒रि॒ऽभूः । असि॑ ।
स इद्दे॒वेषु॑ गच्छति ॥	सः । इत् । दे॒वेषु॑ । ग॒च्छ॒ति॒ ॥

4 **Ágne, yáṃ yajñám adhvaráṃ**	*O Agni, the worship and sacrifice*
viśvátaḥ paribhū́r ási,	*that thou encompassest on every side,*
sá íd devéṣu gachati.	*that same goes to the gods.*

yajñám adhvarám: again co-ordination without **ca**; the former has a wider sense = *worship* (prayer and offering); the latter = *sacrificial act*. **viśvá-tas**: the prn. adj. **víśva** usually shifts its accent to the second syllable before adv. suffixes and as first member of a cd. (p. 454, 10). **ási** is accented as the vb. of a subordinate clause (p. 467, B). **sá íd**: all successively unmarked syllables at the beginning of a hemistich have the Udātta (p. 449, 2). On the particle **íd** see p. 218. **devéṣu**: the loc. of the goal reached (p. 325, 1 *b*); the acc., which might be used, would rather express the goal to which the motion is directed. **gachati**: as the vb. of a principal sentence has no Udātta (19 A); nor has it any accent mark in the Saṃhitā text because all unaccented syllables following a dependent Svarita remain unmarked; on the other hand, all the syllables of an unaccented word are marked with the Anudātta in the Pada text (cp. note on 2 d). The first syllable of **gachati** is long by position (p. 437, *a* 3).

५ अग्निहोंता कविक्रतुः
स॒त्यश्चि॒त्रश्रवस्तमः ।
दे॒वो दे॒वेभिरा गमत् ॥

अ॒ग्निः । होंता । क॒विऽक्रतुः ।
स॒त्यः । चि॒त्रऽश्रवःऽतमः ।
दे॒वः । दे॒वेभिः । आ । गमत् ॥

5 Agnír hótā kavíkratuḥ
satyáś citráśravastamaḥ,
devó devébhir á gamat.

May Agni the invoker, of wise intelligence, the true, of most brilliant fame, the god come with the gods.

Both kaví-kratus and citrá-śravas have the regular Bv. accent (p. 455 c); the latter cd. is not analysed in the Pada text because it forms a unit as first member, from which tama is separated as the second; cp. notes on tama in 1 c and 3 c. devébhis: the inst. often expresses a sociative sense without a prp. (like saha in Skt.): see 199 A 1. devó devébhiḥ: the juxtaposition of forms of the same word, to express a contrast, is common in the RV. gam-a-t: root ao. sb. of gam (p. 171); on the accentuation of á gamat see p. 468, 20 A a.

६ यदङ्ग दा॒शुषे॒ त्वम्
अ॒ग्ने भ॒द्रं क॒रिष्यसि ।
तवेत्तत्सत्य॒मङ्गिरः ॥

यत् । अ॒ङ्ग । दा॒शुषे । त्वम् ।
अ॒ग्ने । भ॒द्रम् । क॒रिष्यसि ।
तव । इत् । तत् । सत्यम् । अ॒ङ्गिरः ॥

6 yád aṅgá dāśúṣe tuám,
Ágne, bhadrám kariṣyási,
távét tát satyám, Aṅgiraḥ.

Just what good thou, O Agni, wilt do for the worshipper, that (purpose) of thee (comes) true, O Aṅgiras.

aṅgá: on this pcl. see 180 (p. 213). dāśúṣe: dat. of dāś-váṃs, one of the few pf. pt. stems in the RV. formed without red. (140, 5; 157 b), of which only vid-váṃs survives in Skt. tvám: here, as nearly everywhere in the RV., to be read as tuám on account of the metre. Though the Pādas forming a hemistich constitute a metrical unit, that is, are not divided from each other either in Sandhi or in the marking of the accent, the second Pāda is syntactically separated from the first inasmuch as it is treated as a new sentence, a voc. or a vb. at its beginning being always accented (p. 465, 18 a; 19 b).

Hence **Agne** is accented (the Udātta being, as always, on the first syllable, p. 465, 18), while Aṅgiras is not (p. 466, 18 b). kariṣyási (ft. of kṛ do): that is, whatever good thou intendest to do to the worshipper will certainly be realized. táva ít tát: *that* intention *of thée.*

७ उप॑ त्वाग्ने दि॒वेदि॑वे   उप॑ । त्वा॒ । अ॒ग्ने॒ । दि॒वेऽदि॑वे ।
दो॒षाव॑स्तर्धि॒या व॒यम् ।   दो॒षाऽव॑स्तः । धि॒या । व॒यम् ।
नमो॑ भर॑न्त॒ एम॑सि ॥   नमः॑ । भर॑न्तः । आ । ए॒म॑सि ॥ ॰

7 úpa tvāgne divé-dive,   *To thee, O Agni, day by day, O*
dóṣāvastar, dhiyā́ vayám,   *illuminer of gloom, we come with*
námo bháranta émasi;   *thought bringing homage;*

    tvā as the enc. form of tvā́m (109 a) and **Agne** as a voc. in the middle of a Pāda (p. 466 b) are unaccented. The acc. tvā is most naturally to be taken as governed by the preposition úpa (p. 209), though it might otherwise be quite well dependent on the cd. vb. úpa ā́-imasi (a common combination of úpa and ā́ with verbs meaning *to go*), as the first prp. is often widely separated from the verb (191 f; p. 468, 20 a). dóṣā-vastar: Sāyaṇa explains this cd. (which occurs here only) as *by night and day*, but vastar never occurs as an adv. and the accent of doṣā́ is shifted (which is not otherwise the case in such cds., as sāyám-prātar *evening and morning*, from sāyám); the explanation as *O illuminer* (from 1. vas *shine*) *of darkness* (with voc. accent on the first syllable) is much more probable, being supported by the description of Indra (iii. 49, 4) as kṣapā́m vastā́ janitā́ sū́ryasya *illuminer of nights, generator of the Sun*. dhiyā́ inst. of dhī́ *thought* (accent, p. 458, 1), used in the sense of *mental prayer*. námas, lit. *bow*, implies a gesture of adoration. bhárantas: N. pl. pr. pt. of bhṛ *bear*. ā́-imasi: the ending masi is five times as common as mas in the RV. (p. 125, f. n. 2).

८ राज॑न्तमध्व॒राणां॑   राज॑न्तम् । अ॒ध्व॒राणा॑म् ।
गो॒पामृ॒तस्य॒ दी॑दि॒विम् ।   गो॒पाम् । ऋ॒तस्य॑ । दी॒दि॒विम् ।
वर्ध॑मानं॒ स्वे दमे॑ ॥   वर्ध॑मानम् । स्वे । दमे॑ ॥

8 rā́jantam adhvarā́ṇām̐,
gopā́m ṛtásya dī́divim,
várdhamānam̐ sué dáme.

(to thee) *ruling over sacrifices, the shining guardian of order, growing in thine own house.*

rā́jantam: this and the other accusatives in this stanza are in agreement with **tvā** in the preceding one. **adhvarā́ṇām**: governed by the preceding word, because verbs of ruling take the gen. (202 A *a*); the final syllable **ām** must be pronounced with a slur equivalent to two syllables (like a vowel sung in music). **go-pā́m**: one of the many m. stems in final radical **ā** (p. 78), which in Skt. is always shortened to **a** (as **go-pa**). **ṛtá** means the regular order of nature, such as the unvarying course of the sun and moon, and of the seasons; then, on one hand, the regular course of sacrifice (rite); on the other, moral order (right), a sense replaced in Skt. by **dharma**. Agni is specially the guardian of **ṛtá** in the ritual sense, because the sacrificial fire is regularly kindled every day; Varuṇa (vii. 86) is specially the guardian of **ṛtá** in the moral sense. **várdhamānam**: *growing in thine own house*, because the sacrificial fire after being kindled flames up in its receptacle on the altar. **své**: to be read as **sué**; this prn. meaning *own* refers to all three persons and numbers in the RV., *my own, thy own, his own*, &c. (cp. p. 112 *c*). **dáme**: this word (= Lat. *domu-s*) is common in the RV., but has disappeared in Skt.

९ स नः पितेव सूनवे
ऽग्ने सूपायनो भव ।
सचस्वा नः स्वस्तये ॥

सः । नः । पिताऽइव । सूनवे ।
अग्ने । सुऽउपायनः । भव ।
सचस्व । नः । स्वस्तये ॥

9 sá naḥ pitéva sūnáve,
Ágne, sūpāyanó bhava;
sácasvā naḥ suastáye.

So, O Agni, be easy of access to us, as a father to his son; abide with us for our well-being.

sá is here used in its frequent anaphoric sense of *as such, thus* (p. 294 *b*). **nas** enc. dat. (109 *a*) parallel to **sūnáve**. **pitā́ iva**: the enc. pcl. **iva** is regularly treated by the Pada text as the second member of a cd.; in the RV. **pitṛ́** is usually coupled with **sūnú**, **mātṛ́** with **putrá**. **sūnávé**: this word as written in the Saṃhitā text appears with two Udāttas, because the Udātta of the elided **á**

is thrown back on the preceding syllable (p. 465, 3); but this á must be restored, as the metre shows, and **sūnáve Ágne** read. Though **a** is elided in about 75 per cent. of its occurrences in the written Saṃhitā text, it remains in the rest; it must be pronounced in about 99 per cent. (cp. p. 23, f. n. 4 and 5). The vowel Sandhi which is invariably applied between the final and initial sounds of the two Pādas of a hemistich, must always be resolved to restore the metre. This is another indication (see note on **Ágne** in 6 b) that the second and the first Pāda were originally as independent of each other as the second and the third. On the accentuation of **sūpāyaná** as a Bv. see p. 455, *c a*. **sácasvā**: this verb (which is exclusively Vedic) is construed with the acc. (here **nas**) or the inst.; the vowel of **sva**, the ending of the 2. s. ipv. Ā., is here (like many other final vowels) lengthened in the Saṃhitā, but is regularly short in the Pada text. **svastáye** must be read as **su-astáye**; it has the sense of a final dat. (200 B 2). It is not analysed in the Pada text because **asti** does not occur as an independent nominal stem.

SAVITṚ́

This god is celebrated in eleven entire hymns and in many detached stanzas as well. He is pre-eminently a golden deity: the epithets golden-eyed, golden-handed, and golden-tongued are peculiar to him. His car and its pole are golden. It is drawn by two or more brown, white-footed horses. He has mighty golden splendour which he diffuses, illuminating heaven, earth, and air. He raises aloft his strong golden arms, with which he arouses and blesses all beings, and which extend to the ends of the earth. He moves in his golden car, seeing all creatures, on a downward and an upward path. Shining with the rays of the sun, yellow-haired, Savitṛ raises up his light continually from the east. His ancient paths in the air are dustless and easy to traverse, and on them he protects his worshippers; for he conveys the departed spirit to where the righteous dwell. He removes evil dreams, and makes men sinless; he drives away demons and sorcerers. He observes fixed laws; the waters and the wind are subject to him. The other gods follow his lead; and no being can resist his will. In one stanza (iii. 62, 10) he is besought to stimulate the thoughts of worshippers who desire to think of the glory of god Savitṛ. This is the celebrated Sāvitrī stanza which has been a morning prayer in India for more than three thousand years. Savitṛ is often distinguished from Sūrya (vii. 63), as when he is said to shine with the rays of the sun, to impel the sun, or to declare men sinless to the sun. But in other passages it is hardly possible to keep the two deities apart.

Savitṛ is connected with the evening as well as the morning; for at his command night comes and he brings all beings to rest.

The word Savitṛ is derived from the root sū *to stimulate*, which is constantly and almost exclusively used with it in such a way as to form a perpetual play on the name of the god. In nearly half its occurrences the name is accompanied by devá *god*, when it means the 'Stimulator god'. He was thus originally a solar deity in the capacity of the great stimulator of life and motion in the world.

i. 35. In this hymn Savitṛ appears as the regulator of time, bringing day and especially night.

The metre of this hymn is Triṣṭubh (p. 441), the commonest in the RV., about two-fifths of which are composed in it. It consists of four verses of eleven syllables identical in construction, and is divided into two hemistichs. The cadence (the last four syllables) is trochaic (– ⏑ – ⏓); the opening, consisting of either four or five syllables followed by a caesura or metrical pause, is predominantly iambic (⏓ – ⏓ – or ⏓ – ⏓ – ⏓), and the break between the caesura and the cadence is regularly ⏑ ⏑ – or ⏑ ⏑. Thus the scheme of the whole normal verse is either ⏓ – ⏓ –, ⏑ ⏑ – | – ⏑ – ⏓ | or ⏓ – ⏓ – ⏓, ⏑ ⏑ | – ⏑ – ⏓ |. The metre of stanzas 1 and 9 is Jagatī (p. 442), which consists of four verses of twelve syllables. The Jagatī is identical with the Triṣṭubh verse extended by one syllable, which, however, gives the cadence an iambic character (– ⏑ – ⏑ ⏓). In the first stanza the caesura is always after the fifth syllable, in the second Pāda following the first member of a compound.

१ ह्वयाम्यग्निं प्रथमं स्वस्तये	ह्वयामि । अग्निम् । प्रथमम् । स्वस्तये ।
ह्वयामि मित्रावरुणाविहावसे ।	ह्वयामि । मित्रावरुणौ । इह । अवसे ।
ह्वयामि रात्रीं जगतो निवेशनीं	ह्वयामि । रात्रीम् । जगतः । निऽवेशनीम् ।
ह्वयामि देवं सवितारमूतये ॥	ह्वयामि । देवम् । सवितारम् । ऊतये ॥

1 **hváyāmi Agníṃ prathamáṃ suastáye;**	*I call on Agni first for welfare;*
hváyāmi Mitrā́váruṇāv ihā́vase;	*I call on Mitra-Varuṇa here for aid; I call on Night that brings the*

hváyāmi Rā́trīṃ jágato nivéś-anīṃ ;	*world to rest ; I call on god Savitṛ for help.*
hváyāmi deváṃ Savitā́ram ūtá-ye.	

hváyāmi: pr. ind. from **hvā** *call* ; note the anaphoric repetition of this word at the beginning of each verse. **prathamám** is in apposition to **Agním**. **su-astáye**: this, **ávase**, and **ūtáye** are final datives (p. 314, B 2) ; the last two words are derived from the same root, **av** *help*. **svastí** (cp. note on i. 1, 9 c) evidently means *well-being* ; by Sāyaṇa, following Yāska (Nirukta, iii. 21), it is explained negatively as **a-vināśa** *non-destruction*. **Mitrā́-váruṇā**: one of the numerous Dvandvas both members of which are dual and accented (p. 269) ; note that Dv. cds. are not analysed in the Pada text. **ihā́vase** for **ihá ávase**: on the accent see p. 464, 17, 1. **jágatas**: the objective gen. (p. 320, B 1 *b*), dependent on **nivéśanīm** = that causes the world to 'turn in' (cp. x. 127, 4. 5) ; the cs. **niveśáyan** is applied to Savitṛ in the next stanza.

२ आ कृष्णेन रजसा वर्तमानो	आ । कृष्णेन । रजसा । वर्तमानः ।
निवेशयन्नमृतं मर्त्यं च ।	निऽवेशयन् । अमृतम् । मर्त्यम् । च ।
हिरण्ययेन सविता रथेना	हिरण्ययेन । सविता । रथेन ।
देवो याति भुवनानि पश्यन् ॥	आ । देवः । याति । भुवनानि । पश्यन् ॥

2 **ā́ kṛṣṇéna rájasā vártamāno,**	*Rolling hither through the dark*
niveśáyann amṛ́taṃ mártiaṃ ca,	*space, laying to rest the immortal and the mortal, on his golden car*
hiraṇyáyena Savitā́ ráthena,	*god Savitṛ comes seeing* (all) *crea-*
ā́ devó yāti bhúvanāni páśyan.	*tures.*

ā́ vártamānas: the prp. may be separated from a pt. as from a finite vb., p. 462, 13 *a* ; when it immediately precedes, as in **ni-veśáyan**, it is usually compounded, *ibid.* **kṛṣṇéna rájasā**: = *through the darkness* ; loc. sense of the inst., 119 A 4. **amṛ́taṃ mártiaṃ ca** s. m. used collectively = *gods and men.* **ráthenā́** must of course be read **ráthena|ā́** ; see note on **Ágne**, i. 1, 9 b. **ā́ devó yāti**: cp. note on ā́ ihá vakṣati, i. 1, 2 c. In this and the two following stanzas Savitṛ is connected with evening.

३ याति देवः प्रवता यात्युद्वता
याति शुभ्राभ्यां यजतो हरिभ्याम्।
आ देवो याति सविता परावतो
ऽप विश्वा दुरिता बाधमानः॥

याति। देवः। प्रऽवता। याति। उत्ऽवता।
याति। शुभ्राभ्याम्। यजतः। हरिऽभ्याम्।
आ। देवः। याति। सविता। पराऽवतः।
अप। विश्वा। दुःऽइता। बाधमानः॥

3 yā́ti deváḥ pravátā, yā́ti udvátā;
yā́ti śubhrā́bhyām yajató háribhyām.
ā́ devó yāti Savitā́ parāváto,
ápa víśvā duritā́ bā́dhamānaḥ.

The god goes by a downward, he goes by an upward path; adorable he goes with his two bright steeds. God Savitṛ comes from the distance, driving away all hardships.

In this stanza a Jagatī verse is combined with a Triṣṭubh in each hemistich. This is quite exceptional in the RV.: see p. 445, β 1 and f. n. 7. pra-vát-ā and ud-vát-ā: local sense of the inst. (199 A 4); note that the suffix vat (p. 263) is in the Pada text treated like the second member of a cd. The downward and upward path refer to the sun's course in the sky. The second yā́ti is accented as beginning a new sentence. háribhyām: inst. in sociative sense; cp. devébhis in i. 1, 5. On the different treatment of śubhrā́bhyām and háribhyām in the Pada text see note on pū́rvebhis in i. 1, 28. parāvátó ऽ pa: see note on Ágne in i. 1, 9. parāvátas: abl. with verb of motion (201 A 1). ápa bā́dhamānas: cp. note on ā́ in 2 c. víśvā duritā́: this form of the n. pl. is commoner in the RV. than that in āni; p. 78, f. n. 14.

४ अभीवृतं कृशनैर्विश्वरूपं
हिरण्यशम्यं यजतो बृहन्तम्।
आस्थाद्रथं सविता चित्रभानुः
कृष्णा रजांसि तविषीं दधानः॥

अभिऽवृतम्। कृशनैः। विश्वऽरूपम्।
हिरण्यऽशम्यम्। यजतः। बृहन्तम्।
आ। अस्थात्। रथम्। सविता। चित्रऽभानुः।
कृष्णा। रजांसि। तविषीम्। दधानः

4 **abhī́vṛtaṃ kṛ́śanair, viśvárūpaṃ,**
híraṇyaśamyaṃ, yajató bṛhántam,
ā́sthād ráthaṃ Savitā́ citrábhānuḥ,
kṛṣṇā́ rájāṃsi, táviṣīṃ dádhānaḥ.

His car adorned with pearls, omniform, with golden pins, lofty, the adorable Savitṛ brightly lustrous, putting on the dark spaces and his might, has mounted.

The final vowel of **abhí** is lengthened in the Saṃhitā text, as often when a long vowel is favoured by the metre. The prp. is also accented, this being usual when a prp. is compounded with a pp. (p. 462, 13 *b*). **kṛ́śanais**: stars are probably meant, as is indicated by x. 68, 11: 'the Fathers adorned the sky with stars, like a dark horse with pearls'. **viśvá-rūpam**: on the accent cp. note on i. 1, 4 b. **-śamyam**: inflected like rathī́, p. 87; the **śamī** is probably a long pin fixed at each end of the yoke to prevent its slipping off the horse's neck. **ā́ asthāt**: root ao. of sthā. **kṛṣṇā́ rájāṃsi**: = *darkness*. **dádhānas** (pr. pt.; the pf. would be dadhānás) governs both rájāṃsi and táviṣīm = *clothing himself in darkness* (cp. 2 a) *and might*, that is, bringing on evening by his might.

५ वि जनाञ्छ्यावाः शितिपादो अख्यन्	वि । जनान् । श्यावाः । शितिऽपादः । अख्यन् ।
रथं हिरण्यप्रउगं वहन्तः ।	रथम् । हिरण्यऽप्रउगम् । वहन्तः ।
शश्वद्विशः सवितुर्दैव्यस्यो-	शश्वत् । विशः । सवितुः । दैव्यस्य ।
पस्थे विश्वा भुवनानि तस्थुः ॥	उपऽस्थे । विश्वा । भुवनानि । तस्थुः ॥

5 **ví jánāñ chyāvā́ḥ śitipā́do akhyan,**
rátham híraṇyapraügaṃ váhantaḥ.
śáśvad víśaḥ Savitúr dáiviasya
upásthe víśvā bhúvanāni tasthuḥ.

His dusky steeds, white-footed, drawing his car with golden pole, have surveyed the peoples. For ever the settlers and all creatures have rested in the lap of divine Savitṛ.

ví: separated from vb.; see note on **á vakṣati, i. 1, 2 c. jánāñ chyāvā́ḥ**: for **jánān śyāvā́ḥ** (40, 1). **śiti-pā́das**: on the accentuation of this Bv. on the final member, see **p.** 455, *c a*. Note that the initial **a** of **akhyan** remains after **o** (cp. note on i. 1, 9 b). **akhyan**: **a ao.** of **khyā** *see* (p. 168, *a* 1), cp. 7 a and 8 a, and **páśyan** in 2 d; the ao. expresses a single action that has just taken place (p. 345 C); the pf. **tasthur** expresses an action that has constantly (**śáśvat**) taken place in the past down to the present (113 A *a*). In **-praügam** (analysed by the Pāda text of x. 130, 3 as **pra-uga**), doubtless = **pra-yugam** (as explained in a Prātiśākhya), there is a remarkable hiatus caused by the dropping of **y. víśvā bhúvanāni**: here the old and the new form of the n. pl. are used side by side, as very often. On the Sandhi of **dáivyasyopásthe** cp. note on **Ágne, i.** 1, 9 b. **dáivya** *divine* is a variation of the usual **devá** accompanying the name of Savitṛ. **upásthe**: the idea that all beings are contained in various deities, or that the latter are the soul (ātmá) of the animate and inanimate world, is often expressed in the RV.

६ तिस्रो द्यावः सवितुर्द्वा उपस्थाँ
एका यमस्य भुवने विराषाट् ।
आणिं न रथ्यममृताधि तस्थुर्
इह ब्रवीतु य उ तच्चिकेतत् ॥

तिस्रः । द्यावः । सवितुः । द्वौ । उपऽस्था ।
एका । यमस्य । भुवने । विराषाट् ।
आणिम् । न । रथ्यम् । अमृता । अधि ।
तस्थुः ।
इह । ब्रवीतु । यः । ऊं इति । तत् । चिकेतत् ॥

6 **tisró dyā́vaḥ; Savitúr dvā́ upá-sthā́m̐,**
ékā Yamásya bhúvane virāṣā́ṭ.
āṇím ná ráthyam amṛ́tā́dhi tasthur:
ihá bravītu yá u tác cíketat.

(There are) *three heavens: two* (are) *the laps of Savitṛ, one overcoming men,* (is) *in the abode of Yama. All immortal things rest* (on him) *as on the axle-end of a car: let him who may understand this tell it here.*

The interpretation of this stanza is somewhat difficult; for it is meant, as the last Pāda indicates, as an enigma (like several others in the RV.). The first Pāda is evidently intended to explain the last two of the preceding stanza: of the three worlds Savitṛ occupies two (air and earth). The second Pāda adds: the third world (the highest heaven) is the abode of Yama, in which dwell men after death (that is, the Pitṛs). The third Pāda means: on Savitṛ, in these two (lower) worlds, the gods rest. **dyā́vas**: N. pl. of **dyó**, here f. (which is rare); probably an elliptical pl. (193, 3 *a*) = heaven, air, and earth. **dvā́**: for **dváu** before **u** (22); after **tisró dyā́vaḥ** the f. form **dvé** should strictly be used (like **ékā** in b), but it is attracted in gender by the following **upásthā** (cp. 194, 3). **upá-sthā̃**: the dual ending **ā** (which in the RV. is more than seven times as common as **au**), appears before consonants, in pausā at the end of a Pāda, and in the middle of a Pāda before vowels, with which it coalesces. Here it is nasalized (as often elsewhere) before the initial vowel of the following Pāda to avoid the hiatus; this is another indication (cp. note on **Ágne**, i. 1, 9 b) that there was in the original text of the RV. no vowel Sandhi between the Pādas of a hemistich. **virā-ṣā́ṭ**: N. s. of **virā-sáh** (81 *b*), in which there is cerebralization of **s** by assimilation to the final cerebral **ṭ** (for **-sā́ṭ**); in the first member the quantity of the vowels (for **vīra**) is interchanged for metrical convenience; the Pada text does not analyse the cd. because the form **virā** does not occur as an independent word (cp. note on **ṛtvíj**, i. 1, 1 b). **amṛ́tā**: n. pl. = the gods. **āṇím ná**: on him, as the car rests on the two ends of the axle which pass through the nave of the wheels. **ádhi tasthur**: the pf. of **sthā** here takes the acc. by being compounded with **ádhi**; in 5 d the simple verb takes the loc. The third Pāda is only a modification in sense of 5 c d. **bravītu**: 3. s. ipv. of **brū** *speak* (p. 143, 3 *c*). The pcl. **u** is always written in the Pada text as a long vowel and nasalized: **ū̃m íti**. **ciketat**: pf. sb. of **cit** *observe*.

७ वि सुपर्णो अन्तरिक्षाण्यख्यद्
गभीरवेपा असुरः सुनीथः ।
क्वे३दानीं सूर्यः कश्चिकेत
कतमां द्यां रश्मिरस्या ततान ॥

वि । सुऽपर्णः । अन्तरिक्षाणि । अख्यत् ।
गभीरऽवेपाः । असुरः । सुऽनीथः ।
क्व । इदानीन् । सूर्यः । कः । चिकेत ।
कतमाम् । द्याम् । रश्मिः । अस्य । आ ।
ततान ॥

7 ví suparṇó antárikṣāṇi akhyad,
gabhīrávepā ásuraḥ sunītháḥ.
kúedā́nīṃ sū́riaḥ? káś ciketa?
katamā́ṃ dyā́ṃ raśmír asyā́
tatāna?

The bird has surveyed the atmospheric regions, the divine spirit, of deep inspiration, of good guidance. Where is now the sun? Who has understood (it)? *To what heaven has his ray extended?*

7–9 deal with Savitṛ as guiding the sun.

ví . . . akhyat: cp. 5 a and 8 a. **suparṇás**: Savitṛ is here called a bird. as the sun-god Sūrya (vii. 63) often is. On the accent of this Bv. and of su-nīthás see p. 455, *c a*. **antárikṣāṇi**: equivalent to **kṛṣṇā́** rájāṃsi (4 d), the aerial spaces when the sun is absent. **ásuras**: this word, which is applied to various gods in the RV., but especially to Varuṇa, and in the Avesta, as *ahura*, is the name of the highest god, means a divine being possessed of occult power; towards the end of the Rigvedic period it gradually lost this sense and came to mean a higher hostile power, celestial demon. **sunīthás**: *guiding well* here means that the sun illumines the paths with his light. **kvèdā́nīm**: when an independent Svarita is in the Saṃhitā text immediately followed by an Udātta, the Svarita vowel, if long, has added to it the figure 3. which is marked with both Svarita and Anudātta (p. 450 *b*). **idā́nīm**: *now* = *at night*. **ciketa**: pf. of cit *observe* (139, 4). **dyā́m**: acc. of dyó (p. 94, 3), here again (cp. 6 a) f. **asyā́**: = asya ā́. **tatāna**: pf. of tan *stretch* (cp. 137, 2 *b*). The question here asked, where the sun goes to at night, is parallel to that asked about the stars in i. 24, 10: 'those stars which are seen at night placed on high, where have they gone by day?'

८ अष्टौ व्यख्यत्ककुभः पृथिव्यास्
त्री धन्व योजना सप्त सिन्धून्।
हिरण्याक्षः सविता देव आगाद्
दधद्रत्ना दाशुषे वार्याणि॥

अष्टौ। वि। अख्यत्। ककुभः। पृथिव्याः।
त्री। धन्व। योजना। सप्त। सिन्धून्।
हिरण्यऽअक्षः। सविता। देवः। आ।
अगात्।
दधत्। रत्ना। दाशुषे। वार्याणि॥

8 **aṣṭáu ví akhyat kakúbhaḥ pṛthivyā́s,**
trī́ dhánva, yójanā, saptá síndhūn.
hiraṇyākṣáḥ Savitā́ devá ā́gād,
dádhad rátnā dāśúṣe vā́riāṇi.

He has surveyed the eight peaks of the earth, the three waste lands, the leagues, the seven rivers. Golden-eyed god Savitṛ has come, bestowing desirable gifts on the worshipper.

The general meaning of this stanza is that Savitṛ surveys all space: the mountains, the plains, the rivers, and the regions between heaven and earth. **aṣṭáu**: 106 *b*. **pṛthivyā́s**: on the accentuation see p. 458, 2. **trī́**: n. pl. (105, 3) to be read disyllabically. **dhánva**: acc. pl. of **dhánvan** n., 90, 3 (p. 70; cp. p. 67, bottom). The long syllable after the caesura in b and d (– ◡ – for ◡ ◡ –) is rare in the RV. (p. 440, 4 B). **yójanā**: probably the thirty leagues that Dawn traverses in the sky (i. 123, 8), the number of each of the other features being expressly stated. **hiraṇyākṣás**: the accent of this cd. as a Bv. is quite exceptional: p. 455 *c*. **ā́-agāt**: root ao. of **gā** *go*. **dádhat**: on the accent cp. 127, 2; on the formation of the stem, 156.

९ हिरण्यपाणिः सविता विचर्षणिर्
उभे द्यावापृथिवी अन्तरीयते ।
अपामीवां बाधते वेति सूर्यम्
अभि कृष्णेन रजसा द्यामृणोति ॥

हिरण्यऽपाणिः । सविता । विऽचर्षणिः ।
उभे इति । द्यावापृथिवी इति । अन्तः ।
ईयते ।
अप । अमीवाम् । बाधते । वेति । सूर्यम् ।
अभि । कृष्णेन । रजसा । द्याम् । ऋणोति ॥

9 **híraṇyapāṇiḥ Savitā́ vícarṣaṇir**
ubhé dyā́vāpṛthivī́ antár īyate.
ápā́mīvām bā́dhate; véti sū́riam;
abhí kṛṣṇéna rájasā dyā́m ṛṇoti.

Golden-handed Savitṛ, the active, goes between both heaven and earth. He drives away disease; he guides the sun; through the dark space he penetrates to heaven.

Dyā́vā-pṛthivī́: with the usual double accent of Devatā-dvandvas (p. 457, *e β*) and not analysed in the Pada text (cp. note on 1 b). Its final ī, as well as the e of **ubhé**, being Pragṛhya (25 *a*, 26 *a*), is followed by **íti** in the Pada text (p. 25, f. n. 2). **antár** (46) combined with ī *go* governs the acc. ; cp. the two laps of Savitṛ in 6 a. **ápa bā́dhate**: he drives away disease, cp. 3 d ; contrary to the general rule (p. 466, 19 A) the vb. is here accented ; this irregularity not infrequently occurs when in the same Pāda a compound verb is immediately followed by a simple vb. **véti**: accented because it begins a new sentence ; Savitṛ guides the sun: cp. 7 c. **kṛṣṇéna rájasā**: cp. 2 a and 4 d. **abhí . . . dyā́m ṛṇoti**: cp. 7 d. The metre of d is irregular : it is a Triṣṭubh of twelve syllables, the first two syllables (abhí) taking the place of a long one. Cp. p. 441, 4 *a* and p. 445, B 1.

१० हिरण्यहस्तो असुरः सुनीथः	हिरण्यऽहस्तः । असुरः । सुऽनीथः ।
सुमृळीकः स्ववाँ यात्वर्वाङ् ।	सुऽमृळीकः । स्वऽवान् । यातु । अर्वाङ् ।
अपसेधन्रक्षसो यातुधानान्	अपऽसेधन् । रक्षसः । यातुऽधानान् ।
अस्थाद्देवः प्रतिदोषं गृणानः ॥	अस्थात् । देवः । प्रतिऽदोषम् । गृणानः ॥

10 **híraṇyahasto ásuraḥ sunītháḥ,** **sumṛḷīkáḥ suávām̐ yātu arvā́ṅ.** **apasédhan rakṣáso yātudhā́nān,** **ásthād deváḥ pratidoṣám gṛṇā-náḥ.**	*Let the golden-handed divine spirit, of good guidance, most gracious, aiding well, come hither. Chasing away demons and sorcerers, the god being lauded has arisen towards eventide.*

ásuras: cp. 7 b. **svávān**: the analysis of the Pada text, **svá-vān** = *possessed of property*, is followed by Sāyaṇa who renders it by **dhanavān** *wealthy* ; this would mean that Savitṛ bestows wealth (cp. **dádhad rátnā** in 8 d, and vi. 71, 4 **ā́ dāśúṣe suvati bhū́ri vāmám** *he*, Savitṛ, *brings much wealth to the worshipper*). This nom. occurs several times in the RV., and is always analysed in the same way by the Padapāṭha. On the other hand, three oblique cases of **su-ávas** *giving good help* occur (**svávasam, svávasā, svávasas**). Roth takes **svávān** to be a nom. of this stem irregularly formed by analogy for **su-ávās** (cp. 83, 2 *a*). I follow the Pada text as the meaning is sufficiently good. Final **ān**, which regularly becomes **ām̐** before vowels (39), sometimes undergoes the same change before y (40, 4). **rakṣásas** has the accent of a m. in **as** (83, 2 *a*) ; the n. form is **rákṣāṃsi**. **yātudhā́nān** is added, as is often the case, without

a connecting **ca**: cp. note on **rayím**, in i. **1, 3 a**; note that the Sandhi of ān before vowels (39) does not apply at the end of an internal Pāda. If Savitṛ in this stanza is connected with morning rather than evening, **ásthāt** would here be equivalent to **úd asthāt**; cp. RV. vi. 71, 4: **úd u ṣyá deváḥ Savitā́ dámunā híraṇyapāṇiḥ pratidoṣám ásthāt** *that god Savitṛ, the domestic friend, the golden-handed, has arisen towards eventide*; it may, however, be equivalent to **ā́ asthāt**, that is, he has mounted his car, cp. **4 c**. **gṛṇānás**: pr. pt. Ā., with ps. sense, of **1. gṛ** *sing, greet.*

११ ये ते पन्थाः सवितः पूर्व्यासो	ये । ते । पन्थाः । सवितरिति । पूर्व्यासः ।
ऽरेणवः सुकृता अन्तरिक्षे ।	अरेणवः । सुऽकृताः । अन्तरिक्षे ।
तेभिर्नो अद्य पथिभिः सुगेभी	तेभिः । नः । अद्य । पथिऽभिः । सुऽगेभिः ।
रक्षा च नो अधि च ब्रूहि देव ॥	रक्ष । च । नः । अधि । च । ब्रूहि । देव ॥

11 **yé te pánthāḥ, Savitaḥ, pūrviáso,**	*Thine ancient paths, O Savitṛ,*
areṇávaḥ súkṛtā antárikṣe,	*the dustless, the well made, in the*
tébhir nŏ adyá pathíbhiḥ sugé-	*air,* (going) *by those paths easy to*
bhī	*traverse protect us to-day, and speak*
rákṣā ca no, ádhi ca brūhi,	*for us, O god.*
deva.	

te: the dat. and gen. of **tvám**, is always unaccented; while **té**, N. pl. m. and N. A. du. f. n. of **tá**, is always **té**. **pánthās**: N. pl. of **pánthā**, m. *path*, which is the only stem (not **pánthan**) in the RV. (99, 1 *a*). **Savitaḥ**: when final Visarjanīya in the Saṃhitā text represents original **r**, this is always indicated by the word being written with r followed by íti in the Pada text; here **Savitar íti**. **'reṇávas**: the initial **a** must be restored (see note on **Ágne**, i. 1, 9 b; but **a** is not elided after **o** in c and d); on the accent of a Bv. formed with privative **a**, see p. 455, *c a*. **sú-kṛtās**: Karmadhārayas, in which the first member is an **adv.** and the last a pp., accent the former; p. 456, 1 *a*. **tébhis**: inst. of **tá**, p. 106; p. 457, 11 *b*. In **c** **nŏ adyá** should be pronounced because **e** and **o** are shortened before **a** (p. 437, *a* 4); this rule does not apply when **e** and **o** are separated from **a** by the caesura; hence in d **ō**, **ádhi** should be pronounced. **sugébhī**: see 47. The final **a** of **rákṣā** is lengthened because the second syllable of the Pāda favours a long vowel. **ádhi . . . brūhi**: *be our advocate;* the meaning of this expression is illustrated by other passages: in i. 123, 3 Savitṛ is besought to report to Sūrya that his worshippers are sinless; in vii. 60, 2 Sūrya is implored to make a similar report to the Ādityas.

MARÚTAS

This group of deities is prominent in the RV., thirty-three hymns being addressed to them alone, seven to them with Indra, and one each to them with Agni and Pūṣan (vi. 54). They form a troop (**gaṇá, śárdhas**), being mentioned in the plural only. Their number is thrice sixty or thrice seven. They are the sons of Rudra (ii. 33) and of Pṛ́śni, who is a cow (probably representing the mottled storm-cloud). They are further said to have been generated by Vāyu, the god of Wind, in the wombs of heaven, and they are called the sons of heaven; but they are also spoken of as self-born. They are brothers equal in age and of one mind, having the same birthplace and the same abode. They have grown on earth, in air, and in heaven, or dwell in the three heavens. The goddess Rodasī́ is always mentioned in connexion with them; she stands beside them on their car, and thus seems to have been regarded as their bride.

The brilliance of the Maruts is constantly referred to: they are golden, ruddy, shine like fires, and are self-luminous. They are very often associated with lightning: all the five compounds of **vidyút** in the RV. are almost exclusively descriptive of them. Their lances represent lightning, as their epithet **ṛṣṭí-vidyut** '*lightning-speared* shows. They also have golden axes. They are sometimes armed with bows and arrows, but this trait is probably borrowed from their father Rudra. They wear garlands, golden mantles, golden ornaments, and golden helmets. Armlets and anklets (**khādí**) are peculiar to them. The cars on which they ride gleam with lightning, and are drawn by steeds (generally feminine) that are ruddy or tawny, spotted, swift as thought. They are great and mighty; young and unaging; dustless, fierce, terrible like lions, but also playful like children or calves.

The noise made by them, and often mentioned, is thunder and the roaring of the winds. They cause the mountains to quake and the two worlds to tremble; they rend trees, and, like wild elephants, devour the forests. One of their main activities is to shed rain: they cover the eye of the sun with rain; they create darkness with the cloud when they shed rain; and they cause the heavenly pail and the streams of the mountains to pour. The waters they shed are often clearly connected with the thunder storm. Their rain is often figuratively called milk, ghee, or honey. They avert heat, but also dispel darkness, produce light, and prepare a path for the sun.

They are several times called singers: they are the singers of heaven; they sing a song; for Indra when he slew the dragon, they sang a song and pressed Soma. Though primarily representing the sound of the winds, their song is also conceived as a hymn of praise. Thus they come to be compared with priests, and are addressed as priests when in the company of Indra.

Owing to their connexion with the thunderstorm, the Maruts are constantly associated with Indra (ii. 12) as his friends and allies, increasing his strength and prowess with their prayers, hymns, and songs, and generally assisting him in the fight with Vṛtra. Indra indeed accomplishes all his celestial exploits in their company. Sometimes, however, the Maruts accomplish these exploits alone. Thus they rent Vṛtra joint from joint, and disclosed the cows.

When not associated with Indra, the Maruts occasionally exhibit the maleficent traits of their father Rudra. Hence they are implored to ward off the lightning from their worshippers and not to let their ill-will reach them, and are besought to avert their arrow and the stone which they hurl, their lightning, and their cow- and man-slaying bolt. But like their father Rudra, they are also supplicated to bring healing remedies. These remedies appear to be the waters, for the Maruts bestow medicine by raining.

The evidence of the RV. indicates that the Maruts are Storm-gods. The name is probably derived from the root mar, *to shine*, thus meaning 'the shining ones'.

i. 85. Metre: Jagatī; 5 and 12 Triṣṭubh.

१ प्र ये शुम्भन्ते जनयो न सप्तयो
यामन्रुद्रस्य सूनवः सुदंससः ।
रोदसी हि मरुतश्चक्रिरे वृधे
मदन्ति वीरा विदथेषु घृष्वयः ॥

प्र । ये । शुम्भन्ते । जनयः । न । सप्तयः ।
यामन् । रुद्रस्य । सूनवः । सुऽदंससः ।
रोदसी इति । हि । मरुतः । चक्रिरे ।
वृधे ।
मदन्ति । वीराः । विदथेषु । घृष्वयः ॥

1 **prá yé śúmbhante, jánayo ná, sáptayo**
yā́man, Rudrásya sūnávaḥ su-dáṃsasaḥ,

The wondrous sons of Rudra, the racers, who on their course adorn themselves like women, the Maruts have indeed made the two

ródasī hí Marútaś cakriré vṛdhé. mádanti vīrā́ vidátheṣu ghṛ́ṣvayaḥ.	*worlds to increase. The impetuous heroes rejoice in rites of worship.*

jánayas: 99, 1 *a*. **yā́man**: loc., 90, 2. **sudáṃsasas**: accent, p. 455, 10 *c a*. **cakriré**: 3. pl. Ā. pf. of kṛ; with dat. inf., p. 334, b. **mádanti**: with loc., 204, 1 *a*. **vidátheṣu**: the etymology and precise meaning of this word have been much discussed. It is most probably derived from vidh *worship* (cp. p. 41, f. n. 1), and means *divine worship*.

२ त उक्षितासो महिमानमाशत	ते। उक्षितासः। महिमानम्। आशत।
दिवि रुद्रासो अधि चक्रिरे सदः।	दिवि। रुद्रासः। अधि। चक्रिरे। सदः।
अर्चन्तो अर्कं जनयन्त इन्द्रियम्	अर्चन्तः। अर्कम्। जनयन्तः। इन्द्रियम्।
अधि श्रियो दधिरे पृश्निमातरः॥	अधि। श्रियः। दधिरे। पृश्निऽमातरः॥

2 tá ukṣitā́so mahimā́nam āśata: diví Rudrā́so ádhi cakrire sádaḥ. árcanto arkám, janáyanta indriyám, ádhi śríyo dadhire Pṛ́śnimātaraḥ.	*They having waxed strong have attained greatness: in heaven the Rudras have made their abode. Singing their song and generating the might of Indra, they whose mother is Pṛśni have put on glory.*

té: N. pl. m. of **tá** *that*, 110. **ukṣitā́sas**: pp. of 2. ukṣ (= vakṣ) *grow*. **āśata**: 3. pl. Ā. root ao. of **aṃś** *attain*. **Rudrā́sas**: the Maruts are often called 'Rudras' as equivalent to 'sons of Rudra'. **ádhi**: prp. with the loc. **diví**; 176, 2. **janáyanta indriyám**: that is, by their song. **ádhi dadhire**: 3. pl. Ā. pf. of **ádhi dhā**, which is especially often used of putting on ornaments. **śríyas**: A. pl. of **śrī́** *glory*; referring to the characteristic brilliance of the Maruts.

३ गोमातरो यच्छुभयन्ते अञ्जिभिस्	गोऽमातरः। यत्। शुभयन्ते। अञ्जिऽभिः।
तनूषु शुभ्रा दधिरे विरुक्मतः।	तनूषु। शुभ्राः। दधिरे। विरुक्मतः।
बाधन्ते विश्वमभिमातिनमप	बाधन्ते। विश्वम्। अभिऽमातिनम्। अप।
वर्त्मान्येषामनु रीयते घृतम्॥	वर्त्मानि। एषाम्। अनु। रीयते। घृतम्॥

3 **gómātaro yác chubháyantĕ añjíbhis,**
tanū́ṣu śubhrā́ dadhire virúkmataḥ.
bā́dhante víśvam abhimātínam ápa.
vártmāni eṣām ánu rīyate ghṛtám.

When they whose mother is a cow deck themselves with ornaments, shining they put on their bodies brilliant weapons. They drive off every adversary. Fatness flows along their tracks.

gómātaras : as the sons of the cow **Pṛśni. yác chubháyante** : Sandhi, 53. **dadhire** : pf. with pr. sense, *they have put on = they wear.* **ápa** : prp. after the vb. and separated from it by other words, 191 *f*; p. 468, 20. **ánu rīyate** : 3. pl. Ā. pr. of **ri** *flow.* **ghṛtám** : *ghee* = fertilizing rain. The meaning of d is : the course of the Maruts is followed by showers of rain. **eṣām** : unemphatic G. pl. m. of **ayám**, p. 452, 8 B *c.*

४ वि ये भ्राजन्ते सुमखास ऋष्टिभिः
प्रच्यावयन्तो अच्युता चिदोजसा।
मनोजुवो यन्मरुतो रथेष्वा
वृषव्रातासः पृषतीरयुग्ध्वम्॥

वि। ये। भ्राजन्ते। सुऽमखासः। ऋष्टिऽभिः।
प्रऽच्यवयन्तः। अच्युता। चित्। ओजसा।
मनःऽजुवः। यत्। मरुतः। रथेषु। आ।
वृषऽव्रातासः। पृषतीः। अयुग्ध्वम्॥

4 **ví yé bhrā́jante súmakhāsa ṛṣṭíbhiḥ,**
pracyāváyanto ácyutā cid ójasā,
manojúvo yán, Maruto, rátheṣu ā́
vṛ́ṣavrātāsaḥ pṛ́ṣatīr áyugdhuam ;

Who as great warriors shine forth with their spears, overthrowing even what has never been overthrown with their might : when ye, O Maruts, that are swift as thought, with your strong hosts, have yoked the spotted mares to your cars,

súmakhāsas : a Karmadhāraya cd. according to its accent (cp. p 455 10 *c a*), but the exact meaning of **makhá** is still somewhat uncertain. **pra-cyāváyantas** : pr. pt. of cs. of **cyu** *move* ; though this cs., which occurs frequently in the RV., always has a long radical vowel in the Saṃhitā text, it invariably has a short vowel in the Padapāṭha. **Marutas**: change from the 3. to the 2. prs., in the same sentence, a not infrequent transition in the RV. **manojúvas**: N. pl. radical ū stem **mano-jū́**, 100, II *a* (p. 88). **rátheṣu ā́**: 176, 2. **pṛ́ṣatīs**: the spotted mares that draw the cars of the Maruts. **áyugdhvam**: 2. pl. Ā. root ao. of **yuj** *yoke*.

५ प्र यद्रथेषु पृषतीरयुग्ध्वं	प्र । यत् । रथेषु । पृषतीः । अयुग्ध्वम् ।
वाजे अद्रिं मरुतो रंहयन्तः ।	वाजे । अद्रिम् । मरुतः । रंहयन्तः ।
उतारुषस्य वि ष्यन्ति धाराश्	उत । अरुषस्य । वि । स्यन्ति । धाराः ।
चर्मेवोदभिर्व्युन्दन्ति भूम ॥	चर्मऽइव । उदऽभिः । वि । उन्दन्ति । भूम ॥

5 **prá** yád ráthesu pṛ́ṣatīr áyugdhvam,	*when ye have yoked the spotted mares before your cars, speeding, O*
vā́je ádrim, Maruto, raṃháyantaḥ,	*Maruts, the stone in the conflict, they discharge the streams of the*
utā́ruṣásya ví ṣianti dhā́rāś	*ruddy* (steed) *and moisten the earth*
cármevodábhir ví undanti bhū́ma.	*like a skin with waters.*

áyugdhvam: with loc., cp. 204, 1 b. **ádrim**: the Maruts hold lightning in their hands and cast a stone. **utá**: here comes before the first instead of the second of two clauses, as ca sometimes does (p. 228. 1). **áruṣasya**: the ruddy steed of heaven; cp. v. 83, 6 where the Maruts are invoked to pour forth the streams of the stallion; and in v. 56, 7 their *ruddy steed* (vājī́ áruṣaḥ) is spoken of. **ví ṣyanti**: 3. pl. pr. of **sā** *bind*; Sandhi, 67 *a*; change back from 2. to 3. prs.; cp. 4 c d. **undanti**: 3. pl. pr. of **ud** *wet*. **bhū́ma**: N. of **bhū́man** n. *earth* (but **bhūmán** m. *abundance*).

६ आ वो वहन्तु सप्तयो रघुष्यदो	आ । वः । वहन्तु । सप्तयः । रघुऽस्यदः ।
रघुपत्वानः प्र जिगात बाहुभिः ।	रघुऽपत्वानः । प्र । जिगात । बाहुऽभिः ।
सीदता बर्हिरुरु वः सदस्कृतं	सीदत । आ । बर्हिः । उरु । वः । सदः । कृतम् ।
मादयध्वं मरुतो मध्वो अन्धसः ॥	मादयध्वम् । मरुतः । मध्वः । अन्धसः ॥

6 ā́ vo vahantu sáptayo raghu-
ṣyádo;
raghupátvānaḥ prá jigāta bāhú-
bhiḥ.
sī́datā́ barhír: urú vaḥ sádas
kṛtáṃ.
mādáyadhvaṃ, Maruto, mádh-
vŏ ándhasaḥ.

Let your swift-gliding racers bring you hither. Swift-flying come forward with your arms. Sit down on the sacrificial grass: a wide seat is made for you. Rejoice, O Maruts, in the sweet juice.

raghu-ṣyádas: Sandhi, 67 *b*. **raghupátvānas**: as belonging to this Pāda to be taken with **prá** **jigāta** (**gā** *go*). **bāhúbhis**: with outstretched arms as they drive. **sī́data ā́**: 2. pl. ipv. pr. of **sad** *sit* with prp. following (p. 468, 20). **sádas**: Sandhi, 43, 2 *a*. **kṛtám**: as finite vb., 208. **mādáyadhvam**: cs. of **mad** *rejoice*, with gen., 202 A *b*. **mádhvas**: gen. n. of **mádhu**, p. 81, f. n. 12; the sweet juice is Soma.

७ तेऽवर्धन्त स्वतवसो महित्वना
नाकं तस्थुरुरु चक्रिरे सदः ।
विष्णुर्यद्धावद्वृषणं मदच्युतं
वयो न सीदन्नधि बर्हिषि प्रिये ॥

ते । अवर्धन्त । स्वऽतवसः । महिऽत्वना ।
आ । नाकम् । तस्थुः । उरु । चक्रिरे । सदः ।
विष्णुः । यत् । ह । आवत् । वृषणम् ।
मदऽच्युतम् ।
वयः । न । सीदन् । अधि । बर्हिषि ।
प्रिये ॥

7 tè ’vardhanta svátavaso mahi-
tvanā́:
ā́ nā́kaṃ tasthúr; urú cakrire
sádaḥ.
Víṣṇur yád dhā́vad vṛ́ṣaṇaṃ
madacyútaṃ,
váyo ná sīdann ádhi barhíṣi
priyé.

Self-strong they grew by their greatness: they have mounted to the firmament; they have made for themselves a wide seat. When Viṣṇu helped the bull reeling with intoxication, they sat down upon their beloved sacrificial grass like birds.

tè ’vardhanta: Sandhi accent, p. 465 17, 3. **mahitvanā́**: inst. of **mahitvaná**, p. 77, f. n. 3 **ā́ tasthúr**: vb. of a principal sentence accented according to p. 468, *β*. **Víṣṇus**: the mention of wide space (a conception intimately connected with Viṣṇu, cp. **uru-gāyá**, &c.) in 6 c and 7 b has here probably suggested the introduction of Viṣṇu (i. 154), who is in various passages associated with the Maruts (especially in v. 87) and who also forms a dual divinity (Índrā-Víṣṇū) with Indra. **dha**: Sandhi, 54. **ávat**: 3. s. ipf. of **av** *favour*; Viṣṇu helps Indra, aided by the Maruts, in his conflicts. **vṛ́ṣan**: dec., 90, 1; both this word and **madacyút** are applied to Soma as well as Indra, but the meaning of the vb. **av** and the use of the ipf. are in favour of Indra being intended, the sense then being: 'when Viṣṇu and Indra, associated in conflict, came to the Soma offering, the Maruts, their companions, came also.' **váyas**: N. pl. of **ví** *bird*. **sīdan**: unaugmented ipf. of **sad** *sit*.

८ शूरा इवेद्युयुधयो न जग्मयः
श्रवस्यवो न पृतनासु येतिरे ।
भयन्ते विश्वा भुवना मरुद्भ्यो
राजान इव त्वेषसंदृशो नरः ॥

शूराःऽइव । इत् । युयुधयः । न । ज-
ग्मयः ।
श्रवस्यवः । न । पृतनासु । येतिरे ।
भयन्ते । विश्वा । भुवना । मरुत्ऽभ्यः ।
राजानःऽइव । त्वेषऽसंदृशः । नरः ॥

8 śū́rā ivéd yúyudhayo ná jágmayaḥ,
śravasyávo ná pṛ́tanāsu yetire.
bháyante víśvā bhúvanā Marúdbhio:
rā́jāna iva tveṣásaṃdṛśo náraḥ.

Like heroes, speeding like warriors, like fame-seeking (men) *they have arrayed themselves in battles. All creatures fear the Maruts: the men are like kings of terrible aspect.*

iva: note how this pcl. interchanges with **ná** in this stanza. **yetire**: 3. pl. pf. Ā. of **yat**: 137, 2 *a*. **bháyante**: 3. pl. pr. Ā. of **bhī** *fear*; the pr. stem according to the **bhū** class is much commoner in the RV. than that according to the third class. **Marúdbhyas**: 201 A *b*. **náras**: the Maruts; N. pl. of **nṛ** *man*, 101, 1.

९ त्वष्टा यद्वज्रं सुकृतं हिरण्ययं
सहस्रभृष्टिं स्वपा अवर्तयत् ।

त्वष्टा । यत् । वज्रम् । सुऽकृतम् । हिर-
ण्ययम् ।

धत्त इन्द्रो नर्यपांसि कर्तवे
ऽहन्वृत्रं निरपामौब्जदर्णवम् ॥

सहस्रऽभृष्टिम् । सुऽअपाः । अवर्तयत् ।
धत्ते । इन्द्रः । नरि । अपांसि । कर्तवे ।
अहन् । वृत्रम् । निः । अपाम् । औब्जत् ।
अर्णवम् ॥

9 **Tváṣṭā yád vájram súkṛtam hiraṇyáyam**
sahásrabhṛṣṭim suápā ávartayat,
dhattá Índro náriápāṃsi kártave:
áhan Vṛtrám, nír apā́m aubjad arṇavam.

When the skilful Tvaṣṭr had turned the well-made, golden, thousand-edged bolt, Indra took it to perform manly deeds: he slew Vṛtra, and drove out the flood of waters.

The association of ideas connecting Indra with the Maruts is continued from 7 c d. That Tvaṣṭr fashioned Indra's bolt for him is mentioned, in a similar context, in i. 32, 1 c and 2 b: **áhann áhim, ánv apás tatarda; Tváṣṭā asmai vájram svaryàṃ tatakṣa** *he slew the serpent, he released the waters; Tvaṣṭr fashioned for him the whizzing bolt.* **dhatté**: 3. s. pr. Ā. used in the past sense (212 A 2). **kártave**: dat. inf. of purpose, *in order to perform* (**kṛ**), 211. **náryápāṃsi** is here and in viii. 96, 19 analysed by the Pada text as **nári ápāṃsi**. The only possible sense of these words would be *deeds against the hero* (Vṛtra). On the other hand **náryāṇi** appears once (vii. 21, 4) and **náryā** twice (iv. 19, 10; viii. 96, 21) as an attribute of **ápāṃsi**; the epithet **náryāpasam**, analysed by the Padapāṭha (viii. 93, 1) as **nárya-apasam** *doing manly deeds* is applied to Indra. It thus seems preferable to make the slight emendation **náryápāṃsi** (to be read **náriápāṃsi**) in the Saṃhitā text, and **náryā|ápāṃsi** in the Pada text. **nír aubjat**: 3. s. ipf. of **ubj** *force* (cp. 23 c).

१० ऊर्ध्वं नुनुद्रेऽवतं त ओजसा
दादृहाणं चिद्बिभिदुर्वि पर्वतम् ।
धमन्तो वाणं मरुतः सुदानवो

ऊर्ध्वम् । नुनुद्रे । अवतम् । ते । ओजसा ।
दादृहाणम् । चित् । बिभिदुः । वि ।
पर्वतम् ।

मदे॒ सोम॑स्य॒ रण्या॑नि चक्रिरे ॥ धम॑न्तः । वा॒णम् । म॒रुतः॑ । सु॒ऽदान॑वः । मदे॑ । सोम॑स्य । रण्या॑नि । च॒क्रि॒रे॒ ॥

10 ūrdhvám̐ nunudre avatám̐ tá ójasā;
dádr̥hāṇám̐ cid bibhidur ví párvatam.
dhámanto vāṇám̐ Marútah̐ sudā́navo
máde sómasya ráṇiāni cakrire.

They have pushed up the well with might; they have split even the firm mountain. Blowing their pipes the bountiful Maruts have performed glorious deeds in the intoxication of Soma.

ūrdhvám: *have pressed* (the bottom) *upward*, that is, *overturned, poured out*; **avatám**: the cloud; = they have shed rain. **dādr̥hāṇám**: pf. pt. Ā. of **dr̥h** *make firm*, with long red. vowel (139, 9), shortened in the Pada text. **bibhidur ví**: p. 468, 20. **párvatam**: cloud mountain; another way of saying the same thing. **dhámantas**: with reference to the sound made by the Maruts; cp. **árcantas**, 2 c. **máde sómasya**: Indra is constantly said to perform his mighty deeds in the intoxication of Soma, so his associates the Maruts are here similarly described.

११ जि॒ह्मं नु॑नुद्रेऽव॒तं तया॑ दि॒शा-
सि॑ञ्चन्नुत्सं॒ गोत॑माय तृष्णजे॑ ।
आ ग॑च्छन्ती॒मव॑सा चि॒त्रभा॑नवः
कामं॒ विप्र॑स्य तर्पयन्त॒ धाम॑भिः ॥

जि॒ह्मम् । नु॒नु॒द्रे॒ । अ॒व॒तम् । तया॑ । दि॒शा । असि॑ञ्चन् । उत्स॑म् । गोत॑माय । तृ॒ष्ण॒ऽजे॑ । आ । ग॒च्छ॒न्ति॒ । ई॒म् । अव॑सा । चि॒त्रऽभा॑नवः । काम॑म् । विप्र॑स्य । त॒र्प॒य॒न्त॒ । धाम॑ऽभिः ॥

11 jihmám̐ nunudre avatám̐ táyā diśā́:
ásiñcann útsam̐ Gótamāya tr̥ṣṇáje.
ā́ gachantīm ávasā citrábhānavaḥ:
kā́mam̐ víprasya tarpayanta dhā́mabhiḥ.

They have pushed athwart the well in that direction: they poured out the spring for the thirsty Gotama. Of brilliant splendour they approach him with help; may they satisfy the desire of the sage by their powers.

jihmám: so as to be horizontal and pour out the water, much the same as **ūrdhvám** in 10 a. **táyā diśā́**: this expression is obscure; it may mean, in the quarter in which Gotama was; cp. 199 A 4. **īm**: *him*, Gotama, p. 220. **víprasya**: of Gotama. **tarpayanta**: cs. of **tṛp** *be pleased*; the inj. is more natural here, coming after a pr., than an unaugmented ipf. would be.

१२ या वः शर्म शशमानाय सन्ति	या । वः । शर्म । शशमानाय । सन्ति ।
त्रिधातूनि दाशुषे यछताधि ।	त्रिऽधातूनि । दाशुषे । यछत । अधि ।
अस्मभ्यं तानि मरुतो वि यन्त	अस्मभ्यम् । तानि । मरुतः । वि । यन्त ।
रयिं नो धत्त वृषणः सुवीरम् ॥	रयिम् । नः । धत्त । वृषणः । सुऽवीरम् ॥

12 **yā́ vaḥ śárma śaśamānā́ya sánti,**	*The shelters which you have for*
tridhā́tūni dāśúṣe yachatā́dhi.	*the zealous man, extend them three-*
asmábhyaṃ tā́ni, Maruto, ví yanta.	*fold to the worshipper. Extend*
rayím no dhatta, vṛṣaṇaḥ, su-vī́ram.	*them to us, O Maruts. Bestow on us wealth together with excellent heroes, mighty ones.*

śárma: N. pl. n. (90, 2) **śaśamānā́ya**: pf. pt. Ā. of **śam** *labour*. **tridhā́tūni**: used appositionally (198). **dāśúṣe**: dat. of **dāśvā́ṃs**, 157 *b*. **yachata ádhi**: prp. after vb., p. 468, 20; ipv. pr. of **yam** *stretch*. **asmábhyam**: p. 104. **ví yanta**: 2. pl. ipv. root ao. of **yam** *stretch* (cp. p. 172, 5). **dhatta**: 2. pl. ipv. of **dhā** *put* (p. 144 B *b*). **su-vī́ram**: that is, accompanied by warrior sons; cp. **vīrávattamam**, i. 1, 3 c.

VÍṢṆU

This deity occupies a subordinate position in the RV., being celebrated in only five or six hymns. The only anthropomorphic traits mentioned about him are the strides he takes, and the description of him as a youth vast in body who is no longer a child. The central feature of his nature consists in his three steps, connected with which are his exclusive epithets 'wide-going' (uru-gāyá) and 'wide-striding' (uru-kramá). With these steps he traverses the earth or the terrestrial spaces. Two of his steps are visible to men, but the third or highest is beyond the flight of birds or mortal ken. His highest step is like an eye fixed in heaven; it shines brightly down. It is his dear abode, where pious men and the gods rejoice. There can be no doubt that these three steps refer to the course of the sun, and in all probability to its passage through the three divisions of the world: earth, air, and heaven. Viṣṇu sets in motion like a revolving wheel his ninety steeds (= days) with their four names (= seasons), an allusion to the three hundred and sixty days of the solar year. Thus Viṣṇu seems to have been originally a personification of the activity of the sun, the swiftly-moving luminary that with vast strides passes through the whole universe. Viṣṇu takes his steps for man's existence, to bestow the earth on him as a dwelling. The most prominent secondary characteristic of Viṣṇu is his friendship for Indra, with whom he is often allied in the fight with Vṛtra. In hymns addressed to Viṣṇu alone, Indra is the only other deity inci-dentally associated with him. One hymn (vi. 69) is dedicated to the two gods conjointly. Through the Vṛtra myth the Maruts, Indra's companions, are drawn into alliance with Viṣṇu, who throughout one hymn (v. 87) is praised in combination with them.

The name is most probably derived from **viṣ** *be active*, thus meaning 'the active one'.

i. 154. Metre: Triṣṭubh.

१ विष्णोर्नु कं वीर्याणि प्र वोचं
यः पार्थिवानि विममे रजांसि ।
यो अस्कभायदुत्तरं सधस्थं
विचक्रमाणस्त्रेधोरुगायः ॥

विष्णोः । नु । कम् । वीर्याणि । प्र ।
वोचम् ।
यः । पार्थिवानि । वि॒ऽममे । रजांसि ।
यः । अस्कभायत् । उत्ऽतरम् । सधऽस्थम् ।
विऽचक्रमाणः । त्रेधा । उरुऽगायः ॥

1 Víṣṇor nú kaṃ vīríāṇi prá vo-
    caṃ,
  yáḥ párthivāni vimamé rájāṃsi;
  yó áskabhāyad úttaraṃ sadhá-
    sthaṃ,
  vicakramāṇás trēdhórugāyáḥ.

I will now proclaim the heroic powers of Viṣṇu, who has measured out the terrestrial regions; who established the upper gathering-place, having wide-paced, strode out triply.

kam: this pcl. as an encl. always follows nú, sú or hí (p. 225, 2).
vīryáṇi: the syllable preceding the so-called independent Svarita

(p. 448) is marked with the Anudātta in the same way as that preceding the Udātta; here we have, as usual, in reality the dependent Svarita, the word having to be pronounced vīriàṇi. **prá vocam**: inj. ao. of **vac**, 147, 3. **pā́rthivāni rájāṃsi**: the earth and the contiguous air. **vi-mamé**: this refers to the sun traversing the universe; cp. what is said of Varuṇa in v. 85, 5: **mā́neneva tasthivā́m̐ antárikṣe ví yó mamé pṛthivī́ṃ sū́ryeṇa** *who standing in the air has measured out the earth with the sun, as with a measure.* **áskabhāyat**: ipf. of **skabh** *prop*; the cosmic action of supporting the sky is also attributed to Savitṛ, Agni, and other deities. **úttaraṃ sadhástham**: that is, heaven, as opposed to the terrestrial spaces in b, according to the twofold division of the world. **vicakramāṇás**: pf. pt. Ā. of **kram**. **tre-dhā́**: with his three steps; the first syllable must be pronounced with a slur equivalent to two short syllables (⏑⏑); the resolution **tredhā́ urugāyáḥ** would produce both an abnormal break and an abnormal cadence (p. 441, top).

२ प्र तद्विष्णुः स्तवते वीर्येण
मृगो न भीमः कुचरो गिरिष्ठाः ।
यस्योरुषु त्रिषु विक्रमणेष्व्
अधिक्षियन्ति भुवनानि विश्वा ॥

प्र । तत् । विष्णुः । स्तवते । वीर्येण ।
मृगः । न । भीमः । कुचरः । गिरिऽस्थाः ।
यस्य । उरुषु । त्रिषु । विऽक्रमणेषु ।
अधिऽक्षियन्ति । भुवनानि । विश्वा ॥

2 **prá tád Víṣṇuḥ stavate vīríeṇa,**
mṛgó ná bhīmáḥ kucaró giri-ṣṭhā́ḥ,
yásyorúṣu triṣú vikrámaṇeṣu
adhikṣiyánti bhúvanāni víśvā.

By reason of his heroic power, like a dread beast that wanders at will, that haunts the mountains, Viṣṇu is praised aloud for that: he in whose three wide strides all beings dwell.

prá stavate: Ā. of **stu** in the ps. sense, as is often the case when the pr. stem is formed according to the first (and not the second) class. **tád**: the cognate acc. (p. 300, 4) referring to the heroic powers of Viṣṇu attributed to him in the preceding stanza. **vīryèṇa**: cp. note on **vīryā̀ṇi** in 1 a. **mṛgás**: Sāyaṇa here interprets this word to mean a beast of prey such as a lion; but though **bhīmá** occurs as an attribute both of **siṃhá** *lion* and of **vṛṣabhá** *bull* in the RV., **giriṣṭhā́** is found three or four times applied to the latter and never to the former, and in the next stanza Viṣṇu is called a 'mountain-dwelling bull'; hence the simile appears to allude to a bull rather than a lion. **ku-cará**: Yāska, followed by Sāyaṇa, has two explanations of this word, *doing ill* (**ku = kutsitaṃ karma** *blameworthy deed*) or *going anywhere* (**kva ayaṃ na gachati** *where does he not go?*). Note that the word is not analysed in the Pada text because **ku** does not occur as an independent word. Sāyaṇa has two explanations of **giriṣṭhā́s**: *dwelling in a lofty world* or *always abiding in speech* (**giri** as loc. of **gir**) *consisting of Mantras*, &c. (!); on the inflexion see 97, 2; note that in the analysis of the Pada text the change caused by internal Sandhi in the second member is, as always, removed. **vikrámaneṣu**: note that the final vowel of the Pāda must be restored at the junction with the next Pāda. **adhi-kṣiyánti**: the root 1. **kṣi** follows the **ad** class (**kṣéti**) when it means *dwell*, but the **bhū** class (**kṣáyati**) when it means *rule over*. With c and d cp. what is said of Savitṛ in i. 35, 5.

३ प्र विष्णवे शूषमेतु मन्म	प्र । विष्णवे । शूषम् । एतु । मन्म ।
गिरिक्षित उरुगायाय वृष्णे ।	गिरिऽक्षिते । उरुऽगायाय । वृष्णे ॥
य इदं दीर्घं प्रयतं सधस्थम्	यः । इदम् । दीर्घम् । प्रऽयतम् । सधऽस्थम् ।
एको विममे त्रिभिरित्पदेभिः ॥	एकः । विऽममे । त्रिऽभिः । इत् । पदेभिः ॥

3 **prá Víṣṇave śūṣám etu mánma,**	*Let my inspiring hymn go forth*
girikṣíta urugāyā́ya vṛ́ṣṇe,	*for Viṣṇu, the mountain-dwelling*
yá idáṃ dīrgháṃ práyataṃ sadhástham	*wide-pacing bull, who alone with*
éko vimamé tribhír ít padébhiḥ;	*but three steps has measured out this long far-extended gathering-place;*

śūṣám: the **ū** must be slurred disyllabically (= ◡◡). **idáṃ sadhástham**: of course the earth as opposed to **úttaraṃ sadhástham** in 1 c. **ékas** and **tribhís** are antithetical. **íd** emphasizes the latter word: *with only three.* The second Pāda of this stanza is parallel to the third of the preceding, the epithets in the former being applied direct to Viṣṇu, in the latter to the wild beast to which Viṣṇu is compared: **girikṣít** = **giriṣṭhā́**; **urugāyá** = **kucará**; **vṛ́ṣan** = **mṛgó bhīmáḥ**. This correspondence of **kucará** (besides V.'s alternative exclusive epithet **urukramá** in 5 c and elsewhere) confirms the explanation of **urugāyá** as *wide-pacing* from **gā** *go* (Yāska, **mahāgati** *having a wide gait*), and not *widely sung* from **gā** *sing* (Sāyaṇa).

4 यस्य त्री पूर्णा मधुना पदान्य्
अक्षीयमाणा स्वधया मदन्ति ।
य उ त्रिधातु पृथिवीमुत द्याम्
एको दाधार भुवनानि विश्वा ॥

यस्य । त्री । पूर्णा । मधुना । पदानि ।
अक्षीयमाणा । स्वधया । मदन्ति ।
यः । ऊं इति । त्रिऽधातु । पृथिवीम् ।
उत । द्याम् ।
एकः । दाधार । भुवनानि । विश्वा ॥

4 **yásya trī́ pūrṇā́ mádhunā padā́ni**
ákṣīyamāṇā svadháyā mádanti;
yá u tridhā́tu pṛthivī́m utá dyā́m
éko dādhā́ra bhúvanāni víśvā.

Whose three steps filled with mead, unfailing, rejoice in bliss; and who in threefold wise alone has supported earth and heaven, and all beings.

trī́: n. pl. of **trí** (105, 3). **padā́ny**: the final vowel of the Pāda must be restored; cp. 2 c. **pūrṇā́**: cp. p. 308 d. **ákṣīyamāṇā**: *never failing* in mead; the privative pcl. **a** is almost invariably accented in Karmadhārayas, p. 456 a (top); such negative cds. are not analysed in the Pada text. **svadháyā**: inst. with verbs of rejoicing (p. 308 *c*). **mádanti**: his footsteps rejoice, that is, those dwelling in them do so. **u**: = *also* (p. 221, 2). **tri-dhā́tu**: this n. form is best taken adverbially = **tredhā́** in 1 d, *in a threefold way,* by taking his three steps. It might, however, mean the threefold world, loosely explained by the following *earth and heaven.* **ékas**: *alone* in antithesis to **víśvā**, cp. 3 d. **dādhā́ra**: pf. of **dhṛ**, with long red. vowel (139, 9), which is here not shortened in the Pada text.

5 तदस्य प्रियमभि पाथो अश्यां
नरो यत्र देवयवो मदन्ति ।
उरुक्रमस्य स हि बन्धुरित्था
विष्णोः पदे परमे मध्व उत्सः ॥

तत् । अस्य । प्रियम् । अभि । पाथः ।
अश्याम् ।
नरः । यत्र । देवऽयवः । मदन्ति ।
उरुऽक्रमस्य । सः । हि । बन्धुः । इत्था ।
विष्णोः । पदे । परमे । मध्वः । उत्सः ॥

5 **tád asya priyám abhí pā́tho aśyām,**
náro yátra devayávo mádanti:
urukramásya sá hí bándhur itthā́,
Víṣṇoḥ padé paramé mádhva útsaḥ.

I would attain to that dear domain of his, where men devoted to the gods rejoice: for that, truly akin to the wide-strider, is a well of mead in the highest step of Viṣṇu.

abhí aśyām: op. root ao. of **aṃś** *reach*. **yátra**: in the third step of Viṣṇu = heaven, where the Fathers drink Soma with Yama (cp. i. 35, 6). **náras**: that is, pious men who dwell in **heaven**; N. pl. of **nṛ́**, 101, 1. **sá**: referring to **pā́thas** is attracted in gender to **bándhus**, 194, 3. **itthā́**: p. 218. **mádhvas** (gen., p. 81, n. 12): cp. 4 a, where the three steps are filled with mead; but the third step is its special abode.

6 ता वां वास्तून्युश्मसि गमध्यै
यत्र गावो भूरिशृङ्गा अयासः ।
अत्राह तदुरुगायस्य वृष्णः
परमं पदमव भाति भूरि ॥

ता । वाम् । वास्तूनि । उश्मसि । गमध्यै ।
यत्र । गावः । भूरिऽशृङ्गाः । अयासः ।
अत्र । अह । तत् । उरुऽगायस्य । वृष्णः ।
परमम् । पदम् । अव । भाति । भूरि ॥

6 **tā́ vām vā́stūni uśmasi gámadhyai,**
yátra gā́vo bhū́riśṛṅgā ayā́saḥ:
átrā́ha tád urugāyásya vṛ́ṣṇaḥ
paramám padám áva bhāti bhū́ri.

We desire to go to those abodes of you two, where are the many-horned nimble kine: there indeed that highest step of the wide-pacing bull shines brightly down.

vām : *of you two*, that is, of Indra and Viṣṇu. The former, being the only other god with whom Viṣṇu is intimately associated, would easily be thought of incidentally in a hymn addressed to Viṣṇu alone; this dual also anticipates the joint praise of these two gods as a dual divinity (Índrā-Víṣṇū) in the first two stanzas of the next hymn (i. 155). **uśmasi** : 1. pl. pr. of vaś *desire* (134, 2 *a*). **gám-adhyai** : dat. inf., p. 193, 7. **gā́vas** : N. pl. of **gó** *cow* (102, 2); it is somewhat doubtful what is meant by the cows; they are explained by Yāska and Sāyaṇa as rays; this is a probable sense, as the rays of dawn are compared with cattle, and something connected with sunlight is appropriate to the third step of Viṣṇu, the realm of light. Roth explains **gā́vas** as stars, but there is little to support this interpretation. **bhū́ri-śr̥ṅgas** : *many-horned* would allude to the diffusion of the sunbeams in many directions. **ayā́sas** : this form is understood as a N. pl. of **aya** (from **i** *go*) by Yāska, who explains it as **ayanās** *moving*, and by Sāyaṇa as **gantāras** *goers* = **ativistr̥tās** *very widely diffused*; but the occurrence of the A. s. **ayā́sam**, the G. pl. **ayā́sām**, as well as the A. pl. **ayā́sas**, indicates that the stem is **ayā́s**; while its use as an attribute of **siṃhá** *lion*, **áśva** *horse*, and often of the Maruts, shows that the meaning must be *active, swift, nimble*. **áha** : on the use of this pcl. see p. 216. **vŕ̥ṣṇas** : cp. 3 b.

DYÁVĀ-PR̥THIVÍ

Heaven and Earth are the most frequently named pair of deities in the RV. They are so closely associated that, while they are invoked as a pair in six hymns, Dyáus is never addressed alone in any hymn, and Pr̥thiv in only one of three stanzas. The dual compound Dyā́vā-Pr̥thivī́, moreover, occurs much oftener than the name of Dyáus alone. Heaven and Earth are also mentioned as **ródasī** *the two worlds* more than 100 times. They are parents, being often called **pitárā**, **mātárā**, **jánitrī**, besides being separately addressed as 'father' and 'mother'. They have made and sustain all creatures; they are also the parents of the gods. At the same time they are in different passages spoken of as themselves created by individual gods. One of them is a prolific bull, the other a variegated cow, being both rich in seed. They never grow old. They are great and wide-extended; they are broad and vast abodes. They grant food and wealth, or bestow great fame and dominion. Sometimes moral qualities are attributed to them. They are wise and promote righteousness. As father and mother they guard beings, and protect from disgrace and misfortune. They are sufficiently personified to be called leaders of the sacrifice and to be conceived as seating themselves around the offering; but they never attained to a living personification or importance in worship. These two deities are quite co-ordinate, while in most of the other pairs one of the two greatly predominates.

i. 160. Metre: **Jagatī.**

१ ते हि द्यावापृथिवी विश्वशंभुव
ऋतावरी रजसो धारयत्कवी ।
सुजन्मनी धिषणे अन्तरीयते
देवो देवी धर्मणा सूर्यः शुचिः ॥

ते इति । हि । द्यावापृथिवी इति । विश्व-
ऽशंभुवा ।
ऋतवरी इत्यृतऽवरी । रजसः । धार-
यत्कवी इति धारयत्ऽकवी ।
सुजन्मनी इति सुऽजन्मनी । धिषणे इति ।
अन्तः । ईयते ।
देवः । देवी इति । धर्मणा । सूर्यः । शुचिः ॥

**1 té hí Dyā́vā-Pṛthiví́ viśváśaṃ-
bhuvā,
ṛtā́varī, rájaso dhārayátkavī:
sujánmanī dhiṣáṇe antár īyate
devó deví́ dhármaṇā Sū́riaḥ
śúciḥ.**

These two, indeed, Heaven and Earth, are beneficial to all, observing order, supporting the sage of the air: between the two divine bowls that produce fair creations the divine bright Sūrya moves according to fixed law.

The first two Pādas form an independent sentence; otherwise **hí** (p. 252) would accent **īyate** in c. **Dyā́vā-Pṛthiví́**: on the accent, and treatment in the Pada text, see note on i. 35, 1 b. **viśvá-śaṃbhuvā**: dec., p. 89; accent, note on i. 1, 4 b; final **a** and **ā** are never contracted with **ṛ** (19 *a* and note 5). **ṛtā-varī**: note that, when the final vowel of a cd. is Pragṛhya, this is in the Pada text first indicated by **íti**, and the cd. is then repeated and analysed; in the present case the suffix **varī** (f. of **van**, pp. 67 and 69, f. n. 2) is treated like the final member of a cd., and the final vowel of **ṛtā** is treated as metrically lengthened. **dhārayát-kavī**: a governing cd. (189 A 2 *a*); the gen. **rájasas** is dependent on **-kavi**, probably = Agni, who (in x. 2, 7) is said to have been begotten by Dyāvā-pṛthivī. **dhiṣáṇe**: the exact meaning of this word, here a designation of dyā́vā-pṛthivī́, is uncertain. **antár īyate** *goes between* with acc.; the same thing is said of Savitṛ in i. 35, 9 b. **dhárman** n. *ordinance* (**dharmán** m. *ordainer*) is the only stem in the RV. (**dhárma** is a later one).

२ उरुव्यचसा महिनी असश्चता
पिता माता च भुवनानि रक्षतः ।
सुधृष्टमे वपुष्ये३ न रोदसी
पिता यत्सीमभि रूपैरवासयत् ॥

उरुऽव्यचसा । महिनी इति । असश्चता ।
पिता । माता । च । भुवनानि । रक्षतः ।
सुधृष्टमे इति सुऽधृष्टमे । वपुष्ये३ इति ।
न । रोदसी इति ।
पिता । यत् । सीम् । अभि । रूपैः । अवासयत् ॥

2 uruvyácasā mahínī asaścátā,
pitā́ mātā́ ca, bhúvanāni rakṣataḥ.
sudhṛ́ṣṭame vapuṣíe ná ródasī,
pitā́ yát sīm abhí rūpáir ávāsayat.

As Father and Mother, far-extending, great, inexhaustible, the two protect (all) beings. Like two most proud fair women are the two worlds, since the Father clothed them with beauty.

uru-vyácasā: on the accent of this Bv. *having wide extension*, see p. 455 *c a*. The du. **a-saścát-ā** is a Bv. (as the accent shows, p. 455 *c a*) *having no second*, while **á-saścant** (also an epithet of Dyāvā-pṛthivī) is a Karmadhāraya (p. 455, f. n. 2), *not a second* = *unequalled*. **su-dhṛ́ṣṭame**: on the Pada analysis cp. note on i. 1, 1 c. **vapuṣyè**: cp. note on vīryā̀ṇi, i. 154, 1 a. **pitā́**: the god here meant as the father of Dyāvā-pṛthivī may be Viśvakarman, who in RV. x. 81, 1. 2 is called 'our father' and is described as creating the earth and heaven. **sīm**: see p. 249. **abhí avāsayat**: ipf. cs. of 2. vas *wear*.

३ स वह्निः पुत्रः पित्रोः पवित्रवान्
पुनाति धीरो भुवनानि मायया ।

सः । वह्निः । पुत्रः । पित्रोः । पवित्रऽवान् ।
पुनाति । धीरः । भुवनानि । मायया ।

धेनुं च पृश्निं वृषभं सुरेतसं
विश्वाहा शुक्रं पयो अस्य दुक्षत ॥

धेनुम् । च । पृश्निम् । वृषभम् । सुऽरेतसम् ।
विश्वाहा । शुक्रम् । पयः । अस्य । धुक्षत ॥

3 sá váhniḥ putráḥ pitaróḥ pavítravān
punā́ti dhī́ro bhúvanāni māyáyā.
dhenúṃ ca pṛ́śniṃ vṛṣabháṃ surétasaṃ
viśvā́hā śukráṃ páyŏ asya dukṣata.

That son of the two parents, the driver, the purifier, wisely purifies beings by his mysterious power. He has always milked from the speckled cow and from the bull abounding in seed his shining moisture.

putrás: by the son of the parents (Heaven and Earth) Agni is meant; for he is expressly said to have been begotten by Heaven and Earth (RV., x. 2, 7), cp. note on 1 b; he is especially called **váhni** as the one who conveys (vahati) the gods to the sacrifice; he is very frequently called **pāvaká** *purifier* (a term seldom applied to any other deity); he purifies beings in his character of priest. Sāyaṇa thinks the Sun is meant, and explains *purifies* by *illumines*. **dhenúm**: the term *cow* is often used in the RV. in the sense of earth. **ca** is here used with the first acc. instead of the second (cp. p. 228, 1). **vṛṣabhám**: Dyaus is called a bull in other passages also, and is said to have been made by Agni to roar for man (i. 31, 4). **su-rétasam**: alludes to the shedding of rain. **viśvā́hā** is a cd. adv. resulting from the juxtaposition of **víśvā áhā** as an acc. of time (cp. p. 300, 5) = *for all days* equivalent to **áhā víśvā** which also occurs. **dukṣata**: unaugmented **sa** ao. (141 *a*) without initial aspiration (which is, however, restored in the Pada text), from **duh** *milk* (with two acc., 198, 2). The general meaning of c d is that Agni as the priest of sacrifice causes heaven to fertilize the earth, and the latter to be productive.

४ अयं देवानामपसामपस्तमो
यो जजान रोदसी विश्वशंभुवा ।
वि यो ममे रजसी सुक्रतूयया-

अयम् । देवानाम् । अपसाम् । अपःऽतमः ।
यः । जजान । रोदसीऽइति । विश्वऽशंभुवा ।

जरेभिः स्कम्भनेभिः समानृचे ॥

वि । यः । ममे । रजसी इति । सुक्रतुऽयया ।
अजरेभिः । स्कम्भनेभिः । सम् । आनृचे ॥

4 **ayám̥ devā́nām apásām apás-
tamo
yó jajā́na ródasī viśváśam̥-
bhuvā.
ví yó mamé rā́jasī sukratūyáyā
ajárebhiḥ skámbhanebhiḥ, sám
ānṛce.**

He of the active gods is the most active who has created the two worlds that are beneficial to all. He who with insight has measured out the two spaces (and upheld them) *with unaging supports, has been universally praised.*

In this stanza (cp. 2) the father of Heaven and Earth is celebrated. **apásām** : partitive gen. (p. 321, *b* a). **ví . . . mamé** : this expression is also used of Viṣṇu (see i. 154, 1. 3) and other gods. **rájasī** : the heavenly and the terrestrial spaces. The initial vowel of d must be restored. **sám ānṛce** : red. pf. of **arc** *sing* (139, 6), the Ā. being used in the ps. sense ; Sāyaṇa explains it in an act. sense as **pūjitavān** *has honoured*, which he further interprets to mean **sthāpitavān** *has established!*

५ ते नो गृणाने महिनी महि श्रवः
क्षत्रं द्यावापृथिवी धासथो बृहत् ।
येनाभि कृष्टीस्ततनाम विश्वहा
पनाय्यमोजो अस्मे समिन्वतम् ॥

ते इति । नः । गृणाने इति । महिनी
इति । महि । श्रवः ।
क्षत्रम् । द्यावापृथिवी इति । धासथः ।
बृहत् ।
येन । अभि । कृष्टीः । ततनाम । विश्वहा ।
पनाय्यम् । ओजः । अस्मे इति । सम् ।
इन्वतम् ॥

5 **té no gṛṇāné, mahinī, máhi śrá-
vaḥ,
kṣatrám̥, Dyāvā-Pṛthivī, dhā-
satho bṛhát.**

So being lauded, O great ones bestow on us, O Heaven and Earth, great fame and ample dominion. Bring for us praiseworthy strength

yénābhí kṛṣṭī́s tatánāma viśváhā — *by which we may always extend over the peoples.*
panā́yiam ójŏ asmé sám invatam.

té: N. du. f., used anaphorically (p. 294, *b*). **gṛṇāné**: pr. pt. of 1. **gṛ** *sing*, Ā. used in ps. sense. **mahinī**: there are six adjectives meaning *great*, formed from the root **mah** *be great*: by far the commonest is **máh** (81); **mahánt** (85 *a*) is also common; **mahá** and **mahín** are not common, but are inflected in several cases; **máhi** and **mahás** (83, 2 *a* α) are used in the N. A. sing. only, the former very often, the latter rarely. **kṣatrám**: without **ca**. **dhāsathas**: 2. du. sb. **s** ao. (p. 162, 2) of **dhā** *bestow*, to be construed with the dat. **nas**. **abhí . . . tatánāma**: pf. sb. of **tan** *stretch* (140, 1, p. 156). **viśvá-hā** is an adv. formed with the suffix **hā** = **dhā** (p. 212 *β*) meaning literally *in every manner* = *always* (cp. **viśvā́hā** in 3 d); on the accent cp. note on **viśvátas** in i. 1, 4 b. **panā́yya**: see 162, 2. **ójŏ**: final **o** is pronounced short before **ă** (p. 437, *a* 4), but the rhythm of the break here (– ◡ –) is abnormal (p. 440, f. n. 6). **asmé**: properly loc. of **vayám** (p. 104), but also used as a dat., is Pragṛhya; it is dat. here (200 A 1). **invatam**: 2. du. ipv. of **inv**, a secondary root produced by a transfer from the fifth class (**i-nu**) to the first, **ínv-a** (133, 3 *b*).

ÍNDRA

sá janāsa índrah

Indra is invoked alone in about one-fourth of the hymns of the RV., far more than are addressed to any other deity; for he is the favourite national god of the Vedic people. He is more anthropomorphic on the physical side, and more invested with mythological imagery, than any other member of the pantheon. He is primarily a god of the thunderstorm who vanquishes the demons of drought or darkness, and sets free the waters or wins the light. He is secondarily the god of battle who aids the victorious Āryan in overcoming his aboriginal foes.

His physical features, such as body and head, are often referred to; after he has drunk Soma he agitates his jaws and his beard; and his belly is many times mentioned in connexion with his great powers of drinking Soma. Being tawny (**hári**) in colour, he is also tawny-haired and tawny-bearded. His arms are especially often referred to because they wield the thunderbolt (**vájra**), which, mythologically representing the lightning stroke, is his exclusive weapon. This bolt was fashioned for him by Tvaṣṭṛ, being made of iron (**āyasá**), golden, tawny, sharp, many-pointed, sometimes spoken of as a stone or rock. Several epithets, compounds or derivatives of **vájra**, such as **vájra-bāhu** *bearing the bolt in his arm* and **vajrín** *wielder of the bolt* are almost without exception applied to him. Sometimes he is described as armed with bow and arrows; he also carries a hook (**aṅkuśá**).

Having a golden car, drawn by two tawny steeds (**hárī**), he is a car-fighter (**rathesṭhā̆**). Both his car and his steeds were fashioned by the Ṛbhus, the divine artificers.

As Indra is more addicted to Soma than any of the other gods, the common epithet 'Soma-drinker' (**Somapā́**) is characteristic of him. This beverage stimulates him to carry out his warlike deeds; thus for the slaughter of Vṛtra he is said to have drunk three lakes of Soma. One whole hymn (x. 119) is a monologue in which Indra, intoxicated with Soma, boasts of his greatness and his might.

Indra is often spoken of as having been born, and two whole hymns deal with the subject of his birth. His father, the same as Agni's, appears to be Dyaus; but the inference from other passages is that he is Tvaṣṭṛ, the artificer among the gods. Agni is called Indra's twin brother, and Pūṣan (vi. 54) is also his brother. His wife, who is often mentioned, is Indrāṇī. Indra is associated with various other deities. The Maruts (i. 85) are his chief allies, who constantly help him in his conflicts. Hence the epithet **Marútvant** *accompanied by the Maruts* is characteristic of him. Agni is the god most often conjoined with him as a dual divinity. Indra is also often coupled with Varuṇa (vii. 86) and Vāyu, god of Wind, less often with Soma (viii. 48), Bṛhaspati (iv. 50), Pūṣan, and Viṣṇu.

Indra is of vast size; thus it is said that he would be equal to the earth even if it were ten times as large as it is. His greatness and power are constantly dwelt on: neither gods nor men have attained to the limit of his might; and no one like him is known among the gods. Thus various epithets such as **śakrá** and **śácīvant** *mighty*, **śácīpáti** *lord of might*, **śatá-kratu** *having a hundred powers*, are characteristic of him.

The essential myth forming the basis of his nature is described with extreme frequency and much variation. Exhilarated by Soma and generally escorted by the Maruts, he attacks the chief demon of drought, usually called Vṛtra, but often also the serpent (**áhi**). Heaven and Earth tremble when the mighty combat takes place. With his bolt he shatters Vṛtra who encompasses the waters, hence receiving the exclusive epithet **apsu-jít** *conquering in the waters*. The result of the conflict, which is regarded as being constantly renewed, is that he pierces the mountain and sets free the waters pent up like imprisoned cows. The physical elements in the conflict are nearly always the bolt, the mountain, waters or rivers, while lightning, thunder, cloud, rain are seldom directly named. The waters are often terrestrial, but also often aerial and celestial. The clouds are the mountains (párvata, girí), on which the demons lie or dwell, or from which Indra casts them down, or which he cleaves to release the waters. Or the cloud is a rock (ádri) which encompasses the cows (as the waters are sometimes called), and from which he releases them. Clouds, as containing the waters, figure as cows also; they further appear under the names of udder (ū́dhar), spring (útsa), cask (kávandha), pail (kóśa). The clouds, moreover, appear as the fortresses (púras) of the aerial demons, being described as moving, autumnal, made of iron or stone, and as 90, 99, or 100 in number. Indra shatters them and is characteristically called the 'fort-destroyer' (pūrbhíd). But the chief and specific epithet of Indra is 'Vṛtra-slayer' (Vṛtra-hán), owing to the essential importance, in the myth, of the fight with the demon. In this fight the Maruts are his regular allies, but Agni, Soma, and Viṣṇu also often assist him. Indra also engages in conflict with numerous minor demons; sometimes he is described as destroying demons in general, the Rakṣases or the Asuras.

With the release of the waters is connected the winning of light, sun, and dawn. Thus Indra is invoked to slay Vṛtra and to win the light. When he had slain Vṛtra, releasing the waters for man, he placed the sun visibly in the heavens. The sun shone forth when Indra blew the serpent from the air. There is here often no reference to the Vṛtra fight. Indra is then simply said to find the light; he gained the sun or found it in the darkness, and made a path for it. He produces the dawn as well as the sun; he opens the darkness with the dawn and the sun. The cows mentioned along with the sun and dawn, or with the sun alone, as found, released, or won by Indra, are here probably the morning beams, which are elsewhere compared with cattle coming out of their dark stalls. Thus when the dawns went to meet Indra, he became the lord of the cows; when he overcame Vṛtra he made visible the cows of the nights. There seems to be a confusion between the restoration of the sun after the darkness of the thunderstorm, and the recovery of the sun from the darkness of night at dawn. The latter feature is probably an extension of the former. Indra's connexion with the thunderstorm is in a few passages divested of mythological imagery, as when he is said to have created the lightnings of heaven and to have directed the action of the waters downwards. With the Vṛtra-fight, with the winning of the cows and of the sun, is also connected the gaining of Soma. Thus when Indra drove the serpent from the air, there shone forth fires, the sun, and Soma; he won Soma at the same time as the cows.

Great cosmic actions are often attributed to Indra. He settled the quaking mountains and plains. He stretches out heaven and earth like a hide; he holds asunder heaven and earth as two wheels are kept apart by the axle; he made the non-existent into the existent in a moment. Sometimes the separation and support of heaven and earth are described as a result of Indra's victory over a demon who held them together.

As the destroyer of demons in combat, Indra is constantly invoked by warriors. As the great god of battle he is more frequently called upon than any other deity to help the Aryans in their conflicts with earthly enemies. He protects the Aryan colour and subjects the black skin. He dispersed 50,000 of the black race. He subjected the Dasyus to the Aryan, and gave land to the Aryan.

More generally Indra is praised as the protector, helper, and friend of his worshippers. He is described as bestowing on them wealth, which is considered the result of victories. His liberality is so characteristic that the frequent attribute maghávan *bountiful* is almost exclusively his.

Besides the central myth of the Vṛtra-fight, several minor stories are connected with Indra. In various passages he is described as shattering the car of Uṣas, goddess of Dawn (iv. 51); this trait is probably based on the notion of Indra's bringing the sun when kept back by the delaying dawn. He is also said to have stopped the steeds of the Sun, apparently by causing the latter to lose a wheel of his car. Indra is further associated with the myth of the winning of Soma; for it is to him that the eagle brings the draught of immortality from the highest heaven. Another myth is the capture by Indra, with the help of Saramā, of the cows confined in a cave by demons called Paṇis.

Various stories which, though mixed with mythological elements, probably have an historical basis, are told of Indra's having fought in aid of individual protégés, such as king Sudās, against terrestrial foes.

The attributes of Indra are chiefly those of physical superiority and rule over the physical world. He is energetic and violent in action, an irresistible fighter, an inexhaustible lavisher of the highest goods on mankind, but at the same time sensual and immoral in various ways, such as excess in eating and drinking, and cruelty in killing his own father Tvaṣṭṛ. He forms a marked contrast to Varuṇa, the other great universal monarch of the RV., who wields passive and peaceful sway, who uniformly applies the laws of nature, who upholds moral order, and whose character displays lofty ethical features.

The name of Indra is pre-Indian; for it occurs in the Avesta as that of a demon; the term *verethraghna* (=Vṛtrahán) is also found there as the designation of the God of Victory, though unconnected with Indra. Thus it seems likely that there was already in the Indo-Iranian period a god resembling the Vṛtra-slaying Indra of the RV. The etymology of the word is doubtful, but its radical portion ind may be connected with that in índ-u *drop*.

ii. 12. Metre: Triṣṭubh.

१ यो जात एव प्रथमो मनस्वान्
देवो देवान्क्रतुना पर्यभूषत् ।
यस्य शुष्माद्रोदसी अभ्यसेतां
नृम्णस्य मह्ना स जनास इन्द्रः ॥

यः । जातः । एव । प्रथमः । मनस्वान् ।
देवः । देवान् । क्रतुना । परिऽअभूषत् ।
यस्य । शुष्मात् । रोदसी इति । अभ्यसेताम् ।
नृम्णस्य । मह्ना । सः । जनासः । इन्द्रः ॥

1 **yó jātá evá prathamó mánasvān**
devó devā́n krátunā paryábhūṣat;
yásya śúṣmād ródasī ábhyasetām
nṛmṇásya mahnā́: sá, janāsa, Índraḥ.

The chief wise god who as soon as born surpassed the gods in power; before whose vehemence the two worlds trembled by reason of the greatness of his valour: he, O men, is Indra.

evá: see p. 224, 2. **mánas-vān**: note that the suffix **vān** is not separated in the Pada text, as it is in **pavítra-vān** (i. 160, 3); had the Sandhi of the word, however, been **máno-vān** it would have been analysed as **mánaḥ**ऽ**vān**. **devó devā́n**: cp. i. 1, 5 c. **paryá-bhūṣat**: the exact meaning of the vb. **pári bhūṣ** is somewhat uncertain here, but as the greatness of Indra is especially emphasized in this hymn, *surpass* seems the most probable. Sāyaṇa explains it here as *encompassed with protection*; in the AV. as *ruled over*; in the TS. as *surpassed*. **ródasī**: the Pragṛhya **ī** of duals is not shortened in pronunciation before vowels (p. 437, f. n. 3). **ábhyasetām**: ipf. of **bhyas** = **bhī** *be afraid of*, with abl. (p. 316, *b*). **mahnā́**: inst. of **mahán** *greatness* (cp. p. 458, 2). The refrain **sá, janāsa, Índraḥ** ends every stanza (except the last) of this hymn; similarly **víśvasmād Índra úttaraḥ** ends all the twenty-three stanzas of x. 86.

२ यः पृथिवीं व्यथमानामदृंहद्
यः पर्वतान्प्रकुपिताँ अरम्णात् ।
यो अन्तरिक्षं विममे वरीयो

यः । पृथिवीम् । व्यथमानाम् । अदृंहत् ।
यः । पर्वतान् । प्रऽकुपितान् । अरम्णात् ।
यः । अन्तरिक्षम् । विऽममे । वरीयः ।

यो द्यामस्तभ्नात्स जनास इन्द्रः ॥ यः । द्याम् । अस्तभ्नात् । सः । जनासः । इन्द्रः ॥

2 yáḥ pṛthivīṃ vyáthamānām ádṛṃhad,
yáḥ párvatān prákupitām̐ áramṇāt,
yó antárikṣaṃ vimamé várīyo,
yó dyā́m ástabhnāt: sá, janāsa, Índraḥ.

Who made firm the quaking earth, who set at rest the agitated mountains; who measures out the air more widely, who supported heaven: he, O men, is Indra.

yás: note that every Pāda of this stanza, as well as of nearly every other stanza of this hymn, begins with a form of the relative prn. corresponding to the **sá** of the refrain. The cosmic deeds of Indra in all the three divisions of the universe, earth, air, and heaven, are here described. **áramṇāt**: ipf. of **ram** *set at rest.* **vimamé várīyas** (cpv. of **urú**, 103, 2 *a*): here the cpv. is used predicatively, *extended* so as to be *wider*; cp. vi. 69, 5, where it is said of Indra and Viṣṇu: 'ye made the air wider and stretched out the spaces for us to live.' **dyā́m**: acc. of **dyó** *sky.* **ástabhnāt**: ipf. of **stabh** *prop*; in this and the preceding stanza the ipf. of narration is used throughout excepting **vimamé** (a form of constant occurrence, cp. 154, 1. 3; 160, 4): cp. 213 *d* (p. 343).

3 यो हत्वाहिमरिणात्सप्त सिन्धून्
यो गा उदाजदपधा वलस्य ।
यो अश्मनोरन्तरग्निं जजान
संवृक्समत्सु स जनास इन्द्रः ॥

यः । हत्वा । अहिम् । अरिणात् । सप्त । सिन्धून् ।
यः । गाः । उत्ऽआजत् । अपऽधा । वलस्य ।
यः । अश्मनोः । अन्तः । अग्निम् । जजान ।
सम्ऽवृक् । समत्ऽसु । सः । जनासः । इन्द्रः ॥

3 yó hatvā́him áriṇāt saptá síndhūn,
yó gā́ udā́jad apadhā́ Valásya,
yó áśmanor antár agníṃ jajā́na,
saṃvṛ́k samátsu: sá, janāsa, Índraḥ.

Who having slain the serpent released the seven streams, who drove out the cows by the unclosing of Vala, who between two rocks has produced fire, victor in battles: he, O men, is Indra.

The first hemistich refers to the two well-known myths, the release of the waters by the conquest of Vṛtra, and the capture of the cows imprisoned by Vala; cp. ii. 14, 2: **yó apó vavṛvā́ṃsaṃ Vṛtrā́ṃ jaghā́na** *who slew Vṛtra who had enclosed the waters*, and *ibid.* 3: **yó gā́ udā́jad, ápa hí Valā́ṃ vā́ḥ** *who drove out the cows, for he unclosed Vala.* **áriṇāt**: ipf. of **ri** *release.* **saptá síndhūn**: the seven rivers of the Panjāb. **gā́s**: A. pl. of **gó** *cow.* **ud-ā́jat**: ipf. of **aj** *drive.* There is some doubt as to the exact interpretation of **apadhā́**, a word that occurs here only. In form it can only be an I. s. of **apa-dhā́** (cp. 97, 2). The parallel use of **ápa-vṛ** in ii. 14, 3 (quoted above) indicates that **apa-dhā́** means the *unclosing* by Indra of the cave of Vala in which the cows are imprisoned; cp. also i. 11, 5: **tvā́ṃ Valásya gómató 'pāvar bílam** *thou hast unclosed the aperture of Vala rich in cows.* The form is explained by Durga, the commentator on the Nirukta, by **apadhānena** as meaning **udghāṭanena Valasya** *by the unclosing of Vala.* Sāyaṇa interprets it as an irregularity for the abl. = *from the enclosure of Vala.* **Valásya**: the objective gen. (p. 320, B 1 *b*) = by opening (the cave of) Vala. **áśmanor antár**: between two clouds, according to Sāyaṇa; between heaven and earth accord ng to Durga; the allusion is to the lightning form of Agni who in several passages is said to be 'in the rock', to be 'produced from the rock' and is called 'son of the rock' (**ádreḥ sūnúḥ**).

४ येनेमा विश्वा च्यवना कृतानि
यो दासं वर्णमधरं गुहाकः ।
श्वघ्नीव यो जिगीवाँ लक्षमाददद्
अर्यः पुष्टानि स जनास इन्द्रः ॥

येन । इमा । विश्वा । च्यवना । कृतानि ।
यः । दासम् । वर्णम् । अधरम् । गुहा ।
अकरित्यकः ।
श्वघ्नीऽइव । यः । जिगीवान् । लक्षम् ।
आदत ।
अर्यः । पुष्टानि । सः । जनासः । इन्द्रः ॥

4 **yénemā́ víśvā cyávanā kṛtā́ni,**
yó dā́saṃ várṇam ádharaṃ gú-
hā́kaḥ;

By whom all things here have been made unstable, who has made subject the Dāsa colour and has

śvaghnī́va yó jigīvā́m̐ lakṣám ā́dad aryáḥ puṣṭā́ni : sá, janāsa, Índraḥ.

made it disappear; who, like a winning gambler the stake, has taken the possessions of the foe: he, O men, is Indra.

imā́ víśvā : *all these things*, that is, *all things on earth.* cyávanā is used predicatively after kṛtā́ni, just as ádharam is in b after ákar; cp. iv. 30, 22 : yás tā́ víśvāni cicyuṣé *who hast shaken the whole world.* dā́sam várṇam : *the non-Aryan colour* (= kṛṣṇám várṇam), the aborigines; note the difference of accent in the substantive dāsá and the adj. dā́sa. ákar : root ao. of kṛ (148, 1 *b*), to be construed with both ádharam (*make inferior* = *subject*) and gúhā (*put in hiding* = *cause to disappear, drive away*). When a final Visarjanīya in the Saṃhitā text represents an etymological r, this is indicated in the Pada text by putting íti after the word and repeating the latter in its pause form : ákar íty ákaḥ. jigīvā́m̐ : pf. pt. of ji *win* (139, 4) ; on the Sandhi see 40, 3. Since the normal metre requires ⏑ ⏑ – after the caesura (p. 441, top), this word was here perhaps metrically pronounced jigivā́m̐ as it came to be regularly written in B. ā́dat : irr. a ao. (147 *a* 1) from dā *give*; though not analysed in the Pada text, it must owing to the sense be = ā-ádat *has taken.* aryás : gen of arí (99, 3) ; this word appears to be etymologically a Bv. = *having no wealth* (ri = rai), either for oneself (whence the sense *needy, suppliant*) or to bestow on others (whence the sense *niggard, foe*). [If a single meaning has to be given, *devout* is misleading, and *suppliant* should be substituted for it in the *Vedic Grammar*, p. 81, f. n. 1 ; 99, 3 ; and in the Index, p. 473.]

५ यं स्मा पृच्छन्ति कुह सेति घोरम्
उतेमाहुर्नैषो अस्तीत्येनम् ।
सो अर्यः पुष्टीर्विज इवा मिनाति
श्रदस्मै धत्त स जनास इन्द्रः ॥

यम् । स्म । पृच्छन्ति । कुह । सः । इति । घोरम् ।
उत । ईम् । आहुः । न । एषः । अस्ति । इति । एनम् ।
सः । अर्यः । पुष्टीः । विजःऽइव । आ । मिनाति ।
श्रत् । अस्मै । धत्त । सः । जनासः । इन्द्रः ॥

5 yáṃ smā pṛchánti kúha séti ghorám,
utém āhur náiṣó astī́ti enam ;
só 'ryáḥ puṣṭī́r víja ivā́ mināti.
śrád asmai dhatta : sá, janāsa, Índraḥ.

The terrible one of whom they ask ‘where is he’, of whom they also say ‘he is not’; he diminishes the possessions of the niggard like the (player's) *stake. Believe in him: he, O men, is Indra.*

smā (p. 250) is metrically lengthened, the second syllable of the Pāda favouring a long vowel (p. 441, top). **pṛchánti** : pr. of **prach.** **séti** for **sá íti** : the irr. contraction of **sá** with a following vowel is common (48 *a*). **īm** anticipates **enam** : see p. 220. **āhur** : pf. of **ah** *say*, 139, 4 ; this vb. not being accented, b has the form of a principal clause, though the almost invariable use of relative clauses in this hymn would lead one to expect that the **yám** of the first clause would accentuate the second also. **só aryás** : the initial **a**, though written, should be dropped ; otherwise the irr. contraction **víjevā́** is just possible, but ◡ – for ◡ ◡ following a caesura after the fifth syllable is rare. 5 c is parallel to 4 c : **ā́ mināti** to **ā́dat** ; **aryáḥ puṣṭī́ḥ** to **āryáḥ puṣṭā́ni** ; **víjaḥ** to **lakṣám.** Uṣas (iv. 51) is in i. 92, 10 described as wearing away the life of mortals, **śvaghnī́va kṛtnúr víja ā́minānā** *diminishing* it *as a skilful gambler the stakes.* **mināti** : pr. of **mī** *damage.* **śrád dhatta** (2. pl. ipv. of **dhā**) *believe*, with dat. (200 A. 1 *e*). The Pādas a b mention doubts as to the existence of Indra ; c implies that he does exist ; and d calls for belief in him.

६ यो रध्रस्य चोदिता यः कृशस्य
यो ब्रह्मणो नाधमानस्य कीरेः ।
युक्तग्राव्णो योऽविता सुशिप्रः
सुतसोमस्य स जनास इन्द्रः ॥

यः । रध्रस्य । चोदिता । यः । कृशस्य ।
यः । ब्रह्मणः । नाधमानस्य । कीरेः ।
युक्तऽग्राव्णः । यः । अविता । सुऽशिप्रः ।
सुतऽसोमस्य । सः । जनासः । इन्द्रः ॥

6 yó radhrásya coditā́, yáḥ kṛśásya,
yó brahmáṇo nā́dhamānasya kīréḥ ;

Who is furtherer of the rich, of the poor, of the suppliant Brahmin singer ; who, fair-lipped, is the helper of him that has pressed Soma

yuktágrāvṇo yó avitā́ suśipráḥ
sutásomasya : sá, janāsa, Índraḥ.

and has set to work the stones : he, O men, is Indra.

coditā́ governs the three genitives (the rich, the poor, the priestly poet) of a b, as the three relatives show; while avitā́ governs that of c. su-śiprás : Bv. cd., p. 455, *c a*. The exact meaning of śipra is somewhat doubtful, but as it is regularly dual, has the attributive *tawny,* hári-śipra being parallel to hári-śmaśāru *tawny-bearded,* and is associated with Indra's drinking of Soma, it can hardly mean anything but lips or moustaches ; it could not well mean *jaws* which are hánū. yuktá-grāvṇas : of him who has set in motion the stones with which the Soma shoots are pounded.

७ यस्याश्वासः प्रदिशि यस्य गावो
यस्य ग्रामा यस्य विश्वे रथासः ।
यः सूर्यं य उषसं जजान
यो अपां नेता स जनास इन्द्रः ॥

यस्य । अश्वासः । प्रऽदिशि । यस्य । गावः ।
यस्य । ग्रामाः । यस्य । विश्वे । रथासः ।
यः । सूर्यम् । यः । उषसम् । जजान ।
यः । अपाम् । नेता । सः । जनासः । इन्द्रः ॥

7 yásyā́śvāsaḥ pradíśi, yásya gā́vo,
yásya grā́mā, yásya víśve ráthāsaḥ ;
yáḥ sū́riaṃ, yá uṣásaṃ jajā́na ;
yó apā́ṃ netā́ : sá, janāsa, Índraḥ.

In whose control are horses, kine, clans, all chariots ; who creates the sun, the dawn ; who is the guide of the waters : he, O men, is Indra.

uṣásam : often also uṣā́sam ; du. N. A. uṣásā and uṣā́sā ; N. pl. uṣásas and uṣā́sas ; see 83, 2 *a*, f. n. 1.

८ यं क्रन्दसी संयती विह्वयेते
परेऽवर उभया अमित्राः ।
समानं चिद्रथमातस्थिवांसा
नाना हवेते स जनास इन्द्रः ॥

यम् । क्रन्दसी इति । संयती इति सम्ऽयती । विह्वयेते इति विऽह्वयेते ।
परे । अवरे । उभयाः । अमित्राः ।
समानम् । चित् । रथम् । आतस्थिऽवांसा ।
नाना । हवेते इति । सः । जनासः । इन्द्रः ॥

8 **yáṃ krándasī saṃyatī́ vihváyete,**
párĕ ávara ubháyā amítrāḥ;
samānáṃ cid rátham ātasthivā́ṃsā
nā́nā havete: sá, janāsa, Índraḥ.

Whom the two battle-arrays, coming together, call upon divergently, both foes, the farther and the nearer; two having mounted the self-same chariot invoke him separately: he, O men, is Indra.

saṃ-yatī́: pr. pt. du. n. of **sám-i** *go together.* **vi-hváyete** (from **hvā**) and **nā́nā havete** (from **hū**, the Samprasāraṇa form of **hvā**) are synonymous = *call on variously*; cp. i. 102, 5. 6: **nā́nā hí tvā hávamānā jánā imé** *these men calling on thee* (Indra) *variously*; and **átha jánā ví hvayante siṣāsávaḥ** *so men call* on thee *variously, desiring gains.* **páré 'vara**: must be read **párĕ ávara**, though the succession of five short syllables before the caesura is irregular (p. 440, 4). The second Pāda explains **krándasī**: **ubháyās** (never used in the dual) = both groups of foes, that on the farther and that on the nearer side, from the point of view of the speaker; according to Sāyaṇa, *the superior and the inferior.* **samānám** contrasted with **nā́nā**: two who are on the same chariot, that is, the fighter and the driver, invoke him separately. **havete**: not being accented must be taken as the vb. of a principal clause; cp. note on 5 b.

९ यस्मान्न ऋते विजयन्ते जनासो
यं युध्यमाना अवसे हवन्ते ।
यो विश्वस्य प्रतिमानं बभूव
यो अच्युतच्युत्स जनास इन्द्रः ॥

यस्मात् । न । ऋते । विऽजयन्ते । जनासः ।
यम् । युध्यमानाः । अवसे । हवन्ते ।
यः । विश्वस्य । प्रतिऽमानम् । बभूव ।
यः । अच्युतऽच्युत् । सः । जनासः । इन्द्रः ॥

9 yásmān nárté vijáyante jánāso,
yáṃ yúdhyamānā ávase hávante;
yó víśvasya pratimā́naṃ babhū́va,
yó acyutacyút: sá, janāsa, Índraḥ.

Without whom men do not conquer, whom they when fighting call on for help; who has been a match for every one, who moves the immovable: he, O men, is Indra.

ná ṛté: must be pronounced **nárté** (19 *a*). **vi-jáyante**: pr. of **ji** *conquer*. **hávante**: cp. **vihváyete** in 8 a. **ávase**: final dat. (p. 314, B 2). **pratimā́nam**: cp. iv. 18, 4: **nahī́ nú asya pratimā́nam ásti antár jātéṣu utá yé jánitvāḥ** *for there is no match for him among those who have been born nor those who will be born.* **acyuta-cyút**: cp. 4 a; also iii. 30, 4: **tvám cyāváyann ácyutāni . . . cárasi** *thou continuest shaking unshaken things.*

१० यः शश्वतो मह्येनो दधानान्
अमन्यमानाञ्छर्वा जघान ।
यः शर्धते नानुददाति शृध्यां
यो दस्योर्हन्ता स जनास इन्द्रः ॥

यः । शश्वतः । महि । एनः । दधानान् ।
अमन्यमानान् । शर्वा । जघान ।
यः । शर्धते । न । अनुऽददाति । शृध्याम् ।
यः । दस्योः । हन्ता । सः । जनासः । इन्द्रः ॥

10 **yáḥ śáśvato máhi éno dádhānān**
ámanyamānāñ chárvā jaghā́na;
yáḥ śárdhate nā́nudádāti śṛdhyā́m,
yó dásyor hantā́: sá, janāso, índraḥ.

Who slays with his arrow the unexpecting many that commit great sin; who forgives not the arrogant man his arrogance, who slays the Dasyu: he, O men, is Indra.

dádhānān: pr. pt. Ā. of **dhā**. The Sandhi of **ān** (39) is not applied between Pādas (cp. i. 35, 10 c). **ámanyamānān**: *not thinking* scil. that he would slay them; on the Sandhi of **n + ś**, see 40, 1. **śárvā**: *with his arrow* (inst., p. 80); with his characteristic weapon, the **vájra**, he slays his foes in battle. **jaghā́na**: *has slain* (and still slays) may be translated by the present (213 A *a*). **anudádāti**: 3. s. pr. of **ánu + dā** *forgive*, with dat. (cp. 200 A *f*). **dásyos**: *of the demon*, a term applied to various individual demons, such as Śambara (11 a).

११ यः शम्बरं पर्वतेषु क्षियन्तं
चत्वारिंश्यां शरद्यन्वविन्दत् ।
ओजायमानं यो अहिं जघान
दानुं शयानं स जनास इन्द्रः ॥

यः । शम्बरम् । पर्वतेषु । क्षियन्तम् ।
चत्वारिंश्याम् । शरदि । अनुऽअविन्दत ।
ओजायमानम् । यः । अहिम् । जघान ।
दानुम् । शयानम् । सः । जनासः । इन्द्रः ॥

11 **yáḥ Śámbaram párvateṣu kṣiyántam**
catvāriṃśyā́ṃ śarádi anvávindat;
ojāyámānaṃ yŏ áhiṃ jaghā́na,
Dā́nuṃ śáyānaṃ: sá, janāsa, Índraḥ.

Who in the fortieth autumn found out Śambara dwelling in the mountains; who has slain the serpent as he showed his strength, the son of Dānu, as he lay: he, O men, is Indra.

Śambara, next to Vṛtra, Vala, and Śuṣṇa, is the most frequently mentioned demon foe of Indra, who strikes him down from his mountain. He is often spoken of as possessing many forts. **kṣiyántam**: see note on i. 154, 2 d. **catvāriṃśyā́m**: that is, Indra found him after a very long search, as he was hiding himself. **anvávindat**: ipf. of 2. **vid** *find*. The second hemistich refers to Indra's slaughter of Vṛtra. **ojāyámānam**: cp. iii. 32, 11: **áhann áhiṃ pariśáyānam árṇa ojāyámānam** *thou slewest the serpent showing his strength as he lay around the flood*. **Dā́num**: this is strictly the name of Vṛtra's mother, here used as a metronymic = **Dānava**; cp. i. 32, 9: **Dā́nuḥ śaye sahávatsā ná dhenúḥ** *Dānu lay like a cow with her calf* (i. e. Vṛtra). **śáyānam**: pr. pt. Ā. of **śī** *lie* (134, 1 *c*).

१२ यः सप्तरश्मिर्वृषभस्तुविष्मान्
अवासृजत्सर्तवे सप्त सिन्धून् ।
यो रौहिणमस्फुरद्वज्रबाहुर्
द्यामारोहन्तं स जनास इन्द्रः ॥

यः । सप्तऽरश्मिः । वृषभः । तुविष्मान्
अवऽअसृजत् । सर्तवे । सप्त । सिन्धून् ।
यः । रौहिणम् । अस्फुरत् । वज्रऽबाहुः ।
द्याम् । आऽरोहन्तम् । सः । जनासः । इन्द्रः ॥

12 **yáḥ saptáraśmir vṛṣabhás túviṣmān**
avā́sṛjat sártave saptá síndhūn;
yó Rauhiṇám ásphurad vájrabāhur
dyā́m āróhantaṃ: sá, janāsa, Índráḥ.

The mighty seven-reined bull who let loose the seven streams to flow; who armed with the bolt spurned Rauhiṇa as he scaled heaven: he, O men, is Indra.

The term **vṛṣabhá** is very often applied to gods, but especially to Indra, as expressing mighty strength and fertility. **saptá-raśmis**:

having seven reins probably means ‘hard to restrain’, ‘irresistible’; Sāyaṇa interprets the cd. to mean ‘having seven kinds of clouds (parjanyās) that shed rain on the earth’. **túviṣ-mān**: the suffix **mant** is separated in the Pada text only after vowels, as **gó ऽ mān**; on the Sandhi see 10 a. **ava-ásṛjat**: ipf. of sṛj *emit*. **sártave**: dat. inf. of sṛ *flow* (p. 192, 4). **saptá síndhūn**: cp. 3 a and i. 35, 8 b. **Rauhiṇám**: a demon mentioned in only one other passage of the RV. **dyā́m ā-róhantam**: *ascending to heaven* in order to attack Indra.

१३ द्यावा चिदस्मै पृथिवी नमेते
शुष्माच्चिदस्य पर्वता भयन्ते ।
यः सोमपा निचितो वज्रबाहुर्
यो वज्रहस्तः स जनास इन्द्रः ॥

द्यावा । चित् । अस्मै । पृथिवी इति ।
नमेते इति ।
शुष्मात् । चित् । अस्य । पर्वताः । भयन्ते ।
यः । सोमऽपाः । निऽचितः । वज्रऽबाहुः ।
यः । वज्रऽहस्तः । सः । जनासः । इन्द्रः ॥

13 **Dyā́vā cid asmai Pṛthivī́ namete;**
śúṣmāc cid asya párvatā bhayante;
yáḥ somapā́ nicitó vájrabāhur,
yó vájrahastaḥ: sá, janāsa, Índraḥ.

Even Heaven and Earth bow down before him; before his vehemence even the mountains are afraid. Who is known as the Soma-drinker, holding the bolt in his arm, who holds the bolt in his hand: he, O men, is Indra.

Dyā́vā . . . Pṛthivī́: the two members of Devatā-dvandvas are here, as often, separated by other words (186 A 1). **asmai**: dat. with nam *bow* (cp. 200 A 1 *k*, p. 311). **bháyante**: see note on i. 85, 8 c. **śúṣmād**: cp. 1 e. **soma-pā́s** (97, 2): predicative nom., (196 *b*). **ni-citás**: on the accent see p. 462, f. n. 4.

१४ यः सुन्वन्तमवति यः पचन्तं
यः शंसन्तं यः शशमानमूती ।
यस्य ब्रह्म वर्धनं यस्य सोमो
यस्येदं राधः स जनास इन्द्रः ॥

यः । सुन्वन्तम् । अवति । यः । पचन्तम् ।
यः । शंसन्तम् । यः । शशमानम् । ऊती ।
यस्य । ब्रह्म । वर्धनम् । यस्य । सोमः ।
यस्य । इदम् । राधः । सः । जनासः । इन्द्रः ॥

14 yáḥ sunvántam ávati, yáḥ pácantam,
yáḥ śáṃsantam, yáḥ śaśamānám ūtī́;
yásya bráhma várdhanaṃ, yásya sómo,
yásyedáṃ rā́dhaḥ: sá, janāsa, Índraḥ.

Who with his aid helps him that presses Soma, him that bakes, him that offers praise, him that has prepared the sacrifice; whom prayer, whom Soma, whom this gift strengthens: he, O men, is Indra.

sunvántam: all the participles in a and b refer to some act of worship: pressing Soma; baking sacrificial cakes, &c.; praising the gods; having prepared the sacrifice. **śaśamānám**: explained by Sāyaṇa as **stotraṃ kurvāṇam** *offering a Stotra*; by the Naighaṇṭuka, iii. 14, as **arcantam** *singing*; by the Nirukta, vi. 8, as **śaṃsamānam** *praising*. **ūtī́**: contracted inst. of ūtí (p. 80) to be construed with **ávati**; cp. i. 185, 4: **ávasā ávantī** *helping with aid*. **várdhanam**: to be taken predicatively with each of the three subjects **bráhma, sómas, rā́dhas**, *of whom prayer*, &c. *is the strengthening*, that is, whom prayer, &c. strengthens; **yásya** being an objective gen. (p. 320, B 1 *b*). **idáṃ rā́dhas** *this gift* = this sacrificial offering.

१५ यः सुन्वते पचते दुध्र आ चिद्
वाजं दर्दर्षि स किलासि सत्यः ।
वयं त इन्द्र विश्वह प्रियासः
सुवीरासो विदथमा वदेम ॥

यः । सुन्वते । पचते । दुध्रः । आ । चित् ।
वाजम् । दर्दर्षि । सः । किल । असि । सत्यः ।
वयम् । ते । इन्द्र । विश्वह । प्रियासः ।
सुऽवीरासः । विदथम् । आ । वदेम ॥

15 yáḥ sunvaté pácate dudhrá ā́ cid
vā́jaṃ dárdarṣi, sá kílāsi satyáḥ.
vayáṃ ta, Indra, viśváha priyā́saḥ,
suvī́rāso vidátham ā́ vadema.

As he who, most fierce, enforces booty for him that presses and him that bakes, thou indeed art true. We ever dear to thee, O Indra, with strong sons, would utter divine worship.

This concluding stanza is the only one that does not end with the refrain **sá, jánāsa, Índraḥ**. Instead, the poet, changing the from 3 to the 2. prs., substitutes at the end of b the words **sá kíla‿asi satyáḥ** *as such thou art indeed true* = to be depended on (cp. note on satyám in i. 1, 6 c); while c and d are a prayer ending with an adaptation of the favourite refrain of the Gautamas, the poets of the second Maṇḍala: **bṛhád vadema vidáthe suvī́rāḥ** *we would, accompanied by strong sons, speak aloud at divine worship.* **ā́ cid:** perhaps better taken as emphasizing **dudhrás** (cp. p. 216) than with **dárdarṣi** (int. of **dṝ**). **te:** gen. with **priyā́sas** (p. 322, C). **vidátham:** the etymology and precise sense of this word have been much discussed. There can now be hardly any doubt that it is derived from the root **vidh** *worship*, and that it means *divine worship*, scarcely distinguishable from **yajñá**, of which it is given as a synonym in Naighaṇṭuka, iii. 17; cp. note on i. 85, 1.

RUDRÁ

This god occupies a subordinate position in the RV., being celebrated in only three entire hymns, in part of another, and in one conjointly with Soma. His hand, his arms, and his limbs are mentioned. He has beautiful lips and wears braided hair. His colour is brown; his form is dazzling, for he shines like the radiant sun, like gold. He is arrayed with golden ornaments, and wears a glorious necklace (niṣká). He drives in a car. His weapons are often referred to: he holds the thunderbolt in his arm, and discharges his lightning shaft from the sky; but he is usually said to be armed with a bow and arrows, which are strong and swift.

Rudra is very often associated with the Maruts (i. 85). He is their father, and is said to have generated them from the shining udder of the cow Pṛśni.

He is fierce and destructive like a terrible beast, and is called a bull, as well as the ruddy (aruṣá) boar of heaven. He is exalted, strongest of the strong, swift, unassailable, unsurpassed in might. He is young and unaging, a lord (ī́śāna) and father of the world. By his rule and univeral dominion he is aware of the doings of men and gods. He is bountiful (mīḍhvā́ṃs), easily invoked and auspicious (śivá). But he is usually regarded as malevolent; for the hymns addressed to him chiefly express fear of his terrible shafts and deprecation of his wrath. He is implored not to slay or injure, in his anger, his worshippers and their belongings, but to avert his great malignity and his cow-slaying, man-slaying bolt from them, and to lay others low. He is, however, not purely maleficent like a demon. He not only preserves from calamity, but bestows blessings. His healing powers are especially often mentioned; he has a thousand remedies, and is the greatest physician of physicians. In this connexion he has two exclusive epithets, **jálāṣa**, *cooling*, and **jálāṣa-bheṣaja**, *possessing cooling remedies*.

The physical basis represented by Rudra is not clearly apparent. But it seems probable that the phenomenon underlying his nature was the storm, not pure and simple, but in its baleful aspect seen in the destructive agency of lightning. His healing and beneficent powers would then have been founded partly on the fertilizing and purifying action of the thunderstorm, and partly on the negative action of sparing those whom he might slay. Thus the deprecations of his wrath led to the application of the euphemistic epithet **śivá**, which became the regular name of Rudra's historical successor in post-Vedic mythology.

The etymological sense of the name is somewhat uncertain, but would be 'Howler' according to the usual derivation from **rud** *cry*.

ii. 33. Metre: **Triṣṭubh.**

१ आ ते॑ पितर्मरुतां सु॒म्नमे॑तु॒
मा न॒ः सूर्य॑स्य सं॒दृशो॑ युयोथाः ।
अ॒भि नो॑ वी॒रो अर्व॑ति क्षमेत॒
प्र जा॑येमहि रुद्र प्र॒जाभि॑ः ॥

आ । ते॒ । पि॒त॒रिति॑ । म॒रु॒ता॒म् । सु॒म्नम् । ए॒तु॒ ।
मा । न॒ः । सूर्य॑स्य । स॒म्ऽदृश॑ः । यु॒यो॒था॒ः ।
अ॒भि । न॒ः । वी॒रः । अर्व॑ति । क्ष॒मे॒त॒ ।
प्र । जा॒ये॒म॒हि॒ । रु॒द्र॒ । प्र॒ऽजाभि॑ः ॥

1 ā́ te, pitar Marutāṃ, sumnám etu:
mā́ naḥ sū́ryasya saṃdŕ̥śo yuyothāḥ.
abhí no vīró árvati kṣameta;
prá jāyemahi, Rudᵃra, prajā́bhiḥ.

Let thy good will, O Father of the Maruts, come (to us): sever us not from the sight of the sun. May the hero be merciful to us in regard to our steeds; may we be prolific with offspring.

pitar Marutām: the whole of a compound voc. expression loses its accent unless it begins a sentence of Pāda; in the latter case only the first syllable would be accented (p. 465, 18 *a*). **yuyothās**: 2. s. inj. Ā. of 2. **yu** *separate*, with irregular strong radical vowel (p. 144, *a*). **saṃdŕ̥śas**: abl. 201 A 1. **vīrás** = Rudra, with change from 2. to 3. prs., as is often the case (cp. i. 85, 5 c). **árvati abhí kṣameta** = may he not injure us in our steeds, may he spare them. **Rudra** must be read as a trisyllable (15, 1 *d*).

२ त्वादत्तेभी रुद्र शंतमेभिः
शतं हिमा अशीय भेषजेभिः ।
व्य१स्मद्द्वेषो वितरं व्यंहो
व्यमीवाश्चातयस्वा विषूचीः ॥

त्वाऽदत्तेभिः । रुद्र । शम्ऽतमेभिः ।
शतम् । हिमाः । अशीय । भेषजेभिः ।
वि । अस्मत् । द्वेषः । विऽतरम् । वि । अंहः ।
वि । अमीवाः । चातयस्व । विषूचीः ॥

2 **tvā́dattebhī, Rud[a]ra, śáṃtamebhiḥ**
śatáṃ hímā aśīya bheṣajébhiḥ.
ví asmád dvéṣo vitarám, ví áṃho,
ví ámīvāś cātayasvā víṣūcīḥ.

By the most salutary medicines given by thee, O Rudra, I would attain a hundred winters. Drive far away from us hatred, away distress, away diseases in all directions.

tvā́-dattebhī: the first member of this cd. retains the inst. case-form (p. 273); Sandhi, 47. **śatám**: on the concord see p. 291, *b*; life extending to a hundred winters or autumns (**śarádas**) is often prayed for. **aśīya**: root ao. op. Ā. of **aṃś** (p. 171, 4). **ví**: the prp. of a cd. vb. is often repeated with each object, the vb. itself being used only once. **vitarám**: adv. of the cpv. of **ví** *farther* (cp. **út-tara**) employed only with verbs compounded with **ví**. **cātayasvā**: ipv. Ā. cs. of **cat**, with metrical lengthening of the final vowel. **víṣūcīs**: A. pl. f. of **víṣvañc** *turned in various directions*, is used predicatively like an adv.

३ श्रेष्ठो जातस्य रुद्र श्रियासि
तवस्तमस्तवसां वज्रबाहो ।
पर्षि णः पारमंहसः स्वस्ति
विश्वा अभीती रपसो युयोधि ॥

श्रेष्ठः । जातस्य । रुद्र । श्रिया । असि ।
तवःऽतमः । तवसाम् । वज्रबाहो इति वज्रऽबाहो ।
पर्षि । नः । पारम् । अंहसः । स्वस्ति ।
विश्वाः । अभिऽइतीः । रपसः । युयोधि ॥

3 **śréṣṭho jātásya, Rud[a]ra, śriyā́si,**
tavástamas tavásāṃ, vajrabāho.
párṣi ṇaḥ pārám áṃhasaḥ suasti;
víśvā abhītī rápaso yuyodhi.

Thou art the best of what is born, O Rudra, in glory, the mightiest of the mighty, O wielder of the bolt. Transport us to the farther shore of distress in safety. Ward off all attacks of mischief.

jātásya: the pp. used as a n. collective noun = *that which has been born, creation.* **vajra-bāho**: it is only here that this specific epithet of Indra is applied to any other deity; the voc. **o** of **u** stems is regularly treated as Pragṛhya by the Pada text, but not in the Saṃhitā text (where for instance **vā́yav ā́** and **vā́ya ukthébhiḥ** are written). **párṣi**: from **pṛ** *take across*, is one of a number of isolated 2. s. pr. indicatives in form, but ipv. in sense (p. 349, β). **ṇas**: initial **n** cerebralized even in external Sandhi (65 A *c*). **pārám**: acc. of the goal (197 A 1). **svastí**: this word is not analysed in the Pada text (like **sumatí**, &c.) because **asti** does not occur as an independent substantive; here it is a shortened form of the contracted inst. **svastí** (p. 80, n. 2); it is several times used in the sense of a final dat. = **svastáye**. **abhī̀tīs**: = **abhí itīs**, hence the Svarita (p. 464, 17, 1 *a*); Sandhi, 47. **yuyodhi**: 2. s. ipv. of **yu** *separate*, with irr. strong radical vowel (p. 144, *a*).

४ मा त्वा रुद्र चुक्रुधामा नमोभिर्
मा दुष्टुती वृषभ मा सहूती ।
उन्नो वीराँ अर्पय भेषजेभिर्
भिषक्तमं त्वा भिषजां शृणोमि ॥

मा । त्वा । रुद्र । चुक्रुधाम । नमःऽभिः ।
मा । दुःऽस्तुती । वृषभ । मा । सऽहूती ।
उत् । नः । वीरान् । अर्पय । भेषजेभिः ।
भिषक्ऽतमम् । त्वा । भिषजाम् । शृणोमि ॥

4 **mā́** tvā, **Rudra, cukrudhāmā** **námobhir,**
mā́ dúṣṭutī, vṛṣabha, mā sá-hūtī.
ún no vīrā́m̐ **arpaya bheṣajé-bhir:**
bhiṣáktamam tvā **bhiṣájām śṛ-ṇomi.**

May we not anger thee, O Rudra, with our obeisances, nor with ill praise, O bull, nor with joint invocation. Raise up our heroes with remedies: I hear of thee as the best physician of physicians.

cukrudhāma: this form, red. (cs.) ao. (149, p. 174) might in itself be either sb. or inj., because the 1. pl. P. of these moods is identical in **a** stems; but the use here of the prohibitive pcl. **mā́**, which is employed with inj. forms only (180), decides the question. **námobhis**: that is, with ill or inadequate worship; cp. **dúṣṭutī** in b; the latter form is a contracted inst. (p. 80); on the internal Sandhi of this word see 43, 3 *a*. **sáhūtī**: contracted inst.; invocation with other deities whom Rudra might consider inferior. **úd arpaya**: cs. of úd ṛ (p. 197, irr. 1) = *raise up, strengthen*. **bhiṣájām**: partitive gen. (see 202 B 2 *b*, p. 321); cp. 3 b. **śṛṇomi**: pr. of śru *hear*; with double acc., 198, 1.

५ हवीमभिर्हवते यो हविर्भिर्
अव स्तोमेभी रुद्रं दिषीय ।
ऋदूदरः सुहवो मा नो अस्यै
बभ्रुः सुशिप्रो रीरधन्मनायै ॥

हवीमऽभिः । हवते । यः । हविःऽभिः ।
अव । स्तोमेभिः । रुद्रम् । दिषीय ।
ऋदूदरः । सुऽहवः । मा । नः । अस्यै ।
बभ्रुः । सुऽशिप्रः । रीरधत् । मनायै ॥

5 **hávīmabhir hávate yó havírbhir,
áva stómebhī Rud^{a}rám diṣīya:
ṛdūdáraḥ suhávo mā́ no asyái
babhrúḥ suśípro rīradhan manā́yai.**

Rudra who is called on with invocations and with oblations, I would appease with songs of praise: may he, the compassionate, easy to invoke, ruddy brown, fair-lipped, not subject us to that jealousy of his.

hávīman: from **hū** *call*, but **havís** from **hu** *sacrifice*. **áva diṣīya**: s ao. op. Ā. of **dā** *give* (144, 3). **ṛdūdáras** is not analysed in the Pada text, perhaps owing to a doubt whether it is = **ṛdu-udára** or **ṛdū-dára** (the former is the view of Yāska who explains it as **mṛdu-udara**); for **ṛdū-pā́** and **ṛdū-vṛ́dh** are separated and **dara** is separated in **puraṃ-dará**. Both this word (according to the former analysis) and **su-háva** are Bv. (p. 455, *c a*). **babhrús**: this colour is attributed to Rudra in viii. 9, 15 also; otherwise it is applied more often to Soma (viii. 48) as well as once to Agni. **su-śípras**: see note on ii. 12, 6 c. **rīradhat**: inj. red. ao. of **randh**. **asyái manā́yai**: that is, Rudra's well-known wrath is deprecated; cp. 4 a b. There is some doubt as to the exact interpretation of this stanza. The chief objection to the above explanation is the necessity to take **hávate** in a ps. sense (= **hūyate** according to Sāyaṇa). The following sense has also been suggested: 'he who invokes Rudra (thinks), "I would buy off Rudra with songs of praise": let not Rudra subject us to that suspicion (on his part).'

६ उन्मा॑ ममन्द वृष॒भो म॒रुत्वा॑न्
त्वक्षी॑यसा॒ वय॑सा॒ नाध॑मानम् ।
घृणी॑व छा॒यामर॒पा अ॑शी॒या
विवा॑सेयं रु॒द्रस्य॑ सु॒म्नम् ॥

उत् । मा॒ । म॒म॒न्द॒ । वृ॒ष॒भः । म॒रुत्वा॑न् ।
त्वक्षी॑यसा । वय॑सा । नाध॑मानम् ।
घृणि॑ऽइव । छा॒याम् । अ॒र॒पाः । अ॒शी॒य॒ ।
आ । वि॒वा॒से॒य॒म् । रु॒द्रस्य॑ । सु॒म्नम् ॥

6 ún mā mamanda vṛṣabhó Marútvān
tvákṣīyasā váyasā nā́dhamānam.
ghṛ́ṇīva chāyā́m arapā́ aśīya :
ā́ vivāseyam Rud^{a}rásya sumnám.

The bull accompanied by the Maruts has gladdened me, the suppliant, with his most vigorous force. I would unscathed attain shade in heat as it were: I would desire to win the good will of Rudra.

úd . . . mamanda: pf. of **mand** (nasalized form of **mad**) *gladden*; intransitive, *be glad*, in Ā. only. **ṛṣabhás**: Rudra. **Marútvān**: though this epithet is characteristic of Indra, it is also twice applied to Rudra (as father of the Maruts, see 1 a) as well as very rarely to a few other gods who are associated with Indra; on the Sandhi see 40, 2. **ghṛ́ṇīva** has been much discussed. The only natural explanation (following the Pada text) is **ghṛ́ṇi iva**, taking **ghṛ́ṇi** as a contracted inst. f. (p. 80) expressing either cause = by *reason of heat* (199 A 3) or time = *in heat* (199 A 5); Sāyaṇa's explanation is **ghṛ́ṇī iva** *like one heated by the rays of the sun*; but a word **ghṛṇín** N. **ghṛṇī́** does not occur, and the accent is wrong. For the simile cp. vi. 16, 38: **úpa chāyā́m iva ghṛ́ṇer áganma śárma te vayám** *we have entered thy shelter like shade* (protecting) *from heat* (p. 317, 2). **aśīya**: see 2 b; on the Sandhi of the final vowel of the Pada, cp. i. 160, 4 c. **ā́ vivāseyam**: op. ds. of **van** *win*.

७ क्व१॒ स्य ते॑ रुद्र मृळ॒याकु॑र्
हस्तो॒ यो अस्ति॑ भेष॒जो जला॑षः ।
अ॒प॒भ॒र्ता रप॑सो॒ दैव्य॑स्या॒-
भी नु मा॑ वृषभ चक्षमीथाः ॥

क्व॑ । स्यः । ते॒ । रु॒द्र॒ । मृ॒ळ॒याकुः॑ ।
हस्तः॑ । यः । अस्ति॑ । भे॒ष॒जः । जला॑षः ।
अ॒प॒ऽभ॒र्ता । रप॑सः । दैव्य॑स्य ।
अ॒भि । नु । मा॒ । वृ॒ष॒भ॒ । च॒क्ष॒मी॒थाः॒ ॥

7 **kúa syá te, Rudᵃra, mṛḷayā́kur**
hásto yṓ ásti bheṣajó jálāṣaḥ?
apabhartā́ rápaso dáiviasya
abhī́ nú mā, vṛṣabha, cakṣam-
īthāḥ.

Where, O Rudra, is that merciful hand of thine which is healing and cooling? As remover of injury coming from the gods, do thou, O Bull, now be compassionate towards me.

kvai̱ sya: see p. 450, *b*. **bheṣajás** is an adj. here and in one other passage; otherwise it is a n. noun meaning *medicine*. **apabhartā́**: on the accent see p. 453, 9 *d*. **dáivyasya**: *derived from the gods*, that is, such as is inflicted by Rudra himself; on the Sandhi of the final vowel, cp. 6 c. **abhī́**: final vowel metrically lengthened in the second syllable of the Pāda, but not in 1 c. **cakṣamīthās**: 2. s. pf. op. of kṣam (p. 156, 3).

८ प्र बभ्रवे वृषभाय श्वितीचे
महो महीं सुष्टुतिमीरयामि ।
नमस्या कल्मलीकिनं नमोभिर्
गृणीमसि त्वेषं रुद्रस्य नाम ॥

प्र । बभ्रवे । वृषभाय । श्वितीचे ।
महः । महीम् । सुऽस्तुतिम् । ईरयामि ।
नमस्य । कल्मलीकिनम् । नमःऽभिः ।
गृणीमसि । त्वेषम् । रुद्रस्य । नाम ॥

8 **prá babhráve vṛṣabhā́ya śvitīcé**
mahó mahī́ṃ suṣṭutím īrayāmi.
namasyā́ kalmalīkínaṃ námo-
bhir,
gṛṇīmási tveṣáṃ Rudrásya
nā́ma.

For the ruddy-brown and whitish bull I utter forth a mighty eulogy of the mighty one. I will adore the radiant one with obeisances. We invoke the terrible name of Rudra.

prá . . . īrayāmi: an example of the prp. at the beginning, and the vb. to which it belongs at the end of a hemistich. **śvitīcé**: D. s. of **śvityáñc** (cp. 93). **mahás**: gen. s. m. of **máh**, beside the acc. s. f. of the same adj. (Sāyaṇa: mahato mahatīm), *of the great one* (Rudra); cp. i. 1, 5 c. **namasyā́**: according to the Pada this form has its final syllable metrically lengthened for **namasyá**, which is the 2. s. ipv.; otherwise it is the 1. s. sb. (p. 128), which is the more likely because the third syllable does not favour metrical lengthening, and because the 1. prs. is used both in the preceding and the following Pāda. The metre of c is abnormal because the caesura follows the third syllable, and there is a secondary caesura after the eighth. **gṛṇīmási**: 1. pl. pr. of gṛ *sing* (p. 138).

९ स्थिरेभिरङ्गैः पुरुरूप उग्रो
बभ्रुः शुक्रेभिः पिपिशे हिरण्यैः ।
ईशानादस्य भुवनस्य भूरेर्
न वा उ योषद्रुद्रादसुर्यम् ॥

स्थिरेभिः । अङ्गैः । पुरुऽरूपः । उग्रः ।
बभ्रुः । शुक्रेभिः । पिपिशे । हिरण्यैः ।
ईशानात् । अस्य । भुवनस्य । भूरेः ।
न । वै । ऊं इति । योषत् । रुद्रात् । असुर्यम् ॥

9 **sthirébhir áṅgaiḥ pururūpa ugró**
babhrúḥ śukrébhiḥ pipiśe híraṇyaiḥ.
ī́śānād asyá bhúvanasya bhū́rer
ná vā́ u yoṣad Rud^a^rā́d asuryàm.

With his firm limbs, having many forms, the mighty one, ruddy-brown, has adorned himself with bright gold ornaments. From the ruler of this great world, from Rudra, let not his divine dominion depart.

sthirébhir áṅgaiḥ: probably to be construed with **pipiśe**, *by means of his firm limbs he has adorned himself with golden ornaments*, that is, his limbs are adorned with golden ornaments; Sāyaṇa supplies **yuktás** *furnished with firm limbs.* **pipiśe**: pf. Ā. of piś. **ī́śānād**: pr. pt. (agreeing with **Rudrād**) of **īś** *rule over* with gen. (202 A *a*); the pf. pt. is **īśāná**. **bhū́res**: agreeing with **bhúvanasya**; cp. vii. 95, 2: **cétantī bhúvanasya bhū́reḥ** *taking note of the wide world* (where **bhū́res** could not agree with any other word); Sāyaṇa takes it with **Rudrā́d**. **yoṣat**: s ao. of yu *separate* (p. 162, 2; 201 A 1). **asuryàm**: an examination of the occurrences of this word indicates that as an adj. it should be pronounced **asuría**, but as a substantive **asuryá**.

१० अर्हन्बिभर्षि सायकानि धन्वा-
र्हन्निष्कं यजतं विश्वरूपम् ।
अर्हन्निदं दयसे विश्वमभ्वं
न वा ओजीयो रुद्र त्वदस्ति ॥

अर्हन् । बिभर्षि । सायकानि । धन्व ।
अर्हन् । निष्कम् । यजतम् । विश्वऽरूपम् ।
अर्हन् । इदम् । दयसे । विश्वम् । अभ्वम् ।
न । वै । ओजीयः । रुद्र । त्वत् । अस्ति ॥

10 **árhan bibharṣi sā́yakāni dhánva**
árhan niṣkám̐ yajatám̐ viśvárūpam ;
árhann idám̐ dayase víśvam ábhvam :
ná vā́ ójīyo, Rudᵃra, tvád asti.

Worthy thou bearest arrows and bow ; worthy thy adorable all-coloured necklace ; worthy thou wieldest all this force : there is nothing mightier than thou, O Rudra.

bibharṣi : 2. s. pr. of **bhṛ** *bear* ; this pr. stem is much less common than that according to the first class, **bhára**. **árhann** : 52. **idám** : *this*, viz. that thou possessest. **dayase** : 2. s. Ā. pr. of 2. **dā** *divide*. Sāyaṇa interprets **idám̐ dayase ábhvam** as *thou protectest this very extensive* (**ábhvam**) *world*. **tvád** : abl. after cpv. (p. 317, 3).

११ स्तुहि श्रुतं गर्तसदं युवानं
मृगं न भीममुपहत्नुमुग्रम् ।
मृळा जरित्रे रुद्र स्तवानो
ऽन्यं ते अस्मन्नि वपन्तु सेनाः ॥

स्तुहि । श्रुतम् । गर्तऽसदम् । युवानम् ।
मृगम् । न । भीमम् । उपऽहत्नुम् । उग्रम् ।
मृळ । जरित्रे । रुद्र । स्तवानः ।
अन्यम् । ते । अस्मत् । नि । वपन्तु । सेनाः ॥

11 **stuhí śrutám̐ gartasádam̐ yúvānam̐,**
mṛgám̐ ná bhīmám upahatnúm, ugrám.
mṛḷā́ jaritré Rudᵃra stávāno :
anyám̐ tĕ asmán ní vapantu sénāḥ.

Praise him, the famous, that sits on the car-seat, the young, the mighty, that slays like a dread beast. O Rudra, being praised be gracious to the singer : let thy missiles lay low another than us.

yúvānam : other gods also, such as Agni, Indra, the Maruts, are spoken of as young. **mṛgám̐ ná bhīmám** : cp. note on i. 154, 2 b ; either a bull (**vṛṣabhó ná bhīmáḥ** vi. 22, 1) or a lion (**simhó ná bhīmáḥ**, iv. 16, 14) may be meant. **mṛḷá** : ipv. of **mṛḍ** ; with dat., p. 311, *f*. **stávānas** : here, as nearly always, in a ps. sense. **asmád** : abl. with **anyá**, p. 317, 3. **sénās** : that this word here means *missiles* is rendered probable by the parallel passage VS. 16, 52 : **yā́s te sahásram̐ hetáyo 'nyám asmán ní vapantu tā́ḥ** *may those thousand missiles of thine lay low another than us.*

१२ कुमारश्चित्पितरं वन्दमानं
प्रति नानाम रुद्रोपयन्तम्।
भूरेर्दातारं सत्पतिं गृणीषे
स्तुतस्त्वं भेषजा रास्यस्मे ॥

कुमारः। चित्। पितरम्। वन्दमानम्।
प्रति। ननाम। रुद्र। उपऽयन्तम्।
भूरेः। दातारम्। सत्ऽपतिम्। गृणीषे।
स्तुतः। त्वम्। भेषजा। रासि। अस्मे इति ॥

12 kumārá́ś cit pitáram vándamā-
nam
práti nānāma Rud[a]ropayántam.
bhū́rer dātā́ram sátpatim gṛṇīṣe:
stutás tuám bheṣajā́ rāsi asmé.

A son bows towards his father who approving approaches him, O Rudra. I sing to the true lord, the giver of much: praised thou givest remedies to us.

The interpretation of a b is doubtful. It seems to mean: Rudra, as a father, approaches with approval the singer, as a son; Rudra, being addressed in the voc., is told this in an indirect manner. I cannot follow Sāyaṇa (**pratinato 'smi** *I have bowed down to*) and several translators in treating **nanāma** as 1. s. pf., which in the RV. could only be **nanama** (p. 149, n. 1). **nānāma**: =pr.; the lengthening of the first syllable is not metrical, see 139, 9. The meaning of c d appears to correspond to that of a b: Rudra, being praised, shows his favour by bestowing his remedies; the singer therefore extols him as the giver of riches. **gṛṇīṣe**: an irr. form of the 1. s. Ā. of **gṛ** *sing*. **asmé**: dat., p. 104; 200 A 1.

१३ या वो भेषजा मरुतः शुचीनि
या शंतमा वृषणो या मयोभु।
यानि मनुरवृणीता पिता नस
ता शं च योश्च रुद्रस्य वश्मि ॥

या। वः। भेषजा। मरुतः। शुचीनि।
या। शम्ऽतमा। वृषणः। या। मयःऽभु।
यानि। मनुः। अवृणीत। पिता। नः।
ता। शम्। च। योः। च। रुद्रस्य। वश्मि ॥

13 yā́ vo bheṣajā́, Marutaḥ, śúcīni,
yā́ śáṃtamā, vṛṣaṇo, yā́ mayo-
bhú,
yā́ni Mánur ávṛṇītā, pitā́ nas:
tā́ śám ca yóś ca Rud[a]rásya
vaśmi.

Your remedies, O Maruts, that are pure, that are most wholesome, O mighty ones, that are beneficent, that Manu, our father, chose: these and the healing and blessing of Rudra I desire.

Marutas: the Maruts, as the sons of Rudra (cp. 1 a) are here incidentally invoked, and their remedies associated with Rudra's. **mayobhú:** the short form of the N. pl. n. (p. 82, n. 7, and p. 83, *d*). **Mánus:** the ancestor of mankind, often spoken of as a father or 'our father', and the institutor of sacrifice. **ávṛṇītā**: 3. s. ipf. Ā. (with metrically lengthened final vowel) of 2. **vṛ** *choose.* **śám, yós**: these words are frequently used in combination, either as adverbs or substantives.

१४ परि णो हेती रुद्रस्य वृज्याः	परि । नः । हेतिः । रुद्रस्य । वृज्याः ।
परि त्वेषस्य दुर्मतिर्मही गात् ।	परि । त्वेषस्य । दुःऽमतिः । मही । गात् ।
अव स्थिरा मघवद्भ्यस्तनुष्व	अव । स्थिरा । मघवत्ऽभ्यः । तनुष्व ।
मीढ्वस्तोकाय तनयाय मृळ ॥	मीढ्वः । तोकाय । तनयाय । मृळ ॥

14 **pári ṇo hetī́ Rud**[a]**rásya vṛjyāḥ,**
pári tveṣásya durmatír mahī́ gāt.
áva sthirā́ maghávadbhyas tanuṣva;
mī́ḍhvas, tokā́ya tánayāya mṛḷa.

May the dart of Rudra pass us by, may the great ill will of the terrible one go by us: slacken thy firm (weapons) *for* (our) *liberal patrons; O bounteous one, be merciful to our children and descendants.*

vṛjyās: 3. s. root ao. prc. (p. 172 *a*) of **vṛj** *twist.* **gāt**: root ao. inj. of **gā** *go.* maghávadbhyas: the I. D. Ab. pl. of **maghávan** are formed from the supplementary stem **maghávant** (91, 5). **áva tanuṣva sthirā́**: *relax the taut,* with reference to the bow, the special weapon of Rudra; used with the dat. because equivalent to mṛḷa *be merciful to* (p. 311 *f*). **mī́ḍhvas**: voc. of the old unreduplicated pf. pt. **mīḍhvā́ṃs, cp. p. 66**; 157 *b* (p. 182). mṛḷa: = **mṛḷa,** p. 437, a 9.

१५ एवा बभ्रो वृषभ चेकितान	एव । बभ्रो इति । वृषभ । चेकितान ।
यथा देव न हृणीषे न हंसि ।	यथा । देव । न । हृणीषे । न । हंसि ।
हवनश्रुन्नो रुद्रेह बोधि	हवनऽश्रुत् । नः । रुद्र । इह । बोधि ।
बृहद्वदेम विदथे सुवीराः ॥	बृहत् । वदेम । विदथे । सुऽवीराः ॥

15 **evā́, babhro vṛṣabha cekitāna,**
yáthā, deva, ná hṛṇīṣé ná hámsi,
havanaśrún no Rud^{a}rehá bodhi.
bṛhád vadema vidáthe suvī́rāḥ.

So, O ruddy brown, far-famed bull, be listening here, O Rudra, to our invocation, inasmuch as thou art not wroth and slayest not, O god. We would, with strong sons, speak aloud at divine worship.

éva: to be taken with c, since in the normal syntactical order it should follow **yáthā** in the sense which it here has (p. 241, 1); when **yathā** meaning *so that* follows, it is normally construed with the sb. (241, 2), not with the ind., as here. **cekitāna**: voc. int. pr. pt. of cit *note*; Sāyaṇa explains it as *knowing all*, but the act. only has this sense (e. g. **cikitvā́ṃs** *knowing*): this and the two preceding vocatives are unaccented because not beginning the Pāda (p. 466, 18 *b*). **hṛṇīṣé**: 2. s. Ā. pr. of 2. **hṛ** *be angry*. **hámsi**: 2. s. pr. of **han**, Sandhi, 66 A 2. **bodhi**: 2. s. root ao. ipv. of **bhū** (p. 172, n. 1). **nas**: dat. to be taken with **bodhi**, lit. *be invocation-hearing for us* (not gen. dependent on **havana**, lit. *hearing the invocation of us*). **vadema**: see note on ii. 12, 15 d.

APÁṂ NÁPĀT

This deity is celebrated in one entire hymn (ii. 35), is invoked in two stanzas of a hymn to the Waters, and is often mentioned incidentally elsewhere. Brilliant and youthful, he shines without fuel in the waters which surround and nourish him. Clothed in lightning, he is golden in form, appearance, and colour. Standing in the highest place, he always shines with undimmed splendour. Steeds, swift as thought, carry the Son of Waters. In the last stanza of his hymn he is invoked as Agni and must be identified with him; Agni, moreover, in some hymns addressed to him, is spoken of as Apāṃ napāt. But the two are also distinguished; for example, 'Agni, accordant with the Son of Waters, confers victory over Vṛtra'. The epithet **āśu-héman** *swiftly-speeding*, applied three times to Apāṃ napāt, in its only other occurrence refers to Agni. Hence Apāṃ napāt appears to represent the lightning form of Agni which lurks in the cloud. For Agni, besides being directly called Apāṃ napāt, is also termed the embryo (**gárbha**) of the waters; and the third form of Agni is described as kindled in the waters.

This deity is not a creation of Indian mythology, but goes back to the Indo-Iranian period. For in the Avesta Apàm napāt̰ is a spirit of the waters, who lives in their depths, who is surrounded by females, who is often invoked with them, who drives with swift steeds, and is said to have seized the brightness in the depth of the ocean.

ii. 35. Metre : Triṣṭubh.

१ उ॒पेम॑सृक्षि वाज॒युर्व॑च॒स्यां
चनो॑ दधीत ना॒द्यो गिरो॑ मे ।
अ॒पां नपा॑दाशु॒हेमा॑ कु॒वित्स
सु॒पेश॑सस्करति॒ जोषि॑ष॒द्धि ॥

उप॑ । ई॒म् । अ॒सृ॒क्षि॒ । वा॒ज॒ऽयुः । व॒च॒स्याम् ।
चनः॑ । द॒धी॒त॒ । ना॒द्यः॑ । गिरः॑ । मे॒ ।
अ॒पाम् । नपा॑त् । आ॒शु॒ऽहेमा॑ । कु॒वित् । सः ।
सु॒ऽपेश॑सः । क॒र॒ति॒ । जोषि॑षत् । हि ॥

1 **úpem asṛkṣi vājayúr vacasyā́m :**
cáno dadhīta nādió gíro me.
Apā́ṃ nápād āśuhémā kuvít sá
supéśasas karati ? jóṣiṣad dhí.

Desirous of gain I have sent forth this eloquence (to him) *: may the son of streams gladly accept my songs. Will he, the Son of Waters, of swift impulse, perchance make* (them) *well-adorned? For he will enjoy* (them).

asṛkṣí : 1. s Ā. s ao. of **sṛj**, which with **úpa** may take two acc., so that nādyám might be supplied. On **īm** see 180 (p. 220). **dadhīta** : 3. s. pr. op. Ā. of **dhā**, which with **cánas** takes the acc. or loc. **nādyá**, which occurs only here, is evidently synonymous with **apā́ṃ nápāt** in c. **āśuhémā**, though a Bv., is accented on the second member : see p. 455 *c a*. **karati** : 3. s. sb. root ao. of **kṛ** : unaccented because **kuvít** necessarily accents the verb only if it is in the same Pāda. **supéśasas** *well-adorned = well-rewarded* ; cp. ii. 34, 6 : dhíyaṃ **vā́japeśasam** *a prayer adorned with gain* ; on the accent see p. 455 *c a* ; on the Sandhi (-s k-) see 43, 2 *a*. **jóṣiṣat** : 3. s. sb. **iṣ** ao. of **juṣ**. **hí** explains why he is likely to accept them ; it accents **jóṣiṣat**, which, however, as beginning a new sentence (p. 466, 19 *a*), would be accented without it.

२ इ॒मं स्व॑स्मै हृ॒द आ सुत॑ष्टं
मन्त्रं॑ वोचेम कु॒विद॑स्य॒ वेद॑त् ।
अ॒पां नपा॑दसु॒र्य॑स्य म॒ह्ना
विश्वा॑न्य॒र्यो भुव॑ना जजान ॥

इ॒मम् । सु । अ॒स्मै॒ । हृ॒दः । आ । सुऽत॑ष्टम् ।
मन्त्र॑म् । वो॒चे॒म॒ । कु॒वित् । अ॒स्य॒ । वेद॑त् ।
अ॒पाम् । नपा॑त् । अ॒सु॒र्य॑स्य । म॒ह्ना ।
विश्वा॑नि । अ॒र्यः । भुव॑ना । ज॒जा॒न॒ ॥

2 imáṃ sú asmai hṛdá ā́ sútaṣṭáṃ
mántraṃ vocema: kuvíd asya védat?
Apā́ṃ nápād, asuríasya mahnā́,
víśvāni aryó bhúvanā jajāna.

We would verily utter from our heart this well-fashioned hymn for him. Perchance he will take note of it. The Son of Waters, the lord, by the greatness of divine dominion, has created all beings.

hṛdá ā́: this expression occurs several times, e.g. iii. 39, 1: **matír hṛdá ā́ vacyámānā** *a prayer welling from the heart.* **sútaṣṭam** *well-fashioned,* like a car, to which the seers frequently compare their hymns; on the accent see p. 456, 1 *a*; cp. p. 462, 13 *b*. **asmai** and **asya**: unaccented, p. 452, 8 B *c*; dat. of prs. with vac: cp. 200, 1 *c*. **védat**: 3. s. pr. sb. of **vid** *know,* with gen., cp. 202 A *c*. **asuryàsya**: see p. 451, 6.

३ सम॒न्या यन्त्युप॑ यन्त्य॒न्याः
स॑मा॒नमू॒र्वं न॒द्यः॑ पृणन्ति ।
तमू॒ शुचिं॒ शुच॑यो दीदि॒वांस॑म्
अ॒पां नपा॑तं॒ परि॑ तस्थु॒रापः॑ ॥

सम् । अ॒न्याः । यन्ति॑ । उप॑ । य॒न्ति॒ । अ॒न्याः ।
स॒मा॒नम् । ऊ॒र्वम् । न॒द्यः॑ । पृ॒ण॒न्ति॒ ।
तम् । ऊँ॒ इति॑ । शुचि॑म् । शुच॑यः । दीदि॒ऽवांस॑म् ।
अ॒पाम् । नपा॑तम् । परि॑ । त॒स्थुः॒ । आपः॑ ॥

3 sám anyā́ yánti, úpa yanti anyā́ḥ:
samānám ūrváṃ nadíaḥ pṛṇanti.
tám ū śúciṃ śúcayo dīdivā́ṃsam
Apā́ṃ nápātaṃ pári tásthur ā́paḥ.

While some flow together, others flow to (the sea)*: the streams fill the common receptacle; him the pure, the shining Son of Waters, the pure waters stand around.*

yánti: accented because of the antithesis expressed by **anyā́ḥ—anyā́ḥ**, the first vb. then being treated as subordinate (see p. 468 β). **ūrvám**: = *ocean.* **samānám**: *common,* because all streams flow into it. **nadyàs**: cp. **asuryàsya** in 2 c. **pṛṇanti**: from **pṝ** *fill.*

ū : u is often lengthened in the second syllable of a Pāda before a single consonant (see p. 220). dīdivā́ṃsam : pf. pt. of dī *shine*, with lengthened red. vowel (139, 9) and shortened radical vowel; the sense is illustrated by 4 d. pári tasthur : = *they tend him.*

४ तमस्मेरा युवतयो युवानं
मर्मृज्यमानाः परि यन्त्यापः ।
स शुक्रेभिः शिक्वभी रेवदस्मे
दीदायानिध्मो घृतनिर्णिगप्सु ॥

तम् । अस्मेराः । युवतयः । युवानम् ।
मर्मृज्यमानाः । परि । यन्ति । आपः ।
सः । शुक्रेभिः । शिक्वऽभिः । रेवत् । अस्मे इति ।
दीदाय । अनिध्मः । घृतऽनिर्निक् । अप्ऽसु ॥

4 tám ásmerā yuvatáyo yúvānaṃ
marmṛjyámānāḥ pári yanti ā́-
paḥ :
sá śukrébhiḥ śíkvabhī revád
asmé
dīdā́yānidhmó ghṛtánirṇig apsú.

Him, the youth, the young maidens, the waters, not smiling, making him bright surround: he with clear flames shines bountifully on us, without fuel in the waters, having a garment of ghee.

ásmerās : it is somewhat uncertain what is the exact sense here implied; but judging by iv. 58, 8, where the drops of ghee are described as hastening 'to Agni like beauteous maidens, smiling, to meeting-places', it may mean that the waters attend seriously on this form of Agni, not as lovers. yúvānam : a term applied to Agni in several passages. marmṛjyámānās : the vb. mṛj is often used of making Agni bright, with ghee, &c. śíkvabhis : the precise sense is somewhat doubtful, but it must mean 'flames' or the like. Note that though in this word the ending bhis is separated in the Pada text, it is not so in śukrébhis because śúkre is not a stem. asmé : dat. Pragṛhya, 26 *c*. dīdā́ya : 3. s. pf. of dī *shine*, with long red. vowel (139, 9). an-idhmás : accent, p. 455 *c a*; cp. x. 30, 4 : yó anidhmó dīdayad apsú antár *who shone without fuel in the waters.* ghṛtá-nirṇik : an epithet otherwise applied only to Agni and (once) to the *sacrifice* (yajñá) : note that the second member appears in the Pada text as nirnik, in accordance with the analysis niḥ-nik when the word occurs uncompounded.

५ अस्मै तिस्रो अव्यथ्याय नारीर्
देवाय देवीर्दिधिषन्त्यन्नम् ।
कृता इवोप हि प्रसर्स्रे अप्सु
स पीयूषं धयति पूर्वसूनाम् ॥

अस्मै । तिस्रः । अव्यथ्याय । नारीः ।
देवाय । देवीः । दिधिषन्ति । अन्नम् ।
कृताःऽइव । उप । हि । प्रऽसर्स्रे । अप्ऽसु ।
सः । पीयूषम् । धयति । पूर्वऽसूनाम् ॥

5 asmái tisró avyathiáya nā́rīr
devā́ya devī́r didhiṣanti ánnam:
kṛ́tā ivópa hí prasarsré apsú;
sá pīyū́ṣaṃ dhayati pūrvasū́nām.

On him, the immovable god, three divine women desire to bestow food: for he has stretched forth as it were to the breasts (?) *in the waters: he sucks the milk of them that first bring forth.*

tisró devī́ḥ: the waters in the three worlds are probably meant; in iii. 56, 5 Agni is spoken of as having three mothers (**trimātā́**), and three maidens of the waters (**yoṣáṇās tisró ápyāḥ**) are there mentioned: they wish to feed him, while he desires to drink their milk. **didhiṣanti**: ds. of 1. **dhā** *bestow*: this is the usual form, while **dhítsa** is rare. **kṛ́tās**: the meaning of this word, which occurs here only, is quite uncertain. **pra-sarsré**: 3. s. pr. int. of **sṛ**. **dhayati**: 3. s. pr. of 2. **dhā** *suck*. **pūrvasū́nām**: i. e. Apāṃ napāt is their first offspring; cp. x. 121, 7: **ā́po janáyantīr Agním** *the waters producing Agni.*

६ अश्वस्यात्र जनिमास्य च स्वर्
द्रुहो रिषः संपृचः पाहि सूरीन् ।
आमासु पूर्षु परो अप्रमृष्यं
नारातयो वि नशन्नानृतानि ॥

अश्वस्य । अत्र । जनिम । अस्य । च । स्वः ।
द्रुहः । रिषः । सम्ऽपृचः । पाहि । सूरीन् ।
आमासु । पूर्षु । परः । अप्रऽमृष्यम् ।
न । अरातयः । वि । नशन् । न । अनृतानि ॥

6 áśvasya átra jánimāsyá ca svàr.
druhó riṣáḥ sampṛ́caḥ pāhi sūrī́n.
āmā́su pūrṣú paró apramṛṣyáṃ
nā́rātayo ví naśan nā́nṛtāni.

The birth of this steed is here and in heaven. Do thou protect the patrons from falling in with malice and injury. Him that is not to be forgotten, far away in unbaked citadels, hostilities shall not reach nor falsehoods.

Though every word is clear in this stanza the meaning of the whole is somewhat uncertain. It seems to be this: Apāṃ napāt is produced from both the terrestrial and the heavenly waters. He is invoked to protect sacrificers from injury. He himself dwells beyond the reach of foes. **áśvasya**: Agni is often spoken of as a steed. **átra**: *here*, i.e. in the waters of earth. **svàr**: this is the only passage in the RV. in which the word is not to be read as súar; it is here a loc. without the ending i (see 82 *c*). **pāhi**: the change from the 3. to the 2. prs. in the same stanza is common in the RV. with reference to deities. On this form depends the abl. inf. **sampṛ́cas** as well as the two preceding ablatives: lit. *protect the patrons from malice and from injury, from falling in with them* (cp. p. 337 *a*). **āmā́su**: *in the unbaked*, i.e. *natural* (cloud) *citadels*. **pūrṣú**: loc. pl. of púr, 82. **parás**: note the difference of accent between this adv. and the N. s. adj. **páras** *yonder, other*. **naśat**: inj. pr. of 3. **naś** *reach*.

७ स्व आ दमे सुदुघा यस्य धेनुः
स्वधां पीपाय सुभ्वन्नमत्ति ।
सो अपां नपादूर्जयन्नप्स्व१न्तर्
वसुदेयाय विधते वि भाति ॥

स्वे । आ । दमे । सुऽदुघा । यस्य । धेनुः ।
स्वधाम् । पीपाय । सुऽभु । अन्नम् । अत्ति ।
सः । अपाम् । नपात् । ऊर्जयन् । अप्ऽसु ।
अन्तः ।
वसुऽदेयाय । विधते । वि । भाति ॥

7 **svá á dáme sudúghā yásya dhenúḥ,**
svadhā́ṃ pīpāya, subhú ánnam atti;
sò 'pā́ṃ nápād ūrjáyann apsú antár,
vasudéyāya vidhaté ví bhāti.

He, in whose own house is a cow yielding good milk, nourishes his vital force, he eats the excellent food; he, the Son of Waters, gathering strength within the waters, shines forth for the granting of wealth to the advantage of the worshipper.

svá á dáme: that is, within the waters; in i. 1, 8 **své dáme** refers to the sacrificial altar on which Agni grows, that is, flames up. The first three Pādas merely vary the sense of 5. The food that he eats is the milk that he receives, and that strengthens him. **svadhā́m** : this word is not analysed in the Padapāṭha of the RV. and AV. (as if derived from a root svadh), but it is separated in that of the TS. as **sva-dhā́**. **pīpāya** : 3. s. pf. of pi *swell*, with lengthened red. vowel (139, 9). só apā́m must be read as sò 'pā́m since a must here be metrically elided (21 *a* ; p. 465, 17, 3). On **apsv àntár** see p. 450, 2 *b* [where apsv1antaḥ should be corrected to apsva1ntaḥ]. **vidhaté** : dat. of advantage (p. 314, B 1) ; on the accent see p. 458, 11, 3. **vasudhéyāya** : dat. of purpose, *ibid.*, B 2. **ví bhāti** : here Apāṃ napāt is thought of as the terrestrial Agni appearing on the sacrificial altar.

८ यो अप्स्वा शुचिना दैव्येन
ऋतावाजस्र उर्विया विभाति ।
वया इदन्या भुवनान्यस्य
प्र जायन्ते वीरुधश्च प्रजाभिः ॥

यः । अप्ऽसु । आ । शुचिना । दैव्येन ।
ऋतऽवा । अजस्रः । उर्विया । विऽभाति ।
वयाः । इत् । अन्या । भुवनानि । अस्य ।
प्र । जायन्ते । वीरुधः । च । प्रऽजाभिः ॥

8 yó apsú ā́ śúcinā dáiviena
ṛtā́vā́jasra urviyā́ vibhā́ti :
vayā́ íd anyā́ bhúvanāni asya
prá jāyante vīrúdhaś ca prajā́-bhiḥ.

Who in the waters, with bright divinity, holy, eternal, widely shines forth : as offshoots of him other beings and plants propagate themselves with progeny.

śúcinā dáivyena : = *divine brightness.* **ṛtā́vā** : note that in the Padapāṭha the original short a is restored (cp. i. 160, 1). **vayā́s** : other beings are his offshoots because he produced them ; cp. 2 d : **víśvāni bhúvanā jajāna.** **prajā́bhis** : cp. ii. 33, 1, prá jāyemahi prajā́bhiḥ.

९ अपां नपादा ह्यस्थादुपस्थं
जिह्मानामूर्ध्वो विद्युतं वसानः ।
तस्य ज्येष्ठं महिमानं वहन्तीर्
हिरण्यवर्णाः परि यन्ति यह्वीः ॥

अपाम् । नपात् । आ । हि । अस्थात् । उप ऽस्थम् ।
जिह्मानाम् । ऊर्ध्वः । विऽद्युतम् । वसानः ।
तस्य । ज्येष्ठम् । महिमानम् । वहन्तीः ।
हिरण्यऽवर्णाः । परि । यन्ति । यह्वीः ॥

9 Apā́ṃ nápād ā́ hí ásthād upá-
sthaṃ
jihmā́nām, ūrdhvó vidyútaṃ
vásānaḥ.
tásya jyéṣṭhaṃ mahimā́nam
váhantīr,
híraṇyavarṇāḥ pári yanti yah-
vī́ḥ.

The Son of Waters has occupied the lap of the prone (waters), (himself) *upright, clothing himself in lightning. Bearing his highest greatness, golden-hued, the swift streams flow around* (him).

The lightning Agni is again described in this stanza. **jihmā́nām ūrdhváh**: these words are in contrast; cp. i. 95, 5 of Agni: **vardhate . . . āsu jihmā́nām ūrdhváḥ . . . upásthe** *he grows in them, upright in the lap of the prone.* **tásya mahimā́nam** *his greatness = him the great one.* **híraṇyavarṇās**: because he is clothed in lightning. **pári yanti**: cp. 3 a and 4 b. **yahvī́s**: the meaning of the word yahvá, though it occurs often, is somewhat uncertain: it may be *great* (Naighaṇṭuka, Sāyaṇa), or *swift* (Roth), or *young* (Geldner).

१० हिरण्यरूपः स हिरण्यसंदृग्
अपां नपात्सेदु हिरण्यवर्णः ।
हिरण्ययात्परि योनेर्निषद्या
हिरण्यदा ददत्यन्नमस्मै ॥

हिरण्यऽरूपः । सः । हिरण्यऽसंदृक् ।
अपाम् । नपात् । सः । इत् । ऊं इति ।
हिरण्यऽवर्णः ।
हिरण्ययात् । परि । योनेः । निऽसद्य ।
हिरण्यऽदाः । ददति । अन्नम् । अस्मै ॥

10 híraṇyarūpaḥ, sá híraṇyasaṃ-
dṛg;
Apā́ṃ nápāt séd u híraṇyavar-
ṇaḥ;
hiraṇyáyāt pári yóner niṣádyā,
hiraṇyadā́ dadati ánnam asmai.

He is of golden form, of golden aspect; this Son of Waters is of golden hue; to him (coming) *from a golden womb, after he has sat down, the givers of gold give food.*

In this stanza the terrestrial Agni is described. He is spoken of as 'golden' because of the colour of his flames. **séd**: 48 a. **pári** as a prp. here governs the abl. (176, 1 *a*). The *golden source* of Agni may be the sun, as Durga thinks; thus the solar deity Savitṛ is spoken of as distinctively golden (cp. i. 35); but hiraṇyáya yóni may = hiraṇyagarbhá (x. 121, 1) at the creation, when Agni was produced from the waters (x. 121, 7). Sāyaṇa wishes to supply **rājate** after **niṣádya** = *having sat down shines*. This is quite unnecessary; it is more natural to take c and d as one sentence, **niṣádya** referring to **asmai**: *to him, after he has sat down, they give* (cp. 210). Note that the Pada text shortens the final vowel of **niṣádyā** (cp. 164, 1). **hiraṇyadā́s**: that is, those who give gold as a sacrificial fee, the patrons of the sacrifice. In a hymn in praise of the dakṣiṇā́ *the sacrificial fee* (x. 107, 2) it is said hiraṇyadā́ amṛtatvám bhajante *the givers of gold partake of immortality*. **dadati**: 3. pl. pr. act. of dā *give* (p. 125, f. n. 4). **ánnam**: the oblation (cp. 11 d).

११ तदस्यानीकमुत चारु नामा-	तत् । अस्य । अनीकम् । उत । चारु । नाम ।
पीच्यं वर्धते नप्तुरपाम् ।	अपीच्यम् । वर्धते । नप्तुः । अपाम् ।
यमिन्धते युवतयः समित्था	यम् । इन्धते । युवतयः । सम् । इत्था ।
हिरण्यवर्णं घृतमन्नमस्य ॥	हिरण्यऽवर्णम् । घृतम् । अन्नम् । अस्य ॥

11 **tád asyā́nīkam utá cā́ru nā́ma**	*That face of his and the dear*
apīcíaṃ vardhate náptur apā́m.	*secret name of the Son of Waters*
yám indháte yuvatáyaḥ sám itthā́	*grow. Of him, whom, golden-coloured, the maidens kindle thus,*
híraṇyavarṇaṃ: ghṛtám ánnam asya.	*ghee is the food.*

ánīkam: the flaming aspect of Agni seen at the sacrifice. **apīcyàm**: *secret*; cp. gúhyaṃ cā́ru nā́ma *the dear secret name* of Soma (ix. 96, 16); *the secret name of the Son of Waters grows* means that the sacrificial Agni, under his secret name of Son of Waters, grows in the waters, cherished by them; another way of expressing what is said in 4 and 7. The cadence of b is irregular, the last syllable but one being short instead of long (cp. p. 440). **yuvatáyas**: the waters (cp. 4 a). **sám**: the prp. after the vb. (p. 468, 20). **ghṛtám ánnam asya**: cp. ghṛtánirṇik in 4 d and subhv ánnam atti in 7 b.

The general meaning of the stanza is: Agni, who in the hidden form of Apāṃ Napāt is nourished in the waters, is at the sacrifice fed with ghee.

१२ अ॒स्मै ब॒हू॒नाम॑व॒माय॒ सख्ये॑	अ॒स्मै । ब॒हू॒नाम् । अ॒व॒माय॑ । सख्ये॑ ।
य॒ज्ञैर्वि॑धेम॒ नम॑सा ह॒विर्भिः॑ ।	य॒ज्ञैः । वि॒धे॒म॒ । नम॑सा । ह॒विःऽभिः॑ ।
सं सानु॒ मार्ज्मि॒ दिधि॑षामि॒ बिल्मै॒र्	सम् । सानु॑ । मार्ज्मि॑ । दिधि॑षामि । बिल्मैः॑ ।
दधा॒म्यन्नैः॒ परि॑ वन्द ऋ॒ग्भिः ॥	दधा॑मि । अन्नैः॑ । परि॑ । व॒न्दे॒ । ऋ॒क्ऽभिः॑ ॥

12 asmái **bahūnā́m avamā́ya sá-khye**
yajñáir vidhema námasā havír-bhiḥ:
sā́ṃ sā́nu **mā́rjmi; dídhiṣāmi** bílmair;
dádhāmi ánnaiḥ; pári vanda ṛgbhíḥ.

To him the nearest friend of many we offer worship with sacrifices, homage, oblations: I rub bright (his) *back; I support* (him) *with shavings; I supply* (him) *with food; I extol* (him) *with stanzas.*

avamā́ya: lit. *the lowest*, that is, *the nearest*; **bahūnā́m** (accent, p. 458, 2 *a*): *of many* (gods). In iv. 1, 5 Agni is invoked as **avamá** and **nédiṣṭha** *nearest*; and in AB. i. 1, 1 Agni is called the *lowest* (**avamá**) of the gods (while Viṣṇu is the *highest* **paramá**), because he is always with men as the terrestrial fire. **sā́ṃ mā́rjmi**: cp. **marmṛjyámānās** in 4 b; on the accent cp. i. 35, 9 c. The prp. **sám** may be supplied with the other two following verbs. **dídhiṣāmi**: pr. ds. of **dhā** *put*; accented as first word of a new sentence. **bílmais**: *with shavings*, to make the newly kindled fire flame up. **ánnais**: with oblations. **dádhāmi**: pr. of **dhā** *put*.

१३ स ईं॒ वृषा॑जनय॒त्तासु॒ गर्भं॑	सः । ई॒म् । वृषा॑ । अ॒ज॒न॒य॒त् । तासु॑ । गर्भ॑म् ।
स ईं॒ शिशु॑र्धयति॒ तं रि॑हन्ति ।	सः । ई॒म् । शिशुः॑ । ध॒य॒ति॒ । तम् । रि॒ह॒न्ति॒ ।
सो अ॒पां नपा॒दन॑भिम्लातवर्णो॒	सः । अ॒पाम् । नपा॑त् । अन॑भिम्लातऽवर्णः ।
ऽन्यस्ये॑वे॒ह त॒न्वा॑ विवेष ॥	अ॒न्यस्य॑ऽइव । इ॒ह । त॒न्वा॑ । वि॒वे॒ष ॥

13 sá īṃ vṛ́ṣājanayat tā́su gárbhaṃ;
sá īṃ śíśur dhayati; tā́ṃ rihanti;
sò 'pā́ṃ nápād ánabhimlāta-varṇo
anyásyeveha tanúā viveṣa.

He, the bull, generated in them that germ; he, as a child, sucks them; they kiss him; he, the Son of Waters, of unfaded colour, works here with the body of another.

In a and b Apāṃ napāt reproduces himself in the waters; in c and d he appears as the sacrificial fire on earth. **īm** anticipates **gárbham**; *him*, that is, *a son*. **tā́su**: in the waters, as his wives. **īm** in b = *them*, the waters, who here are both the wives and mothers of Apāṃ napāt. **dhayati**: cp. 5 d. **rihanti**: lit. *lick*, as a cow the calf. **só apā́m**: here the **a**, though written must be dropped after **o**, as in 7 c. **ánabhimlāta-varṇas**: he is as bright here as in the waters; cp. **híraṇyavarṇas** in 10 b; on the Sandhi, cp. note on i. 1, 9 b. **anyásya iva**: of one who seems to be another, but is essentially the same. **ihá**: on earth, in the form of the sacrificial Agni.

१४ अस्मिन्पदे परमे तस्थिवांसम्
अध्वस्मभिर्विश्वहा दीदिवांसम्।
आपो नप्त्रे घृतमन्नं वहन्तीः
स्वयमत्कैः परि दीयन्ति यह्वीः॥

अस्मिन्। पदे। परमे। तस्थिऽवांसम्।
अध्वस्मऽभिः। विश्वहा। दीदिऽवांसम्।
आपः। नप्त्रे। घृतम्। अन्नम्। वहन्तीः।
स्वयम्। अत्कैः। परि। दीयन्ति। यह्वीः॥

14 asmín padé paramé tasthivā́ṃsam,
adhvasmábhir viśváhā dīdivā́ṃsam,
ā́po, náptre ghṛtám ánnaṃ váhantīḥ,
svayám átkaiḥ pári dīyanti yahvī́ḥ.

Him stationed in this highest place, shining for ever with undimmed (rays), *the Waters, bringing ghee as food to* (their) *son, swift, themselves fly around with their robes.*

padé paramé: in the abode of the aerial waters. **adhvasmábhis**: a substantive has to be supplied: flames or rays; cp. 4 c, **śukrébhiḥ**

śíkvabhir dīdā́ya. **náptre: apā́m** is omitted because **ā́pas** immediately precedes. **átkais:** the meaning of this word is not quite certain, but it most probably means *garment*; the commentators give several senses. The expression perhaps implies that the waters cover him up for protection or concealment. **pári dīyanti** (**dī** *fly*); cp. **pári yanti** in 4 b and 9 d, and **pári tasthur** in 3 d.

१५ अयांसमग्ने सुच्चितिं जनाया-
यांसमु मघवंद्ध्यः सुवृक्तिम् ।
विश्वं तद्भद्रं यदवंन्ति देवा
बृहद्वदेम विदथे सुवीराः ॥

अयांसम् । अग्ने । सुऽच्चितिम् । जनाय ।
अयांसम् । ऊं इति । मघवंत्ऽभ्यः । सुऽवृक्तिम् ।
विश्वंम् । तत् । भद्रम् । यत् । अवंन्ति । देवाः ।
बृहत् । वदेम । विदथे । सुऽवीराः ॥

15 **áyāṃsam, Agne, sukṣitím jánāya;**
áyāṃsam u maghávadbhyaḥ suvṛktím:
víśvaṃ tád bhadrám yád ávanti devā́ḥ.
bṛhád vadema vidáthe suvī́rāḥ.

I have bestowed, O Agni, safe dwelling on the people; I have also bestowed a song of praise on the patrons: auspicious is all that the gods favour. We would, with strong sons, speak aloud at divine worship.

áyāṃsam: 1. s. s ao. of **yam.** **Agne:** the sacrificial Agni is here addressed. **jánāya:** *on* (our) *people*, by means of this hymn. **suvṛktím:** *a hymn* that will produce the fulfilment of their wishes. **bhadrám:** if a hymn finds favour with the gods, it will produce blessings. **vadema:** the poet desires this also as a reward for his hymn. The final hemistich also occurs at the end of ii. 23; and the last Pāda is the refrain of twenty-three of the forty-three hymns of the second Maṇḍala.

MITRA

The association of Mitra with Varuṇa is so intimate that he is addressed alone in one hymn only (iii. 59). Owing to the scantiness of the information supplied in that hymn his separate character appears somewhat indefinite.

Uttering his voice, he marshals men and watches the tillers with unwinking eye. He is the great Āditya who marshals, yātayati, the people, and the epithet yātayáj-jana *arraying men together* appears to be peculiarly his. Savitṛ (i. 35) is identified with Mitra because of his laws, and Viṣṇu (i. 154) takes his three steps by the laws of Mitra: statements indicating that Mitra regulates the course of the sun. Agni, who goes at the head of the dawns (that is to say, is kindled before dawn), produces Mitra, and when kindled is Mitra. In the Atharvaveda, Mitra at sunrise is contrasted with Varuṇa in the evening, and in the Brāhmaṇas Mitra is connected with day, Varuṇa with night.

The conclusion from the Vedic evidence that Mitra was a solar deity, is corroborated by the Avesta and by Persian religion in general, where Mithra is undoubtedly a sun-god or a god of light specially connected with the sun.

The etymology of the name is uncertain, but it must originally have meant 'ally' or 'friend', for the word often means 'friend' in the RV., and the Avestic Mithra is the guardian of faithfulness. As the kindly nature of the god is often referred to in the Veda, the term must in the beginning have been applied to the sun-god in his aspect of a benevolent power of nature.

iii. 59. Metre: Triṣṭubh, 1–5; Gāyatrī, 6–9.

१ मित्रो जनान्यातयति ब्रुवाणो	मित्रः। जनान्। यातयति। ब्रुवाणः।
मित्रो दाधार पृथिवीमुत द्याम्।	मित्रः। दाधार। पृथिवीम्। उत। द्याम्।
मित्रः कृष्टीरनिमिषाभि चष्टे	मित्रः। कृष्टीः। अनिऽमिषा। अभि। चष्टे।
मित्राय हव्यं घृतवज्जुहोत॥	मित्राय। हव्यम्। घृतऽवत्। जुहोत॥

1 Mitró jánān yātayati bruvāṇó; Mitró dādhāra pṛthivī́m utá dyā́m; Mitráḥ kṛṣṭī́r ánimiṣābhí caṣṭe: Mitrā́ya havyám̐ ghṛtávaj juhota.	*Mitra speaking stirs men; Mitra supports earth and heaven; Mitra regards the people with unwinking eye: to Mitra offer the oblation with ghee.*

yātayati: *stirs* to activity. bruvāṇás: by calling, that is, arousing them; cp. what is said of Savitṛ: 'who makes all beings hear him by his call' (v. 82, 9) and 'he stretches out his arms that all may hear him' (ii. 38, 2). Sāyaṇa interprets the word as *being praised or making a noise.* Some scholars take the pt. with Mitrás in the sense of *he who calls himself Mitra,* but this in my opinion is in itself highly improbable, while this construction cannot be shown to exist in the RV., and even later seems only to occur when the name immediately precedes, i. e. **Mitró bruvāṇáḥ**. This Pāda occurs slightly modified in vii. 36, 2 as **jánaṃ ca Mitró yatati bruvāṇáḥ**. **dādhāra**: pf. = pr.; p. 342 *a* (cp. 139, 9); note that the red. syllable of this pf. is never shortened in the Pada text (cp. i. 154, 4). **dyā́m**: acc. of **dyó** (102, 3). **ánimiṣā**: inst. of **á-nimiṣ**; it is characteristic of Mitra and Varuṇa to regard men with unwinking eye. **caṣṭe**: 3. s. of **cakṣ**; on the Sandhi see 66 B 2 *a*. **juhota**: 2. pl. ipv. irr. strong form occurring beside the regular **juhutá** (p. 144, B 3 *a*).

२ प्र स मित्र मर्तो अस्तु प्रयस्वान्
यस्त आदित्य शिक्षति व्रतेन ।
न हन्यते न जीयते त्वोतो
नैनमंहो अश्नोत्यन्तितो न दूरात् ॥

प्र । सः । मित्र । मर्तः । अस्तु । प्रयस्वान् ।
यः । ते । आदित्य । शिक्षति । व्रतेन ।
न । हन्यते । न । जीयते । त्वाऽऊतः ।
न । एनम् । अंहः । अश्नोति । अन्तितः ।
न । दूरात् ॥

2 **prá sá, Mitra, mártŏ astu práyasvān,**
yás ta, Āditya, śíkṣati vraténa.
ná hanyate, ná jīyate tuóto:
náinam áṃho 'śnoty ántito ná dūrā́t.

Let that mortal offering oblations, O Mitra, be pre-eminent who pays obeisance to thee, O Āditya, according to (thy) *ordinance. He who is aided by thee is not slain nor vanquished: trouble reaches him neither from near nor from far.*

tvótas: **tva** must often be read as **tua**; **tuótas** is therefore more natural than the prosodical shortening (p. 437 *a* 4) of **tvă-ū́tas**. The fourth Pāda has one syllable too many as written in the Saṃhitā text. By dropping the **a** after **o** the correct number of syllables is obtained, but the break (– – ⏑) remains quite irregular (p. 440, 4 B).

३ अनमीवास इळया मदन्तो
मितज्ञवो वरिमन्ना पृथिव्याः ।
आदित्यस्य व्रतमुपक्षियन्तो
वयं मित्रस्य सुमतौ स्याम ॥

अनमीवासः । इळया । मदन्तः ।
मितऽज्ञवः । वरिमन् । आ । पृथिव्याः ।
आदित्यस्य । व्रतम् । उपऽक्षियन्तः ।
वयम् । मित्रस्य । सुऽमतौ । स्याम ॥

3 anamīvā́sa íḷayā mádanto,
mitájñavo várimann ā́ pṛthivyā̀ḥ,
Ādityásya vratám upakṣiyánto,
vayám Mitrásya sumatáu siāma.

Free from disease, delighting in the sacred food, firm-kneed on the expanse of earth, abiding by the ordinance of the Āditya, may we remain in the good will of Mitra.

váriman: loc. (90, 2) with ā́; note that váriman is n., varimán, m. (p. 453, 9 *e*). Ādityásya: that is, of Mitra.

४ अयं मित्रो नमस्यः सुशेवो
राजा सुक्षत्रो अजनिष्ट वेधाः ।
तस्य वयं सुमतौ यज्ञियस्या-
पि भद्रे सौमनसे स्याम ॥

अयम् । मित्रः । नमस्यः । सुऽशेवः ।
राजा । सुऽक्षत्रः । अजनिष्ट । वेधाः ।
तस्य । वयम् । सुऽमतौ । यज्ञियस्य ।
अपि । भद्रे । सौमनसे । स्याम ॥

4 ayám Mitró namasíaḥ suśévo,
rā́jā sukṣatró ajaniṣṭa vedhā́ḥ:
tásya vayám sumatáu yajñíyasya,
ápi bhadré saumanasé siāma.

This Mitra, adorable, most propitious, a king wielding fair sway, has been born as a disposer: may we remain in the goodwill of him the holy, in his auspicious good graces.

ajaniṣṭa: 3. s. Ā. iṣ ao. of jan. vedhā́s: that is, as a wise moral ruler; on the dec. see 83, 2 *a*. ápi: to be taken as a verbal prp. with as *be*.

५ महाँ आदित्यो नमसोपसद्यो
यातयज्जनो गृणते सुशेवः ।
तस्मा एतत्पन्यतमाय जुष्टम्
अग्नौ मित्राय हविरा जुहोत ॥

महान् । आदित्यः । नमसा । उपऽसद्यः ।
यातयत्ऽजनः । गृणते । सुऽशेवः ।
तस्मै । एतत् । पन्यंऽतमाय । जुष्टम् ।
अग्नौ । मित्राय । हविः । आ । जुहोत ॥

5 **mahā́m̐ Ādityó námasopasádyo**
yātayájjano gṛṇaté suśévaḥ:
tásmā etát pányatamāya júṣṭam
agnáu Mitrā́ya havír ā́ juhota.

The great Āditya, to be approached with homage, stirring men, to the singer most propitious: to him most highly to be praised, to Mitra, offer in fire this acceptable oblation.

mahā́m̐: 39. **yātayájjanas**: on the accent of governing cds. see p. 455 *b*. **gṛṇaté**: dat. of pr. pt. of **gṛ** *sing*; accent, p. 458, 3. **júṣṭam**: a pp. of **juṣ** *enjoy*, with shift of accent when used as an adj. meaning *welcome* (cp. p. 384). **juhota**: cp. note on 1 d.

६ मि॒त्रस्य॑ चर्षणी॒धृतो
ऽवो॑ दे॒वस्य॑ सान॒सि ।
द्यु॒म्नं चि॒त्रश्र॑वस्तमम् ॥

मि॒त्रस्य॑ । च॒र्ष॒णि॒ऽधृतः॑ ।
अवः॑ । दे॒वस्य॑ । सा॒न॒सि ।
द्यु॒म्नम् । चि॒त्रश्र॑वःऽतमम् ॥

6 **Mitrásya carṣaṇīdhṛ́to,**
ávo devásya sānasí,
dyumnáṃ citráśravastamam.

Of Mitra, the god who supports the folk, the favour brings gain, (his) *wealth brings most brilliant fame.*

carṣaṇīdhṛ́tas: the Pada text restores the metrically lengthened short vowel of **carṣaṇi**. **-dhṛ́tó 'vo**: p. 465, 17, 3; cp. note on i. 1, 9 b. **citráśravastamam**: see note on i. 1, 5 b.

७ अ॒भि यो म॑हि॒ना दिवं॑
मि॒त्रो ब॒भूव॑ स॒प्रथाः॑ ।
अ॒भि श्रवो॑भिः पृथि॒वीम् ॥

अ॒भि । यः । म॒हि॒ना । दिव॑म् ।
मि॒त्रः । ब॒भूव॑ । स॒ऽप्रथाः॑ ।
अ॒भि । श्रवः॑ऽभिः । पृ॒थि॒वीम् ॥

7 **abhí yó mahinā́ dívaṃ**
Mitró babhū́va saprátháḥ,
abhí śrávobhiḥ pṛthivī́m:

Mitra the renowned, who is superior to heaven by his greatness, superior to earth by his glories:

abhí bhū *surpass* takes the acc. **mahinā́** for **mahimnā́**: 90, 2. **dívam**: acc. of **dyú**, 99, 5: cp. **dyó**, 102, 3. **babhū́va**: the pf.

here is equivalent to a pr.; p. 342 *a*. In c babhū́va must be supplied with the repeated prp.; cp. note on ii. 33, 2. The cadence of c is irregular: – ◡ ◡ – instead of ◡ – ◡ –; cp. p. 438, 3 *a*.

८ मित्राय पञ्च येमिरे	मित्राय । पञ्च । येमिरे ।
जना अभिष्टिशवसे ।	जनाः । अभिष्टिऽशवसे ।
स देवान्विश्वान्बिभर्ति ॥	सः । देवान् । विश्वान् । बिभर्ति ॥

8 **Mitrā́ya páñca yemire**
jánā abhíṣṭiśavase:
sá devā́n víśvān bibharti.

To Mitra, strong to help, the five peoples submit: he supports all the gods.

páñca jánāḥ: *the five peoples*, here = all mankind. **yemire**: 3. pl. pf. Ā. of **yam** (see p. 150, f. n. 1). **bibharti**: 3. s. pr. P. of **bhṛ**. **víśvān**: this is the regular word for *all* in the RV.: its place begins to be taken by sárva in late hymns. The general meaning of the stanza is that gods and men are dependent on Mitra. The cadence of c is trochaic instead of iambic (see p. 439 *a*).

९ मित्रो देवेष्वायुषु	मित्रः । देवेषु । आयुषु ।
जनाय वृक्तबर्हिषे ।	जनाय । वृक्तऽबर्हिषे ।
इष इष्टव्रता अकः ॥	इषः । इष्टऽव्रताः । अकरित्यकः ॥

9 **Mitró, devéṣu āyúṣu,**
jánāya vṛktábarhiṣe
íṣa iṣṭávratā akaḥ.

Mitra, among gods and mortals, has provided food, according to the ordinances he desires, for the man whose sacrificial grass is spread.

iṣṭá-vratās: a Bv. agreeing with **íṣas**, food regulated by the ordinances which Mitra desires, i. e. to be eaten according to fixed rules.

BṚ́HASPÁTI

This god is addressed in eleven entire hymns, and in two others conjointly with Indra. He is also, but less frequently, called Bráhmaṇas páti, 'Lord of prayer', the doublets alternating in the same hymn. His physical features are few: he is sharp-horned and blue-backed; golden-coloured and ruddy. He is armed with bow and arrows, and wields a golden hatchet or an iron axe. He has a car, drawn by ruddy steeds, which slays the goblins, bursts open the cow-stalls, and wins the light. Called the father of the gods, he is also said to have blown forth their births like a blacksmith. Like Agni, he is both a domestic and a **brahmán** priest. He is the generator of all prayers, and without him sacrifice does not succeed. His song goes to heaven, and he is associated with singers. In several passages he is identified with Agni, from whom, however, he is much oftener distinguished. He is often invoked with Indra, some of whose epithets, such as **maghávan** *bountiful* and **vajrín** *wielder of the bolt* he shares. He has thus been drawn into the Indra myth of the release of the cows. Accompanied by his singing host he rends Vala with a roar, and drives out the cows. In so doing he dispels the darkness and finds the light. As regards his relation to his worshippers, he is said to help and protect the pious man, to prolong life, and to remove disease.

Bṛ́haspáti is a purely Indian deity. The double accent and the parallel name **Bráhmaṇas páti** indicate that the first member is the genitive of a noun **bṛ́h**, from the same root as **bráhman**, and that the name thus means 'Lord of prayer'.

He seems originally to have represented an aspect of Agni, as a divine priest, presiding over devotion, an aspect which had already attained an independent character by the beginning of the Rigvedic period. As the divine brahmán priest he seems to have been the prototype of Brahmā, the chief of the later Hindu triad.

iv. 50. **Indra is invoked with Bṛhaspati in 10 and 11.**

Metre: **Triṣṭubh; 10 Jagatī.**

१ यस्तस्तम्भ सहसा वि ज्मो अन्तान्	यः। तस्तम्भ। सहसा। वि। ज्मः। अन्तान्।
बृहस्पतिस्त्रिषधस्थो रवेण।	बृहस्पतिः। त्रिऽसधस्थः। रवेण।
तं प्रत्नास ऋषयो दीध्यानाः	तम्। प्रत्नासः। ऋषयः। दीध्यानाः।
पुरो विप्रा दधिरे मन्द्रजिह्वम्॥	पुरः। विप्राः। दधिरे। मन्द्रऽजिह्वम्॥

1 **yás tastámbha sáhasā ví jmó ántān**	*Bṛhaspati who occupying three seats with roar has propped asunder*
Bṛ́haspátis triṣadhasthó rávena,	*with might the ends of the earth,*
tám pratnā́sa ṛ́ṣayo dī́dhiānāḥ	*him, the charming-tongued, the*
puró víprā dadhire mandrájihvam.	*ancient seers, the wise, pondering, placed at their head.*

ví tastámbha: the prp. here follows the vb. and is separated from it by an intervening word: p. 468, 20. **jmás:** gen. of **jmā́** (97, 2). Pronounce **jmŏ́ antā́n** (p. 437 *a* 4). Cosmic actions like that expressed in a are ascribed to various deities. **Bṛ́haspátis:** note that this cd. is not analysed in the Pada text, while its doublet **Bráhmaṇas páti** is treated as two separate words. **triṣadhasthás:** refers to the three sacrificial fires and is a term predominantly applied to Agni, cp. v. 11, 2: **puróhitam Agníṃ náras triṣadhasthé sám īdhire** *men have kindled Agni as their domestic priest in his triple seat*; on the accent see p. 455, 10 *c a*. **rávena:** referring to the loud sound of the spells uttered; the word is especially used in connexion with the release of the cows from Vala; cp. 4 c and 5 b. **puró dadhire:** appointed their Purohita, a term frequently applied to Agni, who is also continually said to have been chosen priest by men.

२ धुनेतयः सुप्रकेतं मदन्तो	धुनऽइतयः । सुऽप्रकेतम् । मदन्तः ।
बृहस्पते अभि ये नस्ततस्रे ।	बृहस्पते । अभि । ये । नः । ततस्रे ।
पृषन्तं सृप्रमदब्धमूर्वं	पृषन्तम् । सृप्रम् । अदब्धम् । ऊर्वम् ।
बृहस्पते रक्षतादस्य योनिम् ॥	बृहस्पते । रक्षतात् । अस्य । योनिम् ॥

2 **dhunétayaḥ supraketáṃ mádanto**
Bṛ́haspate, abhí yé nas tatasré
pṛ́ṣantaṃ sṛprám ádabdham ūrváṃ;
Bṛ́haspate, rákṣatād asya yónim.

Who with resounding gait, rejoicing, O Bṛhaspati, for us have attacked the conspicuous, variegated, extensive, uninjured herd: O Bṛhaspati, protect its dwelling.

This is a very obscure stanza, the allusions in which can only be conjectured. The subject of a–c is not improbably the ancient priests, mentioned in 1 c, who with the aid of Bṛhaspati recaptured the cows confined in the stronghold of Vala. **mádantas:** being exhilarated with Soma. **tatasré:** 3. pl. pf. Ā. of taṃs *shake*. **pṛ́ṣantam:** perhaps in allusion to the dappled cows contained in it. **supraketám:** *easy to recognize*, i.e. by their lowing, cp. i. 62, 3

Bṛhaspati found the cows; the heroes roared (**vāvaśanta**) *with the ruddy kine.* The fourth Pāda is a prayer to Bṛhaspati to protect the recovered kine. Pāda *c* is a Dvipadā hemistich: see p. 443 *a*. **rákṣatāt**: 2. s. ipv. of **rakṣ**: on the accent see p. 467 A *c*.

3 बृहस्पते या परमा परावद्
अत आ त ऋतस्पृशो नि षेदुः।
तुभ्यं खाता अवता अद्रिदुग्धा
मध्वः श्चोतन्त्यभितो विरप्शम्॥

बृहस्पते। या। परमा। पराऽवत्।
अतः। आ। ते। ऋतऽस्पृशः। नि। सेदुः।
तुभ्यम्। खाताः। अवताः। अद्रिऽदुग्धाः।
मध्वः। श्चोतन्ति। अभितः। विऽरप्शम्॥

3 **Bṛ́haspate, yā́ paramā́ parāvád,**
áta ā́ ta ṛtaspṛ́śo ní ṣeduḥ.
túbhyaṃ khātā́ avatā́ ádridugdhā
mádhvaḥ ścotanti abhíto virapśám.

O Bṛhaspati, that which is the farthest distance, from thence (coming) *those that cherish the rite have seated themselves for thee. For thee springs that have been dug, pressed out with stones, drip superabundance of mead on all sides.*

áta ā́ ní ṣedur: cp. ii. 35, 10 c. **ṛtaspṛ́śas**: perhaps the gods; or the ancient seers mentioned in 1 c and perhaps in 2: they have come from the farthest distance and have seated themselves at the Soma libation offered to thee. **khātā́s . . . ádridugdhās**: two figures alluding to the streams of Soma, which flows in channels and is pounded with stones. **mádhvas**: on this form of the gen. see p. 81, f. n. 12.

4 बृहस्पतिः प्रथमं जायमानो
महो ज्योतिषः परमे व्योमन्।
सप्तास्यस्तुविजातो रवेण
वि सप्तरश्मिरधमत्तमांसि॥

बृहस्पतिः। प्रथमम्। जायमानः।
महः। ज्योतिषः। परमे। विऽओमन्।
सप्तऽआस्यः। तुविऽजातः। रवेण।
वि। सप्तऽरश्मिः। अधमत्। तमांसि॥

4 **Bṛ́haspátiḥ prathamáṃ jā́yamāno**

Bṛhaspati when first being born from the great light in the highest

mahó jyótiṣaḥ, paramé víoman,
saptáāsyas tuvijātó rávena
ví saptáraśmir adhamat támāṃsi.

heaven, seven-mouthed, high-born, with his roar, seven-rayed, blew asunder the darkness.

mahás: abl. of máh, agreeing with jyótiṣas (cp. 201 A 1). The Sun is probably meant; cp. ii. 35, 10 c. saptásyas in iv. 51, 4 is an epithet of Áṅgira (in iv. 40, 1 Bṛhaspati is Āṅgirasá); it is parallel to saptáraśmi, an epithet applied also once to Agni and once to Indra. rávena: cp. 1 b and 5 b. ví adhamat: ipf. of dham. Agni and Sūrya are also said to dispel the darkness.

५ स सुष्टुभा स ऋक्वता गणेन
वलं रुरोज फलिगं रवेण ।
बृहस्पतिरुस्रिया हव्यसूदः
कनिक्रदद्वावशतीरुदाजत् ॥

सः । सुऽस्तुभा । सः । ऋक्वता । गणेन ।
वलम् । रुरोज । फलिऽगम् । रवेण ।
बृहस्पतिः । उस्रियाः । हव्यऽसूदः ।
कनिक्रदत् । वावशतीः । उत् । आजत् ॥

5 sá suṣṭúbhā, sá ṛ́kvatā gaṇéna
valáṃ ruroja phaligáṃ rávena:
Bṛ́haspátir usríyā havyasū́daḥ
kánikradad vā́vaśatīr úd ājat.

He with the well-praising, jubilant throng burst open with roar the enclosing cave: Bṛhaspati bellowing drove out the lowing ruddy kine that sweeten the oblation.

gaṇéna: the Aṅgirases, who in i. 62, 3 are associated with Indra and Bṛhaspati in the finding of the cows: Bṛ́haspátir bhinád ádriṃ, vidád gā́ḥ: sám usríyābhir vāvaśanta náraḥ *Bṛhaspati cleft the mountain, he found the cows; the heroes* (= the Aṅgirases) *roared with the ruddy kine.* phaligám: the exact meaning of this word does not clearly appear from its four occurrences; but it must have a sense closely allied to *receptacle*: e.g. viii. 32, 25, yá udnáḥ phaligáṃ bhinán, nyàk síndhūṁr avā́sṛjat *who* (Indra) *cleft the receptacle of water* (and) *discharged the streams downwards*; in three passages it is spoken of as being rent or pierced, and twice is associated with Vala; and in the Naighaṇṭuka it is given as a synonym of megha *cloud.* rávena: with reference both to Bṛhaspati and the kine (cp. 5 d). havya-sū́das: that is, with milk. kánikradat: intv. pr. pt. of krand; cp. 173, 3; 174 *b.* vā́vaśatīs: intv. pr. pt. of vāś (cp. 174).

६ ए॒वा पि॒त्रे वि॒श्वदे॑वाय॒ वृष्णे॑
य॒ज्ञैर्वि॑धेम॒ नम॑सा ह॒विर्भिः॑ ।
बृह॑स्पते सुप्र॒जा वी॒रव॑न्तो
व॒यं स्या॑म॒ पत॑यो र॒यी॒णाम् ॥

ए॒व । पि॒त्रे । वि॒श्वऽदे॑वाय । वृष्णे॑ ।
य॒ज्ञैः । वि॒धे॒म॒ । नम॑सा । ह॒विःऽभिः॑ ।
बृह॑स्पते । सु॒ऽप्र॒जाः । वी॒र॒ऽव॑न्तः ।
व॒यम् । स्या॒म॒ । पत॑यः । र॒यी॒णाम् ॥

6 evā́ pitré viśvádevāya vṛ́ṣṇe
yajñáir vidhema, námasā, havírbhiḥ.
Bṛ́haspate, suprajā́ vīrávanto
vayám̐ siāma pátayo rayīṇā́m.

Then to the father that belongs to all the gods, the bull, we would offer worship with sacrifices, obeisance, and oblations. O Bṛhaspati, with good offspring and heroes we would be lords of wealth.

evā́: with final vowel metrically lengthened. The sense of the pcl. here is: *such being the case* (cp. 180). **pitré**: Bṛhaspati. The term is applied to Agni, Indra, and other gods. **vīrávantas**: that is, possessing warrior sons, cp. i. 1, 3 c. **vayám**: this line occurs several times as the final Pāda of a hymn; cp. viii. 48, 13.

७ स इद्राजा॒ प्रति॑जन्यानि॒ विश्वा॒
शुष्मे॑ण तस्थाव॒भि वी॒र्ये॑ण ।
बृह॒स्पतिं॒ यः सुभृ॑तं बि॒भर्ति॑
वल्गू॒यति॒ वन्द॑ते पूर्व॒भाज॑म् ॥

सः । इत् । राजा॑ । प्रति॑ऽजन्यानि । विश्वा॑ ।
शुष्मे॑ण । त॒स्थौ॒ । अ॒भि । वी॒र्ये॑ण ।
बृह॒स्पति॑म् । यः । सुऽभृ॑तम् । बि॒भर्ति॑ ।
व॒ल्गु॒ऽयति॑ । वन्द॑ते । पूर्व॒ऽभाज॑म् ॥

7 sá íd rā́jā prátijanyāni víśvā
śúṣmeṇa tasthāv abhí vīríeṇa,
Bṛ́haspátim̐ yáḥ súbhṛtam̐ bibhárti,
valgūyáti, vándate pūrvabhā́jam.

That king with his impulse and his heroism overcomes all hostile forces, who keeps Bṛhaspati well-nourished, honours him, and praises him as receiving the first (portion of the offering).

abhí: the prp., as often, here follows the vb. **súbhṛtam̐ bibhárti**: lit. *cherishes him as well-cherished* (predicative). All three verbs depend on **yás**, though the last two, as beginning a Pāda and a sentence, would even otherwise be accented. **valgūyáti**: note that this denominative is treated as a cd. in the Pada text (cp. 175 A 1). **pūrvabhā́jam**: predicative.

८ स इत्क्षेति सुधित ओकसि स्वे
तस्मा इळा पिन्वते विश्वदानीम् ।
तस्मै विशः स्वयमेवा नमन्ते
यस्मिन्ब्रह्मा राजनि पूर्व एति ॥

सः । इत् । क्षेति । सुऽधितः । ओकसि । स्वे ।
तस्मै । इळा । पिन्वते । विश्वऽदानीम् ।
तस्मै । विशः । स्वयम् । एव । नमन्ते ।
यस्मिन् । ब्रह्मा । राजनि । पूर्वः । एति ॥

8 sá ít kṣeti súdhita ókasi své,
tásmā íḷā pinvate viśvadā́nīm;
tásmai víśaḥ svayám evā́ namante,
yásmin brahmā́ rā́jani pū́rva éti.

That king dwells well-established in his own abode, to him the consecrated food always yields abundance; to him his subjects bow down of their own accord, with whom the priest has prrcedence.

kṣeti: from **1. kṣi** *possess* or *dwell.* **sú-dhita**: this form of the pp. of **dhā** is still preserved as the last member of cds. (otherwise **hitá**); the word is explained as **su-hita** in the AB. **ókasi své**: cp. **své dáme** in i. 1, 8 c. **íḷā**: explained as *food* (**annam**) in AB. viii. 26, 7, and as *earth* (**bhūmi**) by Sāyaṇa. **yásmin rā́jani**: the loc. here = *in the presence of whom, in whose case*; the antecedent is here put in the relative clause, while in 7 a it accompanies the corr. (**sá íd rā́jā**). **pū́rva éti**: with reference to this line the AB. viii. 26, 9 remarks, **purohitam evaitad āha** *thus one calls him a Purohita*; cp. also AB. viii. 1, 5: **brahma khalu vai kṣatrāt pūrvam** *the Brāhmaṇa certainly prccedes the Kṣatriya.*

९ अप्रतीतो जयति सं धनानि
प्रतिजन्यान्युत या सजन्या ।
अवस्यवे यो वरिवः कृणोति
ब्रह्मणे राजा तमवन्ति देवाः ॥

अप्रतिऽइतः । जयति । सम् । धनानि ।
प्रतिऽजन्यानि । उत । या । सऽजन्या ।
अवस्यवे । यः । वरिवः । कृणोति ।
ब्रह्मणे । राजा । तम् । अवन्ति । देवाः ॥

9 ápratīto jayati sáṃ dhánāni
prátijanyāni utá yā́ sájanyā.
avasyáve yó várivaḥ kṛṇóti
brahmáṇe rā́jā, tám avanti deváḥ.

Unresisted he wins wealth both belonging to his adversaries and to his own people. The king who for the priest desiring (his) *help procures prosperity, him the gods help.*

After the statement in 7 that the king who honours Bṛhaspati prospers, it is added in 8 and 9 that the king who honours the Brahman, the counterpart among men of Bṛhaspati, also prospers.

jayati sám: prp. after the vb. (p. 285 *f*). **dhánāni**: he wins wealth both abroad and at home. **avasyáve—avanti**: both words from the same root **av**: the gods help the king who helps the Brahman.

१० इन्द्रश्च सोमं पिबतं बृहस्पते
ऽस्मिन्यज्ञे मन्दसाना वृषण्वसू ।
आ वां विशन्त्विन्दवः स्वाभुवो
ऽस्मे रयिं सर्ववीरं नि यच्छतम् ॥

इन्द्रः । च । सोमम् । पिबतम् । बृहस्पते । अस्मिन् । यज्ञे । मन्दसाना । वृषण्वसू इति वृषण्ऽवसू । आ । वाम् । विशन्तु । इन्दवः । सुऽआभुवः । अस्मे इति । रयिम् । सर्वऽवीरम् । नि । यच्छतम् ॥

10 **Índraś ca sómam pibatam, Bṛhaspate,**
asmín yajñé mandasānā́, vṛ́ṣaṇ-vasū:
ā́ vām viśantu índavaḥ suā-bhúvo;
asmé rayím sárvavīram ní yachatam.

O Indra and Bṛhaspati, drink the Soma, rejoicing at this sacrifice, O ye of mighty wealth; let the invigorating drops enter you two; bestow on us riches accompanied altogether with sons.

Índraś ca: nom. for voc. (196 *c a*; cp. **ca**, p. 228, 1 and **1** *a*). **pibatam**: 2. du. ipv. of **pā** *drink*. **mandasānā́**: ao. pt. of **mand** = **mad**. **vṛ́ṣaṇ-vasū**: here **vṛṣan** = *mighty*, *great*; Sāyaṇa explains the word as if it were a governing cd. (189 A), the normal form of which would, however, be **varṣáṇ-vasu** (189 A 2; cp. p. 455 *b*). Note that in the Pada text the cd. is first marked as Pragṛhya with iti and then analysed; also that in the analysis the first member here appears not in its pause form vṛṣan (65) but in its Sandhi form with ṇ as not final. **rayím sárvavīram**: that is, wealth with offspring consisting of sons only: a frequent prayer (cp. i. 1, 3 c). **yachatam**: 2. ipv. pr. of **yam**. Here we have the intrusion of a Jagatī stanza in a Triṣṭubh hymn (cp. p. 445, f. n. 7). In this and the following stanza Indra is associated with Bṛhaspati, as in the whole of the preceding hymn, iv. 49.

११ बृहस्पत इन्द्र वर्धतं नः
सचा सा वां सुमतिर्भूत्वस्मे ।
अविष्टं धियो जिगृतं पुरंधीर्
जजस्तमर्यो वनुषामरातीः ॥

बृहस्पते । इन्द्र । वर्धतम् । नः ।
सचा । सा । वाम् । सुऽमतिः । भूतु । अस्मे इति ।
अविष्टम् । धियः । जिगृतम् । पुरम्ऽधीः ।
जजस्तम् । अर्यः । वनुषाम् । अरातीः ॥

11 **Bṛ́haspata, Ind^{a}ra, várdhatam naḥ;**
sácā sā́ vām sumatír bhūtu asmé.
aviṣṭám dhíyo; jigṛtám púram-dhīr;
jajastám aryó vanúṣām árātīḥ.

O Bṛhaspati and Indra, cause us to prosper; let that benevolence of yours be with us. Favour (our) *prayers; arouse rewards; weaken the hostilities of foe and rivals.*

Bṛ́haspata Indra: contrary to the general rule the second voc. is here unaccented (p. 465, 18 *a*); this is doubtless because the two are here treated as a dual divinity, as in the preceding hymn (iv. 49), in every stanza of which they are invoked as Indrā-Bṛhaspatī. **Indra** must be pronounced trisyllabically (cp. p. 15 *d*). **vām**: gen. (109 *a*). **bhūtu**: 3. s. ipv. root ao. of bhū. **asmé**: loc. with **sácā** (177, 5) and (as in 10 d) Pragṛhya (26 *c*). **aviṣṭám**: 2. s. du. ipv. of the **iṣ** ao. of **av** *favour* (145, 5). **jigṛtám**: 2. du. red. ao. of **gṛ** *waken*; accented because beginning a new sentence (p. 467 *b*). **dhíyas . . . púraṃdhīs**: these words often appear side by side and in contrast: the former then meaning *prayers* for gifts, the latter the *bestowal* (dhi from **dhā** *bestow*) *of plenty* (**púram** an acc.; cp. the Padapāṭha). **púraṃdhīs** here is also opposed to **árātīs** (lit. *lack of liberality*) in d. **jajastám**: 2. du. ipv. pf. of **jas**. **aryás**: gen. of **arí** (99, 3); cp. note on ii. 12, 4. The genitives **aryás** and **vanúṣām** are co-ordinate and dependent on **árātīs**; this appears from various parallel passages, as **aryó árātīḥ** *hostilities of the foe* (vi. 16, 27);

aghány aryó, vanúṣām árātayaḥ *evil deeds of the foe, hostilities of rivals* (vii. 83, 5); **abhîtim aryó, vanúṣām śávāṃsi** *the onset of the foe, the might of rivals* (vii. 21, 9 d). 11 a = vii. 97, 9 d.

UṢÁS

The goddess of Dawn is addressed in about twenty hymns. The personification is but slight, the physical phenomenon always being present to the mind of the poet. Decked in gay attire like a dancer, clothed in light, she appears in the east and unveils her charms. Rising resplendent as from a bath she comes with light, driving away the darkness and removing the black robe of night. She is young, being born again and again, though ancient. Shining with a uniform hue, she wastes away the life of mortals. She illumines the ends of the sky when she awakes; she opens the gates of heaven; her radiant beams appear like herds of cattle. She drives away evil dreams, evil spirits, and the hated darkness. She discloses the treasures concealed by darkness, and distributes them bountifully. She awakens every living being to motion. When Uṣas shines forth, the birds fly up from their nests and men seek nourishment. Day by day appearing at the appointed place, she never infringes the ordinance of nature and of the gods. She renders good service to the gods by awakening all worshippers and causing the sacrificial fires to be kindled. She brings the gods to drink the Soma draught. She is borne on a shining car, drawn by ruddy steeds or kine, which probably represent the red rays of morning.

Uṣas is closely associated with the Sun. She has opened paths for Sūrya to travel; she brings the eye of the gods, and leads on the beautiful white horse. She shines with the light of the Sun, with the light of her lover. Sūrya follows her as a young man a maiden; she meets the god who desires her. She thus comes to be spoken of as the wife of Sūrya. But as preceding the Sun, she is occasionally regarded as his mother; thus she is said to arrive with a bright child. She is also called the sister, or the elder sister, of Night (x. 127), and their names are often conjoined as a dual compound (**uṣā́sā-náktā** and **náktoṣā́sā**). She is born in the sky, and is therefore constantly called the 'daughter of Heaven'. As the sacrificial fire is kindled at dawn, Uṣas is often associated with Agni, who is sometimes called her lover. Uṣas causes Agni to be kindled, and Agni goes to meet the shining Dawn as she approaches. She is also often connected with the twin gods of early morning, the Aśvins (vii. 71). When the Aśvins' car is yoked, the daughter of the sky is born. They are awakened by her, accompany her, and are her friends.

Uṣas brings the worshipper wealth and children, bestowing protection and long life. She confers renown and glory on all liberal benefactors of the poet. She is characteristically bountiful (maghónī).

The name of Uṣas is derived from the root vas, *to shine*, forms of which are often used with reference to her in the hymns in which she is invoked.

iv. 51. Metre : **Triṣṭubh.**

१ इदमु त्यत्पुरुतमं पुरस्ताज्
ज्योतिस्तमसो वयुनावदस्थात् ।
नूनं दिवो दुहितरो विभातीर्
गातुं कृणवन्नुषसो जनाय ॥

इदम् । ऊं इति । त्यत् । पुरुऽतमम् । पुरस्तात् ।
ज्योतिः । तमसः । वयुनऽवत् । अस्थात् ।
नूनम् । दिवः । दुहितरः । विऽभातीः ।
गातुम् । कृणवन् । उषसः । जनाय ॥

1 **idám u tyát purutámam purástāj**
jyótis támaso vayúnāvad asthāt.
nūnáṃ divó duhitáro vibhātī́r
gātúṃ kṛṇavann Uṣáso jánāya.

This familiar, most frequent light in the east, with clearness has stood (forth) *from the darkness. Now may the Dawns, the daughters of the sky, shining afar, make a path for man.*

tyád : see p. 297, 5. **purutámam** : because appearing every morning ; hence **Uṣásas** *the Dawns* in d. **támasas** : abl. dependent on **asthāt** = **úd asthāt**. The word **vayúna**, though very frequently used, is still somewhat uncertain in meaning. The commentators explain it variously as mārga *road,* prajñāna *cognition,* and **kānti** *beauty.* Pischel favours the first of these. Sāyaṇa here explains **vayúnāvat** as 'very beautiful or possessed of knowledge = showing everything'. It probably here means 'making the way clear', cp. **gātúm** in **d**. **nūnám** : note that in the RV. this word always means *now*. **divó duhitáras** : from the point of view of the daily recurrence of the phenomenon, Dawn is pl. throughout this hymn. **gātúm** : cp. vi. 64, 1 : 'she makes all fair paths easy to traverse'. **kṛṇavan** : 3. pl. sb. ; explained by Sāyaṇa as 3. pl. ipf. ind., **akurvan.**

२ अस्थुरु चित्रा उषसः पुरस्तान्
मिता इव स्वरवोऽध्वरेषु ।
व्यू व्रजस्य तमसो द्वारो-
छन्तीरव्रञ्छुचयः पावकाः ॥

अस्थुः । ऊं इति । चित्राः । उषसः । पुर-
स्तात् ।
मिताःऽइव । स्वरवः । अध्वरेषु ।
वि । ऊं इति । व्रजस्य । तमसः । द्वारा ।
उच्छन्तीः । अव्रन् । शुचयः । पावकाः ॥

2 ásthur u citrā́ Uṣásaḥ purástān,
mitā́ iva sváravŏ adhvaréṣu.
ví ū vrajásya támaso duā́rā
uchántīr avrañ chúcayaḥ pa-
vākā́ḥ.

The brilliant Dawns have stood in the east, like posts set up at sacrifices. Shining they have unclosed the two doors of the pen of darkness, bright and purifying.

Uṣásas: that is, each of the preceding Dawns and the present one. **mitā́s**: pp. of **mi** *fix.* **sváravas**: that is, shining with ointment; cp. i. 92, 5: **svárum ná péśo vidátheṣu áñjañ, citrám divó duhitā́ bhānúm** aśret *the daughter of heaven has spread her brilliant beam, like one who at divine worship anoints the post, the ornament* (of the sacrifice). Note that **u** in **c** is lengthened though followed by two consonants (p. 437 *a* 3). **vrajásya**: a simile with **iva** omitted; cp. i. 92, 4; **gā́vo ná vrajám ví Uṣā́ āvar támaḥ** *Dawn has unclosed the darkness as the cows their stall.* **dvā́rā**: the two folds of the door, the dual of **dvā́r** often being used thus. **ví**: to be taken with **avran**, 3. pl. root ao. of **vṛ** *cover.* **uchántīs**: pr. pt. of 1. **vas** *shine.* **śucáyaḥ pāvakā́ḥ**: these two adjectives very often appear in juxtaposition. On the pronunciation of **pāvaká** see p. 437 *a*.

३ उच्छन्तीरद्य चितयन्त भोजान्
राधोदेयायोषसो मघोनीः ।
अचित्रे अन्तः पणयः ससन्त्व-
बुध्यमानास्तमसो विमध्ये ॥

उच्छन्तीः । अद्य । चितयन्त । भोजान् ।
राधःऽदेयाय । उषसः । मघोनीः ।
अचित्रे । अन्तरिति । पणयः । ससन्तु ।
अबुध्यमानाः । तमसः । विऽमध्ये ॥

3 uchántīr adyá citayanta bhojā́n
rādhodéyāya Uṣáso maghónīḥ.

Shining to-day may the bounteous Dawns stimulate the liberal to the

acitré antáḥ paṇáyaḥ sasantu,
ábudhyamānās támaso víma-
dhye.

giving of wealth. In obscurity let the niggards sleep, unwakening in the midst of darkness.

citayanta : 3. pl. Ā. inj. ; explained by Sāyaṇa as an indicative : prajñāpayanti *they instruct.*

४ कुवित्स देवीः सनयो नवो वा
यामो बभूयादुषसो वो अद्य ।
येना नवग्वे अङ्गिरे दशग्वे
सप्तास्ये रेवती रेवदूष ॥

कुवित् । सः । देवीः । सनयः । नवः । वा ।
यामः । बभूयात् । उषसः । वः । अद्य ।
येन । नवऽग्वे । अङ्गिरे । दशऽग्वे ।
सप्तऽआस्ये । रेवतीः । रेवत् । ऊष ॥

4 kuvít sá, devīḥ, sanáyo návo vā
yā́mo babhūyā́d, Uṣaso, vŏ
adyá :
yénā Návagve, Áṅgire, Dáśagve
saptáāsye, revatī, revád ūṣá ?

Should this be an old course or a new for you to-day, O divine Dawns : (is it that) *by which ye have shone wealth, ye wealthy ones, upon Navagva, Aṅgira, and Daśagva the seven-mouthed?*

babhūyā́t : op. pf. of bhū, accented on account of kuvít (cp. notes on ii. 35, 1. 2). The general meaning is the hope that Dawn will bring wealth to-day as of old. Navagva, Aṅgiras, and Daśagva are the names of ancients associated with Indra in the release of the cows enclosed by the Paṇis and by Vala. The allusion in saptā́sye is uncertain ; in iv. 50, 4 it is an epithet of Bṛhaspati, who is also associated with the capture of the cows and may therefore be meant here. The meaning would then be : bring us wealth to-day as ye did to Navagva, Aṅgiras, Daśagva and Bṛhaspati. revatī revát : these words are found connected in other passages also. ūṣá : 2. pl. pf. act. of 1. vas *shine.*

५ यूयं हि देवीर्ऋतयुग्भिरश्वैः
परिप्रयाथ भुवनानि सद्यः ।
प्रबोधयन्तीरुषसः ससन्तं
द्विपाच्चतुष्पाच्चरथाय जीवम् ॥

यूयम् । हि । देवीः । ऋतयुक्ऽभिः । अश्वैः ।
परिऽप्रयाथ । भुवनानि । सद्यः ।
प्रऽबोधयन्तीः । उषसः । ससन्तम् ।
द्विऽपात् । चतुःऽपात् । चरथाय । जीवम् ॥

5 yūyáṃ hí, devīr, ṛtayúgbhir áśvaiḥ
paripraуāthá bhúvanāni sadyáḥ,
prabodháyantīr, Uṣasaḥ, sasántaṃ,
dvipā́c cátuṣpāc caráthāya jīvam.

For you, O goddesses, with your steeds yoked in due time, proceed around the worlds in one day, awakening, O Dawns, him who sleeps, the two-footed and the four-footed living world, to motion.

pariprayāthá: accented owing to **hí**; on the accentuation of verbal prepositions see p. 469 B *a*. **prabodháyantīs**: cp. i. 92, 9, **víśvaṃ jīváṃ carásе bodháyantī** *wakening every living soul to move.* **cátuṣpād**: note that **catúr** when accented as first member of a cd. shifts its accent to the first syllable. This word, **dvipā́d** and **jīvám** are all neuter.

६ क्वं स्विदासां कतमा पुराणी	क्व । स्वित् । आसाम् । कतमा । पुराणी ।
यया विधाना विदधुर्ऋभूणाम् ।	यया । विऽधाना । विऽदधुः । ऋभूणाम् ।
शुभं यच्छुभ्रा उषसश्चरन्ति	शुभम् । यत् । शुभ्राः । उषसः । चरन्ति ।
न वि ज्ञायन्ते सदृशीरजुर्याः ॥	न । वि । ज्ञायन्ते । सऽदृशीः । अजुर्याः ॥

6 kúa svíd āsāṃ katamā́ purāṇī́
yáyā vidhā́nā vidadhúr ṛbhūṇā́m?
śúbhaṃ yác chubhrā́ Uṣásaś cáranti,
ná ví jñāyante sadṛ́śīr ajuryā́ḥ.

Where, pray, and which ancient one of them (was it) *at which they* (the gods) *imposed the tasks of the Ṛbhus? When the beaming dawns proceed on their shining course, they are not distinguished, alike, unaging.*

āsām: of the dawns. **yáyā**: in a temporal sense = at whose time. **vidadhúr**: *they*, the gods, *enjoined*: this probably refers to the most distinctive feat of the Ṛbhus, that of making one bowl into four; cp. i. 161, 2: **ékaṃ camasáṃ catúraḥ kṛṇotana, tád vo devā́ abruvan** *'make the one bowl four', that the gods said to you*; that was one of their **vidhā́nā** *tasks.* **śúbham**: cognate acc. **ná ví jñāyante**: they are always the same; cp. i. 92, 10, **púnaḥ-punar jā́yamānā purāṇī́ samānáṃ várṇam abhí śúmbhamānā** *being* *born again and again, ancient of days, adorning herself with the same colour*, where dawn is, as usually, spoken of as a single goddess reappearing day after day, whereas in this hymn many individual dawns that appear successively are referred to.

७ ता घा ता भद्रा उषसः पुरासुर्
अभिष्टिद्युम्ना ऋतजातसत्याः ।
यास्वीजानः शशमान उक्थैः
स्तुवञ्छंसन्द्रविणं सद्य आप ॥

ताः । घ । ताः । भद्राः । उषसः । पुरा ।
आसुः ।
अभिष्टिऽद्युम्नाः । ऋतजातऽसत्याः ।
यासु । ईजानः । शशमानः । उक्थैः ।
स्तुवन् । शंसन् । द्रविणम् । सद्यः । आप ॥

7 tā́ ghā tā́ bhadrā́ Uṣásaḥ purā́sur,
abhiṣṭídyumnā ṛtájātasatyāḥ;
yā́su ījānáḥ śaśamāná ukthái̇ḥ
stuváñ, cháṃsan, dráviṇaṃ sadyá ā́pa.

Those indeed, those Dawns have formerly been auspicious, splendid in help, punctually true; at which the strenuous sacrificer with recitations praising, chanting, has at once obtained wealth.

On purā́ with pf. see 213 A. **ījānás**: pf. pt. Ā. of **yaj** *sacrifice*. **śaśamāná**: pf. pt. Ā. of **śam** *labour*. **stuváñ cháṃsan** = **stuván** + **śáṃsan** (40, 1). The general meaning of the stanza is: former dawns have brought blessings to the sacrificer; may they do so now.

८ ता आ चरन्ति समना पुरस्तात्
समानतः समना पप्रथानाः ।
ऋतस्य देवीः सदसो बुधाना
गवां न सर्गा उषसो जरन्ते ॥

ताः । आ । चरन्ति । समना । पुरस्तात् ।
समानतः । समना । पप्रथानाः ।
ऋतस्य । देवीः । सदसः । बुधानाः ।
गवाम् । न । सर्गाः । उषसः । जरन्ते ॥

8 tā́ ā́ caranti samanā́ purástāt,
samānátaḥ samanā́ paprathānā́ḥ.
ṛtásya devī́ḥ sádaso budhānā́,
gávāṃ ná sárgā, Uṣáso jarante.

They approach equally in the east, spreading themselves equally from the same place. The goddesses waking from the seat of order, like herds of kine let loose, the Dawns are active.

samanā́: always in the same way. **samānatás**; cp. i. 124, 3: **prajānatī́ iva, ná díśo mināti** *as one who knows* (the way), *she loses not her direction.* **ṛtásya sádasaḥ**: abl. dependent on **budhānā́ḥ** (cp. 10); cp. i. 124, 3; **ṛtásya pánthām ánv eti sādhú** *she follows straight the path of order.* **budhānā́s**: ao. pt., *awaking* (intr.), not = **bodhayantyas** *wakening* (trans.) according to Sāyaṇa; when Ā. and without an object, **budh** is intr.; cp. **ábodhi** *has awoke*, said of Uṣas (i. 92, 11; iii. 61, 6; vii. 80, 2). **gavā́ṃ ná sárgāḥ**: cp. iv. 52, 5, **práti bhadrā́ adṛkṣata gávāṃ sárgā ná raśmáyaḥ** *the auspicious rays* (of dawn) *have appeared like kine let loose.* **jarante**: *are awake = are active, are on the move* (cp. **ā́ caranti** in a and 9 a, b); *are praised* (stūyante) according to Sāyaṇa.

९ ता इन्न्वे३व समना समानीर्
अमीतवर्णा उषसश्चरन्ति ।
गूहन्तीरभ्वमसितं रुशद्भिः
शुक्रास्तनूभिः शुचयो रुचानाः ॥

ताः । इत् । नु । एव । समना । समानीः ।
अमीतऽवर्णाः । उषसः । चरन्ति ।
गूहन्तीः । अभ्वम् । असितम् । रुशत्ऽभिः ।
शुक्राः । तनूभिः । शुचयः । रुचानाः ॥

9 **tā́ ín nú evá samanā́ samānī́r,**
ámītavarṇā Uṣásaś caranti.
gū́hantīr ábhvam ásitam, rúśadbhiḥ
śukrā́s tanū́bhiḥ, śúcayo, rucānā́ḥ.

Those Dawns even now equally the same, of unchanged colour, move on; concealing the black monster, bright with gleaming forms, brilliant, beaming.

On the accentuation of **nv èvá** see p. 450, 2 *b*. **ábhvam**: cp. i. 92, 5, **bā́dhate kṛṣṇám ábhvam** *she drives away the black monster* (of night). **rúśadbhis**: m. form irregularly agreeing with the f. **tanū́bhis**. Note that the Pada text does not separate the endings **bhyām, bhis, bhyas, su** from f. stems in long vowels, nor of m. stems in **a** because the pure stem in these cases appears in an altered form, e. g. **priyébhis**, but **pitṛ́ऽbhis**.

१० रयिं दिवो दुहितरो विभातीः
प्रजावन्तं यच्छतास्मासु देवीः ।

रयिम् । दिवः । दुहितरः । विऽभातीः ।
प्रजाऽवन्तम् । यच्छत । अस्मासु । देवीः ।

स्योनादा वः प्रतिबुध्यमानाः
सुवीर्यस्य पतयः स्याम ॥

स्योनात् । आ । वः । प्रतिऽबुध्यमानाः ।
सुऽवीर्यस्य । पतयः । स्याम ॥

10 **rayíṃ, divo duhitaro, vibhātī́ḥ**
prajā́vantaṃ yachatāsmā́su, devīḥ.
sionā́d ā́ vaḥ pratibúdhyamānāḥ,
suvī́riasya pátayaḥ siāma.

O daughters of Heaven, do ye shining forth bestow on us, goddesses, wealth accompanied by offspring. Awaking from our soft couch towards you, we would be lords of a host of strong sons.

yachata: pr. ipv. of **yam**, here construed with the loc.; the usual case is the dat. (200 A 1). **pratibúdhyamānās**: with **ā́** and abl., cp. **budhānā́** with abl. in 8 c.

११ तद्वो दिवो दुहितरो विभातीर्
उप ब्रुव उषसो यज्ञकेतुः ।
वयं स्याम यशसो जनेषु
तद्द्यौश्च धत्तां पृथिवी च देवी ॥

तत् । वः । दिवः । दुहितरः । विऽभातीः ।
उप । ब्रुवे । उषसः । यज्ञऽकेतुः ।
वयम् । स्याम । यशसः । जनेषु ।
तत् । द्यौः । च । धत्ताम् । पृथिवी । च ।
देवी ॥

11 **tád vo, divo duhitaro, vibhātī́r**
úpa bruva, Uṣaso, yajñáketuḥ:
vayám siāma yaśáso jáneṣu;
tád Dyáuś ca dhattā́ṃ Pṛthivī́ ca devī́.

For that I whose banner is the sacrifice, O daughters of Heaven, implore you that shine forth, O Dawns: we would be famous among men; let Heaven and the goddess Earth grant that.

vibhātī́r: to be taken with **vas**. **úpa bruve**: with two acc. (p. 304, 2). **yajñáketus**: the singer thus describes himself; in i. 113, 19 the Dawn is called **yajñásya ketúḥ** *the signal of the sacrifice.* **yaśáso** (accent, p. 453, 9 A *a*) **jáneṣu**: this phrase frequently occurs in prayers. **vayám**: the poet having in b spoken in the sing. on his own behalf, now changes, as often, to the pl., so as to include the others who are present. **dhattā́m**: 3. du. of **dhā**, accented, though not beginning a sentence, because of **ca . . . ca** (see p. 468 *β*).

AGNI

See Introduction to i. 1 on the nature of Agni.

v. 11. Metre : Jagatī.

१ जनस्य गोपा अजनिष्ट जागृविर्	जनस्य । गोपाः । अजनिष्ट । जागृविः ।
अग्निः सुदक्षः सुविताय नव्यसे ।	अग्निः । सुऽदक्षः । सुविताय । नव्यसे ।
घृतप्रतीको बृहता दिविस्पृशा	घृतऽप्रतीकः । बृहता । दिविऽस्पृशा ।
द्युमद्वि भाति भरतेभ्यः शुचिः ॥	द्युऽमत् । वि । भाति । भरतेभ्यः । शुचिः ॥

1 **Jánasya gopá ajaniṣṭa jágṛvir Agníḥ sudákṣaḥ suvitáya návyase. ghṛtápratīko bṛhatá divispṛ́śā dyumád ví bhāti bharatébhiaḥ śúciḥ.**	*Guardian of the people, watchful, most skilful, Agni has been born for renewed welfare. Butter-faced, bright, he shines forth brilliantly for the Bharatas with lofty, heaven-touching* (flame).

gopás: 97, 2. **ajaniṣṭa**: iṣ ao. of jan *generate*. **su-dákṣas**: a Bv. (p. 455 *c a*). **suvitáya**: final dat. (p. 314, B 2). **návyase**: dat. of cpv. of náva *new*. **ghṛtá-pratīkas**: cp. **yásya prátīkam áhutaṃ ghṛténa** *whose face is sprinkled with butter* (vii. 8, 1) as an analysis of the cd. **bṛhatá**: supply **téjasā**. **bharatébhyas**: for the benefit of (p. 314, 1) the Bharatas, the tribe to which the seer belongs.

२ यज्ञस्य केतुं प्रथमं पुरोहितम्	यज्ञस्य । केतुम् । प्रथमम् । पुरःऽहितम् ।
अग्निं नरस्त्रिषधस्थे समीधिरे ।	अग्निम् । नरः । त्रिऽसधस्थे । सम् । ईधिरे ।
इन्द्रेण देवैः सरथं स बर्हिषि	इन्द्रेण । देवैः । सऽरथम् । सः । बर्हिषि ।
सीदन्नि होता यजथाय सुक्रतुः ॥	सीदत् । नि । होता । यजथाय । सुऽक्रतुः ॥

2 **yajñásya ketúṃ, prathamáṃ puróhitam, Agníṃ náras, triṣadhasthé sám īdhire.**	*As banner of sacrifice, as first domestic priest, men have kindled Agni in the threefold abode.* (Coming) *on the same car with Indra*

índreṇa deváiḥ sarátham̐ sá barhíṣi **sídan ní hótā yajáthāya sukrátuḥ.**	*and the gods may that most wise Invoker sit down on the sacrificial grass for sacrifice.*

ketúm: in apposition to **Agním**, in allusion to the smoke of sacrifice; cp. viii. 44, 10, **hótāram . . . dhūmáketum . . . yajñā́nām ketúm** *the Invoker, the smoke-bannered banner of sacrifices*; cp. 3 d. **prathamám**: first-appointed in order of time. **puróhitam**: see i. 1, 1. **náras**: N. pl. of **nṛ́** (p. 91). **tri-ṣadhasthé**: on the three sacrificial altars; Sandhi 67 *b*. **sám īdhire**: pf. of **idh** *kindle; have kindled* and still kindle (cp. p. 342 *a*). **sarátham**: adv. governing **índreṇa** and **deváis** (cp. p. 309, 2). **sídan ní**: the ipf. expresses that he sat down in the past when he became Purohita; the prp. as often follows the verb (p. 468, 20). **yajáthāya**: final dat. (p. 314, B 2).

३ असंमृष्टो जायसे मात्रोः शुचिर्	असंम्ऽमृष्टः । जायसे । मात्रोः । शुचिः ।
मन्द्रः कविरुदतिष्ठो विवस्वतः ।	मन्द्रः । कविः । उत् । अतिष्ठः । विवस्वतः ।
घृतेन त्वावर्धयन्नग्न आहुत	घृतेन । त्वा । अवर्धयन् । अग्ने । आऽहुत ।
धूमस्ते केतुरभवद्दिवि श्रितः ॥	धूमः । ते । केतुः । अभवत् । दिवि । श्रितः ॥

3 **ásammṛṣṭo jāyase māt^a^róḥ śúcir.** **mandráḥ kavír úd atíṣṭho Vivásvataḥ.** **ghṛténa tvāvardhayann, Agna āhuta,** **dhūmás te ketúr abhavad diví śritáḥ.**	*Uncleansed thou art born bright from thy two parents. Thou didst arise as the gladdening sage of Vivasvant. With butter they strengthened thee, O Agni, in whom the offering is poured. Smoke became thy banner that reached to the sky.*

ásam-mṛṣṭas: pp. of **mṛj** *wipe*, opposed to **śúcis**, though uncleansed, yet bright. **mātrós**: abl. du.: the two fire-sticks, from which Agni is produced by friction. **úd atiṣṭhas**: 3. s. ipf. of **sthā** *stand*. **Vivásvatas**: gen. dependent on **kavís**; *the sage* (a common designation of Agni) *of Vivasvant*, the first sacrificer. **tvā**: the caesura, which **should** follow this word (p. 442, 6), **is** here only apparently neglected because the following augment may be treated as dropped. **avardhayan**: that is, made the fire burn up with the ghee poured into it; explained by **ā-huta**. **dhūmás**, &c.: affords an analysis of Agni's epithet **dhūmáketu** (cp. note on 2 a). **diví**: loc. of the goal (p. 325 *b*). Note the use of the imperfects as referring to past events (p. 345, B).

४ अग्निर्नो यज्ञमुप वेतु साधुया-
ऽग्निं नरो वि भरन्ते गृहेगृहे ।
अग्निर्दूतो अभवद्धव्यवाहनो
ऽग्निं वृणाना वृणते कविक्रतुम् ॥

अग्निः । नः । यज्ञम् । उप । वेतु । साधुऽया ।
अग्निम् । नरः । वि । भरन्ते । गृहेऽगृहे ।
अग्निः । दूतः । अभवत् । हव्यऽवाहनः ।
अग्निम् । वृणानाः । वृणते । कविऽक्रतुम् ॥

4 **Agnír no yajñám úpa vetu sādhuyā́.**
Agním̩ náro ví bharante gṛhé-gṛhe.
Agnír dūtó abhavad dhavyavā́hano.
Agním̩ vṛṇānā́ vṛṇate kavíkratum.

Let Agni come straightway to our sacrifice. Men carry Agni hither and thither in every house. Agni became the messenger, the carrier of oblations. In choosing Agni they choose one who has the wisdom of a seer.

vetu: 3. s. ipv. of **vī**. **bharante**: see note on **bhṛ**, ii. 33, 10 a. **gṛhé-gṛhe**: 189 C *a*. **dūtás**: Agni is characteristically a messenger as an intermediary between heaven and earth. **dhavyavā́hanas**: Sandhi, 54. **vṛṇānā́s**: pr. pt. A. of 2. **vṛ**, *choosing Agni* as their priest. **vṛṇate**: 3. pl. pr. Ā of 2 **vṛ**.

५ तुभ्येदमग्ने मधुमत्तमं वचस्
तुभ्यं मनीषा इयमस्तु शं हृदे ।
त्वां गिरः सिन्धुमिवावनीर्महीर्
आ पृणन्ति शवसा वर्धयन्ति च ॥

तुभ्य । इदम् । अग्ने । मधुमत्ऽतमम् । वचः ।
तुभ्यम् । मनीषा । इयम् । अस्तु । शम् । हृदे ।
त्वाम् । गिरः । सिन्धुम्ऽइव । अवनीः ।
महीः ।
आ । पृणन्ति । शवसा । वर्धयन्ति । च ॥

5 túbhyedám, Agne, mádhumattamam vácas,
túbhyam manīṣā́ iyám astu śam hṛdé.
tuā́m gíraḥ, síndhum ivāvánīr mahī́r,
ā́ pṛṇanti śávasā, vardháyanti ca.

For thee, O Agni, let this most honied speech, for thee this prayer be a comfort to thy heart. The songs fill thee, as the great rivers the Indus, with power, and strengthen thee.

túbhya: this form of the dat. of **tvám** occurs about a dozen times in the Saṃhitā text beside the much commoner **túbhyam** (as in b); it occurs only before vowels with which it is always contracted, having only once (v. 30, 6) to be read with hiatus. **manīṣā́ iyám**: in this and two other passages of the RV. the ā of **manīṣā́** is not contracted in the Saṃhitā text, because it precedes the caesura. **śám**: in apposition, *as a delight* or *comfort*. **síndhum iva**: this simile occurs elsewhere also; thus **Índram ukthā́ni vāvṛdhuḥ, samudrám iva síndhavaḥ** *the hymns strengthen Indra as the rivers the sea.* **ā́ pṛṇanti**: from **pṝ** *fill*. **śávasā**: because hymns, like oblations, are thought to give the gods strength. **vardháyanti**: cs. of **vṛdh** *grow*; accent, p. 466, 19 *a*.

६ त्वामग्ने अङ्गिरसो गुहा हितम्
अन्वविन्दञ्छिश्रियाणं वनेवने ।
स जायसे मथ्यमानः सहो महत्
त्वामाहुः सहसस्पुत्रमङ्गिरः ॥

त्वाम् । अग्ने । अङ्गिरसः । गुहा । हितम् ।
अनु । अविन्दन् । शिश्रियाणम् । वनेऽवने ।
सः । जायसे । मथ्यमानः । सहः । महत् ।
त्वाम् । आहुः । सहसः । पुत्रम् । अङ्गिरः ॥

6 tuā́m, Agne, Áṅgiraso gúhā hitám
ánv avindañ chiśriyāṇáṃ vánevane.
sá jāyase mathyámānaḥ sáho mahát:
tuā́m āhuḥ sáhasas putrám, Aṅgiraḥ.

Thee, O Agni, the Aṅgirases discovered hidden, abiding in every wood. Thus thou art born, when rubbed with mighty strength: they call thee the son of strength, O Aṅgiras.

Áṅgirasas: an ancient priestly family (cp. x. 14, 3–6), Agni being regarded as their chief (cp. d and i. 1, 6). They are said to have designed the first ordinances of sacrifice (x. 67, 2). **gúhā hitám** *placed* (pp. of **dhā**) *in hiding, concealed*, explained by **śiśriyāṇám váne**; *having betaken himself* (pf. pt. of **śri**) *to, resting in*, all *wood*. **ánv avindan**: *they found* him *out* as a means of sacrifice; Sandhi, 40. **váne-vane**: 189 C *a*. **sá**: *as such* = as found in wood (cp. p. 294 *b*). **mathyámānas**: pr. pt. ps. of **math** *stir*, being produced by the friction of the kindling sticks. **sáho mahát**: cognate acc. = *with mighty strength* (cp. **sáhasā yó mathitó jāyate nṛ́bhiḥ** *he who when rubbed by men with strength is born*, vi. 48, 5); this being an explanation of why he is called **sáhasas putrám** *son of strength*: this, or **sáhasaḥ sūnúḥ**, is a frequent epithet of Agni; Sandhi, 43, 2 *a*. **Aṅgiras**: see note on a.

PARJÁNYA

This deity occupies quite a subordinate position, being celebrated in only three hymns. His name often means 'rain-cloud' in the literal sense; but in most passages it represents the personification, the cloud then becoming an udder, a pail, or a water-skin. Parjanya is frequently described as a bull that quickens the plants and the earth. The shedding of rain is his most prominent characteristic. He flies around with a watery car, and loosens the water-skin; he sheds rain-water as our divine (**ásura**) father. In this activity he is associated with thunder and lightning. He is in a special degree the producer and nourisher of vegetation. He also produces fertility in cows, mares, and women. He is several times referred to as a father. By implication his wife is the Earth, and he is once called the son of Dyaus.

v. 83. Metre: 1. 5–8. 10. **Triṣṭubh**; 2–4. **Jagatī**; 9. **Anuṣṭubh**.

१ अच्छा॑ वद त॒वसं॑ गी॒र्भिरा॒भिः	अच्छ॑ । व॒द॒ । त॒वस॑म् । गीः॒ऽभिः । आ॒भिः ।
स्तु॒हि प॒र्जन्यं॒ नम॒सा वि॑वास ।	स्तु॒हि । प॒र्जन्य॑म् । नम॑सा । आ । वि॒वा॒स॒ ।
कनि॑क्रदद्वृष॒भो जी॒रदा॑नू	कनि॑क्रदत् । वृ॒ष॒भः । जी॒रऽदा॑नुः ।
रेतो॑ दधा॒त्योष॑धीषु॒ गर्भ॑म् ॥	रेतः॑ । द॒धा॒ति॒ । ओष॑धीषु । गर्भ॑म् ॥

1 áchā vada tavásam gīrbhír ābhíḥ;
stuhí Parjányam; námasā́ vivāsa.
kánikradad vṛṣabhó jīrádānū
réto dadhāti óṣadhīṣu gárbham.

Invoke the mighty one with these songs; praise Parjanya; seek to win him with obeisance. Bellowing, the bull of quickening gifts places seed in the plants as a germ.

áchā: with final vowel metrically lengthened in the second syllable of the Pāda. **vada**: the poet addresses himself. **vivāsa**: ds. of van *win*. **kánikradat**: see iv. 50, 5 d. **vṛṣabhás**: Parjanya. **jīrádānū**: Sandhi, 47; his quickening gift is rain = **rétas** in d. **gárbham**: as apposition to **rétas**, Parjanya quickens the growth of plants with rain.

२ वि वृक्षान् हंन्त्युत हंन्ति रक्षसो
विश्वं बिभाय भुवनं महावंधात् ।
उतानांगा ईषते वृष्ण्यांवतो
यत्पर्जन्यः स्तनयन् हन्ति दुष्कृतः ॥

वि । वृक्षान् । हन्ति । उत । हन्ति । रक्षसः ।
विश्वम् । बिभाय । भुवनम् । महाऽवंधात् ।
उत । अनांगाः । ईषते । वृष्ण्यंऽवतः ।
यत् । पर्जन्यः । स्तनयंन् । हन्ति । दुःऽकृतः ॥

2 ví vṛkṣā́n hanti utá hanti rakṣáso:
víśvam bibhāya bhúvanam mahā́vadhāt.
utā́nāgā īṣate vṛ́ṣṇiāvato,
yát Parjányaḥ stanáyan hánti duṣkṛ́taḥ.

He shatters the trees and he smites the demons: the whole world fears him of the mighty weapon. Even the sinless man flees before the mighty one, when Parjanya thundering smites the evil-doers.

bibhāya: pf. of **bhī** = pr. (p. 342 *a*). **mahā́vadhāt**: a Bv. owing to its accent (p. 455 *c*). **vṛ́ṣṇyāvatas**: Parjanya; abl. with verbs of fearing (p. 316 *b*). **ánāgās**: with irr. accentuation of the privative **an-** in a Bv. (p. 455 *c a* and f. n. 2). This word is here contrasted with **duṣkṛ́tas**; hence the **utá** before it has the force of *even*. On the internal Sandhi of **duṣkṛ́t** see 43, 2 *a*.

३ रथीव कशयाश्वाँ अभिक्षिपन्न्
आविर्दूतान्कृणुते वर्ष्यांँ३ अहं ।

रथीऽईव । कशंया । अश्वांन् । अभिऽक्षिपन् ।

दूरात्सिंहस्य स्तनथा उदीरते
यत्पर्जन्यः कृणुते वर्ष्यं१ नभः ॥

आविः । दूतान् । कृणुते । वर्ष्यान् । अह ।
दूरात् । सिंहस्य । स्तनथाः । उत् । ईरते ।
यत् । पर्जन्यः । कृणुते । वर्ष्यम् । नभः ॥

3 rathī́ iva káśayā́śvām̐ abhikṣipánn,
āvír dūtā́n kṛṇute varṣíām̐ áha.
dūrā́t siṃhásya stanáthā úd īrate,
yát Parjányaḥ kṛṇuté varṣíam nábhaḥ.

Like a charioteer lashing his horses with a whip he makes manifest his messengers of rain. From afar arise the thunders of the lion, when Parjanya makes rainy the sky.

rathī́ : N. of rathín, much less common than rathī́, N. rathī́s. The contraction rathī́va also occurs in x. 51, 6; rathī́r iva is much commoner and would have been metrically better here. dūtā́n: the clouds. siṃhásya stanáthāḥ: condensed for 'the thunders of Parjanya like the roars of a lion. varṣyàm: predicative acc.; on the accent of this form and of varṣyàn in b, see p. 450, 2 *b*. kṛṇuté: note that kṛ follows the fifth class in the RV., kṛṇóti, &c.; karóti does not appear till the AV., cp. p. 145, 4.

4 प्र वाता वान्ति पतयन्ति विद्युत
उदोषधीर्जिहते पिन्वते स्वः ।
इरा विश्वस्मै भुवनाय जायते
यत्पर्जन्यः पृथिवीं रेतसावति ॥

प्र । वाताः । वान्ति । पतयन्ति । विऽद्युतः ।
उत् । ओषधीः । जिहते । पिन्वते । स्व१रिति स्वः ।
इरा । विश्वस्मै । भुवनाय । जायते ।
यत् । पर्जन्यः । पृथिवीम् । रेतसा । अवति ॥

4 prá vā́tā vā́nti; patáyanti vidyúta;
úd óṣadhīr jíhate; pínvate súaḥ.
írā víśvasmai bhúvanāya jāyate,
yát Parjányaḥ pṛthivī́m rétasā́vati.

The winds blow forth, the lightnings fall; the plants shoot up; heaven overflows. Nurture is born for the whole world when Parjanya quickens the earth with seed.

vā́nti, jíhate (2. hā *go*) are both accented as antithetical (p. 468, 19 *β*) to the two following verbs patáyanti (itv., 168), pínvate, which are accented as beginning new sentences (p. 466, 19 A *a*); cp. also note on bā́dhate, i. 35, 9 c. On the secondary root pinv see 134, 4 *β*. írā: the rain shed by Parjanya makes the earth productive (cp. 1 c, d). Note that the preceding Jagatī triplet (2–4) is bound together by a refrain beginning with yát Parjányaḥ and varying the idea 'when Parjanya rains'.

५ यस्य व्रते पृथिवी नन्नमीति	यस्य । व्रते । पृथिवी । नन्नमीति ।
यस्य व्रते शफवज्जर्भुरीति ।	यस्य । व्रते । शफऽवत् । जर्भुरीति ।
यस्य व्रत ओषधीर्विश्वरूपाः	यस्य । व्रते । ओषधीः । विश्वऽरूपाः ।
स नः पर्जन्य महि शर्म यच्छ ॥	सः । नः । पर्जन्य । महि । शर्म । यच्छ ॥

5 **yásya vraté pṛthivī́ nánnamīti;**	*In whose ordinance the earth*
yásya vraté śapha̍vaj járbhurīti,	*bends low; in whose ordinance*
yásya vratá óṣadhīr viśvá-	*hoofed animals leap about; in*
rūpāḥ:	*whose ordinance plants are omni-*
sá naḥ, Parjanya, máhi śárma	*form, as such, O Parjanya, bestow*
yacha.	*mighty shelter on us.*

yásya vraté: that is, in obedience to whose law. **nánnamīti**: int. of **nam** (see 173, 2 *b*; 172 *a*). **śaphávat**: *that which has hoofs*, used as a n. collective. **járbhurīti**: int. of **bhur** *quiver* (174 *a*). **óṣadhīs**: the following adj. **viśvárūpāḥ** is most naturally to be taken predicatively, like the verbs in **a** and **b**. **sá**: as nom. corr. followed by the voc.: *as such, O Parjanya*. **yacha**: ipv. of **yam**.

६ दिवो नो वृष्टिं मरुतो ररीध्वं	दिवः । नः । वृष्टिम् । मरुतः । ररीध्वम् ।
प्र पिन्वत वृष्णो अश्वस्य धाराः ।	प्र । पिन्वत । वृष्णः । अश्वस्य । धाराः ।
अर्वाङेतेन स्तनयित्नुनेह्य	अर्वाङ् । एतेन । स्तनयित्नुना । आ । इहि ।
अपो निषिञ्चन्नसुरः पिता नः ॥	अपः । निऽसिञ्चन् । असुरः । पिता । नः ॥

6 **divó no vṛṣṭím, Maruto rarī-**	*Give us, O Maruts, the rain*
dhvam;	*of heaven; pour forth the streams*

prá pinvata vŕ̥ṣṇo áśvasya dhā́-rāḥ.	*of your stallion. Hither with this thunder come, pouring down the waters as the divine spirit our father.*
arvā́ṅ eténa stanayitnúnéhi,	
apó niṣiñcánn ásuraḥ pitā́ naḥ.	

divás: this might be abl., *from heaven*, as it is taken to be by Sāyaṇa; but it is more probably gen., being parallel to **áśvasya dhā́rāḥ** in b; cp. ix. 57, 1, **prá te dhā́rā, divó ná, yanti vr̥ṣṭáyaḥ** *thy streams go forth like the rains of heaven.* **rarīdhvam**: 2. pl. pr. ipv. of **rā** *give* (cp. p. 144, B 1 *a*). **Marutas**: the storm gods, as associated with rain, are in a b invoked to bestow rain, which is described as water shed by their steed (as also in i. 64, 6 and ii. 34, 13). **vŕ̥ṣṇo áśvasya**: = *stallion.* In c d Parjanya is again addressed. **stanayitnúnéhi**: the accent alone (apart from the Pada text) shows that this is a contraction not of **-nā ihi** (which would be **-nehi**), but of **-nā éhi**, which would normally be **-náihi**; **-néhi** is based on the artificial contraction **-nā́** (=**-nā ā́**)+**ihi**. The same Sandhi occurs in **Índréhi** (i. 9, 1) for **Índra ā́ ihi**. With **stanayitnúnā** cp. **stanáyan** in 2 d and **stanáthās** in 3 c. **apás** = **vr̥ṣṭím** in a and **dhā́rās** in b. **ásuraḥ pitā́ naḥ**: as appositional subject of the sentence, with the 2. ipv. **íhi**; cp. **sá** in 5 d with the voc. Parjanya and the 2. ipv. **yacha**. The two epithets are applied to other gods also, such as Dyaus, whom in his relation to Earth Parjanya most resembles.

७ अ॒भि क्र॑न्द स्त॒नय॒ गर्भ॒मा धा॑	अ॒भि । क्र॒न्द॒ । स्त॒नय॑ । गर्भ॑म् । आ । धाः॒ ।
उ॒द॒न्वता॒ परि॑ दीया॒ रथे॑न ।	उ॒द॒न्ऽवता॑ । परि॑ । दी॒य॒ । रथे॑न ।
दृतिं॒ सु क॑र्ष॒ विषि॑तं॒ न्य॑ञ्चं	दृति॑म् । सु । क॒र्ष॒ । विऽसि॑तम् । न्य॑ञ्चम् ।
स॒मा भ॑वन्तू॒द्वतो॑ निपा॒दाः ॥	स॒माः । भ॒व॒न्तु॒ । उ॒त्ऽवतः॑ । नि॒ऽपा॒दाः ॥

7 **abhí kranda; stanáya; gárbham ā́ dhā;**	*Bellow towards us; thunder; deposit the germ; fly around with thy water-bearing car. Draw well thy water-skin unfastened downward: let the heights and valleys be level.*
udanvátā pári dīyā ráthena.	
dŕ̥tiṃ sú karṣa víṣitaṃ nía-ñcaṃ:	
samā́ bhavantu udváto nipādā́ḥ.	

stanáya: accented as forming a new sentence. **gárbham**: cp. 1 d, **réto dadhāti óṣadhīṣu gárbham**. **dhās**: 2. s. root ao. sb. of 1. **dhā**. **dīyā**: with final vowel metrically lengthened. **dṛ́tim**: the rain-cloud, here compared with a water-skin, doubtless like the leather bag made of a goat-skin still used in India by water-carriers. **víṣitam** (from **si** *tie*): *untied* so as to let the water run out. **nyàñcam**: predicative: = so that the untied orifice turns downward. **samā́s**: that is, may the high and the low ground be made level by the surface of the water covering both.

८ महान्तं कोशमुदचा नि षिञ्च
स्यन्दन्तां कुल्या विषिताः पुरस्तात् ।
घृतेन द्यावापृथिवी व्युन्धि
सुप्रपाणं भवत्वघ्न्याभ्यः ॥

महान्तम् । कोशम् । उत् । अच । नि । सिञ्च ।
स्यन्दन्ताम् । कुल्याः । विऽसिताः । पुरस्तात् ।
घृतेन । द्यावापृथिवी इति । वि । उन्धि ।
सुऽप्रपानम् । भवतु । अघ्न्याभ्यः ॥

8 **mahā́ntam kóśam úd acā, ní ṣiñca;**
syándantām kulyā́ víṣitāḥ purástāt.
ghṛténa dyā́vāpṛthivī́ ví undhi;
suprapāṇám bhavatu aghniā́bhyaḥ.

Draw up the great bucket, pour it down; let the streams released flow forward. Drench heaven and earth with ghee; let there be a good drinking place for the cows.

The process of shedding rain is here compared with the drawing up of a pail from a well and pouring out its contents. **acā**: metrical lengthening of the final a. **ní ṣiñca**: Sandhi, 67 *c*. **purástāt**: according to Sāyaṇa *eastward*, because 'rivers generally flow eastwards'; but though this is true of the Deccan, where he lived, it is not so of the north-west of India, where the RV. was composed. **ghṛténa**: figuratively of rain, because it produces fatness or abundance. **dyā́vāpṛthivī́**: Pragṛhya, but not analysed in the Pada text (cp. i. 35, 1 b). **undhi**: 2. s. ipv. of **ud** *wet* = **unddhi**. This Pāda is equivalent in sense to 7 d. **suprapāṇám**: note that in the

Pada text this compound is written with a dental *n*, indicating that this was regarded by the compilers of that text as the normal internal Sandhi (see 65 *b*).

९ यत्पर्जन्य कनिक्रदत्
स्तनयन्हंसि दुष्कृतः ।
प्रतीदं विश्वं मोदते
यत्किं च पृथिव्यामधि ॥

यत् । पर्जन्य । कनिक्रदत् ।
स्तनयन् । हंसि । दुःऽकृतः ।
प्रति । इदम् । विश्वम् । मोदते ।
यत् । किम् । च । पृथिव्याम् । अधि ॥

9 **yát, Parjanya, kánikradat,**
stanáyan hámsi duṣkŕtaḥ,
prátīdám viśvam modate,
yát kím ca pṛthivyā́m ádhi.

When, O Parjanya, bellowing aloud, thundering, thou smitest the evil-doers, this whole world exults, whatever is upon the earth.

yát Parjanya: cp. 2 d. **hámsi**: 2. s. pr. of han (66 A 2). **yát kim ca**: indefinite prn., *whatever* (19 *b*), explains idám **víśvam** *this world*; if a verb were expressed it would be bhávati.

१० अवर्षीर्वर्षमुदु षू गृभाया-
कर्धन्वान्यत्येतवा उ ।
अजीजन ओषधीर्भोजनाय कम्
उत प्रजाभ्योऽविदो मनीषाम् ॥

अवर्षीः । वर्षम् । उत् । ऊं इति । सु ।
गृभाय ।
अकः । धन्वानि । अतिऽएतवै । ऊं इति ।
अजीजनः । ओषधीः । भोजनाय । कम् ।
उत । प्रऽजाभ्यः । अविदः । मनीषाम् ॥

10 **ávarṣīr varṣám: úd u ṣū́ gṛbhāya;**
ákar dhánvāni átietavā́ u.
ájījana óṣadhīr bhójanāya kám;
utá prajā́bhyo avido manīṣā́m.

Thou hast shed rain: now wholly cease; thou hast made the deserts passable again. Thou hast made the plants to grow for the sake of food; and thou hast found a hymn of praise from (thy) *creatures.*

This concluding stanza, implying that Parjanya has shed abundant rain, describes its results.

ávarṣīs: 2. s. **s** ao. of **vṛṣ**. **u ṣū́**: on the Sandhi see 67 *c*; on the meaning of the combination, see under **u** and **sú**, 180. **gṛbhāya**: this pr. stem is sometimes used beside **gṛbhṇā́ti**. **ákar**: 2. s. root ao. of **kṛ**. **áti-etavái**: cp. p. 463, 14 *b a*. **ájījanas**: cp. I d and 4 b. **kám**: see 180. Here we have the exceptional intrusion of a Jagatī Pāda in a Triṣṭubh stanza (p. 445, f. n. 7). **avidas**: **a** ao. of **vid** *find, thou hast found = received.* **prajā́bhyas**: abl., *from creatures* in gratitude for the bestowal of rain.

PŪṢÁN

This god is celebrated in eight hymns, five of which occur in the sixth Maṇḍala. His individuality is vague, and his anthropomorphic traits are scanty. His foot and his right hand are mentioned; he wears braided hair and a beard. He carries a golden spear, an awl, and a goad. His car is drawn by goats instead of horses. His characteristic food is gruel (**karambhá**).

He sees all creatures clearly and at once. He is the wooer of his mother and the lover of his sister (Dawn), and was given by the gods to the Sun-maiden Sūryā as a husband. He is connected with the marriage ceremonial in the wedding hymn (x. 85). With his golden aerial ships Pūṣan acts as the messenger of Sūrya. He moves onward observing the universe, and makes his abode in heaven. He is a guardian who knows and beholds all creatures. As best of charioteers he drove downward the golden wheel of the sun. He traverses the distant path of heaven and earth; he goes to and returns from both the beloved abodes. He conducts the dead on the far-off path of the Fathers. He is a guardian of roads, removing dangers out of the way; and is called 'son of deliverance' (vimúco nápāt). He follows and protects cattle, bringing them home unhurt and driving back the lost. His bounty is often mentioned. 'Glowing' (ā́ghṛṇi) is one of his exclusive epithets. The name means 'prosperer', as derived from **puṣ**, *cause to thrive*. The evidence, though not clear, indicates that Pūṣan was originally a solar deity, representing the beneficent power of the sun manifested chiefly in its pastoral aspect.

vi. 54. Metre: **Gāyatrī**.

१ सं पूषन्विदुषा नय	सम् । पूषन् । विदुषा । नय ।
यो अञ्जसानुशासति ।	यः । अञ्जसा । अनुऽशासति ।
य एवेदमिति ब्रवत् ॥	यः । एव । इदम् । इति । ब्रवत् ॥

1 sáṃ, Pūṣan, vidúṣā naya,
yŏ́ áñjasānuśā́sati,
yá evédám íti brávat.

Conjoin us, O Pūṣan, with one that knowṣ, who shall straightway instruct us, and who shall say (it is) '*just here*'.

vidúṣā: inst. governed by the sense of association produced by the combination of **naya** (nī *lead*) with **sám**: cp. p. 308, 1 *a*. The meaning is: 'provide us with a guide'. **anu-śā́sati** (3. s. pr. sb.): who shall instruct us where to find what we have lost. **idám**: not infrequently, as here, used adverbially when it does not refer to a particular substantive. **brávat**: 3. s. pr. sb. of **brū**.

२ समु पूष्णा गमेमहि
यो गृहाँ अभिशासति ।
इम एवेति च ब्रवत् ॥

सम् । ऊं इति । पूष्णा । गमेमहि ।
यः । गृहान् । अभिऽशासति ।
इमे । एव । इति । च । ब्रवत् ॥

2 sám u Pūṣṇā́ gamemahi,
yó gṛhā́m̐ abhiśā́sati,
imá evéti ca brávat.

We would also go with Pūṣan, who shall guide us to the houses, and shall say (it is) '*just these*'.

u: see p. 221, 2; on its treatment in the Pada text, p. 25, f. n. 2. **Pūṣṇā́**: see note on vidúṣā, 1 a. **gamemahi** (a ao. op. of **gam**): *we would* preferably *go with Pūṣan* as our guide. **gṛhā́n**: that is, the sheds in which our lost cattle are.

३ पूष्णश्चक्रं न रिष्यति
न कोशोऽव पद्यते ।
नो अस्य व्यथते पविः ॥

पूष्णः । चक्रम् । न । रिष्यति ।
न । कोशः । अव । पद्यते ।
नो इति । अस्य । व्यथते । पविः ॥

3 Pūṣṇáś cakráṃ ná riṣyati,
ná kóśŏ áva padyate;
nŏ́ asya vyathate pavíḥ.

Pūṣan's wheel is not injured, the well (of his car) *falls not down; nor does his felly waver.*

nó: = ná u, *also not*; on the Sandhi cp. 24. **kóśó va**: on the Sandhi accent, see p. 465, 17, 3. **asya**: unaccented, p. 452, B *c*. Sāyaṇa explains **cakrám** as Pūṣan's weapon, and **pavís** as the edge of that weapon. But this is in the highest degree improbable because the weapon of Pūṣan is a spear, an awl, or a goad; while his car is elsewhere mentioned, as well as the goats that draw it, and he is called a charioteer.

यो॑ अ॒स्मै॒ ह॒वि॒षाविध॑न्
न॒ तं पू॒षापि॑ मृ॒ष्यते ।
प्रथ॒मो विन्द॑ते॒ वसु॑ ॥

यः॑ । अ॒स्मै॒ । ह॒वि॒षा । अ॒विध॑त् ।
न । तम् । पू॒षा । अपि॑ । मृ॒ष्यते॑ ।
प्रथ॒मः॑ । विन्द॑ते । वसु॑ ॥

4 yó asmai havíṣā́vidhan,
ná tám Pūṣā́pi mṛṣyate :
prathamó vindate vásu.

*Him who has worshipped him with
oblation Pūṣan forgets not: he is
the first that acquires wealth.*

asmai: Pūṣan; on the syntax, see 200, A 1 *f*; on loss of accent, see p. 452 B *c*. ápi: verbal prp. to be taken with mṛṣ. prathamás: the man who worships Pūṣan.

पू॒षा गा अन्वे॑तु॒ नः॒
पू॒षा र॑क्ष॒त्वर्वतः॑ ।
पू॒षा वाजं॑ सनोतु॒ नः॒ ॥

पू॒षा । गाः । अनु॑ । ए॒तु॒ । नः॒ ।
पू॒षा । र॒क्ष॒तु॒ । अर्व॑तः ।
पू॒षा । वाज॑म् । स॒नो॒तु॒ । नः॒ ॥

5 Pūṣā́ gā́ ánu etu naḥ;
Pūṣā́ rakṣatu árvataḥ;
Pūṣā́ vā́jam sanotu naḥ.

*Let Pūṣan go after our cows;
let Pūṣan protect our steeds; let
Pūṣan gain booty for us.*

ánu etu: to be with them and prevent injury or loss. rakṣatu: to prevent their being lost.

पू॒षन्न॒नु प्र गा इ॒हि
य॒जमा॑नस्य सु॒न्वतः॑ ।
अ॒स्माकं॑ स्तुव॒तामुत ॥

पू॒षन् । अनु॑ । प्र । गाः । इ॒हि ।
य॒जमा॑नस्य । सु॒न्वतः॑ ।
अ॒स्माक॑म् । स्तु॒व॒ताम् । उत ॥

6 Pūṣann, ánu prá gā́ ihi
yájamānasya sunvatáḥ,
asmā́kam stuvatā́m utá.

*O Pūṣan, go forth after the cows
of the sacrificer who presses Soma,
and of us who praise thee.*

ánu prá ihi: cp. p. 468, 20 *a*. yájamānasya: of the institutor of the sacrifice. stuvatā́m: of the priests as a body.

७ माकिर्नेशन्माकीं रिषन्
माकीं सं शारि केवटे ।
अथारिष्टाभिरा गहि ॥

माकिः । नेशत् । माकीम् । रिषत् ।
माकीम् । सम् । शारि । केवटे ।
अथ । अरिष्टाभिः । आ । गहि ॥

7 mā́kir neśan; mā́kīṃ riṣan;
mā́kīṃ sáṃ śāri kévaṭe:
áthā́riṣṭābhir ā́ gahi.

Let not any one be lost; let it not be injured; let it not suffer fracture in a pit: so come back with them uninjured.

neśat: inj. ao. of **naś** *be lost* (see 149 *a* 2). **riṣat**: a ao. inj. of **riṣ**. **śāri**: ps. ao. inj. of **śṝ** *crush.* **áriṣṭābhis**: supply **góbhis**.

८ शृण्वन्तं पूषणं वयम्
इर्यमनष्टवेदसम् ।
ईशानं राय ईमहे ॥

शृण्वन्तम् । पूषणम् । वयम् ।
इर्यम् । अनष्टऽवेदसम् ।
ईशानम् । रायः । ईमहे ॥

8 śṛṇvántaṃ Pūṣáṇaṃ vayám,
íryam ánaṣṭavedasam,
ī́śānaṃ rāyá īmahe.

Pūṣan, who hears, the watchful, whose property is never lost, who disposes of riches, we approach.

ánaṣṭa-vedasam: who always recovers property that has been lost; he is also called **ánaṣṭa-paśu**: *whose cattle are never lost*; cp. 1, 2, 5, 6, 7. **rāyás**: gen. dependent on **ī́śānam** (see 202 A *a*). **īmahe**: 1. pl. pr. Ā. of **ī** *go* governing the acc. **Pūṣáṇam**: cp. 197 A 1.

९ पूषन्तव व्रते वयं
न रिष्येम कदा चन ।
स्तोतारस्त इह स्मसि ॥

पूषन् । तव । व्रते । वयम् ।
न । रिष्येम । कदा । चन ।
स्तोतारः । ते । इह । स्मसि ॥

9 Pū́ṣan, táva vraté vayáṃ
ná riṣyema kádā caná:
stotā́ras ta ihá smasi.

O Pūṣan, in thy service may we never suffer injury: we are thy praisers here.

Pū́ṣan táva: note the Sandhi (40, 2). **vraté**: that is, while abiding in thy ordinance. **smasi**: 1. pl. of **as** *be*; c gives the reason for the hope expressed in a b.

१० परिं पूषा परस्ताद्	परिं। पूषा। परस्तात्।
धस्तं दधातु दक्षिणम्।	हस्तम्। दधातु। दक्षिणम्।
पुनर्नो नष्टमाजतु ॥	पुनः। नः। नष्टम्। आ। अजतु॥

10 **pári Pūṣā́ parástā̆d**
dhástaṃ dadhātu dákṣiṇam:
púnar no naṣṭám ā́jatu.

Let Pūṣan put his *right hand around* us *from afar: let him drive up for us again what has been lost.*

parástād: the ā to be pronounced dissyllabically (cp. p. 437. a 8). **pári dadhātu**: for protection. **dhastam** = **hástam**: 54. **naṣṭám**: from **naś** *be lost*; cp. **ánaṣṭavedasam** in 8 b. **ā́jatu**: the meaning of the vb. shows that by the n. **naṣṭám** *what is lost* cows are intended.

ÁPAS

The Waters are addressed in four hymns, as well as in a few scattered verses. The personification is only incipient, hardly extending beyond the notion of their being mothers, young wives, and goddesses who bestow boons and come to the sacrifice. They follow the path of the gods. Indra, armed with the bolt, dug out a channel for them, and they never infringe his ordinances. They are celestial as well as terrestrial, and the sea is their goal. They abide where the gods dwell, in the seat of Mitra-Varuṇa, beside the sun. King Varuṇa moves in their midst, looking down on the truth and the falsehood of men. They are mothers and as such produce Agni. They give their auspicious fluid like loving mothers. They are most motherly, the producers of all that is fixed and that moves. They purify, carrying away defilement. They even cleanse from moral guilt, the sins of violence, cursing, and lying. They also bestow remedies, health, wealth, strength, long life, and immortality. Their blessing and aid are often implored, and they are invited to seat themselves on the sacrificial grass to receive the offering of the Soma priest.

The Waters are several times associated with honey. They mix their milk with honey. Their wave, rich in honey, became the drink of Indra, whom it exhilarated and to whom it gave heroic strength. They are invoked to pour the wave which is rich in honey, gladdens the gods, is the draught of Indra, and is produced in the sky. Here the celestial Waters seem to be identified with the heavenly Soma, the beverage of Indra. Elsewhere the Waters used in preparing the terrestrial Soma seem to be meant. When they appear bearing ghee, milk, and honey, they are accordant with the priests that bring well-pressed Soma for Indra. Soma (viii. 48) delights in them like a young man in lovely maidens; he approaches them as a lover; they are maidens who bow down before the youth.

The deification of the Waters is pre-Vedic, for they are invoked as *āpo* in the Avesta also.

vii. 49. Metre: Triṣṭubh.

१ समुद्रज्येष्ठाः सलिलस्य मध्यात्	समुद्रऽज्येष्ठाः । सलिलस्य । मध्यात् ।
पुनाना यन्त्यनिविशमानाः ।	पुनानाः । यन्ति । अनिऽविशमानाः ।
इन्द्रो या वज्री वृषभो रराद	इन्द्रः । याः । वज्री । वृषभः । ररद ।
ता आपो देवीरिह मामवन्तु ॥	ताः । आपः । देवीः । इह । माम् । अवन्तु ॥

1 **samudrájyeṣṭhāḥ salilásya mádhyāt**	*Having the ocean as their chief, from the midst of the sea, purifying, they flow unresting: let those Waters, the goddesses, for whom Indra, the bearer of the bolt, the mighty one, opened a path, help me here.*
punānā́ yanti ániviśamānāḥ:	
Índro yā́ vajrī́ vṛṣabhó rarā́da,	
tā́ ā́po devī́r ihá mā́m avantu.	

samudrá-jyeṣṭhās: that is, of which the ocean is the largest. **salilásya:** the aerial waters, referred to as divyā́s in 2 a, are meant. **punānā́s:** cp. pāvakā́s in c. **ániviśamānās:** cp. i. 32, 10, where the waters are alluded to as átiṣṭhantīs and ániveśanās *standing not still* and *resting not.* **rarā́da:** of Indra, it is said elsewhere (ii. 15, 3), **vájreṇa khā́ny atṛṇan nadī́nām** *with his bolt he pierced channels for the rivers.* **tā́ ā́po,** &c. is the refrain of all the four stanzas of this hymn.

२ या आपो दिव्या उत वा स्रवन्ति	याः । आपः । दिव्याः । उत । वा । स्रवन्ति ।
खनित्रिमा उत वा याः स्वयंजाः ।	खनित्रिमाः । उत । वा । याः । स्वयम्ऽजाः ।
समुद्रार्था याः शुचयः पावकास्	समुद्रऽअर्थाः । याः । शुचयः । पावकाः ।
ता आपो देवीरिह मामवन्तु ॥	ताः । आपः । देवीः । इह । माम् । अवन्तु ॥

2 yā́ Ā́po divyā́ utá vā srávanti
khanítrimā utá vā yā́ḥ svayaṃ-
jā́ḥ;
samudrā́rthā yā́ḥ śúcayaḥ pa-
vākā́s:
tā́ Ā́po devī́r ihá mā́m avantu.

The Waters that come from heaven or that flow in channels or that arise spontaneously, that clear and purifying have the ocean as their goal: let those Waters, the goddesses, help me here.

divyā́s: that fall from the sky as rain: cp. **salilásya mádhyāt** in 1 a. **khanítrimās**: that flow in artificial channels: cp. **Índro yā́ rarā́da** in 1 c. **svayaṃjā́s**: that come from springs. **samudrā́rthās**: that flow to the sea; cp. **samudrájyeṣṭhāḥ punānā́ yanti** in 1 a, b. **pāvakā́s**: this word here and elsewhere in the RV. must be pronounced **pavākā́** (p. 437 *a* 9).

३ यासां राजा वरुणो याति मध्ये
सत्यानृते अवपश्यञ्जनानाम् ।
मधुश्चुतः शुचयो याः पावकास्
ता आपो देवीरिह मामवन्तु ॥

यासाम् । राजा । वरुणः । याति । मध्ये ।
सत्यानृते इति । अवऽपश्यन् । जनानाम् ।
मधुऽश्चुतः । शुचयः । याः । पावकाः ।
ताः । आपः । देवीः । इह । माम् । अवन्तु ॥

3 **yā́sāṃ rā́jā Váruṇo yā́ti má-**
dhye,
satyānṛté avapáśyañ jánānām,
madhuścútaḥ śúcayo yā́ḥ pa-
vākā́s:
tā́ Ā́po devī́r ihá mā́m avantu.

In the midst of whom King Varuṇa goes looking down upon the truth and untruth of men, who distil sweetness, clear and purifying: let those Waters, the goddesses, help me here.

Váruṇas: this god (vii. 86) is closely connected with the waters, for the most part those of heaven. **avapáśyan**: this shows that the celestial waters are here meant; on the Sandhi see 40, 1. **satyānṛté**: Pragṛhya (26; cp. p. 437, note 3); accent: p. 457, 10 *e*. Note that Dvandvas are not analysed in the Pada text. **madhuścútas**: that is, inherently sweet.

४ यासु राजा वरुणो यासु सोमो
विश्वे देवा यासूर्जं मदन्ति ।

यासु । राजा । वरुणः । यासु । सोमः ।
विश्वे । देवाः । यासु । ऊर्जम् । मदन्ति ।

वैश्वानरो यास्वग्निः प्रविष्टस् वैश्वानरः। यासु। अग्निः। प्रऽविष्टः।
ता आपो देवीरिह मामवन्तु॥ ताः। आपः। देवीः। इह। माम्। अवन्तु॥

4 yā́su rā́jā Váruṇo, yā́su Sómo, Víśve devā́ yā́su ū́rjam mád-anti;
vaiśvānaró yā́su Agníḥ prá-viṣṭas:
tā́ Ā́po devī́r ihá mā́m avantu.

In whom King Varuṇa, in whom Soma, in whom the All-gods drink exhilarating strength, into whom Agni Vaiśvānara has entered: let those Waters, the goddesses, help me here.

ū́rjam: cognate acc. with **mádanti** (cp. 197 A 4) = obtain vigour in exhilaration, that is, by drinking Soma which is associated with the Waters. **vaiśvānarás**: *belonging to all men*, a frequent epithet of Agni. **právistas**: Agni's abode in the Waters is very often referred to; cp. also his aspect as **Apā́ṃ nápāt** 'Son of Waters' (ii. 35).

MITRÁ-VÁRUṆA

This is the pair most frequently mentioned next to Heaven and Earth. The hymns in which they are conjointly invoked are much more numerous than those in which they are separately addressed. As Mitra (iii. 59) is distinguished by hardly any individual traits, the two together have practically the same attributes and functions as Varuṇa alone. They are conceived as young. Their eye is the sun. Reaching out they drive with the rays of the sun as with arms. They wear glistening garments. They mount their car in the highest heaven. Their abode is golden and is located in heaven; it is great, very lofty, firm, with a thousand columns and a thousand doors. They have spies that are wise and cannot be deceived. They are kings and universal monarchs. They are also called Asuras, who wield dominion by means of māyā́ *occult power*, a term mainly connected with them. By that power they send the dawns, make the sun traverse the sky, and obscure it with cloud and rain. They are rulers and guardians of the whole world. They support heaven, and earth, and air.

They are lords of rivers, and they are the gods most frequently thought of and prayed to as bestowers of rain. They have kine yielding refreshment, and streams flowing with honey. They control the rainy skies and the streaming waters. They bedew the pastures with ghee (= rain) and the spaces with honey. They send rain and refreshment from the sky. Rain abounding in heavenly water comes from them. One entire hymn dwells on their powers of bestowing rain.

Their ordinances are fixed and cannot be obstructed even by the immortal gods. They are upholders and cherishers of order. They are barriers against falsehood, which they dispel, hate, and punish. They afflict with disease those who neglect their worship.

The dual invocation of these gods goes back to the Indo-Iranian period, for Ahura and Mithra are thus coupled in the Avesta.

vii. 61. **Metre: Triṣṭubh.**

१ उद्वां चक्षुर्वरुण सुप्रतीकं
देवयोरेति सूर्यस्ततन्वान् ।
अभि यो विश्वा भुवनानि चष्टे
स मन्युं मर्त्येष्वा चिकेत ॥

उत । वाम् । चक्षुः । वरुणा । सुऽप्रतीकम् ।
देवयोः । एति । सूर्यः । ततन्वान् ।
अभि । यः । विश्वा । भुवनानि । चष्टे ।
सः । मन्युम् । मर्त्येषु । आ । चिकेत ॥

1 **úd vāṃ cákṣur, Varuṇā, suprá-tīkaṃ**
deváyor eti Sū́rias tatanvā́n.
abhí yó víśvā bhúvanāni cáṣṭe,
sá manyúṃ mártieṣu ā́ ciketa.

Up the lovely eye of you two gods, O (Mitra and) *Varuṇa, rises, the Sun, having spread* (his light); *he who regards all beings observes* their *intention among mortals.*

cákṣus: cp. vii. 63, 1, úd u eti ... **Sū́ryaḥ** ... **cákṣur Mitrásya Váruṇasya** *up rises the Sun, the eye of Mitra and Varuṇa.* **Varuṇa**: has the form of the voc. s., which could be used elliptically; but the Padapāṭha takes it as the shortened form of the elliptical dual Varuṇā (cp. 193, 2 *a*); cp. deva in 7 *a*. It is, however, difficult to see why the ā should have been shortened, because it conforms to the normal break (◡ ◡ –) of the Triṣṭubh line (see p. 441). **abhí ... cáṣṭe**: the Sun is elsewhere also said to behold all beings and the good and bad deeds of mortals. **manyúm**: that is, their good or evil intentions. **ciketa**: pf. of **cit** *perceive* (cp. 139, 4). In d the caesura irregularly follows the third syllable.

२ प्र वां स मित्रावरुणावृतावा
विप्रो मन्मानि दीर्घश्रुदियर्ति ।

प्र । वाम् । सः । मित्रावरुणौ । ऋतऽवा ।
विप्रः । मन्मानि । दीर्घऽश्रुत् । इयर्ति ।

यस्य ब्रह्माणि सुक्रतू अवाथ
आ यत्क्रत्वा न शरदः पृणैथे ॥

यस्य । ब्रह्माणि । सुक्रतू इति सुऽक्रतू । अवाथः ।
आ । यत् । क्रत्वा । न । शरदः । पृणैथे इति ॥

2 prá vām̐ sá, Mitrā-Varuṇāv, ṛtā́vā
vípro mánmāni dīrghaśrúd iyarti,
yásya bráhmāṇi, sukratū, á-vātha,
ā́ yát krátvā ná śarádaḥ pṛṇáithe.

Forth for you two, O Mitra-Varuṇa, this pious priest, heard afar, sends his hymns, that ye may favour his prayers, ye wise ones, that ye may fill his autumns as it were with wisdom.

iyarti: 3. s. pr. of ṛ *go.* **yásya . . . ávāthas = yát tásya ávāthas**: on the sb. with relatives see p. 356, 2. **sukratū**: see note on ṛtā́varī, i. 160, 1 b. The repeated unaccented word in the Pada text here is not marked with Anudāttas because all unaccented syllables following a Svarita are unmarked. **ā́ pṛṇáithe**: 2. du. sb. pr. of **pṛṇ** *fill.* The meaning of d is not quite certain, but is probably 'that ye who are wise may make him full of wisdom all his life'. **śarádas**: *autumns,* not varṣā́ṇi *rains* (which only occurs in the AV.), regularly used in the RV. to express years of life, because that was the distinctive season where the RV. was composed.

3 प्रोरोर्मित्रावरुणा पृथिव्याः
प्र दिव ऋष्वाद्बृहतः सुदानू ।
स्पशो दधाथे ओषधीषु विक्ष्व्
ऋधग्यतो अनिमिषं रक्षमाणा ॥

प्र । उरोः । मित्रावरुणा । पृथिव्याः ।
प्र । दिवः । ऋष्वात् । बृहतः । सुदानू इति सुऽदानू ।
स्पशः । दधाथे इति । ओषधीषु । विक्षु ।
ऋधक् । यतः । अनिऽमिषम् । रक्षमाणा ॥

3 prá urór, Mitrā-Varuṇā, pṛthivyā́ḥ,

From the wide earth, O Mitra-Varuṇa, from the high lofty sky,

prá divá ṛṣvā́d bṛhatáḥ, sudānū,
spáśo dadhāthe óṣadhīṣu vikṣú
ŕ̥dhag yató, ’nimiṣam rákṣamāṇā.

O bounteous ones, ye have placed your spies that go separately, in plants and abodes, ye that protect with unwinking eye.

urós : here used as f. (as adjectives in u may be: 98), though the f. of this particular adj. is otherwise formed with ī : **urv-ī́**. **sudānū** : see note on sukratū in 2 c. **spáśas** : the spies of Varuṇa (and Mitra) are mentioned in several passages. **dadhāthe** : Pragṛhya (26 *b*). **óṣadhīṣu** : the use of this word seems to have no special force here beyond expressing that the spies lurk not only in the houses of men, but also outside. **yatás** : pr. pt. A. pl. of i *go*. **ánimiṣam** : acc. of **á-nimiṣ** f. *non-winking*, used adverbially, to be distinguished from the adj. **a-nimiṣá** also used adverbially in the acc. The initial **a** must be elided for the sake of the metre.

४ शंसा मित्रस्य वरुणस्य धाम
शुष्मो रोदसी बद्बधे महित्वा ।
अयन्मासा अयज्वनामवीराः
प्र यज्ञमन्मा वृजनं तिराते ॥

शंस । मित्रस्य । वरुणस्य । धाम ।
शुष्मः । रोदसी इति । बद्बधे । महिऽत्वा ।
अयन् । मासाः । अयज्वनाम् । अवीराः ।
प्र । यज्ञऽमन्मा । वृजनम् । तिराते ॥

4 **śámsā Mitrásya Váruṇasya dhā́ma :**
suṣmo ródasī badbadhe mahitvā́.
áyan mā́sā áyajvanām avī́rāḥ ;
prá yajñámanmā vṛjánam tirāte.

I will praise the ordinance of Mitra and Varuṇa: their force presses apart the two worlds with might. May the months of non-sacrificers pass without sons; may he whose heart is set on sacrifice extend his circle.

śáṃsā : this form may be the 2. s. P. ipv. with metrically lengthened final vowel, as the Pada text interprets it; or the 1. s. sb. P. (p. 125). The latter seems more likely because the poet speaks of himself in the 1. prs. (twice) in 6 a, b also. **badbadhe** : int. of **bādh** (174 *a*); cp. vii. 23, 3, **ví bādhiṣṭa syá ródasī mahitvā́** *he has pressed asunder the two worlds with his might.* **mahitvā́** : inst.

(p. 77). **áyan**: 3. pl. pr. sb. of i *go* (p. 130). **avī́rās**: predicative = *as sonless*; on the accent see p. 455, 10 *c a*. **yajñámanmā**: contrasted with **áyajvanām** (accent p. 455, f. n. 2). **prá tirāte**: 3. s. sb. pr. of tṝ *cross*; this cl. vb. is often used in the sense of prolonging life (Ā. one's own, P. that of others), here of increasing the number of one's sons (as opposed to **avī́ras** in c); cp. **prá yé bándhuṃ tiránte, gávyā pṛñcánto áśvyā maghā́ni** *who further their kin, giving abundantly gifts of cows and horses* (vii. 67, 9).

5 अमूरा विश्वा वृषणाविमा वां
न यासु चित्रं ददृशे न यक्षम् ।
द्रुहः सचन्ते अनृता जनानां
न वां निण्यान्यचिते अभूवन् ॥

अमूरा । विश्वा । वृषणौ । इमाः । वाम् ।
न । यासु । चित्रम् । ददृशे । न । यक्षम् ।
द्रुहः । सचन्ते । अनृता । जनानाम् ।
न । वाम् । निण्यानि । अचिते । अभूवन् ॥

5 **ámūrā, víśvā, vṛṣaṇāv, imā́ vāṃ,**
ná yā́su citráṃ dádṛśe, ná yakṣám.
drúhaḥ sacante ánṛtā jánānāṃ:
ná vāṃ niṇyā́ni acite abhūvan.

O wise mighty ones, all these (praises) are *for you two, in which no marvel is seen nor mystery. Avengers follow the falsehoods of men: there have been no secrets for you not to know.*

The interpretation of this stanza is uncertain. Following the Padapāṭha I take **ámūrā** to be a du. m. agreeing with **vṛṣaṇau**, but **víśvā** for **víśvās** (contrary to the Pada) f. pl. N. agreeing with **imā́s** *these* (sc. **stutáyas**). **ná citrám**: that is, no deceit or falsehood. **dádṛśe**: 3. s. pf. Ā. with ps. sense, as often (cp. p. 342 *a*). **drúhas**: the spies of Varuṇa (cp. 3 c). **ná niṇyā́ni**: explains c: there is nothing hidden from you. **a-cíte**: dat. inf. (cp. 167, 1 *a*).

6 समु वां यज्ञं महयं नमोभिर्
हुवे वां मित्रावरुणा सबाधः ।
प्र वां मन्मान्यृचसे नवानि
कृतानि ब्रह्म जुजुषन्निमानि ॥

सम् । ऊं इति । वाम् । यज्ञम् । महयम् ।
नमःऽभिः ।
हुवे । वाम् । मित्रावरुणा । सऽबाधः ।
प्र । वाम् । मन्मानि । ऋचसे । नवानि ।
कृतानि । ब्रह्म । जुजुषन् । इमानि ॥

6 **sám u vāṃ yajñáṃ mahayaṃ námobhir;**
huvé vāṃ, Mitrā-Varuṇā, sabā́dhaḥ.
prá vāṃ mánmāni **ṛcáse** návāni;
kṛtā́ni bráhma jujuṣann imā́ni.

With reverence I will consecrate for you the sacrifice; I call on you two, Mitra-Varuna, with zeal. (These) *new thoughts are to praise you; may these prayers that have been offered be pleasing.*

sám mahayam: 1. s. inj. cs. of **mah. huvé**: 1. s. pr. Ā. of **hū** *call.* **sabā́dhas**: note that the pcl. **sa** is separated in the Pada text, though the privative pcl. a is not. **prá . . . ṛcáse**: dat. inf. from **arc** *praise* (see p. 192, *b* 1; cp. p. 463, notes 2 and 8). **návāni**: the seers often emphasize the importance of new prayers. **bráhma**: n. pl.; see **90,** p. 67 (bottom) and note **4. jujuṣan**: 3. pl. sb. pf. of **juṣ** (140, **1**).

७ इयं देव पुरोहितिर्युवभ्यां
यज्ञेषु मित्रावरुणावकारि ।
विश्वानि दुर्गा पिपृतं तिरो नो
यूयं पात स्वस्तिभिः सदा नः ॥

इयम् । देवा । पुरःऽहितिः । युवऽभ्याम् ।
यज्ञेषु । मित्रावरुणौ । अकारि ।
विश्वानि । दुःऽगा । पिपृतम् । तिरः । नः ।
यूयम् । पात । स्वस्तिऽभिः । सदा । नः ॥

7 **iyáṃ,** devā, **puróhitir yuvábhyāṃ**
yajñéṣu, Mitrā-Varuṇāv, **akāri;**
víśvāni durgā́ piprtaṃ tiró no.
yūyáṃ pāta suastíbhiḥ sádā naḥ.

This priestly service, O gods, has been rendered to you two at sacrifices, O Mitra-Varuṇa. Take us across all hardships. Do ye protect us evermore with blessings.

This final stanza is a repetition of the final stanza of the preceding hymn (vii. 60); d is the refrain characteristic of the hymns of the Vasiṣṭha family, concluding three-fourths of the hymns of the seventh Maṇḍala.

deva: voc. du., shortened for **devā** (cp. **Varuṇa** in 1 a) as restored in the Pada text. **yuvábhyām**: note the difference between this form and yúvabhyām, dat. du. of **yúvan** *youth.* **Mitrā-Varuṇau**: note that in the older parts of the RV. the du. ending **au** occurs only within a Pāda before vowels, in the Sandhi form of **āv.** **akāri**: ps. ao. of **kṛ** *do.* **piprtam**: 2. du. ipv. pr. of **pṛ** *put across.* **yūyám**: pl., scil. **devās**, because the line is a general refrain addressed to the gods, not to Mitra-Varuṇa.

SŪ́RYA

Some ten hymns are addressed to Sūrya. Since the name designates the orb of the sun as well as the god, Sūrya is the most concrete of the solar deities, his connexion with the luminary always being present to the mind of the seers. The eye of Sūrya is several times mentioned; but Sūrya himself is also often called the eye of Mitra and Varuṇa, as well as of Agni and of the gods. He is far-seeing, all-seeing, the spy of the whole world; he beholds all beings, and the good and bad deeds of mortals. He arouses men to perform their activities. He is the soul or guardian of all that moves or is stationary. His car is drawn by one steed called **etaśá**, or by seven swift mares called **hárit** *bays*.

The Dawn or Dawns reveal or produce Sūrya; he shines from the lap of the Dawns; but Dawn is also sometimes Sūrya's wife. He also bears the metronymic Āditya or Āditeya, son of the goddess Aditi. His father is Dyaus or Heaven. The gods raised him who had been hidden in the ocean, and they placed him in the sky; various individual gods, too, are said to have produced Sūrya or raised him to heaven.

Sūrya is in various passages conceived as a bird traversing space; he is a ruddy bird that flies; or he is a flying eagle. He is also called a mottled bull, or a white and brilliant steed brought by Dawn. Occasionally he is described as an inanimate object: he is a gem of the sky, or a variegated stone set in the midst of heaven. He is a brilliant weapon (**ā́yudha**) which Mitra-Varuṇa conceal with cloud and rain, or their felly (**paví**), or a brilliant car placed by them in heaven. Sūrya is also sometimes spoken of as a wheel (**cakrá**), though otherwise the wheel of Sūrya is mentioned. Sūrya shines for all the world, for men and gods. He dispels the darkness, which he rolls up like a skin, or which his rays throw off like a skin into the waters. He measures the days and prolongs life. He drives away sickness, disease, and evil dreams. All creatures depend on him, and the epithet 'all-creating' (**viśvá-karman**) is once applied to him. By his greatness he is the divine priest (**asuryà puróhita**) of the gods. At his rising he is besought to declare men sinless to Mitra-Varuṇa and to other gods.

The name **Sū́rya** is a derivative of **svàr** *light*, and cognate with the Avestic **hvare** *sun*, which has swift horses and is the eye of Ahura Mazda

vii. 63. Metre: **Triṣṭubh.**

१ उद्वेति सुभगो विश्वचक्षाः
साधारणः सूर्यो मानुषाणाम् ।
चक्षुर्मित्रस्य वरुणस्य देवश्
चर्मेव यः समविव्यक्तमांसि ॥

उत् । ऊं इति । एति । सुऽभगः । विश्वऽचक्षाः ।
साधारणः । सूर्यः । मानुषाणाम् ।
चक्षुः । मित्रस्य । वरुणस्य । देवः ।
चर्मऽइव । यः । सम्ऽअविव्यक् । तमांसि ॥

1 **úd u eti subhágo viśvácakṣāḥ**
sádhāraṇaḥ Sū́rio mánuṣāṇām,
cákṣur Mitrásya Váruṇasya devás,
cármeva yáḥ samávivyak támāṃsi.

Up rises the genial all-seeing Sun, common to all men, the eye of Mitra and Varuṇa, the god who rolled up the darkness like a skin.

víśvácakṣās: cp. **urucákṣās** in 4 a; on the accentuation of these two words cp. p. 454, 10 and p. 455, 10 *c a.* **cákṣus**: cp. vii. 61, 1. **sam-ávivyak**: 3. s. ipf. of **vyac** *extend.* **cárma iva**: cp. iv. 13, 4, **raśmáyaḥ Sū́riasya cármevā́vādhus támo apsú antáḥ** *the rays of the sun have deposited the darkness like a skin within the waters.*

२ उद्वेति प्रसवीता जनानां
महान्केतुरर्णवः सूर्यस्य ।
समानं चक्रं पर्याविवृत्सन्
यदेतशो वहति धूर्षु युक्तः ॥

उत् । ऊं इति । एति । प्रऽसविता । जनानाम् ।
महान् । केतुः । अर्णवः । सूर्यस्य ।
समानम् । चक्रम् । परिऽआविवृत्सन् ।
यत् । एतशः । वहति । धूःऽसु । युक्तः ॥

2 **úd u eti prasavītā́ jánānām**
mahā́n ketúr arṇaváḥ Sū́riasya,
samānám cakrám pariāvívṛtsan,
yád Etaśó váhati dhūrṣú yuktáḥ.

Up rises the rouser of the people, the great waving banner of the Sun, desiring to revolve hither the uniform wheel, which Etaśa, yoked to the pole, draws.

prasavītā: with metrically lengthened i (cp. p. 440, 4) for prasavitā as restored by the Padapāṭha; cp. 4 c, jánāḥ Sū́ryeṇa prásūtāḥ. samānám: *uniform*, with reference to the regularity of the sun's course. cakrám: a single wheel of the sun, doubtless with reference to the shape of the luminary, is regularly spoken of. paryāvívṛtsan: ds. of vṛt *turn*; cp. p. 462, 13 *a*. Etaśás: as the name of the sun's steed, is several times mentioned; but Sūrya is also often said to be drawn by seven steeds; cp. i. 164, 2, saptá yuñjanti rátham ékacakram, ékŏ áśvo vahati saptánāmā *seven yoke the one-wheeled car, one steed with seven names draws it.* dhūrṣú: the loc. pl. as well as the s. of this word is used in this way.

३ विभ्राजमान उषसामुपस्थाद्	विऽभ्राजमानः । उषसाम् । उपऽस्थात् ।
रेभैरुदेत्यनुमद्यमानः ।	रेभैः । उत् । एति । अनुऽमद्यमानः ।
एष मे देवः सविता चच्छन्द	एषः । मे । देवः । सविता । चच्छन्द ।
यः समानं न प्रमिनाति धाम ॥	यः । समानम् । न । प्रऽमिनाति । धाम ॥

3 vibhrā́jamāna uṣásām upásthād	*Shining forth he rises from the*
rebháir úd eti anumadyámānaḥ.	*lap of the dawns, greeted with*
eṣá me deváḥ Savitā́ cachanda,	*gladness by singers. He has seemed*
yáḥ samānám ná pramināti dhā́-	*to me god Savitṛ who infringes not*
ma.	*the uniform law.*

cachanda: here the more concrete god Sūrya is approximated to Savitṛ (i. 35), who is in several passages spoken of as observing fixed laws. In this hymn Sūrya is also referred to with terms (prasavitā́, prásūtās) specially applicable to Savitṛ. ná pramināti: cp. what is said of Dawn in i. 123, 9, ṛtásya ná mināti dhā́ma *she infringes not the law of Order.*

४ दिवो रुक्म उरुचक्षा उदेति	दिवः । रुक्मः । उरुऽचक्षाः । उत् । एति ।
दूरेअर्थस्तरणिर्भ्राजमानः ।	दूरेऽअर्थः । तरणिः । भ्राजमानः ।
नूनं जनाः सूर्येण प्रसूता	नूनम् । जनाः । सूर्येण । प्रऽसूताः ।
अयन्नर्थानि कृणवन्नपांसि ॥	अयन् । अर्थानि । कृणवन् । अपांसि ॥

4 divó rukmá urucákṣā úd eti,
dūréarthas taránir bhrā́jamānaḥ.
nūnáṃ jánāḥ Sū́rieṇa prásūtā
áyann árthāni, kṛṇávann ápāṃsi.

The golden gem of the sky, far-seeing rises, whose goal is distant, speeding onward, shining: Now may men, aroused by the Sun, attain their goals and perform their labours.

divó rukmáḥ: cp. vi. 51, 1, **rukmó ná divá úditā vy àdyaut** *like a golden gem of the sky he has shone forth at sunrise*; and v. 47, 3, **mádhye divó níhitaḥ pṛ́śnir áśmā** *the variegated stone set in the middle of the sky*. **dūréarthas**: Sūrya has far to travel before he reaches sunset. **áyan**: 3. pl. pr. sb. of **i** *go*. **árthāni**: note that this word is always n. in the RV. except in two hymns of the tenth book, in which it is **m.** **kṛṇávan**: 3. pl. pr. sb. of **kṛ** *do*; accented because beginning a new sentence (p. 465, 18 *a*).

५ यत्रा॑ च॒क्रुर॒मृता॑ गा॒तुम॑स्मै
श्ये॒नो न दीय॒न्नन्वे॑ति॒ पाथः॑ ।
प्रति॑ वां॒ सूर॒ उदि॑ते विधेम॒
नमो॑भिर्मित्रावरुणो॒त ह॒व्यैः ॥

यत्र॑ । च॒क्रुः । अ॒मृताः॑ । गा॒तुम् । अ॒स्मै॒ ।
श्ये॒नः । न । दीय॑न् । अनु॑ । एति॑ । पाथः॑ ।
प्रति॑ । वा॒म् । सूरे॑ । उत्ऽइ॑ते । वि॒धे॒म॒ ।
नमः॑ऽभिः । मि॒त्रा॒व॒रु॒णा॒ । उ॒त । ह॒व्यैः ॥

5 yátrā cakrúr amṛ́tā gātúm asmai,
śyenó ná dī́yann ánu eti páthaḥ.
práti vām, sū́ra údite, vidhema
námobhir Mitrā-Varuṇotá havyáiḥ.

Where the immortals have made a way for him, like a flying eagle he follows his path. To you two, when the sun has risen, we would pay worship with adorations, O Mitra-Varuṇa, and with offerings.

yátrā: the final vowel metrically lengthened. **amṛ́tās**: various gods, as Varuṇa, Mitra, and Aryaman (vii. 60, 4), are said to have made paths for the sun. **práti** to be taken with **vidhema**. **sū́ra údite**: loc. abs. (205 *b*).

६ नू मि॒त्रो वरु॑णो अर्य॒मा न॒स्
त्मने॑ तो॒काय॒ वरि॑वो दधन्तु ।

नु । मि॒त्रः । वरु॑णः । अ॒र्य॒मा । नः॒ ।
त्मने॑ । तो॒काय॑ । वरि॑वः । द॒ध॒न्तु॒ ।

सुगा नो विश्वा सुपथानि सन्तु
यूयं पात स्वस्तिभिः सदा नः ॥

सुऽगा । नः । विश्वा । सुऽपथानि । सन्तु ।
यूयम् । पात । स्वस्तिऽभिः । सदा । नः ॥

6 **nū́ Mitró Váruṇŏ Aryamā́ nas**
tmáne tokā́ya várivo dadhantu:
sugā́ no víśvā supáthāni santu.
yūyáṃ pāta suastíbhiḥ sádā naḥ.

Now may Mitra, Varuṇa, and Aryaman grant wide space to us ourselves and *to* our *offspring. Let all our paths be fair* and *easy to traverse. Do ye protect us evermore with blessings.*

nū́: to be pronounced with a slur as equivalent to two syllables (◡ –, cp. p. 437 *a* 8); only **nū́** occurs as the first word of a sentence, never **nú** (p. 238); the Pada text always has **nú**. **tmáne**: this word (cp. 90, 2, p. 69) is often used in the sense of *self*, while **ātmán** is only just beginning to be thus used in the RV. (115 *b* α) and later supplants **tanū́** *body* altogether. **dadhantu**: 3. pl. pr. according to the **a** conj. (p. 144, B 3 β) instead of **dadhatu**. **sugā́**: lit. *may all* (paths) *be easy to travel and easy to traverse.* This final stanza is a repetition of the final stanza of the preceding hymn (vii. 62). On d see note on vii. 61, 6.

AŚVÍNĀ

These two deities are the most prominent gods after Indra, Agni, and Soma, being invoked in more than fifty entire hymns and in parts of several others. Though their name (aśv-ín *horseman*) is purely Indian, and though they undoubtedly belong to the group of the deities of light, the phenomenon which they represent is uncertain, because in all probability their origin is to be sought in a very early pre-Vedic age.

They are twins and inseparable, though two or three passages suggest that they may at one time have been regarded as distinct. They are young and yet ancient. They are bright, lords of lustre, of golden brilliancy, beautiful, and adorned with lotus-garlands. They are the only gods called golden-pathed (híraṇya-vartani). They are strong and agile, fleet as thought or as an eagle. They possess profound wisdom and occult power. Their two most distinctive and frequent epithets are dasrá *wondrous* and nā́satya *true*.

They are more closely associated with honey (mádhu) than any of the other gods. They desire honey and are drinkers of it. They have a skin filled with honey; they poured out a hundred jars of honey. They have a honey-goad; and their car is honey-hued and honey-bearing. They give honey to the bee and are compared with bees. They are, however, also fond of Soma, being invited to drink it with Uṣas and Sūrya. Their car is sunlike and, together with all its parts, golden. It is threefold and has three wheels. It is swifter than thought, than the twinkling of an eye. It was fashioned by the three divine artificers, the Ṛbhus. It is drawn by horses, more commonly by birds or winged steeds; sometimes by one or more buffaloes, or by a single ass (rásabha). It passes over the five countries; it moves around the sky; it traverses heaven and earth in one day; it goes round the sun in the distance. Their revolving course (vartís), a term almost exclusively applicable to them, is often mentioned. They come from heaven, air, and earth, or from the ocean; they abide in the sea of heaven, but sometimes their locality is referred to as unknown. The time of their appearance is between dawn and sunrise: when darkness stands among the ruddy cows; Uṣas awakens them; they follow after her in their car; at its yoking Uṣas is born. They yoke their car to descend to earth and receive the offerings of worshippers. They come not only in the morning, but also at noon and sunset. They dispel darkness and chase away evil spirits.

The Aśvins are children of Heaven; but they are also once said to be the twin sons of Vivasvant and Tvaṣṭṛ's daughter Saraṇyū́ (probably the rising Sun and Dawn). Pūṣan is once said to be their son; and Dawn seems to be meant by their sister. They are often associated with the Sun conceived as a female called either Sūryā or more commonly the daughter of Sūrya. They are Sūryā's two husbands whom she chose and whose car she mounts. Sūryā's companionship on their car is indeed characteristic. Hence in the wedding hymn (x. 85) the Aśvins are invoked to conduct the bride home on their car, and they (with other gods) are besought to bestow fertility on her.

The Aśvins are typically succouring divinities. They are the speediest deliverers from distress in general. The various rescues they effect are of a peaceful kind, not deliverance from the dangers of battle. They are characteristically divine physicians, healing diseases with their remedies, restoring sight, curing the sick and the maimed. Several legends are mentioned about those whom they restored to youth, cured of various physical defects, or befriended in other ways. The name oftenest mentioned is that of Bhujyu, whom they saved from the ocean in a ship.

The physical basis of the Aśvins has been a puzzle from the time of the earliest interpreters before Yāska, who offered various explanations, while modern scholars also have suggested several theories. The two most probable are that the Aśvins represented either the morning twilight, as

half light and half dark, or the morning and the evening star. It is probable that the Aśvins date from the Indo-European period. The two horsemen, sons of Dyaus, who drive across the heaven with their steeds, and who have a sister, are parallel to the two famous horsemen of Greek mythology, sons of Zeus, brothers of Helena; and to the two Lettic God's sons who come riding on their steeds to woo the daughter of the Sun. In the Lettic myth the morning star comes to look at the daughter of the Sun. As the two Aśvins wed the one Sūryā, so the two Lettic God's sons wed the one daughter of the Sun; the latter also (like the Dioskouroi and the Aśvins) are rescuers from the ocean, delivering the daughter of the Sun or the Sun himself.

vii. 71. **Metre: Triṣṭubh.**

१ अप स्वसुरुषसो नग्जिहीते	अप । स्वसुः । उषसः । नक् । जिहीते ।
रिणक्ति कृष्णीररुषाय पन्थाम् ।	रिणक्ति । कृष्णीः । अरुषाय । पन्थाम् ।
अश्वामघा गोमघा वां हुवेम	अश्वऽमघा । गोऽमघा । वाम् । हुवेम ।
दिवा नक्तं शरुमस्मद्युयोतम् ॥	दिवा । नक्तम् । शरुम् । अस्मत् । युयोतम् ॥

1 **ápa svásur Uṣáso Nág jihīte:**	*Night departs from* her *sister*
riṇákti kṛṣṇír aruṣā́ya pánthām.	*Dawn. The black one yields a*
áśvāmaghā, gómaghā, vāṃ hu-	*path to the ruddy* (sun). *O ye that*
vema:	*are rich in horses, rich in cows,*
dívā náktaṃ śárum asmád yu-	*on you two we would call: by day*
yotam.	and *night ward off the arrow*
	from us.

Nák (N. of **náś**): this word occurs here only. **ápa jihīte**: 3. s. Ā. from 2. **hā**. Uṣásas: abl., with which **svásur** agrees. Night and Dawn are often called sisters, **e. g. svásā svásre jyā́yasyai yónim āraik** *the* (one) *sister has yielded her place to her greater sister* (i. 124, 8); and their names are often joined as a dual divinity, **náktoṣā́sā**. The hymn opens thus because the Aśvins are deities of the early dawn. **kṛṣṇís** (dec., p. 87): night; cp. i. 113, 2, **śvetyā́ ā́gād ā́raig u kṛṣṇā́ sádanāni asyāḥ** *the bright one has come; the black one has yielded her abodes to her.* **riṇákti**: 3. s. pr. of ric *leave.* **aruṣā́ya**: to the sun; cp. i. 113, 16, **ā́raik pánthāṃ yā́tave sū́ryāya** *she has* *yielded a path for the sun to go.* **pánthām**: on the dec. see 97, 2 *a*. **gómaghā**: on the accentuation of this second voc., see p. 465, 18 *a*. **śárum**: *the arrow* of death and disease; for the Aśvins are characteristically healers and rescuers. **asmád**: p. 104. **yuyotam**: 2. du. of **yu** *separate*, for **yuyutam**; cp. 2 c and note on ii. 33, 1 b.

२ उपायातं दाशुषे मर्त्याय
रथेन वाममश्विना वहन्ता ।
युयुतमस्मदनिराममीवां
दिवा नक्तं माध्वी त्रासीथां नः ॥

उपऽआयातम् । दाशुषे । मर्त्याय ।
रथेन । वामम् । अश्विना । वहन्ता ।
युयुतम् । अस्मत् । अनिराम् । अमीवाम् ।
दिवा । नक्तम् । माध्वी इति । त्रासीथाम् । नः ॥

2 **upā́yātaṃ dāśúṣe mártiāya**
ráthena vāmám, Aśvinā, váh-antā.
yuyutám asmád ánirām ámī-vāṃ:
dívā naktáṃ, mādhvī, trā́sī-thāṃ naḥ.

Come hither to the aid of the pious mortal, bringing wealth on your car, O Aśvins. Ward off from us languor and disease: day and *night, O lovers of honey, may you protect us.*

upa-ā́-yātam: 2. du. ipv. of **yā** *go*; on the accent see p. 469, 20 A *a a*. **mādhvī**: an epithet peculiar to the Aśvins. **trā́sīthām**: 2. du. Ā. **s** ao. op. of **trā** *protect* (143, 4); irregularly accented as if beginning a new sentence.

३ आ वां रथमवमस्यां व्युष्टौ
सुम्नायवो वृषणो वर्तयन्तु ।
स्यूमगभस्तिमृतयुग्भिरश्वैर्
आश्विना वसुमन्तं वहेथाम् ॥

आ । वाम् । रथम् । अवमस्याम् । विऽउष्टौ ।
सुम्नऽयवः । वृषणः । वर्तयन्तु ।
स्यूमऽगभस्तिम् । ऋतयुक्ऽभिः । अश्वैः ।
आ । अश्विना । वसुऽमन्तम् । वहेथाम् ॥

3 **ā́ vāṃ rátham avamásyāṃ víu-ṣṭau**
sumnāyávo vṛ́ṣaṇo vartayantu.

Let your kindly stallions whirl hither your car at (this) *latest day-break. Do ye, O Aśvins, bring it*

syū́magabhastim ṛtayúgbhir áśvair,
ā́, Aśvinā, vásumantaṃ vahethām.

that is drawn with thongs with your horses yoked in due time, hither, laden with wealth.

avamásyām: prn. adj. (120 *c* 1). **sumnāyávas**: the vowel is metrically lengthened in the second syllable, but, when this word occupies another position in the Pada, the short vowel remains.

4 यो वां रथो नृपती अस्ति वोळ्हा
त्रिवन्धुरो वसुमाँ उस्रयामा ।
आ न एना नासत्योप यातम्
अभि यद्वां विश्वप्स्न्यो जिगाति ॥

यः । वाम् । रथः । नृपती इति नृऽपती । अस्ति । वोळ्हा ।
त्रिऽवन्धुरः । वसुऽमान् । उस्रऽयामा ।
आ । नः । एना । नासत्या । उप । यातम् ।
अभि । यत् । वाम् । विश्वऽप्स्न्यः । जिगाति ॥

4 yó vāṃ rátho, nṛpatī, ásti voḷhā́,
trivandhuró vásumām̐ usráyāmā,
ā́ na enā́, Nāsatyā, úpa yātam,
abhí yád vāṃ viśvápsnio jígāti.

The car, O lords of men, that is your vehicle, three-seated, filled with riches, faring at daybreak, with that come hither to us, Nāsatyas, in order that, laden with all food, for you it may approach us.

trivandhurás: accent, p. **455** *c a*. **vásumān**: Sandhi, 39. **ā́ úpa yātam**: p. 468, 20 *a*; cp. note on **upā́yātam** in 2 a. **enā́**: p. 108. **yád**: p. 357. **vām**: ethical dat. **viśvápsnyas**: the meaning of this word being doubtful, the sense of the whole Pāda remains uncertain. **jígāti** 3. s. sb. of **gā** *go*, indistinguishable from the ind.

5 युवं च्यवानं जरसोऽमुमुक्तं
नि पेदव ऊहथुराशुमश्वम् ।
निरंहसस्तमसः स्पर्तमत्रिं
नि जाहुषं शिथिरे धातमन्तः ॥

युवम् । च्यवानम् । जरसः । अमुमुक्तम् ।
नि । पेदवे । ऊहथुः । आशुम् । अश्वम् ।
निः । अंहसः । तमसः । स्पर्तम् । अत्रिम् ।
नि । जाहुषम् । शिथिरे । धातम् । अन्तरिति ॥

5 yuvám Cyávānam jaráso 'mumuktam,
ní Pedáva ūhathur āśúm áśvam;
nír ámhasas támasaḥ spartam Átrim,
ní Jāhuṣám śithiré dhātam antáḥ.

Ye two released Cyavāna from old age, ye brought a swift horse to Pedu; ye rescued Atri from distress and darkness; ye placed Jāhuṣa in freedom.

yuvám: note that this is the nom., **yuvā́m** being the acc.: p. 105. **Cyávāna** is several times mentioned as having been rejuvenated by the Aśvins. **jarásas**: abl. (p. 316 *b*). **amumuktam**: ppf. of **muc** (140, 6, p. 158). **ní ūhathur**: 2. du. pf. of **vah**. **Pedáve**: Pedu is several times mentioned as having received a swift, white, serpent-killing steed from the Aśvins. **níḥ spartam**: 2. du. root ao. of **spṛ** (cp. 148, 1 *a*). The ao. in c and d is irregularly used in a narrative sense. **ní dhātam**: 2. du. root ao. of **dhā**. In i. 116, 20 it is said of the Aśvins: 'ye carried away at night Jāhusa who was encompassed on all sides'.

६ इयं मनीषा इयमश्विना गीर्
इमां सुवृक्तिं वृषणा जुषेथाम् ।
इमा ब्रह्माणि युवयून्यग्मन्
यूयं पात स्वस्तिभिः सदा नः ॥

इयम् । मनीषा । इयम् । अश्विना । गीः ।
इमाम् । सुऽवृक्तिम् । वृषणा । जुषेथाम् ।
इमा । ब्रह्माणि । युवऽयूनि । अग्मन् ।
यूयम् । पात । स्वस्तिऽभिः । सदा । नः ॥

6 iyáṃ manīṣā́, iyám, Aśvinā, gír.
imā́ṃ suvṛktíṃ, vṛṣaṇā, juṣethām.
imā́ bráhmāṇi yuvayū́ni agman.
yūyáṃ pāta suastíbhiḥ sádā naḥ.

This is my thought, this, O Aśvins, my song. Accept gladly this song of praise, ye mighty ones. These prayers have gone addressed to you. Do ye protect us evermore with blessings.

manīṣā́: this is one of the four passages in which the nom. of the der. **ā** dec. does not contract with a following vowel in the Saṃhitā text, here owing to its preceding the caesura (cp. note on v. 11, 5 b).

gír: 82. **agman**: 3. pl. root ao. of **gam** (148, 1 *e*). **This stanza is a repetition of the last stanza of the preceding hymn (vii. 70), which also is addressed to the Aśvins. On d see note on vii. 61, 6.**

VÁRUṆA

Beside Indra (ii. 12) Varuṇa is the greatest of the gods of the RV., though the number of the hymns in which he is celebrated alone (apart from Mitra) is small, numbering hardly a dozen.

His face, eye, arms, hands, and feet are mentioned. He moves his arms, walks, drives, sits, eats, and drinks. His eye with which he observes mankind is the sun. He is far-sighted and thousand-eyed. He treads down wiles with shining foot. He sits on the strewn grass at the sacrifice. He wears a golden mantle and puts on a shining robe. His car, which is often mentioned, shines like the sun, and is drawn by well-yoked steeds. Varuṇa sits in his mansions looking on all deeds. The Fathers behold him in the highest heaven. The spies of Varuṇa are sometimes referred to: they sit down around him; they observe the two worlds; they stimulate prayer. By the golden-winged messenger of Varuṇa the sun is meant. Varuṇa is often called a king, but especially a universal monarch (**samráj**). The attribute of sovereignty (**kṣatrá**) and the term **ásura** are predominantly applicable to him. His divine dominion is often alluded to by the word **māyā́** *occult power*; the epithet **māyín** *crafty* is accordingly used chiefly of him.

Varuṇa is mainly lauded as upholder of physical and moral order. He is a great lord of the laws of nature. He established heaven and earth, and by his law heaven and earth are held apart. He made the golden swing (the sun) to shine in heaven; he has made a wide path for the sun; he placed fire in the waters, the sun in the sky, Soma on the rock. The wind which resounds through the air is Varuṇa's breath. By his ordinances the moon shining brightly moves at night, and the stars placed up on high are seen at night, but disappear by day. Thus Varuṇa is lord of light both by day and by night. He is also a regulator of the waters. He caused the rivers to flow; by his occult power they pour swiftly into the ocean without filling it. It is, however, with the aerial waters that he is usually connected. Thus he makes the inverted cask (the cloud) to pour its waters on heaven, earth, and air, and to moisten the ground.

Varuṇa's ordinances being constantly said to be fixed, he is pre-eminently called **dhṛtávrata** *whose laws are established.* The gods themselves follow his ordinances. His power is so great that neither the birds as they fly nor the rivers as they flow can reach the limits of his dominion. He embraces the universe, and the abodes of all beings. He is all-knowing, and his omniscience is typical. He knows the flight of the birds in the sky, the path of the ships in the ocean, the course of the far-travelling wind beholding all the secret things that have been or shall be done, he witnesses men's truth and falsehood. No creature can even wink without his knowledge.

As a moral governor Varuṇa stands far above any other deity. His wrath is aroused by sin, the infringement of his ordinances, which he severely punishes. The fetters (**pā́śās**) with which he binds sinners are often mentioned, and are characteristic of him. On the other hand, Varuṇa is gracious to the penitent. He removes sin as if untying a rope. He releases even from the sin committed by men's fathers. He spares him who daily transgresses his laws when a suppliant, and is gracious to those who have broken his laws by thoughtlessness. There is in fact no hymn to Varuṇa in which the prayer for forgiveness of guilt does not occur. Varuṇa is on a footing of friendship with his worshipper, who communes with him in his celestial abode, and sometimes sees him with the mental eye. The righteous hope to behold in the next world Varuṇa and Yama, the two kings who reign in bliss.

The original conception of Varuṇa seems to have been the encompassing sky. It has, however, become obscured, because it dates from an earlier age. For it goes back to the Indo-Iranian period at least, since the Ahura Mazda (the wise spirit) of the Avesta agrees with the Asura Varuṇa in character, though not in name. It may even be older still; for the name Varuṇa is perhaps identical with the Greek *οὐρανός sky*. In any case, the word appears to be derived from the root **vṛ** *cover* or *encompass*.

vii. 86. **Metre: Triṣṭubh.**

१ धीरा त्वस्य महिना जनूंषि
वि यस्तस्तम्भ रोदसी चिदुर्वी ।
प्र नाकमृष्वं नुनुदे बृहन्तं
द्विता नक्षत्रं पप्रथच्च भूम ॥

धीरा । तु । अस्य । महिना । जनूंषि ।
वि । यः । तस्तम्भ । रोदसी इति । चित् ।
उर्वी इति ।
प्र । नाकम् । ऋष्वम् । नुनुदे । बृहन्तम् ।
द्विता । नक्षत्रम् । पप्रथत् । च । भूम ॥

1 dhī́rā tú asya mahinā́ janū́ṃṣi,
ví yás tastámbha ródasī cid urvī́.

Intelligent indeed are the generations by the might of him who has propped asunder even the two wide

**prá nā́kam ṛṣvám̐ nunude bṛh-
ántam,
dvitā́ nákṣatram̐; paprā́thac ca
bhū́ma.**

worlds. He has pushed away the high, lofty firmament and the day-star as well; and he spread out the earth.

dhī́rā: cp. 7 c, **ácetayad acítaḥ**; and vii. 60, 6, **acetásam̐ cic cilayanti dákṣaiḥ** *they with their skill make even the unthinking think.* **asya** = Váruṇasya. **mahinā́** = **mahimnā́** (see 90, 2, p. 69). Varuṇa (as well as other gods) is several times said to hold apart heaven and earth (e. g. vi. 70, 1), which were supposed to have originally been united. **prá nunude**: pushed away from the earth; cp. vii. 99, 2 of Viṣṇu: **úd astabhnā nā́kam ṛṣvám̐ bṛhántam** *thou didst prop up the high lofty firmament.* **nā́kam**: means the *vault of heaven*; there is nothing to show that it ever has the sense of *sun* which Sāyaṇa gives it here. Sāyaṇa also makes the verb **nunude**, though unaccented, depend on the relative in b; c is, however, equivalent to a relative clause (cp. ii. 12, 5 b. 8 d). **nákṣatram**: in the sing. this word regularly refers to the sun, in the pl. to the stars. Varuṇa and other gods are often said to have raised the sun to, or to have placed it in, heaven. **dvitā́**: *doubly* to be taken with **nunude**; that is, he raised up from the earth both the vault of heaven and the sun. **paprā́that**: ppf. of **prath** (140, 6); accented because it begins a new sentence. **bhū́ma**: note the difference between **bhū́man** n. *earth* and **bhūmán** m. *multitude* (p. 259).

२ उत स्वया तन्वा३ सं वदे तत्
कदा न्व१न्तर्वरुणे भुवानि ।
किं मे हव्यमहृणानो जुषेत
कदा मृळीकं सुमना अभि ख्यम् ॥

उत । स्वया । तन्वा । सम् । वदे । तत् ।
कदा । नु । अन्तः । वरुणे । भुवानि ।
किम् । मे । हव्यम् । अहृणानः । जुषेत ।
कदा । मृळीकम् । सुऽमनाः । अभि ।
ख्यम् ॥

2 **utá svā́yā tanúā sám̐ vade tát:
kadā́ nú antár Váruṇe bhuvāni?
kím̐ me havyám áhṛṇāno juṣeta?
kadā́ mṛḷīkám̐ sumánā abhí
khyam?**

And I converse thus with myself: 'when, pray, shall I be in communion with Varuṇa? What oblation of mine would he, free from wrath, enjoy? When shall I, of good cheer, perceive his mercy?'

sváyā tanvā: *with my own body* = *with myself* (cp. p. 450, 2 *b*). **nv àntár**; *loc. cit.* Note that when a final original r appears in the Saṃhitā text, it is represented by Visarjanīya only in the Pada text; on the other hand, **antáḥ** in vii. 71, 5 appears as **antár íti**; *within Varuṇa* = *united with Varuṇa.* **bhuvāni**: 1. s. sb. root ao. of **bhū** *be.* **khyam**: 1. s. inj. a ao. of **khyā**.

३ पृच्छे तदेनो वरुण दिदृक्षू-	पृच्छे । तत् । एनः । वरुण । दिदृक्षु ।
पो एमि चिकितुषो विपृच्छम् ।	उपो इति । एमि । चिकितुषः । विऽपृच्छम् ।
समानमिन्मे कवयश्चिदाहुर्	समानम् । इत् । मे । कवयः । चित् । आहुः ।
अयं ह तुभ्यं वरुणो हृणीते ॥	अयम् । ह । तुभ्यम् । वरुणः । हृणीते ॥

3 pṛché tád éno, Varuṇa, didṛ́kṣu;	*I ask about that sin, O Varuṇa, with a desire to find out; I approach the wise in order to ask;*
úpo emi cikitúṣo vipṛ́cham;	
samānám ín me kaváyaś cid āhur:	*the sages say one and the same thing to me: 'this Varuṇa is wroth with thee.'*
ayáṃ ha túbhyaṃ Váruṇo hṛṇīte.	

pṛché: 1. s. pr. ind. Ā. of **prach** *ask.* **didṛ́kṣu** is a difficulty: it has been explained as L. pl. of a supposed word **didṛ́ś**, a very improbable formation = *among those who see*; also as N. s. of a ds. adj. **didṛ́kṣu**, with wrong accent (p. 461 *f*) and wrong Sandhi, for **didṛ́kṣur** (**úpo**) = *desirous of seeing* (i. e. *finding out*). It is probably best, following the Padapāṭha, to take the word as n. of the ds. adj. used adverbially (with adv. shift of accent) = *with a desire to see*, i. e. *find out.* **úpo** = **úpa u** (24). **cikitúṣas**: A. pl. of the pf. pt. of **cit** *perceive.* **vi-pṛ́cham** acc. inf. (167, 2 *a*). **hṛṇīte**: 3. s. pr. Ā. of **hṛ** *be angry*; w. dat. (200 *l*).

४ किमाग आस वरुण ज्येष्ठं	किम् । आगः । आस । वरुण । ज्येष्ठम् ।
यत्स्तोतारं जिघांससि सखायम् ।	यत् । स्तोतारम् । जिघांससि । सखायम् ।

प्र तन्मे वोचो दूळभ स्वधावो — प्र । तत् । मे । वोचः । दुःऽदभ । स्वधाऽवः ।
ऽव त्वानेना नमसा तुर इयाम् ॥ — अव । त्वा । अनेनाः । नमसा । तुरः । इयाम् ॥

4 **kím ā́ga āsa, Varuṇa, jyéṣṭhaṃ** — *What has been that chief sin,*
yát stotā́raṃ jíghāṃsasi sákhāyam ? — *O Varuṇa, that thou desirest to slay thy praiser, a friend? Pro-*
prá tán me voco, dūḷabha svadhāvo : — *claim that to me, thou that art hard to deceive, self-dependent one : thee*
áva tvānenā́ námasā turá͜iyām. — *would I, free from sin, eagerly appease with adoration.*

jyéṣṭham = **jyăiṣṭham**, to be pronounced as a trisyllable (15, 1 *f*). **yát** : *that* as a cj. (p. 242). **jíghāṃsasi** : ds. of han *slay*. **prá vocas** : inj. ao. of vac *say*. **dūḷabha** : 49 *c*. **turá͜iyām** = **turáḥ iyām** (op. of i *go*), to be pronounced, with irr. secondary contraction (cp. 22 *a* ; 48 *a*), as **turéyām**. **áva** to be taken with **iyām** (cp. 5 a–c).

५ अव द्रुग्धानि पित्र्या सृजा नो — अव । द्रुग्धानि । पित्र्या । सृज । नः ।
ऽव या वयं चकृमा तनूभिः । — अव । या । वयम् । चकृम । तनूभिः ।
अव राजन्पशुतृपं न तायुं — अव । राजन् । पशुऽतृपम् । न । तायुम् ।
सृजा वत्सं न दाम्नो वसिष्ठम् ॥ — सृज । वत्सम् । न । दाम्नः । वसिष्ठम् ॥

5 **áva drugdhā́ni pítriā sṛjā no,** — *Set us free from the misdeeds*
áva yā́ vayáṃ cakṛmā́ tanū́bhiḥ. — *of our fathers, from those that we have committed by ourselves. Re-*
áva, rājan, paśutṛ́paṃ ná tāyuṃ, — *lease Vasiṣṭha, O King, like a cattle-stealing thief, like a calf from*
sṛjā́, vatsáṃ ná dā́mᵃno, Vásiṣṭham. — *a rope.*

áva sṛjā (metrically lengthened final, also in d) : note the different construction in a : acc. of object and dat. of prs. ; and in c d : acc. of prs. and abl. of that from which V. is set free. **drugdhā́ni** : pp.

of druh. cakṛmā́: metrical lengthening of final vowel tanū́bhis: in the sense of a ref. prn. ává sṛjā: i.e. from sin tāyum: as one releases (after he has expiated his crime) a thief who has been bound; cp. viii. 67, 14: té ná, Ā́dityāso, mumócata stenám baddhám iva *as such set us free, O Ādityas, like a thief who is bound.* dā́mnas: distinguish dā́man n. *bond* and dā́man n. *act of giving* from dāmán m. *giver* and *gift.*

६ न स स्वो दक्षो वरुण ध्रुतिः सा
सुरा मन्युर्विभीदको अचित्तिः ।
अस्ति ज्यायान्कनीयस उपारे
स्वप्नश्चनेदनृतस्य प्रयोता ॥

न । सः । स्वः । दक्षः । वरुण । ध्रुतिः । सा ।
सुरा । मन्युः । विऽभीदकः । अचित्तिः ।
अस्ति । ज्यायान् । कनीयसः । उपऽअरे ।
स्वप्नः । चन । इत् । अनृतस्य । प्रऽयोता ॥

6 ná sá svó dákṣo, Varuṇa, dhrú-
tiḥ sā́:
súrā manyúr vibhī́dako ácittiḥ;
ásti jyā́yān kánīyasa upāré;
svápnaś canéd ánṛtasya pra-
yotā́.

It was not my own intent, O Varuṇa, it was seduction: liquor, anger, dice, thoughtlessness; the elder is in the offence of the younger; not even sleep is the warder off of wrong.

The general meaning of this stanza is clear: the sin with which Varuṇa is angry has not been due to Vasiṣṭha's intention, but to seduction of one kind or another. The exact sense of three important words is, however, somewhat doubtful, because none of them occurs in any other passage. It can therefore be made out from the etymology and the context only. dhrútis: from the root dhru = dhvṛ (cp. 167 *b*, 9; 171, 2), which occurs at the end of one or two cds., as Varuṇa-dhrú-t *deceiving Varuṇa*; cp. also v. 12, 5: ádhūrṣata svayám eté vácobhir ṛjūyaté vṛjinā́ni bruvántaḥ *these have deceived themselves with their own words, uttering crooked things to the straightforward man.* Thus the meaning of dhrúti appears to be *deception, seduction.* The meaning of c depends on the interpretation of upāré. This word is naturally to be derived (in accordance with the analysis of the Pada text) from upa + ara (ṛ *go*). The cd. vb. úpa ṛ occurs two or three times, e. g. AV. vii. 106, 1: yád ásmṛti cakṛmá kím cid, upārimá cáraṇe *if through forgetfulness we have done anything, have offended in our conduct.* The sense of the noun would therefore be *offence*, the whole Pāda meaning: *the elder is* (involved) *in the* (= *is the cause of the*) *offence of the younger*, that is, an elder has led me, the younger, astray. The use of the loc. here is illustrated by vi. 71, 2: **yáḥ . . . prasavé . . . ási bhū́manaḥ** *who* (Savitṛ) *art in the stimulation of the world*, i. e. *art the cause of the stimulation of the world.* **prayotā́**: this word might be derived from **pra + yu** *join* or **pra + yu** *separate*; the latter occurs in the RV. in the sense of *drive away*, while the former does not occur in the RV., and later means *stir, mingle.* The probability is therefore in favour of the sense *warder off.* **caná** then would have the original sense of *not even* (pp. 229–30). **svápnas**: i.e. by producing evil dreams.

७ अरं दासो न मीळ्हुषे कराण्य-
हं देवाय भूर्णयेऽनागाः ।
अचेतयदचितो देवो अर्यो
गृत्सं राये कवितरो जुनाति ॥

अरम् । दासः । न । मीळ्हुषे । कराणि ।
अहम् । देवाय । भूर्णये । अनागाः ।
अचेतयत् । अचितः । देवः । अर्यः ।
गृत्सम् । राये । कविऽतरः । जुनाति ॥

7 **áraṃ, dāsó ná, mīḷhúṣe karāṇi**
aháṃ devā́ya bhū́rṇaye ánāgāḥ.
ácetayad acíto devó aryó;
gṛ́tsaṃ rāyé kavítaro junāti.

I will, like a slave, do service sinless to the bounteous angry god. The noble god made the thoughtless think; he, the wiser, speeds the experienced man to wealth.

mīḷhúṣe: dat. s. of **mīḍhvā́ṃs.** **karāṇi**: 1. s. sb. root ao. of **kṛ** *do*; to be taken with the adv. **áram** (p. 313, 4). **ácetayat**: see cit. **gṛ́tsam**: even the thoughtful man Varuṇa with his greater wisdom urges on. **rāyé**: final dat. (of **rái**), p. 314, 2. **junāti**: 3. s. pr. of **jū** *speed.*

८ अयं सु तुभ्यं वरुण स्वधावो
हृदि स्तोम उपश्रितश्चिदस्तु ।
शं नः क्षेमे शमु योगे नो अस्तु
यूयं पात स्वस्तिभिः सदा नः ॥

अयम् । सु । तुभ्यम् । वरुण । स्वधाऽवः ।
हृदि । स्तोमः । उपऽश्रितः । चित् । अस्तु ।
शम् । नः । क्षेमे । शम् । ऊं इति । योगे ।
नः । अस्तु ।
यूयम् । पात । स्वस्तिऽभिः । सदा । नः ॥

8 **ayám sú túbhyam, Varuṇa svadhāvo,**
hṛdí stóma upasritaś cid astu.
śám naḥ kṣéme, śám u yóge nŏ astu.
yuyam pāta suastíbhiḥ sádā naḥ.

Let this praise be well impressed on thy heart, O self-dependent Varuṇa. Let us have prosperity in possession, prosperity also in acquisition. Do ye protect us evermore with blessings.

túbhyam : dat. of advantage (p. 314, B 1). **astu naḥ :** p. 320 *f.* On d see note on vii. 61, 6.

MAṆḌŪKĀS

The following hymn, intended as a spell to produce rain, is a panegyric of frogs, who are compared during the drought to heated kettles, and are described as raising their voices together at the commencement of the rains like Brahmin pupils repeating the lessons of their teacher.

vii. 103. Metre: **Triṣṭubh ; 1. Anuṣṭubh.**

१ संवत्सरं शशयाना
ब्राह्मणा व्रतचारिणः।
वाचं पर्जन्यजिन्विताम्
प्र मण्डूका अवादिषुः॥

संवत्सरम्। शशयानाः।
ब्राह्मणाः। व्रतऽचारिणः।
वाचम्। पर्जन्यऽजिन्विताम्।
प्र। मण्डूकाः। अवादिषुः॥

1 samvatsarám śaśayānā́
brāhmaṇā́ vratacāríṇaḥ,
vā́cam Parjányajinvitām
prá maṇḍū́kā avādiṣuḥ.

The frogs having lain for a year, like *Brāhmans practising a vow, have uttered forth their voice roused by Parjanya.*

saṃvatsarám : acc. of duration of time (197, 2). **śaśayānā́s :** pf. pt. Ā. of **śī** *lie* (p. 155, f. n. 1). **brāhmaṇā́s :** i. e. like Brahmins. **vratacāríṇas :** i. e. *practising a vow* of silence. **Parjánya-jinvitām :** because the frogs begin to croak at the commencement of the rainy season ; on the accent see p. 456, 2 *a.* **avādiṣur :** iṣ ao. of vad (145, 1).

२ दिव्या आपो अभि यदेनमायन्
दृतिं न शुष्कं सरसी शयानम् ।
गवामह न मायुर्वत्सिनीनां
मण्डूकानां वग्नुरत्रा समेति ॥

दिव्याः । आपः । अभि । यत् । एनम् ।
आयन् ।
दृतिम् । न । शुष्कम् । सरसी इति ।
शयानम् ।
गवाम् । अह । न । मायुः । वत्सिनीनाम् ।
मण्डूकानाम् । वग्नुः । अत्र । सम् । एति ॥

2 **divyā́ ā́po abhí yád enam ā́yan,**
dŕ̥tiṃ ná śúṣkaṃ, sarasī́ śáyā-nam,
gávām áha ná māyúr vatsínī-nāṃ,
maṇḍū́kānāṃ vagnúr átrā sám eti.

When the heavenly waters came upon him lying like a dry leather-bag in a lake, then the sound of the frogs unites like the lowing of cows accompanied by calves.

divyā́ ā́paḥ: the rains. **enam**: collective = the frogs; cp. the sing. **maṇḍū́kaḥ** in 4 c used collectively. **ā́yan**: ipf. of **i** (p. 130). **sarasī́**: loc. of **sarasī́** according to the primary ī dec. (cp. p. 87). A dried-up lake is doubtless meant. **gávām**: 102, 2; p. 458, *c.* 1. **átrā** (metrically lengthened): here as corr. to **yád** (cp. p. 214).

३ यदीमेनाँ उशतो अभ्यवर्षीत्
तृष्यावतः प्रावृष्यागतायाम् ।
अख्खलीकृत्या पितरं न पुत्रो
अन्यो अन्यमुप वदन्तमेति ॥

यत् । ईम् । एनान् । उशतः । अभि ।
अवर्षीत् ।
तृष्याऽवतः । प्रावृषि । आऽगतायाम् ।
अख्खलीऽकृत्य । पितरम् । न । पुत्रः ।
अन्यः । अन्यम् । उप । वदन्तम् । एति ॥

3 **yád īm enām̐ uśató abhy ávar-ṣīt**
tr̥ṣyā́vataḥ, prāvŕ̥ṣi ā́gatāyām,
akhkhalīkŕ̥tyā, pitáraṃ ná pu-tró,
anyó anyám úpa vádantam eti.

When he has rained upon them the eager, the thirsty, the rainy season having come, one with a croak of joy approaches the other while he speaks, as a son (approaches) *his father.*

īm : see p. 220, 2. uśatás (pr. pt. A. pl. of vaś *desire*) : *longing* for rain. ávarṣīt : iṣ ao. of vṛṣ : if the subject were expressed it would be Parjanya. prāvṛ́ṣi : loc. abs. (see 205, 1 *b*). akhkhalīkṛ́tyā : see 184 *d* ; the final of this gd. may be regarded as retaining the original long vowel rather than metrically lengthening a short vowel, though it always appears with ă in the Pada text. anyás : i. e. maṇḍū́kas.

४ अन्यो अन्यमनु गृभ्णात्येनोर्
अपां प्रसर्गे यदमन्दिषाताम् ।
मण्डूको यदभिवृष्टः कनिष्कन्
पृश्निः संपृङ्क्ते हरितेन वाचम् ॥

अन्यः । अन्यम् । अनु । गृभ्णाति । एनोः ।
अपाम् । प्रऽसर्गे । यत् । अमन्दिषाताम् ।
मण्डूकः । यत् । अभिऽवृष्टः । कनिस्कन् ।
पृश्निः । सम्ऽपृङ्क्ते । हरितेन । वाचम् ॥

4 anyó anyám ánu gṛbhṇāti enor,
apā́ṃ prasargé yád ámandiṣātām.
maṇḍū́ko yád abhívṛṣṭaḥ kániṣkan,
pṛ́śniḥ saṃpṛṅkté háritena vā́cam.

One of the two greets the other when they have revelled in the discharge of the waters. When the frog, rained upon, leaps about, the speckled one mingles his voice with (that of) *the yellow one.*

enos : gen. du., *of them two* (112 *a*). gṛbhṇāti : 3. s. pr. of grabh. ámandiṣātām : 3. du. Ā. iṣ ao. of mand *exhilarate*. maṇḍū́kas : in a collective sense. kániṣkan : 3. s. inj. int. of skand *leap* (= kániṣkandt), see 174 *b*. Note that this form in the Pada text is kániskan, because in the later Sandhi s is not cerebralized before k (cp. 67). The use of the inj. with yád is rare. saṃ-pṛṅkté : 3. s. Ā. pr. of pṛc *mix*.

५ यदेषामन्यो अन्यस्य वाचं
शाक्तस्येव वदति शिक्षमाणः ।
सर्वं तदेषां समृधेव पर्व
यत्सुवाचो वदथनाध्यप्सु ॥

यत् । एषाम् । अन्यः । अन्यस्य । वाचम् ।
शाक्तस्यऽइव । वदति । शिक्षमाणः ।
सर्वम् । तत् । एषाम् । समृधाऽइव । पर्व ।
यत् । सुऽवाचः । वदथन । अधि । अपऽसु ॥

5 yád eṣām anyó aniásya vā́cam,
śāktásyeva vádati śíkṣamāṇaḥ,

When one of them repeats the speech of the other, as the learner

sárvam̥ tád eṣām̥ samṛ́dheva párva
yát suvā́co vádathanā́dhi apsú.

that of his teacher, all that of them is in unison like a lesson that eloquent ye repeat upon the waters.

eṣām̥ : cp. **enos** in 4 a. **samṛ́dhā** : the interpretation of c is uncertain because of the doubt as to the form and meaning of this word, and because of the many senses of **párva**. It has accordingly been very variously explained. The above rendering is perhaps the most probable. **samṛ́dhā** : inst. of **samṛ́dh**, lit. *growing together*, then *unison, harmony*. **párvan**, *joint*, then a *section* in Vedic recitation. Thus c would be an explanation of b, the voices of the frogs sounding together like those of pupils reciting a lesson after their teacher. **vádathana** : see p. 125, f. n. 3; change, as often, from 3. prs. to 2. **ádhi** : 176, 2 *a* (p. 209).

6 गोमायुरेको अजमायुरेकः
पृश्निरेको हरित एक एषाम् ।
समानं नाम बिभ्रतो विरूपाः
पुरुत्रा वाचं पिपिशुर्वदन्तः ॥

गोऽमायुः । एकः । अजऽमायुः । एकः ।
पृश्निः । एकः । हरितः । एकः । एषाम् ।
समानम् । नाम । बिभ्रतः । विऽरूपाः ।
पुरुऽत्रा । वाचम् । पिपिशुः । वदन्तः ॥

6 **gómāyur éko, ajámāyur ékaḥ;**
pṛ́śnir éko; hárita éka eṣām.
samānám̥ nā́ma bíbhrato vi-rūpāḥ.
purutrā́ vā́cam̥ pipiśur vád-antaḥ.

One lows like a cow, one bleats like a goat; one is speckled, one of them is yellow. Bearing a common name, they have different colours. In many ways they adorn their voice in speaking.

gómāyus : cp. 2 c. **pṛ́śnis, háritas** : cp. 4 d. **samānám** : they are all called frogs, though they have different voices and colours. **bíbhratas** : N. pl. pr. pt. of **bhṛ** (p. 132). **purutrā́** : note that the suffix in words in which the vowel is always long in the Saṃhitā text (as in **devatrā́, asmatrā́**, &c.) is long in the Pada text also; while in others like **átra**, in which it is only occasionally lengthened metrically, the vowel is always short in that text. **pipiśur** : they modulate the sound of their voices (cp. a).

७ ब्राह्मणासो अतिरात्रे न सोमे — ब्राह्मणासः । अतिऽरात्रे । न । सोमे ।
सरो न पूर्णमभितो वदन्तः । — सरः । न । पूर्णम् । अभितः । वदन्तः ।
संवत्सरस्य तदहः परि ष्ठ — संवत्सरस्य । तत् । अहरिति । परि । स्थ ।
यन्मण्डूकाः प्रावृषीणं बभूव ॥ — यत् । मण्डूकाः । प्रावृषीणम् । बभूव ॥

7 **brāhmaṇā́so atirātré ná sóme,**
sáro ná pūrṇám abhíto, vádantaḥ,
saṃvatsarásya tád áhaḥ pári ṣṭha,
yán, maṇḍū́kāḥ, prāvṛṣíṇam babhū́va.

Like Brahmins at the over-night Soma sacrifice speaking around as it were a full lake, ye celebrate that day of the year which, O Frogs, has begun the rains.

atirātré: this is the name of a part of the Soma sacrifice in the ritual of the Yajurveda. Its performance lasted a day and the following night. Its mention in the RV. shows that it is ancient. **sáro ná**: *as it were a lake*, a hyperbolic expression for a large vessel filled with Soma. **abhítas**: 177, 1. **pári ṣṭha**: lit. *be around*, then *celebrate*; cp. **pári car** *go round*, then *attend upon*, *honour*; on the Sandhi, cp. 67 *c*. **prāvṛṣíṇam babhū́va**: *has become one that belongs to the rainy season.*

८ ब्राह्मणासः सोमिनो वाचमक्रत — ब्राह्मणासः । सोमिनः । वाचम् । अक्रत ।
ब्रह्म कृण्वन्तः परिवत्सरीणम् । — ब्रह्म । कृण्वन्तः । परिवत्सरीणम् ।
अध्वर्यवो घर्मिणः सिष्विदाना — अध्वर्यवः । घर्मिणः । सिस्विदानाः ।
आविर्भवन्ति गुह्या न के चित् ॥ — आविः । भवन्ति । गुह्याः । न । के । चित् ॥

8 brāhmaṇā́saḥ **somíno vā́cam akrata,**
bráhma kṛṇvántaḥ parivatsarī́ṇam.
adhvaryávo gharmíṇaḥ siṣvidānā́,
āvír bhavanti; gúhiā ná ké cit.

Soma-pressing Brahmins, they have raised their voice, offering their *yearly prayer. Adhvaryu priests, heated, sweating, they appear; none of them are hidden.*

brāhmaṇā́sas: **ná** need not be supplied (as in 1 b), the frogs being identified with priests. **somínas**: *celebrating a Soma sacrifice*, which expresses much the same as **sáro ná pūrṇám abhítaḥ** in 7 b. **vā́cam akrata**: cp. **vádantas** in 7 b. **akrata**: 3. pl. Ā. root ao. of **kṛ** (148, 1 b). **bráhma**: with b cp. 7 c, d. **gharmíṇas** is meant to be ambiguous: oppressed with the heat of the sun (frogs), *busied with hot milk* (priests). Here we already have a reference to the Pravargya ceremony in which milk was heated in a pot, and which was familiar in the ritual of the Brāhmaṇas. **siṣvidānā́s**: pf. pt. Ā. of **svid**; note that the cerebralized initial of the root is restored in the Pada text; cp. **kániṣkan** in 4 c. **āvís**: see p. 266, *b*.

९ देवहितिं जुगुपुर्द्वादशस्य
ऋतुं नरो न प्र मिनन्त्येते ।
संवत्सरे प्रावृष्यागतायां
तप्ता घर्मा अश्नुवते विसर्गम् ॥

देवऽहितिम् । जुगुपुः । द्वादशस्य ।
ऋतुम् । नरः । न । प्र । मिनन्ति । एते ।
संवत्सरे । प्रावृषि । आऽगतायाम् ।
तप्ताः । घर्माः । अश्नुवते । विऽसर्गम् ॥

9 **deváhitiṃ jugupur dvādaśásya:**
ṛtúm náro ná prá minanti eté.
saṃvatsaré, prāvṛ́ṣi ā́gatāyāṃ,
taptā́ gharmā́ aśnuvate visargám.

They have guarded the divine order of the twelvemonth: these men infringe not the season. In a year, the rain time having come, the heated milk-offerings obtain release.

deváhitim: on the accent see p. 456, 2 a. **jugupur**: pf. of **gup** *protect*. **dvādaśásya**: note the difference of accent and inflexion between **dvā́dasa** *twelve* (104) and **dvādaśá** *consisting of twelve, twelfth* (107); supply **saṃvatsarásya** from c. In the Aitareya Brāhmaṇa the year, **saṃvatsara**, is called **dvādaśa** *consisting of twelve* months and **caturviṃsa** *consisting of twenty-four* half-months. The gen. naturally depends on **deváhitim**, as being in the same Pāda. Prof. Jacobi understands **dvādasasya** as the ordinal *twelfth* supplying **mā́sasya** *month*, and making it depend on **ṛtúm** in the next Pāda. This interpretation is then used as evidence to show that the beginning of the year was held in the period of the RV. to commence with the rainy season at the time of the summer solstice, and taken in conjunction with another reference in the RV. to the rainy season at the period to furnish an argument for the very early date of the RV. But there is no trace here of any reference to the end of the year: **saṃvatsaré** in c denotes 'in the course of the year at the rainy season'. **náras**: here again no particle of comparison. **minanti**: from **mī** *damage*; cp. 7 c, d. **saṃvatsaré**: cp. 203, 3 *a*. **prāvṛ́ṣi ā́gatāyām**: loc. abs. as in 3 b. **taptā́ gharmā́ḥ** is meant to be ambiguous: *heated milk-pots* with reference to the priests (cp. **adhvaryávo gharmíṇaḥ** in 8 c) and *dried up cavities* with reference to the frogs (cp. **tṛṣyā́vatas** in 3 b). **aśnuvate** (3. pl. Ā. pr. of **aṃś** *obtain*) **visargám** *obtain release* or *discharge*, i. e. the milk-pots are emptied (and become cool), and the cavities in which the frogs are hidden let them out (and are cooled by the rain), cp. **āvír bhavanti** in 8 d.

१० गोमायुरदादजमायुरदात्
पृश्निरदाद्धरितो नो वसूनि ।
गवां मण्डूका ददतः शतानि
सहस्रसावे प्र तिरन्त आयुः ॥

गोऽमायुः । अदात् । अजऽमायुः । अदात् ।
पृश्निः । अदात् । हरितः । नः । वसूनि ।
गवाम् । मण्डूकाः । ददतः । शतानि ।
सहस्रऽसावे । प्र । तिरन्ते । आयुः ॥

10 **gómāyur adād, ajámāyur adāt,**
pṛśnir adād, dhárito no vásūni.
gavām maṇḍū́kā dadataḥ śatani,
sahasrasāvé prá tiranta ā́yuḥ.

He that lows like a cow has given us riches, he that bleats like a goat has given them, *the speckled one has given* them, and *the yellow one. The frogs giving* us *hundreds of cows prolong our life in a thousandfold Soma pressing.*

gómāyus &c. (cp. 6 a): the various kinds of frogs are here represented as taking the place of liberal institutors of sacrifice in giving bountiful gifts. **dádatas**: N. pl. of pr. pt. of **dā** *give* (cp. 156). **sahasrasāvé**: loc. of time like **saṃvatsaré** in 9 c; the term probably refers to a Soma sacrifice lasting a year with three pressings a day (amounting roughly to a thousand). d is identical with iii. 53, 7 d.

VÍŚVE DEVĀ́Ḥ

The comprehensive group called **Víśve deváḥ** or All-Gods occupies an important position, for at least forty entire hymns are addressed to them. It is an artificial sacrificial group intended to include all the gods in order that none should be left out in laudations meant for the whole pantheon. The following hymn though traditionally regarded as meant for the Viśve devāḥ is a collection of riddles, in which each stanza describes a deity by his characteristic marks, leaving his name to be guessed. The deities meant in the successive stanzas are: 1. Soma, 2. Agni, 3. Tvaṣṭṛ, 4. Indra, 5. Rudra, 6. Pūṣan, 7. Viṣṇu, 8. Aśvins, 9. Mitra-Varuṇa, 10. Aṅgirases.

viii. 29. Metre: Distichs of a Jagatī + Gāyatrī (p. 445, *a.*).

१ बभ्रुरेको विषुणः सूनरो युवा- ञ्ज्यङ्क्ते हिरण्ययम् ॥	बभ्रुः । एकः । विषुणः । सूनरः । युवा । अञ्जि । अङ्क्ते । हिरण्ययम् ॥
1 babhrúr éko víṣuṇaḥ sūnáro yúvā. añjí aṅkte hiraṇyáyam.	*One is brown, varied in form, bountiful, young. He adorns himself with golden ornament.*

babhrús: this epithet is distinctive of Soma, to whom it is applied eight times, while it otherwise refers to Agni only once, and to Rudra in one hymn only (ii. 33). It alludes to the colour of the juice, otherwise described as aruṇá *ruddy*, but most often as hári *tawny*. **víṣuṇas**: probably referring to the difference between the plant and the juice, and the mixtures of the latter with milk and honey. **yúvā**: here and in a few other passages Soma, like Agni, is called a youth, as produced anew every day. **añjí**: cognate acc. (p. 300, 4). **aṅkte**: 3. s. Ā. of añj *anoint*, with middle sense *anoints himself*. **hiraṇyáyam**: cp. ix. 86, 43, **mádhunā abhí añjate . . hiraṇyapāvā́ āsu gṛbhṇate** *they anoint him* (Soma) *with mead; purifying with gold, they seize* him *in them* (the waters), in allusion to fingers with golden rings.

२ योनिमेक आ ससाद द्योतनो- ऽन्तर्देवेषु मेधिरः ॥	योनिम् । एकः । आ । ससाद । द्योतनः । अन्तः । देवेषु । मेधिरः ॥
2 yónim éka ā́ sasāda dyótano, antár devéṣu médhiraḥ.	*One has, shining, occupied his receptacle, the wise among the gods.*

yónim: the sacrificial fireplace; cp. iii. 29, 10, **ayáṃ te yónir ṛtvíyo, yáto jātó árocathāḥ: táṃ jānánn, Agna, ā́ sīda** *this is thy regular receptacle, born from which thou didst shine: knowing it, Agni,* *occupy* it. **dyótanas**: the brightness of Agni is constantly dwelt on. **médhiras**: the wisdom of Agni is very frequently mentioned; in i. 142, 11 he is called **devó devéṣu médhiraḥ** *the wise god among the gods.*

३ वाशीमेको बिभर्ति हस्त आयसीम् वाशीम् । एकः । बिभर्ति । हस्ते । आयसीम् ।
अन्तर्देवेषु निध्रुविः ॥ अन्तः । देवेषु । निऽध्रुविः ॥

3 **vā́śīm éko bibharti hásta āya-sī́m,**
antár devéṣu nídhruviḥ.

One bears in his hand an iron axe, strenuous among the gods.

vā́śīm: this weapon is connected elsewhere only with Agni, the Ṛbhus, and the Maruts. But Agni cannot be meant because he has already been described in 2; while the Ṛbhus and the Maruts would only be referred to in the plural (cp. 10). But x. 53, 9 indicates sufficiently what god is here meant: **Tváṣṭā . . apásām apástamaḥ . . śíśīte nūnám paraśúm suāyasám** *Tvaṣṭṛ, most active of workers, now sharpens his axe made of good iron.* **nídhruvis**: *strenuous* as the artificer of the gods, a sense supported by **apástamas** in the above quotation.

४ वज्रमेको बिभर्ति हस्त आहितं वज्रम् । एकः । बिभर्ति । हस्ते । आऽहितम् ।
तेन वृत्राणि जिघ्नते ॥ तेन । वृत्राणि । जिघ्नते ॥

4 **vájram éko bibharti hásta ā́hi-taṃ:**
téna vṛtrā́ṇi jighnate.

One bears a bolt placed in his hand: with it he slays his foes.

ā́-hitam: pp. of **dhā** *place*; accent, p. 462, 13 *b*. **jighnate**: 3. s. pr. Ā. of **han** *slay*, see p. 432. **vájram**: this, as his distinctive weapon, shows that Indra is meant.

५ तिग्ममेको बिभर्ति हस्त आयुधं तिग्मम् । एकः । बिभर्ति । हस्ते । आयुधम् ।
शुचिरुग्रो जलाषभेषजः ॥ शुचिः । उग्रः । जलाषऽभेषजः ॥

5 **tigmám éko bibharti hásta ā́yu-dhaṃ,**
śúcir ugró jálāṣabheṣajaḥ.

One, bright, fierce, with cooling remedies, bears in his hand a sharp weapon.

ā́yudham: bow and arrows are usually the weapons of Rudra; in vii. 46 1 he is described by the epithets **sthirádhanvan** *having a strong bow*, **kṣipréṣu** *swift-arrowed*, **tigmā́yudha** *having a sharp weapon*. and in vii. 46, 3 his *lightning shaft*, **didyút**, is mentioned. **ugrás**: this epithet is several times applied to Rudra (cp. ii. 33). **jálāṣa-bheṣajas**: this epithet is applied to Rudra in i. 43, 4; Rudra is also called **jálāṣa**, and his hand is described as **jálāṣa** (as well as **bheṣajá**) in ii. 33, 7; these terms are applied to no other deity. b has the irregularity of two redundant syllables (p. 438, 2 *a*).

६ पथ एकः पीपाय तस्करो यथाँ
एष वेद निधीनाम् ॥

पथः । एकः । पीपाय । तस्करः । यथा ।
एषः । वेद । निऽधीनाम् ॥

6 **pathá ékaḥ pīpāya; táskaro yathā**
eṣá veda nidhīnā́m.

One makes the paths prosperous; like a thief he knows of treasures.

pathás: it is characteristic of Pūṣan (vi. 54) to be a knower and guardian of paths. **pīpāya**: pf., with lengthened red. vowel, from pi (= pyā) *make full* or *abundant*; cp. vi. 53, 4: **ví pathó vājasātaye cinuhí** *clear the paths for the gain of wealth* (addressed to Pūsan); and x. 59, 7: **dadātu púnaḥ Pūṣā́ pathíām yā́ suastíḥ** *let Pūṣan give us back the path that is propitious*. **táskaras**: to be taken with b.; like a thief he knows where hidden treasure is to be found; cp. vi. 48, 15 (addressed to Pūsan): **āvír gūḷhā́ vásū karat, suvédā no vásū karat** *may he make hidden wealth manifest, may he make wealth easy for us to find*; he also finds lost cattle; cp. vi. 54, 5–10. **yathā̃**: unaccented (p. 453, 8 B *d*); nasalized to avoid hiatus (p. 23, f. n. 1). **veda**: with gen. (202 A *c*). **nidhīnā́m**: accent (p. 458, 2 *a*); the final syllable to be pronounced dissyllabically.

७ त्रीण्येकं उरुगायो वि चक्रमे
यत्र देवासो मदन्ति ॥

त्रीणि । एकः । उरुऽगायः । वि । चक्रमे ।
यत्र । देवासः । मदन्ति ॥

7 **tríṇi éka urugāyó ví cakrame,**
yátra devā́so mádanti.

One, wide-pacing, makes three strides to where the gods are exhilarated.

trī́ṇi: cognate acc. (p. 300, 4) supply **vikrámaṇāni** (cp. **yásya urúṣu triṣú vikrámaṇeṣu**, i. 154, 2). The three strides are characteristic of Viṣṇu (see i. 154). **urugāyá**: an epithet distinctive of Viṣṇu (cp. i. 154, 1. 3. 5). **yátra**: to the place (the highest step) *where* (p. 240) the gods drink Soma (cp. i. 154, 5). b has the trochaic variety of the Gāyatrī cadence (see p. 439, 3 *a*, *α*).

८ विभिर्द्वा चरत एकया सह प्र प्रवासेव वसतः ॥	विऽभिः । द्वा । चरतः । एकया । सह । प्र । प्रवासाऽइव । वसतः ॥
8 **víbhir duā́ carata, ékayā sahá: prá pravāséva vasataḥ.**	*With birds two fare, together with one woman: like two travellers they go on journeys.*

víbhis: cp. i. 118, 5, **pári vām áśvāḥ pataṃgā́, váyo vahantu aruṣā́ḥ** *let the flying steeds, the ruddy birds, drive you* (Aśvins) *round.* **dvā́ . . ékayā sahá**: the two Aśvins with their one companion, Sūryā; cp. *l. c.*; **ā́ vāṃ ráthaṃ yuvatís tiṣṭhad . ., duhitā́ Sū́ryasya** *the maiden, the daughter of the Sun, mounted your car*; also v. 73, 5: **ā́ yád vāṃ Sūryā́ ráthaṃ tíṣṭhat** *when Sūryā mounted your car.* **prá vasatas**: *they go on a journey* in traversing the sky in their car. **pravāsā́**: this word occurs here only, apparently in the sense of *one who is abroad on travels* (like the post-Vedic **pravāsin**); in the Sūtras and in classical Sanskrit it means *sojourn abroad.* Some scholars regard **pravāséva** as irr. contraction for **pravāsám iva**: *they travel as it were on a journey.*

९ सदो द्वा चक्राते उपमा दिवि सम्राजा सर्पिरासुती ॥	सदः । द्वा । चक्राते इति । उपऽमा । दिवि । सम्ऽराजा । सर्पिरासुती इति सर्पिःऽआसुती ॥
9 **sádo duā́ cakrāte upamā́ diví: samrā́jā sarpírāsutī.**	***Two, as highest, have made for themselves a seat in heaven: two sovereign kings who receive melted butter as their draught.***

samrā́jā, as N. du., is applied to Mitra-Varuṇa exclusively. **cakrāte**: 3. du. pf. Ā. of **kṛ** with middle sense, *make for oneself*. **upamā́**: N. du. in apposition to **dvā́**, further explained by **samrā́jā**.

१० अर्चन्त एके महि साम मन्वत अर्चन्तः । एके । महि । साम । मन्वत ।
तेन सूर्यमरोचयन् ॥ तेन । सूर्यम् । अरोचयन् ॥

10 **árcanta éke máhi sā́ma manvata:** *Singing, some thought of a great chant: by it they caused the sun to shine.*
téna sū́ryam arocayan.

árcantas: singing is characteristic of the Aṅgirases; e.g. i. 62, 2, **sā́ma yénā .. árcanta Áṅgiraso gā́ ávindan** *the chant by which the Aṅgirases, singing, found the cows*; the Maruts are described in x. 78, 5 as **viśvárūpā Áṅgiraso ná sā́mabhiḥ** *manifold with chants like the Aṅgirases.* The Aṅgirases again are those **yá ṛténa sū́ryam árohayan diví** *who by their rite caused the sun to mount to heaven* (x. 62, 3). Sāyaṇa and some other interpreters think that the Atris are meant. But nothing is ever said of the singing or the chants of the Atris. Again, though in one hymn (v. 40) it is said in the last stanza that the Atris found the sun: **yáṃ vái sū́ryaṃ Svàrbhānus támasā́ ávidhyad, Átrayas tám ánv avindan** *the Atris found the sun which Svarbhānu had assailed with darkness* (9), this is only a repetition of what is attributed to Atri in the sing.: **gūḷháṃ sū́ryaṃ támasā .. bráhmaṇā avindad Átriḥ** *Atri by prayer found the sun hidden by darkness* (6) and **Átriḥ sū́ryasya diví cákṣur ā́dhāt** *Atris placed the eye of the sun in heaven* (8); and in the AV. and the ŚB., it is Atri (not the Atris) who performed a similar act. Thus even this deed is not characteristic of the Atris (plural), but at most of Atri (singular). The Aṅgirases must therefore undoubtedly be meant here. **éke**: the pl. is here used to express an indefinite group beside **ékas** and **dvā́** in the rest of the hymn (cp. 105). **manvata**: 3. pl. ipf. Ā. (without augment) of **man** *think*. **arocayan**: ipf. cs. of **ruc** *shine*.

SÓMA

As the Soma sacrifice formed the centre of the ritual of the RV., the god Soma is one of the most prominent deities. With rather more than 120 hymns (all those in Maṇḍala ix, and about half a dozen in others) addressed to him, he comes next to Agni (i. 1) in importance. The anthropomorphism of his character is less developed than that of Indra or Varuṇa because the plant and its juice are constantly present to the mind of the poet. Soma has terrible and sharp weapons, which he grasps in his hand; he wields a bow and a thousand-pointed shaft. He has a car which is heavenly, drawn by a team like Vāyu's. He is also said to ride on the same car as Indra. He is the best of charioteers. In about half a dozen hymns he is associated with Indra, Agni, Pūṣan, and Rudra respectively as a dual divinity. He is sometimes attended by the Maruts, the close allies of Indra. He comes to the sacrifice and receives offerings on the sacred grass.

The Soma juice, which is intoxicating, is frequently termed **mádhu** or *sweet draught*, but oftenest called índu *the bright drop*. The colour of Soma is brown (**babhrú**), ruddy (**aruṇá**), or more usually tawny (**hári**). The whole of the ninth book consists of incantations chanted over the tangible Soma, while the stalks are being pounded by stones, the juice passes through a woollen strainer, and flows into wooden vats, in which it is offered to the gods on the litter of sacred grass (**barhís**). These processes are overlaid with confused and mystical imagery in endless variation. The pressing stones with which the shoot (**aṃśú**) is crushed are called **ádri** or **grávan**. The pressed juice as it passes through the filter of sheep's wool is usually called **pávamāna** or **punāná** *flowing clear*. This purified (unmixed) Soma is sometimes called **śuddhá** *pure*, but much oftener **śukrá** or **śúci** *bright*; it is offered almost exclusively to Vāyu or Indra. The filtered Soma flows into jars (**kaláśa**) or vats (**dróṇa**), where it is mixed with water and also with milk, by which it is sweetened. The verb **mṛj** *cleanse* is used with reference to this addition of water and milk. Soma is spoken of as having three kinds of admixture (**āśír**): milk (**gó**), sour milk (**dádhi**), and barley (**yáva**). The admixture being alluded to as a garment or bright robe, Soma is described as 'decked with beauty'. Soma is pressed three times a day: the Ṛbhus are invited to the evening pressing, Indra to the midday one, which is his exclusively, while the morning libation is his first drink. The three abodes (**sadhástha**) of Soma which are mentioned probably refer to three tubs used in the ritual.

Soma's connexion with the waters, resulting from the admixture, is expressed in the most various ways. He is the drop that grows in the waters; he is the embryo of the waters or their child; they are his mothers or his sisters; he is lord and king of streams; he produces waters and causes heaven and earth to rain. The sound made by the trickling Soma is often alluded to, generally in hyperbolical language, with verbs meaning to roar or bellow, or even thunder. He is thus commonly called a bull among the waters, which figure as cows. Soma is moreover swift, being often compared with a steed, sometimes with a bird flying to the wood. Owing to his yellow colour Soma's brilliance is the physical aspect most dwelt upon by the poets. He is then often likened to or associated with the sun.

The exhilarating power of Soma led to its being regarded as a divine drink bestowing immortal life. Hence it is called amṛ́ta *draught of immortality.* All the gods drink Soma; they drank it to gain immortality; it confers immortality not only on gods, but on men. It has, moreover, medicinal powers: Soma heals whatever is sick, making the blind to see and the lame to walk. Soma also stimulates the voice, and is called 'lord of speech'. He awakens eager thought: he is a generator of hymns, a leader of poets, a seer among priests. Hence his wisdom is much dwelt upon; thus he is a wise seer, and he knows the races of the gods.

The intoxicating effect of Soma most emphasized by the poets is the stimulus it imparts to Indra in his conflict with hostile powers. That Soma invigorates Indra for the fight with Vṛtra is mentioned in innumerable passages. Through this association Indra's warlike exploits and cosmic actions come to be attributed to Soma independently. He is a victor unconquered in fight, born for battle. As a warrior he wins all kinds of wealth for his worshippers.

Though Soma is several times regarded as dwelling or growing on the mountains (like Haoma in the Avesta), his true origin and abode are regarded as in heaven. Soma is the child of heaven, is the milk of heaven, and is purified in heaven. He is the lord of heaven; he occupies heaven, and his place is the highest heaven. Thence he was brought to earth. The myth embodying this belief is that of the eagle that brings Soma to Indra, and is most fully dealt with in the two hymns iv. 26 and 27. Being the most important of herbs, Soma is said to have been born as the lord (páti) of plants, which also have him as their king; he is a lord of the wood (vánaspáti), and has generated all plants. But quite apart from his connexion with herbs, Soma is, like other leading gods, called a king: he is a king of rivers; a king of the whole earth; a king or father of the gods; a king of gods and mortals. In a few of the latest hymns of the RV. Soma begins to be mystically identified with the moon; in the AV. Soma several times means the moon; and in the Brāhmaṇas this identification has already become a commonplace.

We know that the preparation and the offering of Soma (the Avestan Haoma) was already an important feature of Indo-Iranian worship. In both the RV. and the Avesta it is stated that the stalks were pressed, that the juice was yellow, and was mixed with milk; in both it grows on mountains, and its mythical home is in heaven, whence it comes down to earth; in both the Soma draught has become a mighty god and is called a king; in both there are many other identical mythological traits relating to Soma.

It is possible that the belief in an intoxicating divine beverage, the home of which was in heaven, goes back to the Indo-European period. It must then have been regarded as a kind of honey mead (Skt. mádhu, Gk. *μέθυ*, Anglo-Saxon *medu*).

The name of Soma (= Haoma) means *pressed juice*, being derived from the root su (= Av. hu) *press*.

viii. 48. Metre: Triṣṭubh; 5. Jagatī.

१ स्वादोरभक्षि वयसः सुमेधाः
स्वाध्यो वरिवोवित्तरस्य ।
विश्वे यं देवा उत मर्त्यासो
मधु ब्रुवन्तो अभि संचरन्ति ॥

स्वादोः । अभक्षि । वयसः । सुऽमेधाः ।
सुऽआध्यः । वरिवोवित्ऽतरस्य ।
विश्वे । यम् । देवाः । उत । मर्त्यासः ।
मधु । ब्रुवन्तः । अभि । सम्ऽचरन्ति ॥

1 svādór abhakṣi váyasaḥ sumedhā́ḥ
suādhío varivovíttarasya,
víśve yáṃ devā́ utá mártiāso,
mádhu bruvánto, abhí saṃcáranti.

Wisely I have partaken of the sweet food that stirs good thoughts, best banisher of care, to which all gods and mortals, calling it honey, come together.

ábhakṣi: 1. s. Ā. s ao. of bhaj *share*; with partitive gen. (202 A c). sumedhā́s: appositionally, *as a wise man*; svādhyàs: gen. of svādhī́ (declined like rathī́, p. 85, f. n. 4). yám: m. referring to the n. váyas, as if to sóma. abhí saṃcáranti: p. 469, B *a*.

२ अन्तश्च प्रागा अदितिर्भवास्य्
अवयाता हरसो दैव्यस्य ।
इन्दविन्द्रस्य सख्यं जुषाणः
श्रौष्टीव धुरमनु राय ऋध्याः ॥

अन्तरिति । च । प्र । अगाः । अदितिः ।
भवासि ।
अवऽयाता । हरसः । दैव्यस्य ।
इन्दो इति । इन्द्रस्य । सख्यम् । जुषाणः ।
श्रौष्टीऽइव । धुरम् । अनु । राये । ऋध्याः ॥

2 antáś ca prā́gā, Áditir bhavāsi,
avayātā́ háraso dáiviasya.
Índav, Índrasya sakhiáṃ juṣāṇáḥ,
śráuṣṭīva dhúram, ánu rāyá ṛdhyāḥ.

If thou hast entered within, thou shalt be Aditi, appeaser of divine wrath. Mayest thou, O Indu, enjoying the friendship of Indra, like an obedient mare the pole, advance us to wealth.

antáś: cp. note on vii. 86, 2 b. **Soma is here addressed. prágās**: the Padapāṭha analysis of this as **prá ágāḥ** is evidently wrong, because in a principal sentence it must be **prá agāḥ** (p. 468, 20) or in a subordinate one **pra-ágāḥ** (p. 469, 20 B); here it is the latter, because of **ca** = *if* (p. 229, 3). **Áditis**: because Aditi releases from sin (e. g. **anāgāstvám no Áditiḥ kṛṇotu** *may Aditi produce sinlessness for us*, i. 162, 22); that is, may Soma purify us within. **Índav**: vocatives in **o** are always given as Pragṛhya in the Pada text (**o íti**) even though their Sandhi before vowels may be **av** or **a** in the Saṃhitā text; cp. note on ii. 33, 3 b. **śráuṣṭī**: this word occurs only here, and its meaning is uncertain; the most probable sense is *obedient mare*. **rāyé**: this analysis of the Padapāṭha makes the construction doubtful because an acc. is wanted as parallel to **dhúram**; **nas** may be supplied; then the sense would be: 'as a willing mare advances the yoke (of a car), so mayst thou advance (us or the yoke of the sacrifice) for the attainment of wealth.' **ṛdhyās**: root ao. op. of **ṛdh** *thrive*.

3 अपाम सोमममृता अभूमा-
गन्म ज्योतिरविदाम देवान् ।
किं नूनमस्मान्कृणवदरातिः
किमु धूर्तिरमृत मर्त्यस्य ॥

अपाम । सोमम् । अमृताः । अभूम ।
अगन्म । ज्योतिः । अविदाम । देवान् ।
किम् । नूनम् । अस्मान् । कृणवत् । अरातिः ।
किम् । ऊं इति । धूर्तिः । अमृत । मर्त्यस्य ॥

3 **ápāma sómam; amṛ́tā abhūma;**
áganma jyótir; **ávidāma devā́n.**
kíṃ nūnám **asmā́n kṛṇavad á-**
rātiḥ?
kím u dhūrtír, amṛta, márti-
asya?

We have drunk Soma; we have become immortal; we have gone to the light; we have found the gods. What can hostility now do to us, and what the malice of mortal man, O immortal one?

This stanza describes the mental exaltation produced by drinking Soma. Note the use of the aorist four times and its characteristic sense (p. 345, C.). **ápāma**: root ao. of pā *drink*. **abhūma**: root ao. of bhū *become*. **áganma**: root ao. of gám *go*. **jyótis**: acc. of the goal (197 A 1). **ávidāma**: a ao. of 2. vid *find*. **kṛṇavat**: 3. s. pr. sb. of **kṛ** *do* (p. 134). **amṛta**: Soma.

४ शं नो भव हृद आ पीत इन्दो
पितेव सोम सूनवे सुशेवः ।
सखेव सख्य उरुशंस धीरः
प्र ण आयुर्जीवसे सोम तारीः ॥

शम् । नः । भव । हृदे । आ । पीतः ।
इन्दो इति ।
पिताऽइव । सोम । सूनवे । सुऽशेवः ।
सखाऽइव । सख्ये । उरुऽशंस । धीरः ।
प्र । नः । आयुः । जीवसे । सोम । तारीः ॥

4 śaṃ no bhava hṛdá ā́ pītá, Indo;
pitéva, Soma, sūnáve suśévaḥ,
sákheva sákhya, uruśaṃsa, dhī́raḥ,
prá ṇa ā́yur jīváse, Soma, tārīḥ.

Do good to our heart when drunk, O Indu; kindly like a father, O Soma, to his son, thoughtful like a friend to his friend, O far-famed one, prolong our years that we may live, O Soma.

śáṃ hṛdé *refreshing to the heart* occurs several times; the emphasizing pcl. ā́ is here added to the dat. prá ṇaḥ: Sandhi, 65 c. jīváse: dat. inf. of jīv *live*. tārīs: iṣ ao. inj. from tṝ *cross*.

५ इमे मा पीता यशस उरुष्यवो
रथं न गावः समनाह पर्वसु ।
ते मा रक्षन्तु विस्रसश्चरित्राद्
उत मा स्रामाद्यवयन्त्विन्दवः ॥

इमे । मा । पीताः । यशसः । उरुष्यवः ।
रथम् । न । गावः । सम् । अनाह
पर्वऽसु ।
ते । मा । रक्षन्तु । विऽस्रसः । चरित्रात् ।
उत । मा । स्रामात् । यवयन्तु । इन्दवः ॥

5 imé mā pītā́ yaśása uruṣyávo,
rátham ná gā́vaḥ, sam anāha párvasu;
té mā rakṣantu visrásaś carítrād,
utá mā srā́mād yavayantu índavaḥ.

These glorious, freedom-giving (drops), *ye have knit me together in my joints like straps a car; let those drops protect me from breaking a leg and save me from disease.*

imé: supply índavas from d. yaśásas: p. 59. uruṣyávas: cp. varivovíttarasya in 1 b. anāha: this seems to be an irregular pf.

form from **nah** *bind* for **nanāha**; cp. **góbhiḥ sáṃnaddho asi** *thou art bound together with straps* (said of a car); another irregularity is the 2. pl. strong radical vowel (cp. 137, 2). **visrásas**: abl. inf. (of vi-sraṃs) with attracted object in the abl. **carítrād**: p. 337, 3 *a*. Note that Pāda c is a Triṣṭubh. **yavayantu**: cs. ipv. of yu *separate*. Change in c and d, as often, from 2. to 3. prs.

६ अग्निं न मा मथितं सं दिदीपः
प्र चक्षय कृणुहि वस्यसो नः ।
अथा हि ते मद आ सोम मन्ये
रेवाँ इव प्र चरा पुष्टिमच्छ ॥

अग्निम् । न । मा । मथितम् । सम् । दिदीपः ।
प्र । चक्षय । कृणुहि । वस्यसः । नः ।
अथ । हि । ते । मदे । आ । सोम । मन्ये ।
रेवान्ऽइव । प्र । चर । पुष्टिम् । अच्छ ॥

6 agníṃ ná mā mathitáṃ sáṃ didīpaḥ;
prá cakṣaya; kṛṇuhí vásyaso naḥ.
áthā hí te máda ā́, Soma, mánye
revā́m̐ iva. prá carā puṣṭím ácha.

Like fire kindled by friction inflame me; illumine us; make us wealthier. For then, in thy intoxication, O Soma, I regard myself as rich. Enter (into us) *for prosperity.*

didīpas: red. ao. inj. of dīp *shine*. **prá cakṣaya**: cs. of cakṣ *see* (cp. 3 b). **kṛṇuhí**: cp. p. 134; accented as beginning a sentence. **vásyasas**: A. pl. of vásyāṃs (cpv. of vásu, 103, 2 *a*). **áthā** (metrically lengthened): *then*, when inflamed by Soma. **revā́n**: predicatively with **mánye** (196 *a*), **iva** being sometimes added. **prá carā** (metrically lengthened): cp. 2 a, **antáś ca prā́gāḥ**. **puṣṭím ácha**: give us actual prosperity also.

७ इषिरेण ते मनसा सुतस्य
भक्षीमहि पित्र्यस्येव रायः ।

इषिरेण । ते । मनसा । सुतस्य ।
भक्षीमहि । पित्र्यस्यऽइव । रायः ।

सोम राजन्प्र ण आयूंषि तारीर्
अहानीव सूर्यो वासराणि ॥

सोम । राजन् । प्र । नः । आयूंषि । तारीः ।
अहानिऽइव । सूर्यः । वासराणि ॥

7 iṣiréṇa te mánasā sutásya
bhakṣīmáhi, pítriasyeva rāyáḥ.
Sóma rājan, prá ṇa ā́yūṃṣi tārīr,
áhānīva sū́rio vāsarā́ṇi.

Of thee pressed with devoted mind we would partake as of paternal wealth. King Soma, prolong our years as the sun the days of spring.

bhakṣīmáhi: s ao. op. of **bhaj** *share*. **pítryasya iva**: because Soma is regarded as a father, cp. 4 b. **Sóma rājan**: being a single voc. (rājan is in apposition), **Sóma** alone is accented (p. 465, 18). **prá ṇas**: cp. 4 d. **tārīs**: cp. 4 d. **áhāni**: 91, 2.

८ सोम राजन्मृळया नः स्वस्ति
तव स्मसि व्रत्या३स्तस्य विद्धि ।
अलर्ति दक्ष उत मन्युरिन्दो
मा नो अर्यो अनुकामं परा दाः ॥

सोम । राजन् । मृळय । नः । स्वस्ति ।
तव । स्मसि । व्रत्याः । तस्य । विद्धि ।
अलर्ति । दक्षः । उत । मन्युः । इन्दो इति ।
मा । नः । अर्यः । अनुऽकामम् । परा । दाः ॥

8 Sóma rājan, mṛḷáyā naḥ su-asti;
táva smasi vratíās: tásya vid-dhi.
álarti dákṣa utá manyúr, Indo;
mā́ nŏ aryó anukāmám párā dāḥ.

King Soma, be gracious to us for welfare; we are thy devotees: know that. There arise might and wrath, O Indu: abandon us not according to the desire of our foe.

mṛḷáyā: accented as beginning a sentence after an initial voc. (p. 467, 19 A *c*); final vowel metrically lengthened. **svastí**: shortened inst. s. (p. 80, f. n. 2) used adverbially like a dat.; this word though obviously = **su + asti** is not analysed in the Padapāṭha (cp. note on i. 1, 9). **smasi**: 1. pl. pr. of **as** *be*. **tásya**: with **vid**

know about, 202 A *c*. **viddhi**: 2. s. ipv. of **vid** *know*. **álarti**: 3. s. pr. int. of **ṛ** *go* (174 *a*). **aryás**: gen. of **arí** *foe* (cp. p. 81, f. n. 1; 99, 3), dependent on **anukāmám**; cp. **árātis** in 8 c. **dāḥ**: 2. s. root ao. inj. of **dā** *give*.

९ त्वं हि नस्तन्वः सोम गोपा
गात्रेगात्रे निषसत्था नृचक्षाः ।
यत्ते वयं प्रमिनाम व्रतानि
स नो मृळ सुषखा देव वस्यः ॥

त्वम् । हि । नः । तन्वः । सोम । गोपाः ।
गात्रेऽगात्रे । निऽससत्थ । नृऽचक्षाः ।
यत् । ते । वयम् । प्रऽमिनाम । व्रतानि ।
सः । नः । मृळ । सुऽसखा । देव । वस्यः ॥

9 **tuáṃ hí nas tanúas, Soma, gopá̄,**
gá̄tre-gātre niṣasátthā nṛcákṣāḥ.
yát te vayáṃ praminá̄ma vratá̄ni,
sá no mṛḷa suṣakhá̄, deva, vásyaḥ.

Since thou art the protector of our body, O Soma, thou as surveyor of men hast settled in every limb. If we infringe thine ordinances, then be gracious to us as our good friend, O god, for higher welfare.

tanúas: gen. of **tanú̄** *body*. **gopá̄s**: 97 A 2 (p. 79). **gá̄tre-gātre**: 189 C. **ni-ṣasatthā**: 2. s. pf. of **sad**; cerebralization of **s** (67 *a*); metrical lengthening of final **a** (p. 441, *a*). **yád**: p. 242, 3. **praminá̄ma**: sb. pr. of **pra-mī**. **sá**: p. 294, *b*. **su-ṣakhá̄**; on the cerebralization of **s** see 67 *b*; the accent is that of a Bv. (p. 455, *c a*); that of a Karmadhāraya (p. 455, *d* 1) is **su-ṣákhā**; the former is irregularly used in the latter sense. **vásyas**: the cpv. adj. is here used as an acc. adverb (p. 301, *b*).

१० ऋदूदरेण सख्या सचेय
यो मा न रिष्येद्धर्यश्व पीतः ।
अयं यः सोमो न्यधाय्यस्मे
तस्मा इन्द्रं प्रतिरमेम्यायुः ॥

ऋदूदरेण । सख्या । सचेय ।
यः । मा । न । रिष्येत । हरिऽअश्व ।
पीतः ।
अयम् । यः । सोमः । नि । अधायि ।
अस्मे इति ।
तस्मै । इन्द्रम् । प्रऽतिरम् । एमि । आयुः ॥

10 **ṛdūdáreṇa sákhiā saceya,**
yó mā ná ríṣyed, dhariaśva, pītáḥ.
ayám̐ yá sómo niádhāyi asmé,
tásmā Índram̐ pratíram emi áyuḥ.

I would associate with the wholesome friend who having been drunk would not injure me, O lord of the bays. For (the enjoyment of) *that Soma which has been deposited in us, I approach Indra to prolong our years.*

ṛdūdáreṇa: not analysed in the Padapāṭha (cp. note on ii. 33, 5 c); cp. **tvám̐ nas tanvò gopáḥ** in 9 *a*. **sákhyā:** 99, 2. **yó ná ríṣyet:** cp. 4 a. **haryaśva:** a characteristic epithet of Indra, who as the great Soma drinker is here addressed. **nyádhāyi:** 3. s. ao. ps. of **dhā** *put*; this (like **prágās** in 2 a) is irregularly analysed in the Padapāṭha as **ní ádhāyi** instead of **ni-ádhāyi** (p. 469, B). **asmé:** loc. (p. 104); Pragṛhya (26 *c*). **emi:** 1. s. pr. of **i** *go to* with acc. (197, A 1). **pratíram:** acc. inf. of **tṝ** *cross* (p. 336, 2 *a*) governing the acc. **áyus** (cp. 11 d). **tásmai:** *for the sake of that* = to obtain or enjoy that, final dat. (p. 314, B 2).

११ अप त्या अस्थुरनिरा अमीवा
निरत्रसन्तमिषीचीरभैषुः ।
आ सोमो अस्माँ अरुहद्विहाया
अगन्म यत्र प्रतिरन्त आयुः ॥

अप । त्याः । अस्थुः । अनिराः । अमीवाः ।
निः । अत्रसन् । तमिषीचीः । अभैषुः ।
आ । सोमः । अस्मान् । अरुहत । वि ऽहायाः ।
अगन्म । यत्र । प्रऽतिरन्ते । आयुः ॥

11 **ápa tyá asthur ánirā, ámīvā**
nír atrasan, támiṣīcīr ábhaiṣuḥ.
á sómŏ asmám̐ aruhad víhāyā:
áganma yátra pratiránta áyuḥ.

Those ailments have started off, diseases have sped away, the powers of darkness have been affrighted. Soma has mounted in us with might: we have gone to where men prolong their years.

asthur: 3. pl. root ao. of **sthā**. **atrasan:** the ipf. is here irregularly used beside the two aorists; cp. the uniform use of the ao. in 3. **támiṣīcīs:** this word, as occurring here only, is somewhat doubtful in sense; but it is probably a f. adj. formed from a stem in

anc added to **támis** (in **támis-rā** *darkness*): cp. 93 *a* and 95. The meaning is that a draught of Soma drives away disease and the powers of darkness (cp. 3 b). **ábhaiṣur**: s ao. of bhī *fear*. **á aru-hat**: a ao. of **ruh**: cp. the English phrase, 'go to the head'. **áganma yátra**: = 'we have arrived at the point when'. d is identical with i. 113, 16 d; it refers to the renewal of life at dawn.

१२ यो न इन्दुः पितरो हृत्सु पीतो	यः। नः। इन्दुः। पितरः। हृत्ऽसु। पीतः।
ऽमर्त्यो मर्त्याँ आविवेश।	अमर्त्यः। मर्त्यान्। आऽविवेश।
तस्मै सोमाय हविषा विधेम	तस्मै। सोमाय। हविषा। विधेम।
मृळीके अस्य सुमतौ स्याम॥	मृळीके। अस्य। सुऽमतौ। स्याम॥

12 **yó na índuḥ, pitaro, hṛtsú pītó,**
ámartio mártiām̐ āvivéśa,
tásmai Sómāya havíṣā vidh-ema:
mṛḷīké asya sumatáu siāma.

The drop drunk in our hearts, O Fathers, that immortal has entered us mortals, to that Soma we would pay worship with oblation; we would abide in his mercy and good graces.

pitaras: the Fathers, often spoken of as Soma-loving (**somyá**), are called to witness (cp. 13 a). **hṛtsú pītáḥ**: cp. 2 a **antáś ca prágāḥ** and 10 c **yáḥ sómo niádhāyi asmé**.

१३ त्वं सोम पितृभिः संविदानो	त्वम्। सोम। पितृऽभिः। सम्ऽविदानः।
ऽनु द्यावापृथिवी आ ततन्थ।	अनु। द्यावापृथिवी इति। आ। ततन्थ।
तस्मै त इन्दो हविषा विधेम	तस्मै। ते। इन्दो इति। हविषा। विधेम।
वयं स्याम पतयो रयीणाम्॥	वयम्। स्याम। पतयः। रयीणाम्॥

13 **tuám̐, Soma, pitṛ́bhiḥ saṃvid-ānó,**
ánu dyā́vāpṛthivī́ á tatantha.
tásmai ta, Indo, havíṣā vidh-ema:
vayám̐ siāma pátayo rayīṇā́m.

Thou, O Soma, uniting with the Fathers, hast extended thyself over Heaven and Earth. To thee as such, O Indu, we would pay worship with oblation: we would be lords of riches.

sam̥-vidānás: see x. 14, 4 b. ánu á tatantha: = hast become famous in. d is identical with iv. 50, 6 d.

१४ त्रातारो देवा अधि वोचता नो
मा नो निद्रा ईशत मोत जल्पिः ।
वयं सोमस्य विश्वह प्रियासः
सुवीरासो विदथमा वदेम ॥

त्रातारः । देवाः । अधि । वोचत । नः ।
मा । नः । निऽद्रा । ईशत । मा । उत ।
जल्पिः ।
वयम् । सोमस्य । विश्वह । प्रियासः ।
सुऽवीरासः । विदथम् । आ । वदेम ॥

14 trā́tāro devā, ádhi vocatā no.
mā́ no nidrā́ īśata, mótá jálpiḥ.
vayám̥ Sómasya viśváha priyā́sah,
suvī́rāso vidátham ā́ vadema.

Ye protecting gods, speak for us. Let not sleep overpower us, nor idle talk. We always dear to Soma, rich in strong sons, would utter divine worship.

trā́tāro devāḥ: accent, see note on 7 c. ádhi vocatā: 2. pl. ao. ipv. of vac *speak*; final vowel metrically lengthened; = *take our part, defend us* (nas, dat.). nidrā́: probably for nidrā́ḥ: see note on svadhā, x. 129, 5 d. īśata: 3. s. sb. Ā. (not inj., which correct, p. 372); with gen. nas (202, A a). nidrā́ and jálpiḥ probably refer to the vows of waking and silence in the rite of initiation (dīkṣā) to the Soma sacrifice. c d are identical with ii. 12, 15 c d excepting that there ta Indra takes the place of Sómasya. priyā́sas: with gen. (p. 322 C).

१५ त्वं नः सोम विश्वतो वयोधास
त्वं स्वर्विदा विशा नृचक्षाः ।
त्वं न इन्द ऊतिभिः सजोषाः
पाहि पश्चातादुत वा पुरस्तात् ॥

त्वम् । नः । सोम । विश्वतः । वयःऽधाः ।
त्वम् । स्वःऽवित् । आ । विश । नृऽचक्षाः ।
त्वम् । नः । इन्दो इति । ऊतिऽभिः । स
ऽजोषाः ।
पाहि । पश्चातात् । उत । वा । पुरस्तात् ॥

15 tuám̥ naḥ, Soma, viśváto vayodhā́s.
tuám̥ suarvíd. ā́ viśā nṛcákṣāḥ.

Thou art, O Soma, a giver of strength to us on all sides. Thou art a finder of light. Do thou, as

tuáṃ na, Inda, ūtíbhiḥ sajóṣāḥ
pāhí paśćātād utá vā purástāt.

surveyor of men, enter us. Do thou, O Indu, protect us behind and before with thine aids accordant.

ā viśā: final vowel metrically lengthened. **Inda:** for **Indav** (21 *b*); on the Padapāṭha, cp. note on 2 c. **ūtíbhis** to be taken with **sajóṣās.** **utá vā:** *or = and.*

FUNERAL HYMN

The RV. contains a group of five hymns (x. 14–18) concerned with death and the future life. From them we learn that, though burial was also practised, cremation was the usual method of disposing of the dead, and was the main source of the mythology relating to the future life. Agni conveys the corpse to the other world, the Fathers, and the gods. He is besought to preserve the body intact and to burn the goat which is sacrificed as his portion. During the process of cremation Agni and Soma are besought to heal any injury that bird, beast, ant, or serpent may have inflicted on the body. The way to the heavenly world is a distant path on which Savitṛ (i. 35) conducts and Pūṣan (vi. 54) protects the dead. Before the pyre is lighted, the wife of the dead man, having lain beside him, arises, and his bow is taken from his hand. This indicates that in earlier times his widow and his weapons were burnt with the body of the husband. Passing along by the path trodden by the Fathers, the spirit of the dead man goes to the realm of light, and meets with the Fathers who revel with Yama in the highest heaven. Here, uniting with a glorious body, he enters upon a life of bliss which is free from imperfections and bodily frailties, in which all desires are fulfilled, and which is passed among the gods, especially in the presence of the two kings Yama and Varuṇa.

x. 14. Metre: Triṣṭubh; 13. 14. 16. Anuṣṭubh; 15. Bṛhatī.

१ प॒रे॒यि॒वांसं॑ प्र॒वतो॑ म॒हीरनु॑	प॒रे॒यि॒ऽवांस॑म् । प्र॒ऽवतः॑ । म॒हीः । अनु॑ ।
ब॒हुभ्यः॒ पन्था॑मनुपस्पशा॒नम् ।	ब॒हुऽभ्यः॑ । पन्था॑म् । अ॒नु॒ऽप॒स्प॒शा॒नम् ।
वै॒व॒स्व॒तं सं॒गम॑नं॒ जना॑नां	वै॒व॒स्व॒तम् । स॒म्ऽगम॑नम् । जना॑नाम् ।
य॒मं राजा॑नं ह॒विषा॑ दुवस्य ॥	य॒मम् । राजा॑नम् । ह॒विषा॑ । दु॒व॒स्य॒ ॥

1 pareyivā́ṃsam praváto mahī́r ánu,
bahúbhyaḥ pánthām anupaspaśānám,
Vaivasvatáṃ saṃgamanaṃ jánānām,
Yamáṃ rā́jānaṃ havíṣā duvasya.

Him who has passed away along the mighty steeps and has spied out the path for many, him the son of Vivasvant, the assembler of people, Yama the king, do thou present with oblation.

a is a Jagatī (see p. 445, f. n. 7). **pareyivāṃsam**: pf. pt. act. **īyivā́ṃsam** (89 *a*) of **i** *go*, with **párā** *away*. **pravátas**: the steep paths leading to the highest heaven where Yama dwells; cp. ix. 113, 8, **yátra rā́jā Vaivasvató, yátrāvaródhanaṃ diváḥ . . tátra mā́m amṛ́taṃ kṛdhi** *where the king, the son of Vivasvant, and where the secret place of heaven is, there do thou* (Soma) *make me immortal.* **mahī́s**: A. pl. f. of **máh** *great.* **pánthām**: 97, 2 *a*. **Vaivasvatám**: Yama is in several passages called by this patronymic; cf. also 5 e, and x. 17, 1: **Yamásya mātā́, paryuhyámānā mahó jāyā́ Vívasvataḥ** *the mother of Yama being married* as *the wife of the great Vivasvant.* **bahúbhyas**: for the many that die and go to the other world. **anu-paspaśānám**: pf. pt. Ā. of **spaś** *see.* **saṃgámanam**: as *gathering* the dead *together* in his abode. **rā́jānam**: Yama is several times called a king, but never expressly a god. **duvasya**: addressed to the sacrificer.

२ यमो नो गातुं प्रथमो विवेद	यमः । नः । गातुम् । प्रथमः । विवेद ।
नैषा गव्यूतिरपभर्तवा उं ।	न । एषा । गव्यूतिः । अपऽभर्तवै । ऊं इति ।
यत्रा नः पूर्वे पितरः परेयुर्	यत्र । नः । पूर्वे । पितरः । पराऽईयुः ।
एना जज्ञानाः पथ्या३ अनु स्वाः ॥	एना । जज्ञानाः । पथ्याः । अनु । स्वाः ॥

2 Yamó no gātúṃ prathamó viveda:
náiṣā́ gávyūtir ápabhartavā́ u.
yátrā naḥ pū́rve pitáraḥ pareyúr,
enā́ jajñānā́ḥ pathiā́ ánu svā́ḥ.

Yama has first found out the way for us: this pasture is not to be taken away. Whither our former fathers have passed away, thither those that have been born since (pass away) *along their several paths.*

Yamás: a explains what is said of Yama in the preceding stanza. **viveda**: pf. of 2. **vid** *find*. **gávyūtis**: used figuratively to express the abode which Yama has found for those who die. **ápa-bhartavái**: dat. inf. with double accent (p. 452, 7); here it has a passive force (p. 335, *a*). b is most naturally to be taken as forming a hemistich with a, not as beginning a new sentence antecedent to **yátra**. The exact sense of cd is uncertain owing to the doubtful interpretation of ená and jajñānás. The former word is probably corr. to **yátra**, and the latter the frequent pf. pt. Ā. of jan *generate*. It might be from **jñā** *know* (from which, however, this pt. does not seem to occur elsewhere): the meaning would then be, 'knowing the way thereby (ená),' because Yama found it for them. **svás**: *by their own paths*, each by his own, each going by himself.

३ मातली कव्यैर्यमो अङ्गिरोभिर्
बृहस्पतिर्ऋक्वभिर्वावृधानः ।
यांश्च देवा वावृधुर्ये च देवान्
स्वाहान्ये स्वधयान्ये मदन्ति ॥

मातली । कव्यैः । यमः । अङ्गिरःऽभिः ।
बृहस्पतिः । ऋक्वऽभिः । ववृधानः ।
यान् । च । देवाः । ववृधुः । ये । च । देवान् ।
स्वाहा । अन्ये । स्वधया । अन्ये । मदन्ति ॥

3 **Mā́talī Kavyáir, Yamó Áṅgirobhir,**
Bŕhaspátir Ŕkvabhir vāvṛdhānáḥ,
yā́ṃś ca devā́ vāvṛdhúr, yé ca devā́n,
svā́hā anyé, svadháyānyé madanti.

Mātalī having grown strong with the Kavyas, Yama with the Aṅgirases, Bṛhaspati with the Ṛkvans, whom the gods have made strong and who (have made strong) *the gods, some rejoice in the call Svāhā, others in the offering to the dead.*

Mā́talī: mentioned only here; one of seven m. stems in ī (100, 1 b). Sāyaṇa thinks this means Indra because that god's charioteer (in later times) is mātali and therefore **mā́talī** (N. of **mā́talin**) is 'he who is accompanied by **mātali**'; but the accent of words in **in** is invariably on that syllable (p. 454 B *a*). **Kavyáis**: name of a group of ancestors; the inst. used in the sociative sense (199 A 1). **Áṅgi-**

robhis: another group of ancestors, otherwise associated with Bṛhaspati (who exclusively is called Āṅgirasá). **Ṛ́kvabhis**: another group of ancestors; cp. **sá ṛ́kvatā gaṇéna** *he* (Bṛhaspati) *with the singing host* (iv. 50, 5). **vāvṛdhānás**: by means of oblations. **yā́ṃś ca**: the ancestors whom the gods strengthened by their aid, and who strengthened the gods with their offerings. **svā́hā anyé**: some, by their association with the gods, rejoice in the call svā́hā, which is addressed to the gods, others in the funeral oblations offered to them as ancestors. **madanti**: with inst. (p. 308, 1 *c*).

४ इमं यम प्रस्तरमा हि सीदा-	इमम् । यम । प्रऽस्तरम् । आ । हि । सीद ।
ङ्गिरोभिः पितृभिः संविदानः ।	अङ्गिरःऽभिः । पितृऽभिः । सम्ऽविदानः ।
आ त्वा मन्त्राः कविशस्ता वहन्त्व्	आ । त्वा । मन्त्राः । कविऽशस्ताः । वहन्तु ।
एना राजन्हविषा मादयस्व ॥	एना । राजन् । हविषा । मादयस्व ॥

4 **imáṃ, Yama, prastarám ā́ hí sī́da,**
Áṅgirobhiḥ pitṛ́bhiḥ saṃvidānáḥ.
ā́ tvā mántrāḥ kaviśastā́ vahantu.
enā́, rājan, havíṣā mādayasva.

Upon this strewn grass, O Yama, pray seat thyself, uniting thyself with the Aṅgirases, the fathers. Let the spells recited by the seers bring thee hither. Do thou, O king, rejoice in this oblation.

ā́ sī́da: 2. s. ipv. of **sad** *sit* w. acc. **hí**: p. 252, 2; cp. p. 167, B. **pitṛ́bhis**: apposition to **Áṅgirobhis** (cp. 3 a). **saṃvidānás**: pr. pt. Ā. of 2. **vid** *find* according to the root class (158 *a a*). **kavi-śastā́s**: on the accent cp. p. 456, 2 a and p. 462, f. n. 4. **enā́**: here (cp. 2 d) inst. of **ena** (112 *a*) agreeing with **havíṣā**; accented because beginning the Pāda (and always as an adv., cp. 2 d). **mādayasva**: with inst., cp. **madanti** in 3 d.

५ अङ्गिरोभिरा गहि यज्ञियेभिर्	अङ्गिरःऽभिः । आ । गहि । यज्ञियेभिः ।
यम वैरूपैरिह मादयस्व ।	यम । वैरूपैः । इह । मादयस्व ।

विवस्वन्तं हुवे यः पिता ते
ऽस्मिन्यज्ञे बर्हिष्या निषद्य ॥

विवस्वन्तम् । हुवे । यः । पिता । ते ।
अस्मिन् । यज्ञे । बर्हिषि । आ । निऽसद्य ॥

5 Áṅgirobhir ā́ gahi yajñíyebhir;
Yáma, Vairūpáir ihá mādayasva.
Vívasvantam huve, yáḥ pitā́ te,
asmín yajñé barhíṣi ā́ niṣádya.

Come hither with the adorable Aṅgirases; O Yama, with the sons of Virūpa do thou here rejoice. I call Vivasvant who is thy father, (let him rejoice), *having sat himself down on the strew at this sacrifice.*

Áṅgirobhis: sociative inst. (199 A 1). **ā́ gahi**: root ao. ipv. of gam (148, 5). **Vairūpáis**: sociative inst.; this patronymic form occurs only here; **Virūpa** occurs once in the sing. as the name of one who praised Agni (viii. 64, 6), and three times in the pl. as of seers closely connected with the Aṅgirases, as sons of heaven or of Aṅgiras. **huve**: 1. s. pr. Ā. of hū *call*. **yás**: supply ásti. c is defective by one syllable (p. 441, 4 B *a*). **barhíṣi ā́**: to be taken together (cp. 176, 1, 2). **niṣádya**: gd. of sad *sit*; agreeing with **Vívasvantam** (cp. 210): it is not the priest who sits down on the strew, but the god; d occurs in iii. 35, 6 as applied to Indra.

६ अङ्गिरसो नः पितरो नवग्वा
अथर्वाणो भृगवः सोम्यासः ।
तेषां वयं सुमतौ यज्ञियानाम्
अपि भद्रे सौमनसे स्याम ॥

अङ्गिरसः । नः । पितरः । नवऽग्वाः ।
अथर्वाणः । भृगवः । सोम्यासः ।
तेषाम् । वयम् । सुऽमतौ । यज्ञियानाम् ।
अपि । भद्रे । सौमनसे । स्याम ॥

6 Áṅgiraso, naḥ pitáro, Návagvā,
Átharvāṇo, Bhŕ̥gavaḥ, somiā́saḥ:
téṣām vayám sumatáu yajñíyānām
ápi bhadré saumanasé siāma.

The Aṅgirases, our fathers, the Navagvas, the Atharvans, the Bhr̥gus, the Soma-loving: we would abide in the favour, the good graces of them the adorable ones.

naḥ pitáraḥ: in apposition to the names; cp. 4 b. **Návagvās &c.**, names of ancient priestly families. **ápi syāma** to be taken together; **ápi as** = *to take part in.*

७ प्रेहि प्रेहि पथिभिः पूर्व्येभिर्
यत्रा नः पूर्वे पितरः परेयुः ।
उभा राजाना स्वधया मदन्ता
यमं पश्यासि वरुणं च देवम् ॥

प्र । इहि । प्र । इहि । पथिऽभिः । पूर्व्येभिः ।
यत्र । नः । पूर्वे । पितरः । पराऽईयुः ।
उभा । राजाना । स्वधया । मदन्ता ।
यमम् । पश्यासि । वरुणम् । च । देवम् ॥

7 **préhi, préhi pathíbhiḥ pūrvié-bhir,**
yátrā naḥ pū́rve pitáraḥ pa-reyúḥ.
ubhā́ rā́jānā svadháyā mád-antā,
Yamáṃ paśyāsi Váruṇaṃ ca devám.

Go forth, go forth by those ancient paths on which our fathers of old have passed away. Thou shalt see both kings rejoicing in the offering to the dead, Yama and Váruṇa the god.

préhi préhi: addressed to the dead man; note that this repeated cd. vb. is not treated as an Āmreḍita; in fact only one repeated verbal form is so treated in the RV., viz. píba-piba (p. 282, *g*). Note the remarkable alliteration in a b; cp. the repetition of -ā in c and of -am in d; of a- in 9 c d, and of -au in 10–12. **pū́rve**: prn. adj. (p. 116). **rā́jānā**: note that both Yama and Varuṇa are called kings, but Varuṇa alone a god (cp. note on 1 d). **svadháyā**: cp. 3 d. **paśyāsi**: 2. s. pr. sb. of **paś** *see* (cp. p. 353).

८ सं गच्छस्व पितृभिः सं यमेने-
ष्टापूर्तेन परमे व्योमन् ।
हित्वायावद्यं पुनरस्तमेहि
सं गच्छस्व तन्वा सुवर्चाः ॥

सम् । गच्छस्व । पितृऽभिः । सम् । यमेन ।
इष्टाऽपूर्तेन । परमे । विऽओमन् ।
हित्वाय । अवद्यम् । पुनः । अस्तम् । आ ।
इहि ।
सम् । गच्छस्व । तन्वा । सुऽवर्चाः ॥

8 sáṃ gachasva pitṛ́bhiḥ, sáṃ Yaména,
iṣṭāpūrténa paramé víoman.
hitvā́yāvadyáṃ púnar ástam éhi:
sáṃ gachasua tanúā suvárcāḥ.

Unite with the Fathers, unite with Yama, with the reward of thy sacrifices and good works in the highest heaven. Leaving blemish behind go back to thy home; unite with thy body, full of vigour.

iṣṭā-pūrténa: note that this old Dvandva cd. (see vocab.) is not analysed in the Pada text. **paramé**: the abode of Yama and the Fathers is in the highest heaven; **mádhye diváḥ** in x. 15, 14. **víoman**: loc. without i (p. 69). **hitvā́ya**: gd., 163, 3. **ástam**: the home of the Fathers; cp. 9 b–d. **tanvā̀ suvárcāḥ**: being free from disease and frailties, the dead man unites with a body which is complete and without imperfections. The AV. often speaks of such being the state of things in the next life. In **d** the rare resolution of **v** in -**sva** is required.

९ अपेत वीत वि च सर्पतातो
ऽस्मा एतं पितरो लोकमक्रन् ।
अहोभिरद्भिरक्तुभिर्व्यक्तं
यमो ददात्यवसानमस्मै ॥

अप । इत । वि । इत । वि । च । सर्पत । अतः ।
अस्मै । एतम् । पितरः । लोकम् । अक्रन् ।
अहःऽभिः । अत्ऽभिः । अक्तुऽभिः । विऽअक्तम् ।
यमः । ददाति । अवऽसानम् । अस्मै ॥

9 ápeta, vìta, ví ca sarpatā́to:
asmā́ etáṃ pitáro lokám akran.
áhobhir adbhír aktúbhir víaktaṃ
Yamó dadāti avasā́nam asmai.

Begone, disperse, slink off from here: for him the Fathers have prepared this place. Yama gives him a resting-place distinguished by days and waters and nights.

This stanza is addressed to the demons to leave the dead man alone. **vìta**: for **ví ita** (see p. 464, 17, 1 *a*). **asmái**: accented because emphatic at the beginning of a Pāda, but unaccented at the end of d (cp. p. 452, A *c*). **akran**: 3. pl. act. root ao. of **kṛ** *make.* **áhobhir adbhíḥ**: cp. ix. 113, where the joys of the next world are described, yátra jyótir ájasram, tásmin mā́m dhehi amṛ́te lóke *where there is eternal light, in that immortal world place me* (7), and yátra amū́r yahvátīr ā́pas, tátra mā́m amṛ́tam kṛdhi *where are those swift waters, there make me immortal* (8). aktúbhis: *nights* as alternating with days. vyàktam: pp. of ví + añj *adorn, distinguish.*

१० अति द्रव सारमेयौ श्वानौ
चतुरक्षौ शबलौ साधुना पथा ।
अथा पितॄन्त्सुविदत्राँ उपेहि
यमेन ये सधमादं मदन्ति ॥

अति । द्रव । सारमेयौ । श्वानौ ।
चतुःऽअक्षौ । शबलौ । साधुना । पथा ।
अथ । पितॄन् । सुऽविदत्रान् । उप । इहि ।
यमेन । ये । सधऽमादम् । मदन्ति ॥

10 áti drava sārameyáu śuā́nau,
caturakṣáu śabálau sādhúnā pathā́;
áthā pitṝ́n suvidátrām̐ úpehi,
Yaména yé sadhamā́dam mádanti.

Run by a good path past the two sons of Saramā, the four-eyed, brindled dogs; then approach the bountiful Fathers who rejoice at the same feast as Yama.

sārameyáu: in this and the following duals (including 11 a b) the ending au is irregularly used; in the old parts of the RV. ā is employed before consonants and at the end of a Pāda. śvā́nau: to be read as a trisyllable (cp. 91, 3). caturakṣáu: doubtless meant to imply keen sight; thus this epithet is also applied to Agni. In the Avesta a four-eyed dog watches at the head of the bridge by which the souls of the dead pass to the other world, and scares away the fiend from the holy ones. b is a Jagatī (cp. p. 445, f. n. 7). áthā: the second syllable metrically lengthened. Yaména: sociative inst. (p. 306, 1). sadhamā́dam: cognate acc. with mádanti (p. 300, 4).

११ यौ ते श्वानौ यम रक्षितारौ
चतुरक्षौ पथिरक्षी नृचक्षसौ ।

यौ । ते । श्वानौ । यम । रक्षितारौ ।
चतुःऽअक्षौ । पथिरक्षी इति पथिऽरक्षी ।
नृऽचक्षसौ ।

ताभ्यामेनं परि देहि राजन्
स्वस्ति चास्मा अनमीवं च धेहि ॥

ताभ्याम् । एनम् । परि । देहि । राजन् ।
स्वस्ति । च । अस्मै । अनमीवम् । च ।
धेहि ॥

11 yáu te śuánau, Yama, rakṣitárau,
caturakṣáu pathirákṣī nṛcákṣasau,
tábhiām enam pári dehi, rājan:
svastí cāsmā anamīvám ca dhehi.

Give him over to those two, O King, that are thy dogs, O Yama, the guardians, four-eyed, watchers of the path, observers of men; bestow on him welfare and health.

yáu: au in this and the following duals for ā, as in 10. nṛcákṣasau: as Yama's messengers (cp. 12 b). b is a Jagatī (cp. 10 b). enam: the dead man. dehi (2. s. ipv. of dā *give*): that they may guide him to Yama's abode. dhehi: 2. s. ipv. of dhā *put*.

१२ उरूणसावसुतृपा उदुम्बलौ
यमस्य दूतौ चरतो जनाँ अनु ।
तावस्मभ्यं दृशये सूर्याय
पुनर्दातामसुमद्येह भद्रम् ॥

उरुऽनसौ । असुऽतृपौ । उदुम्बलौ ।
यमस्य । दूतौ । चरतः । जनान् । अनु ।
तौ । अस्मभ्यम् । दृशये । सूर्याय ।
पुनः । दाताम् । असुम् । अद्य । इह । भद्रम् ॥

12 urūṇasā́v, asutṛ́pā, udumbaláu,
Yamásya dūtáu carato jánām̐ ánu;
tā́v asmábhyam dṛśáye sū́riāya
púnar dātām ásum adyéhá bhadrám.

Broad-nosed, life-stealing, . . the two as messengers of Yama wander among men; may these two give us back here to-day auspicious life that we may see the sun.

urū-ṇasáu: the second syllable is metrically lengthened; on the cerebralization of the dental n see 65 *b*; here we have the normal use of au as āv before a vowel within a Pāda; *broad-nosed*, that is, keen-scented. asutṛ́pā u-: on the Sandhi see 22; the literal meaning *delighting in lives* implies delighting in taking them, while they wander among men as Yama's messengers. **udumbaláu**: this word occurs here only, and there is no means of throwing any light on its sense; the au of this dual, as of **dūtáu**, for ā, shows the same irregularity as in the preceding stanzas. **caratas**: in order to seek out the lives of those about to go to the abode of Yama. **asmábhyam**: dat. pl. of ahám. **dṛśáye**: dat. inf., with attracted acc. (200 B 4). **dātām**: 3. du. ipv. root ao. of dā *give*; as having already marked us for their victims, let them give back our life to-day.

१३ यमाय सोमं सुनुत	यमाय । सोमम् । सुनुत ।
यमाय जुहुता हविः ।	यमाय । जुहुत । हविः ।
यमं ह यज्ञो गच्छत्य्	यमम् । ह । यज्ञः । गच्छति ।
अग्निदूतो अरंकृतः ॥	अग्निऽदूतः । अरम्ऽकृतः ॥

13 **Yamā́ya sómam sunuta,**
Yamā́ya juhutā havíḥ;
Yamáṃ ha yajñó gachati,
Agnídūto áraṃkṛtaḥ.

For Yama press the Soma, to Yama offer the oblation; to Yama goes the sacrifice well prepared, with Agni as its messenger.

juhutā: with metrically lengthened final vowel; 2. pl. ipv. of hu *sacrifice* addressed to those officiating at the sacrifice. **Yamám**: acc. of the goal (197, 1; cf. 204, 1 *b*). **Agnídūtas**: the idea underlying this figurative expression is that the smoke of the sacrificial fire goes up to heaven where Yama dwells.

१४ यमाय घृतवद्धविर्	यमाय । घृतऽवत् । हविः ।
जुहोत प्र च तिष्ठत ।	जुहोत । प्र । च । तिष्ठत ।
स नो देवेष्वा यमद्	सः । नः । देवेषु । आ । यमत् ।
दीर्घमायुः प्र जीवसे ॥	दीर्घम् । आयुः । प्र । जीवसे ॥

14 **Yamā́ya ghṛtávad dhavír**
juhóta, prá ca tiṣṭhata;
sá no devéṣu ā́ yamad,
dīrghám ā́yuḥ prá jīváse.

To Yama offer the oblation abounding in ghee, and step forth; may he guide us to the gods that we may live a long life.

juhóta: the irr. strong form (p. 144, B. 3 *a*) with a long vowel in the second syllable is here utilized for metrical purposes, as the regular form **juhuta** has its final vowel lengthened in 13 b. **prá tiṣṭhata**: *step forward*, in order to offer the oblation; cp. the use of **prá bhṛ** *bring forward* an oblation. **ā́ yamat**: inj. of root ao. of **yam** *extend*; this form constitutes a play on the name of Yama. **nas**: acc. governed by **ā́ yamad**; cp. ix. 44, 5, **sá naḥ Sómo devéṣu ā́ yamat** *may he, Soma, guide us to the gods*; on the loc., cp. 204 B 1 *b*. **ā́yus**: cognate acc. (197 A 4). **prá jīváse**: cp. p. 463, f. n. 8. The meaning of cd is: 'may he keep us (the survivors) to the worship of the gods (and not lead us to the Fathers), so that we may enjoy long life on earth' (cp. 12 c, d).

१५ यमाय मधुमत्तमं	यमाय । मधुमत्ऽतमम् ।
राज्ञे हव्यं जुहोतन ।	राज्ञे । हव्यम् । जुहोतन ।
इदं नम ऋषिभ्यः पूर्वजेभ्यः	इदम् । नमः । ऋषिऽभ्यः । पूर्वऽजेभ्यः ।
पूर्वेभ्यः पथिकृद्भ्यः ॥	पूर्वेभ्यः । पथिकृत्ऽभ्यः ॥

15 **Yamā́ya mádhumattamaṃ**	*To Yama the king offer the most*
rā́jñe havyáṃ juhotana.	*honied oblation. This obeisance is*
idáṃ náma ṛ́ṣibhyaḥ pūrvajé-bhiaḥ,	*for the seers born of old, the ancient*
pū́rvebhyaḥ pathikṛ́dbhiaḥ.	*makers of the path.*

juhotana: again the strong form to suit the metre (cp. 14 b). **pathikṛ́dbhyas**: because they were the first, after Yama had shown the way, to tread the path leading to Yama's abode (the **pitṛyā́ṇa** *the road of the Fathers*). This stanza is a Bṛhatī in the middle of Anuṣṭubhs, differing from them only by the addition of four syllables in the third Pāda (see p. 444, 9 *b*).

१६ त्रिकद्रुकेभिः पतति	त्रिऽकद्रुकेभिः । पतति ।
षळुर्वीरेकमिद्बृहत् ।	षट् । उर्वीः । एकम् । इत् । बृहत् ।
त्रिष्टुब्गायत्री छन्दांसि	त्रिऽस्तुप् । गायत्री । छन्दांसि ।
सर्वा ता यम आहिता ॥	सर्वा । ता । यमे । आऽहिता ॥

16 **tríkadrukebhiḥ patati.**	*It flies through the three Soma*
ṣáḷ urvī́r, ékam íd bṛhát,	*vats. The six earths, the one great*
triṣṭúb, gāyatrī́, chándāṃsi,	(world), *triṣṭubh, gāyatrī* and (the
sárvā tā́ Yamá ā́hitā.	other) *metres, all these are placed*
	in Yama.

The meaning of a b in this final stanza is obscure, partly because the subject is not expressed in a, and partly because it is uncertain whether b is syntactically connected with a or not. The probability is that here we have two sentences, one consisting of a, the other of b–d. The first then probably means that the Soma draught is ready for Yama; the second expresses the greatness of Yama by stating that all things are contained in him. **tríkadrukebhis**: this word, occurring six times in the RV., always appears in the pl., and always except here in the locative. It is four times directly connected with Soma, and once alludes to it; e. g. **tríkadrukeṣu apibat sutásya** *he* (Indra) *drank of the pressed Soma in the three vessels* (i. 32, 3). The term **tríkadruka** in the ritual of the Brāhmaṇas is the name of three days in a Soma ceremony. The metaphor of flying is applied to the flowing Soma compared with a bird, as '*the god flies like a bird to settle in the vats*' (ix. 3, 1). The allusion therefore seems to be to the Soma which the priests are called upon to press in 13 a. **ṣáḍ urvī́ḥ**: this expression is probably equivalent to the three heavens and three earths: cp. **tisró dyā́vaḥ níhitā antár asmin, tisró bhū́mīr úparāḥ, ṣáḍvidhānāḥ** *the three heavens are placed within him* (Varuṇa) *and the three earths below, forming a sixfold order* (vii. 87, 5). **ékam íd bṛhát**: by this expression is probably meant the universe, otherwise spoken of as **víśvam ékam, idám ékam** &c., the *one* being contrasted with the *six*; cp. i. 164, 6, **ví yás tastámbha ṣáḷ imā́ rájāṃsi .. kím ápi svid ékam?** *who propped asunder these six spaces; what pray is the one?* **triṣṭúbh, gāyatrī́**: *these two names* of metres are only mentioned in this and one other hymn of the tenth Maṇḍala. This and the following four hymns (x. 15–18) are among the latest in the RV. The concluding stanza here, as in some hymns addressed to other deities, sums up the greatness of the god by saying that he embraces all things; cp. i. 32, 15 (Indra); v. 13, 6 (Agni).

PITÁRAS

Two hymns (x. 15 and 54) are addressed to the Pitaras or Fathers, the blessed dead who dwell in the third heaven, the third or highest step of Viṣṇu. The term as a rule applies to the early or first ancestors, who followed the ancient paths, seers who made the paths by which the recent dead go to join them. Various groups of ancestors are mentioned, such as the Aṅgirases and Atharvans, the Bhṛgus and Vasiṣṭhas, who are identical in name with the priestly families associated by tradition with the composition of the Atharvaveda and of the second and seventh Maṇḍalas of the Rigveda. The Pitaras are classed as higher, lower, and middle, as earlier and later, who though not always known to their descendants, are known to Agni. They revel with Yama and feast with the gods. They are fond of Soma, and thirst for the libations prepared for them on earth, and eat the offerings along with him. They come on the same car as Indra and the gods. Arriving in their thousands they range themselves on the sacrificial grass to the south, and drink the pressed draught. They receive oblations as their food. They are entreated to hear, intercede for, and protect their worshippers, and besought not to injure their descendants for any sin humanly committed against them. They are invoked to give riches, children, and long life to their sons, who desire to be in their good graces. The Vasiṣṭhas are once collectively implored to help their descendants. Cosmical actions, like those of the gods, are sometimes attributed to the Fathers. Thus they are said to have adorned the sky with stars, to have placed darkness in the night and light in the day; they found the light and generated the dawn. The path trodden by the Fathers (pitṛyāṇa) is different from that trodden by the gods (devayāna).

x. 15. Metre: Triṣṭubh; 11 Jagatī.

१ उदी॑रता॒मव॑र॒ उत्परा॑स॒	उत् । ई॒र॒ता॒म् । अव॑रे । उत् । परा॑सः ।
उन्म॑ध्य॒माः पि॒तरः॑ सो॒म्यासः॑ ।	उत् । म॒ध्य॒माः । पि॒तरः॑ । सो॒म्यासः॑ ।
असुं॒ य ई॒युर॑वृ॒का ऋ॑त॒ज्ञास्	असु॑म् । ये । ई॒युः । अ॒वृ॒काः । ऋ॒त॒ऽज्ञाः ।
ते नो॑ऽवन्तु पि॒तरो॒ हवे॑षु ॥	ते । नः॒ । अ॒व॒न्तु॒ । पि॒तरः॑ । हवे॑षु ॥

1 úd īratām ávara, út párāsa,
ún madhyamā́ḥ pitáraḥ somiā́saḥ;
ásuṃ yá īyúr avṛkā́ ṛtajñā́s,
té nŏ avantu pitáro háveṣu.

Let the lower, let the higher, let the middlemost Soma-loving Fathers arise; let those Fathers who, friendly, knowing right, have gone to life eternal, *favour us in our invocations.*

úd īratām: note that cd. verbs are often repeated by means of the prp. (here úd twice) alone. **ávare** (on the dec., see 120 *c* 1) &c.: these three words refer to the Pitṛs dwelling in the three divisions of the world, earth, air, heaven (cp. **yé pā́rthive rájasi** in 2 c; and the division of heaven into three, the lowest, the middlemost, and the third in which the Fathers sit: AV. xviii. 2, 49). Sāyaṇa thinks that here the degrees of their holiness is meant, but in this same stanza, when it appears in the AV. (xviii. 1, 44), he thinks that degrees of merit or of age are intended; but degrees of age are expressly mentioned in 2 b by **pū́rvāsas** and **úparāsas**. **ásum**: life in the heavenly world, immortal life (the Pitaras are called immortal in AV. vi. 41, 3) as opposed to terrestrial life. **īyur**: 3. pl. pf. act. of **i** *go*.

२ इदं पितृभ्यो नमो अस्त्वद्य	इदम् । पितृऽभ्यः । नमः । अस्तु । अद्य ।
ये पूर्वासो य उपरास ईयुः ।	ये । पूर्वासः । ये । उपरासः । ईयुः ।
ये पार्थिवे रजस्या निषत्ता	ये । पार्थिवे । रजसि । आ । निऽसत्ताः ।
ये वा नूनं सुवृजनासु विक्षु ॥	ये । वा । नूनम् । सुऽवृजनासु । विक्षु ॥

2 **idáṃ pitṛ́bhyo námŏ astu adyá,**
yé pū́rvāso, yá úparāsa īyúḥ;
yé pā́rthive rájasi ā́ níṣattā,
yé vā nūnáṃ suvṛjánāsu vikṣú.

Let this obeisance be made to-day to the Fathers who have departed earlier and *later, who have seated themselves in the terrestrial air or who are now in settlements with fair abodes.*

pū́rvāsas: in x. 14, 2. 7 the prn. form **pū́rve** is used (see 120, 2). **īyúr**: in x. 14, 2. 7 the more distinctive cd. **pareyúr** appears. **ā́ níṣattās** (pp. of **sad** *sit*, cp. 67 *a*, *b*; cp. **ā́ niṣádya** in x. 14, 5). **pā́rthive rájasi**: in the atmospheric region above the earth; here the Pitaras in the air intermediate between heaven and earth are meant, while in b and d those in heaven and on earth respectively are intended. **suvṛjánāsu vikṣú**: cp. the frequent **mā́nuṣīṣu vikṣú** *human settlements*, with reference to the Fathers present at the funeral offerings on earth.

3 आहं पितॄन्त्सुविदत्राँ अवित्सि
नपातं च विक्रमणं च विष्णोः ।
बर्हिषदो ये स्वधया सुतस्य
भजन्त पित्वस्त इहागमिष्ठाः ॥

आ । अहम् । पितॄन् । सुऽविदत्रान् ।
अवित्सि ।
नपातम् । च । विऽक्रमणम् । च । वि-
ष्णोः ।
बर्हिऽसदः । ये । स्वधया । सुतस्य ।
भजन्त । पित्वः । ते । इह । आऽगमिष्ठाः ॥

3 **áhám pitṝn suvidátrām̐ avitsi,**
nápātam ca vikrámaṇam ca
Víṣṇoḥ:
barhiṣádo yé svadháyā sutásya
bhájanta pitvás, tá ihā́gami-
ṣṭhāḥ.

I have won hither the bountiful Fathers and the grandson and the wide stride of Viṣṇu: they who, sitting on the strew, shall partake of the pressed drink with the offering to the dead, come most gladly here.

ā́-avitsi (1. s. A. s ao. of 2. vid *find*); = I have induced to come to this offering. **nápātam**: it is somewhat uncertain who is meant by this; according to Prof. Geldner's ingenious explanation Yama (with whom the Pitaras are associated) is intended, because in the VS. (xxix. 60) Viṣṇu (here coupled with **nápātam**) is called the husband of Aditi, whose son (TS. vi. 5, 6, 2) was Vivasvant, the father of Yama (see note on x. 14, 1); but it is doubtful whether this later statement was part of the mythological belief of the RV., where Yama is the grandson of Tvaṣṭṛ (x. 17, 1). On the other hand, the word may be used elliptically to designate Agni = **sáhaso nápātam** (Agni is called **náptre sáhasvate** in viii. 102, 7) = **sáhasaḥ sūnúm** *son of strength*, a frequent epithet of Agni, for which once (vi. 4, 4) **sūno** *son* alone is used in an Agni hymn; and below (9 c) Agni is invoked to come with the Fathers: **ágne yāhi suvidátrebhiḥ pitṛ́bhiḥ**. There is here also a good example of the fanciful interpretations of Sāyaṇa: **Víṣṇor** (= **yajñasya**) **nápātam** (= **vināśābhāvam**) *the non-destruction of the sacrifice.* **vikrámaṇam**: Viṣṇu's third step (= the highest heaven), where the Fathers dwell (cp. i. 154, 5). **bhájanta**: 3. pl. inj. Ā. of **bhaj** *share*, with partitive gen. (202 A *e*). **pitvás**: gen. of **pitú** (p. 81). **ā́-gamiṣṭhās**: accent, p. 453, 9 A *b*.

४ बर्हिषदः पितर ऊत्य१र्वाग्
इमा वो हव्या चकृमा जुषध्वम् ।
त आ गतावसा शंतमेना-
था नः शं योररपो दधात ॥

बर्हिऽसदः । पितरः । ऊती । अर्वाक् ।
इमा । वः । हव्या । चकृम । जुषध्वम् ।
ते । आ । गत । अवसा । शम्ऽतमेन ।
अथ । नः । शम् । योः । अरपः । दधात ॥

4 **bárhiṣadaḥ pitara, ūtī́ arvā́g;**
imā́ vo havyā́ cakṛmā: juṣá-dhvam;
tá ā́ gata ávasā śáṃtamena;
áthā naḥ śáṃ yór arapó da-dhāta.

Ye Fathers that sit on the strew, come hither with aid; these offerings we have made to you: enjoy them; so come with most beneficent aid; then bestow on us health and *blessing free from hurt.*

bárhiṣadaḥ pitaraḥ: see note on viii. 48, 7 c. **ūtī́**: inst. of ūtí (p. 81, f. n. 4). **arvā́k**: *hither*; the vb. **ā́ gata** *come* is easily to be supplied from c. **cakṛmā**: with metrical lengthening of the final syllable. **juṣádhvam**: accented because it forms a new sentence (p. 466, 19 *b*). **té**: *as such*, as enjoying our offerings. **gata**: 2. pl. ipv. root ao. of **gam** *go*. **áthā**: metrically lengthened. **dadhāta**: 2. pl. pr. ipv. of **dhā** *place*, with irr. strong form of the pr. stem instead of the normal dhatta (p. 144 B 1 *b*).

५ उपहूताः पितरः सोम्यासो
बर्हिष्येषु निधिषु प्रियेषु ।
त आ गमन्तु त इह श्रुवन्त्व-
धि ब्रुवन्तु तेऽवन्त्वस्मान् ॥

उपऽहूताः । पितरः । सोम्यासः ।
बर्हिष्येषु । निऽधिषु । प्रियेषु ।
ते । आ । गमन्तु । ते । इह । श्रुवन्तु ।
अधि । ब्रुवन्तु । ते । अवन्तु । अस्मान् ॥

5 **úpahūtāḥ pitáraḥ somiā́so**
barhiṣíeṣu nidhíṣu priyéṣu;
tá ā́ gamantu; tá iha śruvantu;
ádhi bruvantu; té avantu asmā́n.

Invited are the Soma-loving Fathers to the dear deposits placed on the strew; let them come; let them listen here; let them speak for us; let them aid us.

úpa-hūtās: pp. of **hū** *call*. **nidhíṣu**: the offerings deposited on the sacrificial grass. **gamantu**: 3. pl. ipv. root ao. of **gam** *go*. **śru-vantu**: 3. pl. ipv. root aò. of **śru** *hear*.

६ आच्या जानु दक्षिणतो निषद्ये-
मं यज्ञमभि गृणीत विश्वे ।
मा हिंसिष्ट पितरः केन चिन्नो
यद्व आगः पुरुषता कराम ॥

आऽअच्य । जानु । दक्षिणतः । निऽसद्य ।
इमम् । यज्ञम् । अभि । गृणीत । विश्वे ।
मा । हिंसिष्ट । पितरः । केन । चित् । नः ।
यत् । वः । आगः । पुरुषता । कराम ॥

6 ácyā jā́nu, dakṣiṇató niṣádya,
imám yajñám abhí gṛṇīta víśve;
mā́ hiṃsiṣṭa, pitaraḥ, kéna cin no,
yád va ā́gaḥ puruṣátā kárāma.

Bending the knee, sitting down to the south do ye all greet favourably this sacrifice; injure us not, O Fathers, by reason of any sin that we may have committed against you through human frailty.

ā́-acyā (gd. of **ac** *bend*): note that the suffix -yā is much oftener long than short (164), but in the Pada text it is always short. **jā́nu:** probably the left knee; cp. the ŚB. ii. 4, 2, 2, where the gods bend the right knee, the Fathers the left knee. In rites connected with the dead, the auspicious direction is reversed, left being substituted for right. **dakṣiṇatás:** *to the right* (of the **védi** *altar*), that is, *to the south*, because the south is the region of Yama and the Pitaras. **gṛṇīta:** 2. pl. ipv. of 1. **gṛ** *sing*. **hiṃsiṣṭa:** 2. pl. inj. **iṣ** ao. of **hiṃs** *injure*. **kéna cid yád ā́gaḥ** for **kéna cid ā́gasā yád**, the substantive being put into the rel. instead of the principal clause. **vas:** dat. of disadvantage (p. 314 B 1). **puruṣátā:** inst. s. identical in form with the stem (97, 1, p. 77). **kárāma:** 1. pl. root ao. sb. (p. 171); in the sense of an indefinite past.

७ आसीनासो अरुणीनामुपस्थे
रयिं धत्त दाशुषे मर्त्याय ।
पुत्रेभ्यः पितरस्तस्य वस्वः
प्र यच्छत त इहोर्जं दधात ॥

आसीनासः । अरुणीनाम् । उपऽस्थे ।
रयिम् । धत्त । दाशुषे । मर्त्याय ।
पुत्रेभ्यः । पितरः । तस्य । वस्वः ।
प्र । यच्छत । ते । इह । ऊर्जम् । दधात ॥

7 ā́sīnāso aruṇī́nām upásthe
rayíṃ dhatta dāśúṣe mártiāya.

Sitting in the lap of the ruddy (dawns) *bestow wealth on the wor-*

putrébhiaḥ, pitaras, tásya vásvaḥ
prá yachata; tá ihórjam dadhāta.

shipping mortal. To your sons, O Fathers, present a share of those riches; so do ye here bestow strength.

ásīnāsas: irr. pr. pt. Ā. of **ās** *sit*: 158 *a*. **aruṇínām**: **aruṇá** *ruddy* is the colour of dawn, and the f. of this adj. sometimes appears as an epithet of the dawns; that these are here meant is also indicated by vii. 9, 1; 63, 3, where Agni and Sūrya are said to awake or arise **uṣásām upásthāt** *from the lap of the dawns*. **dhatta** and **dadhāta**: here both the regular and the irr. ipv. of **dhā** are used (cp. note on 4 d). **tásya vásvaḥ**: referring to rayím in b; on the form of the gen. see p. 81. **té**: anaphoric use (cp. p. 294 *b*).

८ ये नः पूर्वे पितरः सोम्यासो
ऽनूहिरे सोमपीथं वसिष्ठाः ।
तेभिर्यमः संरराणो हवींष्यु
शन्नुशद्भिः प्रतिकाममत्तु ॥

ये । नः । पूर्वे । पितरः । सोम्यासः ।
अनुऽऊहिरे । सोमऽपीथम् । वसिष्ठाः ।
तेभिः । यमः । सम्ऽरराणः । हवींषि ।
उशन् । उशत्ऽभिः । प्रतिऽकामम् । अत्तु ॥

8 **yé naḥ pū́rve pitáraḥ somiáso,**
anūhiré somapīthám Vásiṣṭhāḥ,
tébhir Yamáḥ saṃrarāṇó havíṃṣi,
uśánn uśádbhiḥ, pratikāmám attu.

Those forefathers of ours, the Soma-loving, the Vasiṣṭhas, who fare after him *to the Soma-draught, with them let Yama, sharing their gifts, eat the oblations at pleasure, he the eager with* them *the eager.*

anu-ūhiré: the derivation and meaning are somewhat doubtful; most probably pf. of **vah** *drive*, in this case meaning *who have driven after* Yama *to the Soma-draught*; it may possibly come from **ūh** *consider*, then meaning *who have been considered worthy of the Soma-draught*. **Vásiṣṭhās**: as one of the groups of ancient seers. **saṃrarāṇás** (pf. pt. Ā. of **rā** *give*): sharing with them their gifts to their descendants (cp. 7 b c).

९ ये तातृषुर्देवत्रा जेहमाना
होत्राविदः स्तोमतष्टासो अर्कैः ।

ये । ततृषुः । देवऽत्रा । जेहमानाः ।
होत्राऽविदः । स्तोमऽतष्टासः । अर्कैः ।

आग्ने याहि सुविदत्रेभिरर्वाङ्
सत्यैः कव्यैः पितृभिर्घर्मसद्भिः ॥

आ । अग्ने । याहि । सुऽविदत्रेभिः ।
अर्वाङ् ।
सत्यैः । कव्यैः । पितृऽभिः । घर्मसत्ऽभिः ॥

9 **yé tātṛṣúr devatrā́ jéhamānā,**
hotrāvídaḥ stómataṣṭāsŏ arkáiḥ:
ágne yāhi suvidátrebhir arvā́ṅ
satyáiḥ kavyáiḥ pitṛ́bhir ghar-
masádbhiḥ.

Who, gasping, have thirsted among the gods, knowing oblations, having praise fashioned for them with songs: with them the bountiful Fathers, the true, the wise that sit at the heating vessel, come hither, O Agni.

tātṛṣúr: pf. of **tṛṣ**, with long red. vowel (139, 9); such vowels regularly appear in their short form in the Pada text (cp. note on iii. 59, 1 b). **devatrā́**: in heaven; **trā** is one of the suffixes which in the Pada text is separated, being treated as the second member of a cd. **stomá-taṣṭāsas**: this Tp., *fashioned with praise*, otherwise used with matí = *hymn*, is here applied to persons and thus comes to have the sense of a Karmadhāraya Bv. (189, 1) = **taṣṭá-stomāsas**; the latter kind of cd., with a pp. as first member, does not exist in the RV. **arkáis**: to be taken with the preceding word = *by means of songs*. **arvā́ṅ**: 93 *b*. **kavyáis**: this word occurs in only two other passages, the original meaning apparently being = **kaví** *wise* (cp. **kavyá-tā** *wisdom*); here it may be intended to denote a particular group of Fathers (cp. x. 14, 3). **gharmasádbhis**: probably in heaven; cp. x. 16, 10, **sá gharmám invāt paramé sadhásthe**: *may he* (Agni) *further the gharma in the highest abode*; this word as well as **jéhamānās** may be intended to contrast with **tātṛṣúr**; cp. vii. 103, 9.

१० ये सत्यासो हविरदो हविष्पा
इन्द्रेण देवैः सरथं दधानाः ।
आग्ने याहि सहस्रं देववन्दैः
परैः पूर्वैः पितृभिर्घर्मसद्भिः ॥

ये । सत्यासः । हविःऽअदः । हविःऽपाः ।
इन्द्रेण । देवैः । सऽरथम् । दधानाः ।
आ । अग्ने । याहि । सहस्रम् । देवऽवन्दैः ।
परैः । पूर्वैः । पितृऽभिः । घर्मसत्ऽभिः ॥

10 **yé satyā́so havirádo haviṣpā́ Índreṇa deváiḥ saráthaṃ dádhānāḥ, ā́gne yāhi sahásraṃ devavandáiḥ páraiḥ pū́rvaiḥ pitṛ́bhir gharmasádbhiḥ.**	*They who are true, eating the oblation, drinking the oblation, having the same car with Indra* and *the gods, with those thousand god-praising remote forefathers that sit at the heating vessel, come, O Agni.*

sa-rátham : this word, primarily a Bv., *having the same car*, is then often used as a cognate acc. (p. 300, 4) with **yā** = *go* (on a journey) *with the same car* (here with **dhā** in place of **yā**); then adverbially (p. 301, 5 *b*). **dádhānās** : pr. pt. Ā. of **dhā** *put* (cp. p. 460, f. n. 3); the pf. pt. Ā. would be **dadhānā́s** (159). **sahásram** : agreeing with **pitṛ́bhis** : more usual would be **sahásreṇa pitṛ́bhis** : cp. 194 B 1 *b* (p. 291); **párais** : the primary meaning of this word is *farther* (opposed to *nearer* **ávara**, less often **úpara**, **ántara**), *more remote*, then also *higher*; there is no opposition here to **pū́rvais** (opposed to which are **ávara** and **úpara**), which in any case would be in the reverse order, **pū́rvaiḥ paráiḥ**; the meaning is *the remote, the early Fathers*; cp. vi. 21, 6, **párāṇi pratnā́** *remote, ancient deeds* opposed to **ávarāsas** *later men*.

११ अग्निष्वात्ताः पितर् एह गच्छत	अग्निऽस्वात्ताः । पितरः । आ । इह । गच्छत ।
सदःसदः सदत सुप्रणीतयः ।	सदःसदः । सदत । सुऽप्रनीतयः ।
अत्ता हवींषि प्रयतानि बर्हिष्य्	अत्त । हवींषि । प्रऽयतानि । बर्हिषि ।
अथा रयिं सर्ववीरं दधातन ॥	अथ । रयिम् । सर्वऽवीरम् । दधातन ॥

11 **Ágniṣvāttāḥ pitara, éhá gachata; sádaḥ-sadaḥ sadata, supraṇītayaḥ; attā́ havíṃṣi práyatāni barhíṣi; áthā rayiṃ sárvavīraṃ dadhātana.**	*Ye Fathers that have been devoured by fire come hither; sit you down each on his seat, ye that have good guidance; eat the oblations proffered on the strew; then bestow wealth accompanied entirely by strong sons.*

Ágni-ṣvāttās: with the voc. accent on the first syllable; the ordinary accent would be **Agni-ṣvāttás** like other Tps. formed with **Agni**, but such cds. with a pp. as second member usually accent the first (cp. p. 456, 2 *a*). **svāttás**: pp. of **svād** *sweeten* (cp. 67 *b*). **sádaḥ-sadaḥ**: itv. cd. (p. 282 *a*; p. 454, 10 *a*), governed by **sadata. sadata**: 2. pl. ipv. **a** ao. of **sad** *sit* (147, 5). **supraṇītayas**: *having good guidance, well led, coming in good order*; the Pada text does not recognize the cerebralization of the **n** (65 *a*, *b*). **attā́**, **áthā**: final **a** metrically lengthened. **prá-yatāni**: pp. of **yam**. **dadhātana**: irr. strong form (cp. note on 7 d) and suffix **tana** (p. 925).

१२ त्वमग्न ईळितो जातवेदो ऽवाड्ढव्यानि सुरभीणि कृत्वी । प्रादाः पितृभ्यः स्वधया ते अक्षन् अद्धि त्वं देव प्रयता हवींषि ॥	त्वम् । अग्ने । ईळितः । जातऽवेदः । अवाट् । हव्यानि । सुरभीणि । कृत्वी । प्र । अदाः । पितृऽभ्यः । स्वधया । ते । अक्षन् । अद्धि । त्वम् । देव । प्रऽयता । हवींषि ॥

12 **tuám, Agna, īḷitó, jātavedo, ávāḍ ḍhavyā́ni surabhī́ṇi kṛtví. prā́dāḥ pitṛ́bhyaḥ; svadháyā tě akṣann; addhí tvám, deva, práyatā hav- íṃṣi.**	*Thou, O Agni, having been implored, O Jātavedas, hast conveyed the oblations, having made them fragrant. Thou hast presented them to the Fathers; with the funeral offering they have eaten* them; *do thou, O god, eat the oblations proffered.*

īḷitás: by us. **jāta-vedas**: a very frequent and exclusive epithet of Agni; it is a Bv. as its accent shows, meaning *having knowledge of created things* as explained by the RV. itself: **víśvā veda jánimā jātávedāḥ** *Jātavedas knows all creations* (vi. 15, 13); this is also the explanation of Sāyaṇa here: **jātam, sarvam jagad, vetti, iti jātavedāḥ. ávāṭ**: 2. s. **s** ao. of **vah** *carry* (144, 5). **ḍhavyā́ni**: for **havyā́ni** (54). **kṛtví**: gd. of **kṛ** (163, 1). **adās**: 2. s. root ao. of **dā** (148, 1 *a*). **akṣan**: 3. pl. root ao. of **ghas** *eat* (p. 170, *c*). **addhí**: 2 s. ipv. of **ad** *eat*.

१३ ये चेह पितरो ये च नेह
यांश्च विद्म याँ उ च न प्रविद्म ।
त्वं वेत्थ यति ते जातवेदः
स्वधाभिर्यज्ञं सुकृतं जुषस्व ॥

ये । च । इह । पितरः । ये । च । न । इह ।
यान् । च । विद्म । यान् । ऊं इति । च । न ।
प्रऽविद्म ।
त्वम् । वेत्थ । यति । ते । जातऽवेदः ।
स्वधाभिः । यज्ञम् । सुऽकृतम् । जुषस्व ॥

13 yé ca ihá pitáro yé ca néhá,
yā́ṃś ca vidmá yā́m̐ u ca ná pravidmá,
tuám vettha yáti té, jātavedaḥ;
svadhā́bhir yajñám súkṛtam juṣasva.

Both the Fathers who are here and who are not here, both those whom we know and whom we know not, thou knowest how many they are, O Jātavedas; enjoy the sacrifice well prepared with funeral offerings.

yé ca: supply sánti. **vidmá** 1. pl. pf. of vid *know* (p. 154, 3); the 1. pl. pr. is vidmás. **yā́ṃś ca**: Sandhi, 40 *a*. **yā́m̐ u**: 39, and p. 25, f. n. 2. **pra-vidmá**: *know exactly*. **vettha**: 2. s. pf. of vid *know* (p. 154, 3). **yáti**: cp. 118 *a*. **té**: supply sánti.

१४ ये अग्निदग्धा ये अनग्निदग्धा
मध्ये दिवः स्वधया मादयन्ते ।
तेभिः स्वराळसुनीतिमेतां
यथावशं तन्वं कल्पयस्व ॥

ये । अग्निऽदग्धाः । ये । अनग्निऽदग्धाः ।
मध्ये । दिवः । स्वधया । मादयन्ते ।
तेभिः । स्वऽराट् । असुऽनीतिम् । एताम् ।
यथाऽवशम् । तन्वम् । कल्पयस्व ॥

14 yé Agnidagdhā́ yé ánagnidagdhā,
mádhye diváḥ svadhā́yā mādáyante,
tébhiḥ suarā́ḷ ásunītim etā́m
yathāvaśám tanúam kalpayasva.

Those who, burnt with fire and not burnt with fire, are exhilarated by the funeral offering in the midst of heaven, as sovereign ruler do thou with them fit his body according to thy power for this spirit-guidance.

yé ánagnidagdhāḥ: that is, buried. **mádhye diváḥ**: note that the Fathers enjoy in heaven the funeral offering conveyed to them by

Agni, as well as eating the oblations offered them on the sacrificial grass (11 c). **tébhis**: in association with them (199 A 1), as they know the path of the dead. **svarā́ṭ**: as sovereign lord who acts according to his will (**yathāvaśám**); the subject is Agni who is addressed in 9 c and 10 c (**Agne**), and in 12 a and 13 c (**jātavedas**) or mentioned in 11 a (**Ágniṣvāttās**), and in this stanza itself (**Agnidagdhā́s**). **tanvàṃ kalpayasva**: *the body* of the deceased; the words **svayáṃ tanvàṃ kalpayasva** (VS. xxiii. 15) are explained in ŚB. xiii. 2, 7, 11: **svayáṃ rūpáṃ kuruṣva yādṛ́śam icchási** *assume thyself the form that thou desirest*; cp. also iii. 48, 4 b and vii. 101, 3 b **yathāvaśáṃ tanvàṃ cakra** (= **cakre**) **eṣáḥ** *he has taken a body according to his will*; the corresponding Pāda in the AV. (xviii. 3, 59) reads **yathāvaśáṃ tanvàḥ kalpayāti** *may he fashion our bodies according to his will*; cp. also in the following funeral hymn (x. 16, 4) the hemistich: **yā́s te śivā́s tanvò, jātavedas, tā́bhir vahainaṃ sukṛ́tām u lokám** *with those which are thy auspicious bodies, O Jātavedas, conduct him to the world of the righteous.* **ásunītim etā́m**: dependent, like **tanvàṃ**, on **kalpayasva**: *prepare his body* and *this spirit-leading* = *prepare* it for *this spirit-leading*; Agni conducts the *spirit* (**ásu**) of the dead man, who is cremated, to the next world (cp. x. 16, 4, just quoted) where it unites with a new *body* (**tanū́**); cp. x. 14, 8 cd: **ástam ehi; sáṃ gachasva tanvā̀** *go home; unite with thy* (new) *body*; and x. 16, 5 **sáṃ gachatā́ṃ tanvā̀, jātavedaḥ** *let him* (the deceased) *unite with a* (new) *body, O Jātavedas.*

HYMN OF THE GAMBLER

This is one, among the secular hymns, of a group of four which have a didactic character. It is the lament of a gambler who, unable to resist the fascination of the dice, deplores the ruin he has brought on himself and his family. The dice (**akṣā́s**) consisted of the nuts of a large tree called **vibhī́daka** (*Terminalia bellerica*), which is still utilized for this purpose in India.

x. 34. Metre: Triṣṭubh; 7. Jagatī.

१ प्रावेपा मा बृहतो मादयन्ति	प्रावेपाः । मा । बृहतः । मादयन्ति ।
प्रवातेजा इरिणे वर्वृतानाः ।	प्रवातेऽजाः । इरिणे । वर्वृतानाः ।

सोमस्येव मौजवतस्य भक्षो
विभीदको जागृविर्मह्यमच्छान् ॥

सोमस्यऽइव । मौजऽवतस्य । भक्षः ।
विऽभीदकः । जागृविः । मह्यम् । अच्छान् ॥

1 **prāvepā́ mā bṛható mādayanti**
pravātejā́ íriṇe várvṛtānāḥ.
sómasyeva Maujavatásya bhakṣó,
vibhī́dako jā́gṛvir máhyam achān.

The dangling ones, born in a windy place, of the lofty (tree) *gladden me as they roll on the dice-board. Like the draught of the Soma from Mūjavant, the enlivening Vibhīdaka has pleased me.*

várvṛtānās: int. pt. of vṛt *turn.* **Maujavatásya**: *coming from Mount Mūjavant* as the best. **achān**: 3. s. s ao. of chand (p. 164, 5). Verbs meaning *to please* take the dat. (p. 311 *h*).

२ न मा मिमेथ न जिहीळ एषा
शिवा सखिभ्य उत मह्यमासीत् ।
अक्षस्याहमेकपरस्य हेतोर्
अनुव्रतामप जायामरोधम् ॥

न । मा । मिमेथ । न । जिहीळे । एषा ।
शिवा । सखिऽभ्यः । उत । मह्यम् । आसीत् ।
अक्षस्य । अहम् । एकऽपरस्य । हेतोः ।
अनुऽव्रताम् । अप । जायाम् । अरोधम् ॥

2 **ná mā mimetha, ná jihīḷa eṣā́:**
śivā́ sákhibhya utá máhyam āsīt.
akṣásyāhám ekaparásya hetór
ánuvratām ápa jāyā́m arodham.

She does not scold me, she is not angry: she was kind to friends and to me. For the sake of a die too high by one I have driven away a devoted wife.

mimetha: pf. of mith *dispute.* **jihīḷa**: pf. of hīḍ *be angry* (cp. p. 3, f. n. 2). **sákhibhyas**: dat. (p. 313, 3). **ekaparásya**: according to the accent this is a Tp. adj., *exceeding by one*, alluding to an unlucky throw (called kali) in which when the number of dice thrown is divided by four one remains over (while in the best throw, the kṛta, nothing remains over). **ápa arodham**: root ao. of rudh *obstruct.* The meaning of the stanza is: 'rejecting the kindly advice of my wife, I gambled and lost'.

3 द्वेष्टि श्वश्रूरप जाया रुणद्धि	द्वेष्टि । श्वश्रूः । अप । जाया । रुणद्धि ।
न नाथितो विन्दते मर्डितारम् ।	न । नाथितः । विन्दते । मर्डितारम् ।
अश्वस्येव जरतो वस्न्यस्य	अश्वस्यऽइव । जरतः । वस्न्यस्य ।
नाहं विन्दामि कितवस्य भोगम् ॥	न । अहम् । विन्दामि । कितवस्य । भोगम् ॥

3 **dvéṣṭi śvaśrūr; ápa jāyā́ ruṇaddhi;**	*My mother-in-law hates me, my wife drives me away: the man in distress finds none to pity him:*
ná nāthitó vindate marḍitā́ram:	*'I find no more use in a gambler*
áśvasyeva járato vásniasya	*than in an aged horse that is for*
nāhám vindāmi kitavásya bhógam.	*sale.'*

ápa ruṇaddhi (3. s. pr. of **rudh**): turns him away when he asks for money to gamble with. **nāthitás**: the gambler speaks of himself in the 3. prs. **áśvasya‿iva**: agreeing with **kitavásya**. **járatas**: pr. pt. of **jṝ** *waste away.* **kitavásya bhógam**: objective gen. (p. 320, B *b*).

4 अन्ये जायां परि मृशन्त्यस्य	अन्ये । जायाम् । परि । मृशन्ति । अस्य ।
यस्यागृधद्वेदने वाज्य१क्षः ।	यस्य । अगृधत् । वेदने । वाजी । अक्षः ।
पिता माता भ्रातर एनमाहुर्	पिता । माता । भ्रातरः । एनम् । आहुः ।
न जानीमो नयता बद्धमेतम् ॥	न । जानीमः । नयत । बद्धम् । एतम् ॥

4 **anyé jāyā́m pári mṛśanti asya,**	*Others embrace the wife of him*
yásyā́gṛdhad védane vājī́ akṣáḥ.	*for whose possessions the victorious*
pitā́ mātā́ bhrā́tara enam āhur:	*die has been eager. Father, mother,*
'ná jānīmo, náyatā baddhám etám'.	*brothers say of him, 'we know him not, lead him away bound'.*

ágṛdhat: a ao. of **gṛdh** *be greedy*, governing **védane**, loc. of the object (p. 325, 1 *c*). **vājī́**: to be read with a short final (p. 437, *a* 4, cp. p. 441, 4 a); accent, p. 450, *b*. **āhur**: pf. of **ah** *say*. **jānīmas**: 1. pl. pr. of **jñā** *know*. **náyatā**: accented as beginning a new sentence (p. 466, 19 *a*); final vowel metrically lengthened (cp. p. 441, line 2). **baddhám**: as a debtor.

५ यदादीध्ये न दविषाण्येभिः
परायद्भ्योऽव हीये सखिभ्यः ।
न्युप्ताश्च बभ्रवो वाचमक्रतँ
एमीदेषां निष्कृतं जारिणीव ॥

यत् । आऽदीध्ये । न । दविषाणि । एभिः ।
परायत्ऽभ्यः । अव । हीये । सखिऽभ्यः ।
निऽउप्ताः । च । बभ्रवः । वाचम् । अक्रत ।
एमि । इत् । एषाम् । निःऽकृतम् । जारिणीऽइव ॥

5 **yád ādídhye: 'ná davişāṇi ebhiḥ;**
parāyádbhyo áva hīye sákhibhyaḥ',
níuptāś ca babhrávo vácam ákratam̐,
émíd eṣām niṣkṛtám jārínīva.

When I think to myself, 'I will not go with them; I shall be left behind by my friends as they depart (to play)', *and the brown ones, thrown down, have raised their voices, I go straight, like a courtesan, to their place of assignation.*

ā-dídhye: 1. s. pr. Ā. of **dhī** *think.* **davişāṇi**: iş ao. sb. of **du** *go* (of which other forms occur in the AA. and the YV.); some scholars think the sense of play to be so necessary that this must be an irr. form (iş ao. sb.) from **div** *play* (like **a-ṣṭhavişam,** in a Sūtra, from **ṣṭhiv** *spit*). **ebhis**: with the friends. **áva hīye**: ps. of 1. **hā** *leave; I am left behind* with abl. (cp. 201 A 1). **uptās**: pp. of **vap** *strew.* **ákrata**: 3. pl. Ā. root ao. of **kṛ**, accented because still dependent on **yád.** Here we have a Jagatī Pāda interposed in a Triṣṭubh stanza (cp. p. 445, f. n. 7); the same expression, **vácam akrata,** by ending a Pāda in vii. 103, 8 produces a Jagatī Pāda in a Triṣṭubh stanza. The final vowel of the vb. is here nasalized to avoid the hiatus at the end of the Pāda (cp. i. 35, 6 a); viii. 29, 6 a; see p. 23, f. n. 1). **émi íd**: *I go at once* (p. 218). **eṣām**: of the dice.

६ सभामेति कितवः पृच्छमानो
जेष्यामीति तन्वा३ शूशुजानः ।
अक्षासो अस्य वि तिरन्ति कामं
प्रतिदीव्ने दधत आ कृतानि ॥

सभाम् । एति । कितवः । पृच्छमानः ।
जेष्यामि । इति । तन्वा । शूशुजानः ।
अक्षासः । अस्य । वि । तिरन्ति । कामम् ।
प्रतिऽदीव्ने । दधतः । आ । कृतानि ॥

6 **sabhā́m eti kitaváḥ pṛcchá-
māno,
jeṣyā́mī́ti, tanúā śū́śujānaḥ.
akṣā́sŏ asya ví tiranti kā́mam,
pratidī́vne dádhata ā́ kṛtā́ni.**

The gambler goes to the assembly hall, asking himself, 'shall I conquer', trembling with his body. The dice run counter to his desire, bestowing on his adversary at play the lucky throws.

tanvā̀: accent, p. 450, 2 *b*. **śū́śujānas**: as this pt. is the only form of the vb. occurring, and is itself only found in one other passage (also with **tanvā̀**), its exact meaning is doubtful; but it must express either fear or confidence. **tiranti**: 3. pl. pr. of **tṝ** *cross*. **pratidī́van**: dec., 90, 3; dat. with verbs of giving (200 A 1). **ā́ dadhatas**: N. pl. pr. pt. of **dhā** (156, p. 181, top) agreeing with **akṣā́sas**; with prp. following (p. 462, 13 *a a*). **kṛtā́ni**: probably in the specific sense of *the highest throws*, pl. of n. **kṛtám**.

७ अक्षास इदङ्कुशिनो नितोदिनो
निकृत्वानस्तपनास्तापयिष्णवः ।
कुमारदेष्णा जयतः पुनर्हणो
मध्वा संपृक्ताः कितवस्य बर्हणा ॥

अक्षासः । इत् । अङ्कुशिनः । निऽतोदिनः ।
निऽकृत्वानः । तपनाः । तापयिष्णवः ।
कुमारऽदेष्णाः । जयतः । पुनःऽहनः ।
मध्वा । सम्ऽपृक्ताः । कितवस्य । बर्हणा ॥

7 **akṣā́sa íd aṅkuśíno nitodíno,
nikṛ́tvānas tápanās tāpayiṣṇá-
vaḥ;
kumārádeṣṇā, jáyataḥ punar-
háṇo,
mádhvā sámpṛktāḥ kitavásya
barháṇā.**

The dice are hooked, piercing, deceitful, burning and *causing to burn; presenting gifts like boys, striking back the victors, sweetened with honey by magic power over the gambler.*

tāpayiṣṇavas: causing the gambler to pain others by his losses. **kumārá-deṣṇās**: giving gifts and then taking them back like children. **punarháṇas**: winning back from the winner, equivalent in sense to the preceding word; Sandhi, 65 *b*. **sam-pṛktās**: pp. of **pṛc** *mix*. **barháṇā**: inst. s. (p. 77); with objective gen. (p. 320).

८ त्रिपञ्चाशः क्रीळति व्रात एषां
देव इव सविता सत्यधर्मा ।
उग्रस्य चिन्मन्यवे ना नमन्ते
राजा चिदेभ्यो नम इत्कृणोति ॥

त्रिऽपञ्चाशः । क्रीळति । व्रातः । एषाम् ।
देवःऽइव । सविता । सत्यऽधर्मा ।
उग्रस्य । चित् । मन्यवे । न । नमन्ते ।
राजा । चित् । एभ्यः । नमः । इत् ।
कृणोति ॥

8 **tripañcāśáḥ krīḷati vrā́ta eṣām,**
devá iva Savitā́ satyádharmā:
ugrásya cin manyáve nā́ namante;
rā́jā cid ebhyo náma ít kṛṇoti.

Their host of three fifties plays like god Savitṛ whose laws are true: they bow not before the wrath of even the mighty; even a king pays them obeisance.

tripañcāśás: the evidence is in favour of interpreting this word as meaning *consisting of three fifties*, not *consisting of fifty-three*, as the number of dice normally used. **devá iva Savitā́**: the point of the comparison is that the action of the dice is as independent of the will of others as the action of Savitṛ, who observes fixed laws of his own (iv. 53, 4; x. 139, 3), and whose will and independent dominion no being, not even Indra, Varuṇa, Mitra, Aryaman, Rudra can resist (ii. 38, 7. 9; v. 82, 2). **nā́**: the only example in the RV. of the metrical lengthening of **ná**. **namante, námas**: with dat. (p. 311, *k* and 312, 2 *a*).

९ नीचा वर्तन्त उपरि स्फुरन्त्य्
अहस्तासो हस्तवन्तं सहन्ते ।
दिव्या अङ्गारा इरिणे न्युप्ताः
शीताः सन्तो हृदयं निर्दहन्ति ॥

नीचाः । वर्तन्ते । उपरि । स्फुरन्ति ।
अहस्तासः । हस्तऽवन्तम् । सहन्ते ।
दिव्याः । अङ्गाराः । इरिणे । निऽउप्ताः ।
शीताः । सन्तः । हृदयम् । निः । दहन्ति ॥

9 **nīcā́ vartanta, upári sphuranti.**
ahastā́so hástavantam sahante.
divyā́ áṅgārā íriṇe níuptāḥ,
śītā́ḥ sánto, hṛ́dayam nír dahanti.

They roll down, they spring upward. Though without hands, they overcome him that has hands. Divine coals thrown down upon the gaming-board, being cold, they burn up the heart.

Every Pāda in this stanza contains an antithesis: **nīcā́—upári**; **ahastā́saḥ — hā́stavantam**; **divyā́ḥ — íriṇe**; **śītā́ḥ — nír dahanti**. **divyā́s**: alluding to their magic power over the gambler; cp. **barhā́ṇā** in 7 d. **áṅgārās**: the dice are compared with bits of charcoal lying in a hollow; cp. ŚB. v. 3, 1, 10: **adhidévanam vā́ agnís, tásya eté 'ṅgārā yád akṣā́ḥ** *the gaming-board is fire, the dice are its coals.*

१० जाया तप्यते कितवस्य हीना
माता पुत्रस्य चरतः क्व स्वित् ।
ऋणावा बिभ्यद्धनमिच्छमानो
ऽन्येषामस्तमुप नक्तमेति ॥

जाया । तप्यते । कितवस्य । हीना ।
माता । पुत्रस्य । चरतः । क्व । स्वित् ।
ऋणऽवा । बिभ्यत् । धनम् । इच्छमानः ।
अन्येषाम् । अस्तम् । उप । नक्तम् । एति ॥

10 **jāyā́ tapyate kitavásya hīnā́,**
mātā́ putrásya cárataḥ kúa svit.
ṛṇāvā́ bíbhyad dhánam ichámāno,
anyéṣām ástam úpa náktam eti.

Forsaken the wife of the gambler is grieved, the mother (too) *of the son that wanders who knows where. Indebted, fearing, desiring money he approaches at night the house of others.*

hīnā́: pp. of **hā** *leave.* **putrásya**: the gambler. **tapyate** must be supplied with **mātā́**. **ṛṇā-vā́**: lengthening of final **a** before **v** (15, 1 *c*). **bíbhyat**: pr. pt. of **bhī** *fear.* **úpa eti**: probably for the purpose of stealing, to explain c. **náktam**: see 178, 2; 195 A 5 *a.*

११ स्त्रियं दृष्ट्वाय कितवं ततापा-
न्येषां जायां सुकृतं च योनिम् ।
पूर्वाह्णे अश्वान्युयुजे हि बभ्रून्
सो अग्नेरन्ते वृषलः पपाद ॥

स्त्रियम् । दृष्ट्वाय । कितवम् । तताप ।
अन्येषाम् । जायाम् । सुऽकृतम् । च । यो-
निम् ।
पूर्वाह्णे । अश्वान् । युयुजे । हि । बभ्रून् ।
सः । अग्नेः । अन्ते । वृषलः । पपाद ॥

11 **stríyaṃ dṛṣṭvā́ya kitaváṃ tatāpa,**
anyéṣāṃ jāyā́ṃ, súkṛtaṃ ca yónim

It pains the gambler when he sees a woman, the wife of others, and their well-ordered home. Since he yokes the brown horses in the

pūrvāhṇé áśvān yuyujé hí babhrū́n,
só agnér ánte vṛṣaláḥ papāda.

morning, he falls down (in the evening) *near the fire, a beggar.*

tatāpa: used impersonally with the acc.; this and the following two perfects may be translated as presents, because they express habitual actions continued into and included in the pr. (213 A *a*). **dṛṣṭvā́ya:** gd. of **dṛś** *see*, agreeing with **kitavám** as the virtual subject (210). **stríyam** (p. 88, *β*): jāyā́m as apposition, *a woman who is the wife of others*; that is, when he sees the wives of others and their comfortable homes, he is reminded of the unhappiness of his own wife and the bareness of his own home. **áśvān:** the brown dice are here figuratively called horses, which he yokes; that is, he begins a long spell of gambling with them. **papāda:** he consequently falls down, exhausted and overcome, on the ground beside the fire in the evening, having lost everything.

१२ यो वः सेनानीर्महतो गणस्य
राजा व्रातस्य प्रथमो बभूव ।
तस्मै कृणोमि न धना रुणध्मि
दशाहं प्राचीस्तदृतं वदामि ॥

यः । वः । सेनाऽनीः । महतः । गणस्य ।
राजा । व्रातस्य । प्रथमः । बभूव ।
तस्मै । कृणोमि । न । धना । रुणध्मि ।
दश । अहम् । प्राचीः । तत् । ऋतम् ।
वदामि ॥

12 yó vaḥ senānī́r maható gaṇásya,
rā́jā vrā́tasya prathamó babhū́va,
tásmai kṛṇomi, 'ná dhanā́ ruṇadhmi';
dáśāhám prā́cīs, 'tád ṛtám vadāmi'.

To him who as the general of your great throng, as king has become the first of your host, I stretch forth my ten fingers—'I withhold no money—this is truth I say'.

yó vaḥ: no specific die is meant, the expression only implying a chief, in the abstract, of the total number of dice played with. **dáśa kṛṇomi prā́cīḥ:** *I put the ten* (sc. fingers) *forward*, that is, I stretch out my two hands. **prā́cīs:** A. pl. f. of **prā́ñc**, used predicatively (198, 1). **tásmai:** dat. of advantage (200 B 1). **ná dhanā́**

ruṇadhmi: that is, 'I have no money left for you;' these words in sense come after **prácīs**, expressing what is implied by that gesture. **ṛtám**: predicative, *I say this as true* (198, 1).

१३ अक्षैर्मा दीव्यः कृषिमित्कृषस्व
वित्ते रमस्व बहु मन्यमानः ।
तत्र गावः कितव तत्र जाया
तन्मे वि चष्टे सवितायमर्यः ॥

अक्षैः । मा । दीव्यः । कृषिम् । इत् । कृषस्व ।
वित्ते । रमस्व । बहु । मन्यमानः ।
तत्र । गावः । कितव । तत्र । जाया ।
तत् । मे । वि । चष्टे । सविता । अयम् ।
अर्यः ॥

13 **akṣáir má dīvyaḥ; kṛṣím ít kṛṣasva;**
vitté ramasva, bahú mányamānaḥ;
tátra gávaḥ, kitava, tátra jāyá:
tán me ví caṣṭe Savitáyám aryáḥ.

'Play not with dice; ply thy tillage; rejoice in thy property, thinking much of it; there are thy cattle, O gambler, there thy wife': this Savitṛ here, the noble, reveals to me.

This stanza is spoken by the gambler, who in a–c quotes the advice of Savitṛ. **dīvyas**: 2. s. inj. of div *play* with má (p. 240). **ramasva**: with loc. (204, 1 *a*). **tátra**: cattle and wife can be regained by acquiring wealth. **caṣṭe**: 3. s. pr. of **cakṣ**. **me**: dat. (200 A *c*). **ayám**: as actually present. **aryás**: *noble*, as upholder of moral law.

१४ मित्रं कृणुध्वं खलु मृळता नो
मा नो घोरेण चरताभि धृष्णु ।
नि वो नु मन्युर्विशतामरातिर्
अन्यो बभ्रूणां प्रसितौ न्वस्तु ॥

मित्रम् । कृणुध्वम् । खलु । मृळत । नः ।
मा । नः । घोरेण । चरत । अभि । धृष्णु ।
नि । वः । नु । मन्युः । विशताम् ।
अरातिः ।
अन्यः । बभ्रूणाम् । प्रऽसितौ । नु । अस्तु ॥

14 **mitrám kṛṇudhvam khálu, mṛḷátā no.**
má no ghoréṇa caratābhí dhṛṣṇú.

Pray make friendship, be gracious to us. Do not forcibly bewitch us with magic power. Let your wrath, your enmity now come to rest. Let

ní vo nú manyúr viśatām, árātir.
anyó babhrūṇā́m prásitau nú astu.

another now be in the toils of the brown ones.

mṛḷátā (2. pl. ipv. of **mṛḍ**, p. 3, n. 2): accented as beginning a new sentence; with final vowel metrically lengthened. **nas**: dat. (p. 311, *f*). **carata‿abhí**: with prp. following the vb. (p. 468, 20 A). **dhṛṣṇú**: acc. adv. (p. 301, *b*). In this final stanza the gambler adjures the dice to release him from their magical power.

PÚRUṢA

There are six or seven hymns dealing with the creation of the world as produced from some original material. In the following one, the well-known Puruṣa-sūkta or Hymn of Man, the gods are the agents of creation, while the material out of which the world is made is the body of a primaeval giant named Puruṣa. The act of creation is here treated as a sacrifice in which Puruṣa is the victim, the parts when cut up becoming portions of the universe. Both its language and its matter indicate that it is one of the very latest hymns of the Rigveda. It not only presupposes a knowledge of the three oldest Vedas, to which it refers by name, but also, for the first and only time in the Rigveda, mentions the four castes. The religious view is moreover different from that of the old hymns, for it is pantheistic: 'Puruṣa is all this world, what has been and shall be'. It is, in fact, the starting-point of the pantheistic philosophy of India.

x. 90. Metre: **Anuṣṭubh**; 16 **Triṣṭubh**.

१ सहस्रशीर्षा पुरुषः
सहस्राक्षः सहस्रपात् ।
स भूमिं विश्वतो वृत्वा-
त्यतिष्ठद्दशाङ्गुलम् ॥

सहस्रऽशीर्षा । पुरुषः ।
सहस्रऽअक्षः । सहस्रऽपात् ।
सः । भूमिम् । विश्वतः । वृत्वा ।
अति । अतिष्ठत् । दशऽअङ्गुलम् ॥

1 sahásraśīrṣā Púruṣaḥ,
sahasrākṣáḥ, sahásrapāt.
sá bhū́mim viśváto vṛtvā́,
áty atiṣṭhad daśāṅgulám.

Thousand-headed was *Puruṣa, thousand-eyed, thousand-footed. He having covered the earth on all sides, extended beyond it the length of ten fingers.*

sahasraśīrṣā &c.: that is, having innumerable heads, eyes, and feet, as representing all created beings (cp. 2). **sahasrākṣás**: of the very numerous Bv. cds. formed with **sahásra** this and **sahasra-arghá** are the only ones with irr. accent (cp. p. 455, 10 *c*). **daśāṅgu-lám**: probably only another way of expressing that his size was greater even than that of the earth. **atiṣṭhat**: ipf. of **sthā** *stand*

२ पुरुष एवेदं सर्वं	पुरुषः । एव । इदम् । सर्वम् ।
यद्भूतं यच्च भव्यम् ।	यत् । भूतम् । यत् । च । भव्यम् ।
उतामृतत्वस्येशानो	उत । अमृतऽत्वस्य । ईशानः ।
यदन्नेनातिरोहति ॥	यत् । अन्नेन । अतिऽरोहति ॥

2 **Púruṣa evédáṃ sárvaṃ**	*Puruṣa is this all, that has been*
yád bhūtáṃ yác ca bháviam.	*and that will be. And he is the*
utámṛtatvásyéśāno,	*lord of immortality, which he grows*
yád ánnenātiróhati.	*beyond through food.*

Puruṣa is coextensive with the whole world including the gods. **bhávyam**: a late and irregular cadence. **amṛtatvásya**: of the immortals, the gods. **yád**: there is some doubt as to the construction of d; the parallelism of **áty atiṣṭhat** in 1 d and of **áty aricyata** in 5 c indicates that Puruṣa is the subject and **yád** (the gods) the object, and that the former exceeds the latter **ánnena**, that is, by means of sacrificial food. The words have also been interpreted to mean: *who* (the gods) *grow up by* (sacrificial) *food*; or, *and of that which grows by food*, that is, creatures other than the gods. In these interpretations the meaning of **áti** does not seem to be sufficiently brought out.

३ एतावानस्य महिमा-	एतावान् । अस्य । महिमा ।
तो ज्यायांश्च पुरुषः ।	अतः । ज्यायान् । च । पुरुषः ।
पादोऽस्य विश्वा भूतानि	पादः । अस्य । विश्वा । भूतानि ।
त्रिपादस्यामृतं दिवि ॥	त्रिऽपात् । अस्य । अमृतम् । दिवि ॥

3 **etávān asya mahimá,**	*Such is his greatness, and more*
áto jyáyāṃś ca Púruṣaḥ.	*than that is Puruṣa. A fourth of*

pā́do 'sya víśvā bhūtā́ni;
tripā́d asyāmŕ̥taṃ diví.

him is all beings, three-fourths of him are what is immortal in heaven.

etā́vān asya: irr. Sandhi for **etā́vām̐ asya** (occurring also in x. 85, 45: **putrā́n ā́**), is a sign of lateness, this being the regular post-Vedic Sandhi (39). **átas**: equivalent to an ab. after the cpv. (201, 3). **jyā́yāṃś ca**: on the Sandhi, see 40 *a*. **Pū́ruṣas**: a metrical lengthening for **Púruṣas** (cp. the Pada text) to avoid a sequence of four short syllables, cp. 5 b. **amŕ̥tam**: equivalent to **amr̥tatvá**.

4 त्रिपादूर्ध्व उदैत्पुरुषः
पादोऽस्येहाभवत्पुनः ।
ततो विष्वङ् व्यक्रामत
साशनानशने अभि ॥

त्रिऽपात् । ऊर्ध्वः । उत् । ऐत् । पुरुषः ।
पादः । अस्य । इह । अभवत् । पुनरिति ।
ततः । विष्वङ् । वि । अक्रामत् ।
साशनानशने इति । अभि ॥

4 tripā́d ūrdhvá úd ait Púruṣaḥ;
pā́do 'syehā́bhavat púnaḥ.
táto víṣvaṅ ví akrāmat
sāśanānaśané abhí.

With three quarters Puruṣa rose upward; one quarter of him here came into being again. Thence he spread asunder in all directions to what eats and does not eat.

úd ait (3. s. ipf. of i *go*, p. 130): to the world of immortals. **ihá**: in this world. **púnar**: that is, from his original form. **tátas**: from the earthly quarter. **ví akrāmat abhi**: distributed himself to, developed into. **sāśana-anaśané**: animate creatures and inanimate things; this cd. represents the latest stage of Dvandvas in the RV. (186 A 1, end).

5 तस्माद्विराळजायत
विराजो अधि पूरुषः ।
स जातो अत्यरिच्यत
पश्चाद्भूमिमथो पुरः ॥

तस्मात् । विऽराट् । अजायत ।
विऽराजः । अधि । पुरुषः ।
सः । जातः । अति । अरिच्यत ।
पश्चात् । भूमिम् । अथो इति । पुरः ॥

5 tásmād Virā́ḷ ajāyata,
Virā́jŏ ádhi Pū́ruṣaḥ.
sá jātó áty aricyata
paśc ā́d bhū́mim átho puráḥ.

From him Virāj was born, from Virāj Puruṣa. When born he reached beyond the earth behind and also before.

tásmād: from the undeveloped quarter of Puruṣa. **Virā́ḷ**: as intermediate between the primaeval Puruṣa and the evolved Puruṣa; cp. x. 72, 4: **Áditer Dákṣo ajāyata, Dákṣād u Áditiḥ pári** *from Aditi Dakṣa was born, and from Dakṣa Aditi.* On the Sandhi, see p. 3, n. 2. With **c d** cp. **1 c d**. **átho**: 24.

६ यत्पुरुषेण हविषा
देवा यज्ञमतन्वत।
वसन्तो अस्यासीदाज्यं
ग्रीष्म इध्मः शरद्धविः॥

यत्। पुरुषेण। हविषा।
देवाः। यज्ञम्। अतन्वत।
वसन्तः। अस्य। आसीत्। आज्यम्।
ग्रीष्मः। इध्मः। शरत्। हविः॥

6 yát Púruṣeṇa havíṣā
devā́ yajñám átanvata,
vasantó asyāsīd ā́jyam,
grīṣmá idhmáḥ, śarád dhavíḥ.

When the gods performed a sacrifice with Puruṣa as an oblation, the spring was its melted butter, the summer its fuel, the autumn its oblation.

Here the gods are represented as offering with the evolved Puruṣa an ideal human sacrifice to the primaeval Puruṣa. **átanvata**: 3. pl. ipf. Ā. of **tan** *stretch*; this vb. is often used figuratively in the sense of *to extend* the web of sacrifice = to carry out, perform. **dhavís**: 54.

७ तं यज्ञं बर्हिषि प्रौक्षन्
पुरुषं जातमग्रतः।
तेन देवा अयजन्त
साध्या ऋषयश्च ये॥

तम्। यज्ञम्। बर्हिषि। प्र। औक्षन्।
पुरुषम्। जातम्। अग्रतः।
तेन। देवाः। अयजन्त।
साध्याः। ऋषयः। च। ये॥

7 táṃ yajñáṃ barhíṣi práukṣan
Púruṣaṃ jātám agratáḥ:

That Puruṣa, born in the beginning, they besprinkled as a sacrifice

téna devā́ ayajanta,
sādhyā́ ṛ́ṣayaś ca yé.

on the strew: with him the gods, the Sādhyas, and the seers sacrificed.

jātám agratás: the evolved Puruṣa, born from Virāj (5 b), the same as in 6 a. **prá-aukṣan**: 3. pl. ipf. of 1. **ukṣ** *sprinkle.* **ayajanta**: = **yajñám átanvata** in 6 b. **Sādhyā́s**: an old class of divine beings (here probably in apposition to **devā́s**), cp. 16 d. **ṛ́ṣayaś ca yé**: *and those who* were *seers,* a frequent periphrastic use of the rel. = simply **ṛ́ṣayas.**

८ तस्माद्यज्ञात्सर्वहुतः
संभृतं पृषदाज्यम् ।
पशून्तांश्चक्रे वायव्यान्
आरण्यान्ग्राम्याश्च ये ॥

तस्मात् । यज्ञात् । सर्वऽहुतः ।
सम्ऽभृतम् । पृषत्ऽआज्यम् ।
पशून् । तान् । चक्रे । वायव्यान् ।
आरण्यान् । ग्राम्याः । च । ये ॥

8 **tásmād yajñā́t sarvahútaḥ**
sámbhṛtam pṛṣadājiám:
paśū́n tā́ṃś cakre vāyavyā̀n,
āraṇyā́n, grāmiā́ś ca yé.

From that sacrifice completely offered was collected the clotted butter: he made that the beasts of the air, of the forest, and those of the village.

tásmād: ab. of the source (201 A 1). **sámbhṛtam**: as finite vb. **pṛṣad-ājyám**: accent, p. 455, 10 *d* 1. **paśū́n**: Sandhi, 40, 2. **tā́ṃś**: attracted to **paśū́n** for **tát (pṛṣadājyám)**; Sandhi, 40, 1 *a.* **vāyavyā̀n**: one of the rare cases where the independent Svarita remains in pronunciation (p. 448, 1); **ā̀n** here remains unaffected by Sandhi because it is at the end of a Pāda (p. 31, f. n. 3); this is one of several indications that the internal Pādas (those within a hemistich) as well as the external Pādas were originally independent (cp. p. 465, f. n. 4). **āraṇyā́n**: that is, *wild.* **grāmyā́ś ca yé** = **grāmyā́n**, that is, *tame*; cp. **ṛ́ṣayaś ca yé** in 7 d.

९ तस्माद्यज्ञात्सर्वहुत
ऋचः सामानि जज्ञिरे
छन्दांसि जज्ञिरे तस्माद्
यजुस्तस्मादजायत ॥

तस्मात् । यज्ञात् । सर्वऽहुतः ।
ऋचः । सामानि । जज्ञिरे ।
छन्दांसि । जज्ञिरे । तस्मात् ।
यजुः । तस्मात् । अजायत ॥

9 tásmād yajñā́t sarvahúta
ṛ́caḥ sā́māni jajñire;
chándāṃsi jajñire tásmād;
yájus tásmād ajāyata.

From that sacrifice completely offered were born the hymns and the chants; the metres were born from it; the sacrificial formula was born from it.

ṛ́cas: the Rigveda. **sā́māni**: the Sāmaveda. **jajñire**: 3. pl. pf. Ā. of jan *beget*. **yájus**: the Yajurveda. This is the first (implicit) mention of the three Vedas. The AV. was not recognized as the fourth Veda till much later.

१० तस्मादश्वा अजायन्त
ये के चोभयादतः ।
गावो ह जज्ञिरे तस्मात्
तस्माज्जाता अजावयः ॥

तस्मात् । अश्वाः । अजायन्त ।
ये । के । च । उभयादतः ।
गावः । ह । जज्ञिरे । तस्मात् ।
तस्मात् । जाताः । अजावयः ॥

10 tásmād áśvā ajāyanta
yé ké ca ubhayā́dataḥ.
gā́vo ha jajñire tásmāt;
tásmāj jātā́ ajāváyaḥ.

From that arose horses and all such as have two rows of teeth. Cattle were born from that; from that were born goats and sheep.

yé ké ca: whatever animals besides the horse, such as asses and mules, have incisors above and below. **ajāváyas**: a pl. Dv. (186 A 2); Dvandvas are not analysed in the Pada text.

११ यत्पुरुषं व्यदधुः
कतिधा व्यकल्पयन् ।
मुखं किमस्य कौ बाहू
का ऊरू पादा उच्येते ॥

यत् । पुरुषम् । वि । अदधुः ।
कतिधा । वि । अकल्पयन् ।
मुखम् । किम् । अस्य । कौ । बाहू इति ।
कौ । ऊरू इति । पादौ । उच्येते इति ॥

11 yát Púruṣaṃ viádadhuḥ,
katidhā́ ví akalpayan?
múkhaṃ kim asya? káu bāhū́?
kā́ ūrū́ pā́dā ucyete?

When they divided Puruṣa, into how many parts did they dispose him? What (did) *his mouth* (become)? *What are* his *two arms,* his *two thighs,* his *two feet called?*

vi-ádadhur: when the gods cut up Puruṣa as the victim; here the Padapāṭha again (see note on viii. 48, 2 a, 10 c) accents the prp. in a subordinate clause (p. 469, 20 B). **káu**: the dual ending **au** for the normal **ā** before consonants (cp. note on x. 14, 10 a); **ká̄** and **pá̄dā** before **ŭ**: 22. **ucyete**: **3.** du. pr. ps. of **vac** *speak*: Pragṛhya, 26 *b*.

१२ ब्रा॒ह्म॒णो॑ऽस्य॒ मुख॑मासीद्
बा॒हू रा॑ज॒न्यः॑ कृ॒तः ।
ऊ॒रू तद॑स्य॒ यद्वैश्यः॑
प॒द्भ्यां शू॒द्रो अ॑जायत ॥

ब्रा॒ह्म॒णः । अ॒स्य॒ । मुख॑म् । आ॒सी॒त् ।
बा॒हू इति॑ । रा॒ज॒न्यः॑ । कृ॒तः ।
ऊ॒रू इति॑ । तत् । अ॒स्य॒ । यत् । वैश्यः॑ ।
प॒त्ऽभ्याम् । शू॒द्रः । अ॒जा॒य॒त॒ ॥

12 **brāhmaṇò 'sya múkham āsīd,**
bāhū́ rājaníaḥ kṛtáḥ;
ūrū́ tád asya yád váiśyaḥ;
padbhyā́m śūdrṓ ajāyata.

His mouth was the Brāhman, his two arms were made the warrior, his two thighs the Vaiśya; from his two feet the Śūdra was born.

In this stanza occurs the only mention of the four castes in the RV. **brāhmaṇò 'sya**: Sandhi accent, p. 465, 17, 3. **rājanyàs**: predicative nom. after a ps. (196 *b*). **kṛtás** attracted in number to **rājanyàḥ**, for **kṛtáu** (cp. 194, 3). **yád váiśyas**: the periphrastic use of the rel. (cp. 7 d and 8 d), lit. *his two thighs became that which* was *the Vaiśya*. **padbhyā́m**: abl. of source (77, 3 *a*, p. 458, 1).

१३ च॒न्द्रमा॒ मन॑सो जा॒तश्
चक्षोः॒ सूर्यो॑ अजायत ।
मुखा॒दिन्द्र॑श्चा॒ग्निश्च॑
प्रा॒णाद्वा॒युर॑जायत ॥

च॒न्द्रमाः॑ । मन॑सः । जा॒तः ।
चक्षोः॑ । सूर्यः॑ । अ॒जा॒य॒त॒ ।
मुखा॑त् । इन्द्रः॑ । च॒ । अ॒ग्निः । च॒ ।
प्रा॒णात् । वा॒युः । अ॒जा॒य॒त॒ ॥

13 **candrámā mánaso jātáś;**
cákṣoḥ sū́ryō ajāyata;
múkhād Índraś ca Agníś ca,
prāṇád Vāyúr ajāyata.

The moon was born from his *mind; from* his *eye the sun was born; from* his *mouth Indra and Agni, from* his *breath Vāyu was born.*

Note that **candrá-mās** is not analysed in the Pada text. **cákṣos**: ab. of **cákṣu** used only in this passage = the usual **cákṣus**; in the Funeral Hymn (x. 16, 3) **sū́ryas** and **cákṣus**, **vā́tas** and **ātmā́** are also referred to as cognate in nature.

१४ नाभ्या आसीदन्तरिक्षं
शीर्ष्णो द्यौः समवर्तत ।
पद्भ्यां भूमिर्दिशः श्रोत्रात्
तथा लोकाँ अकल्पयन् ॥

नाभ्याः । आसीत् । अन्तरिक्षम् ।
शीर्ष्णः । द्यौः । सम् । अवर्तत ।
पत्ऽभ्याम् । भूमिः । दिशः । श्रोत्रात् ।
तथा । लोकान् । अकल्पयन् ॥

14 **nā́bhyā āsīd antárikṣam;**
śīrṣṇó dyáuḥ sám avartata;
padbhyā́m bhū́mir, díśaḥ śró-trāt:
táthā lokā́m̐ akalpayan.

From his *navel was* produced *the air; from* his *head the sky was evolved; from* his *two feet the earth, from* his *ear the quarters: thus they fashioned the worlds.*

nā́bhyās: ab. of **nā́bhi** inflected according to the ī dec. (p. 82 *a*). **śīrṣṇás**: ab. of **śīrṣán** (90, 1 *a*; p. 458, 2). **sám avartata**: this vb. is to be supplied in c; cp. **ádhi sám avartata** in x. 129, 4. **akalpayan**: ipf. cs. of **kḷp**; *they* (the gods) *fashioned.*

१५ सप्तास्यासन्परिधयस्
त्रिः सप्त समिधः कृताः ।
देवा यद्यज्ञं तन्वाना
अबध्नन्पुरुषं पशुम् ॥

सप्त । अस्य । आसन् । परिऽधयः ।
त्रिः । सप्त । सम्ऽइधः । कृताः ।
देवाः । यत् । यज्ञम् । तन्वानाः ।
अबध्नन् । पुरुषम् । पशुम् ॥

15 **saptā́syāsan paridháyas;**
tríḥ saptá samídhaḥ kṛtā́ḥ;
devā́ yád, yajñám tanvānā́,
ábadhnan Púruṣam paśúm.

Seven were his enclosing sticks; thrice seven were the faggots made, when the gods performing the sacrifice bound Puruṣa as the victim.

paridháyas: the green **sticks** put round the sacrificial fire to fence it in, generally three in number. **saptá**: **as a** sacred number. **tanvānā́s**: cp. 8 b. **ábadhnan**: 3. pl. ipf. of **bandh**; cp. **púruṣeṇa havíṣā** in 6 a and **tám yajñám Púruṣam** in 7 a b. **paśúm**: as appositional acc. (198).

१६ यज्ञेन॑ य॒ज्ञम॑यजन्त दे॒वास्
तानि॒ धर्मा॑णि प्रथ॒मान्या॑सन् ।
ते ह॒ नाकं॑ महि॒मान॑: सचन्त
यत्र॒ पूर्वे॑ सा॒ध्याः सन्ति॑ दे॒वाः ॥

य॒ज्ञेन॑ । य॒ज्ञम् । अ॒य॒ज॒न्त॒ । दे॒वाः ।
तानि॑ । धर्मा॑णि । प्र॒थ॒मानि॑ । आ॒स॒न् ।
ते । ह॒ । नाक॑म् । म॒हि॒मान॑: । स॒च॒न्त॒ ।
यत्र॑ । पूर्वे॑ । सा॒ध्याः । सन्ति॑ । दे॒वाः ॥

16 yajñéna yajñám ayajanta devā́s:
tā́ni dhármāṇi prathamā́ni āsan.
té ha nā́kaṃ mahimā́naḥ sacanta,
yátra pū́rve Sādhiā́ḥ sánti, devā́ḥ.

With the sacrifice the gods sacrificed to the sacrifice: these were the first ordinances. These powers reached the firmament where are the ancient Sādhyas, the gods.

ayajanta: this vb. ordinarily takes the acc. of the person worshipped and the inst. of that with which he is worshipped (308, 1 *f*); the meaning here is: they sacrificed to Puruṣa (here appearing as a sacrifice, like Viṣṇu in the Brāhmaṇas) with the sacrifice in which he was the victim. **té mahimā́naḥ**: probably the powers residing in the sacrifice. This stanza is identical with i. 164, 50.

RĀ́TRĪ

The goddess of night, under the name of Rā́trī is invoked in only one hymn (x. 127). She is the sister of Uṣas, and like her is called a daughter of heaven. She is not conceived as the dark, but as the bright starlit night. Decked with all splendour she drives away the darkness. At her approach men, beasts, and birds go to rest. She protects her worshippers from the wolf and the thief, guiding them to safety. Under the name of nákta n., combined with uṣás, Night appears as a dual divinity with Dawn in the form of Uṣā́sā-náktā and Náktoṣā́sā, occurring in some twenty scattered stanzas of the Rigveda.

x. 127. Metre: **Gāyatrī.**

रात्री॒ व्य॑ख्यदाय॒ती
पु॒रु॒त्रा दे॒व्य१॒॑क्षभि॑: ।
विश्वा॒ अधि॒ श्रियो॑ऽधित ॥

रात्री॑ । वि । अ॒ख्य॒त् । आ॒ऽय॒ती ।
पु॒रु॒ऽत्रा । दे॒वी । अ॒क्षऽभि॑: ।
विश्वा॑: । अधि॑ । श्रिय॑: । अ॒धि॒त॒ ॥

1 **Rā́trī ví akhyad āyatī́**
purutrā́ devī́ akṣábhiḥ:
víśvā ádhi śríyo 'dhita.

Night approaching has looked forth in many places with her eyes: she has put on all glories.

ví akhyat: a ao. of **khyā** *see* (147 *a* 1). **ā-yatī́:** pr. pt. f. of **ā + i** *go* (95 *a*). **devī́:** accent, p. 450, *b*; metre, p. 437, *a* 4. **akṣábhis:** 99, 4; the eyes are stars. **ádhi adhita:** root ao. Ā. of **dhā** *put* (148, 1 *a*). **śríyas** (A. pl. of **śrī́**; 100 *b*, p. 87); *the glories* of starlight.

२ ओर्वप्रा अमर्त्या
निवतो देव्युद्वतः ।
ज्योतिषा बाधते तमः ॥

आ । उरु । अप्राः । अमर्त्या ।
निऽवतः । देवी । उत्ऽवतः ।
ज्योतिषा । बाधते । तमः ॥

2 **ā́ urv àprā ámartiā**
niváto devī́ udvátaḥ:
jyótiṣā bādhate támaḥ.

The immortal goddess has pervaded the wide space, the depths, and the heights: with light she drives away the darkness.

ā́ aprās: 3. s. s ao. of **prā** *fill* (144, 5). **devī́:** cp. 1 b. **jyótiṣā:** with starlight.

३ निरु स्वसारमस्कृतो-
षसं देव्यायती ।
अपेदु हासते तमः ॥

निः । ऊं इति । स्वसारम् । अकृत ।
उषसम् । देवी । आऽयती ।
अप । इत् । ऊं इति । हासते । तमः ॥

3 **nír u svásāram askṛta**
Uṣásaṃ devī́ āyatī́:
ápéd u hāsate támaḥ.

The goddess approaching has turned out her sister Dawn; away too will go the darkness.

nír askṛta: 3. s. root ao. of **kṛ** *do*; the **s** is here not original (Padapāṭha akṛta), but is probably due to the analogy of forms such as niṣ-kuru (AV.); it spread to forms in which **kṛ** is compounded with the prps. **pári** and **sám** (**pariṣkṛṇvánti, páriṣkṛta, sáṃskṛta**). **Uṣásam:** *Dawn* here used in the sense of *daylight* (dec., 83, 2 *a*). **nír u — ápa íd u:** in the second clause the pcl. is used anaphorically (p. 221, 2), with special emphasis (**íd**) on the second prp., = and the darkness will also be dispelled by the starlight (cp. 2 c). **hāsate**: 3. s. sb. Ā. of the s ao. of 2. **hā** *go forth* (p. 162, 2).

4 सा नो अद्य यस्या वयं
नि ते यामन्नविक्ष्महि ।
वृक्षे न वसतिं वयः ॥

सा । नः । अद्य । यस्याः । वयम् ।
नि । ते । यामन् । अविक्ष्महि ;
वृक्षे । न । वसतिम् । वयः ॥

4 **sá nŏ adyá, yásyā vayám̱**
ní te yā́mann ávikṣmahi,
vṛkṣé ná vasatím̱ váyaḥ.

So to us to-day thou (hast approached), *at whose approach we have come home, as birds to their nest upon the tree.*

sā́: p. 294, *b*; a vb. has here to be supplied, the most natural one being *hast come*, from **āyatí** in 3 b. **yásyās . . te** for **tvám̱ yásyās**, a prs. prn. often being put in the rel. clause. **yā́man**: loc. (90). **ní . . ávikṣmahi**: s ao. Ā., *we have turned in* (intr.). **vasatím**: governed by a cognate vb. to be supplied, such as *return to*. **váyas**: N. pl. of **ví** *bird* (99, 3 *a*).

5 नि ग्रामासो अविक्षत
नि पद्वन्तो नि पक्षिणः ।
नि श्येनासश्चिदर्थिनः ॥

नि । ग्रामासः । अविक्षत ।
नि । पत्ऽवन्तः । नि । पक्षिणः ।
नि । श्येनासः । चित । अर्थिनः ॥

5 **ní grā́māsŏ avikṣata,**
ní padvánto, ní pakṣíṇaḥ,
ní śyenā́saś cid arthínaḥ.

Home have gone the villages, home creatures with feet, home those with wings, home even the greedy hawks.

ní avikṣata: 3. pl. Ā. s ao. of **viś** *enter*. **grā́māsas**: = *villagers*. **ní**: note the repetition of the prp. throughout, in place of the cd. **vb.**: a common usage.

6 यावया वृक्यं१वृकं
यवय स्तेनमूर्म्ये ।
अथा नः सुतरा भव ॥

यवय । वृक्यम् । वृकम् ।
यवय । स्तेनम् । ऊर्म्ये ।
अथ । नः । सुऽतरा । भव ॥

6 **yāváyā vr̥kíam vŕ̥kam,**	*Ward off the she-wolf and the*
yaváya stenám, ūrmie;	*wolf, ward off the thief, O Night;*
áthā naḥ sutárā bhava.	*so be easy for us to pass.*

yāváyā: cs. of **yu** *separate*; this and other roots ending in **ú**, as well as in **i**, **r̥**, may take Guṇa or Vr̥ddhi in the cs. (168, 1 *c*), but the Padapāṭha invariably gives **yavaya**; the final vowel is metrically lengthened (in b it is long by position before st). **vr̥kyàm:** accent, p. 450, 2 *b*. **áthā:** final metrically lengthened (cp. p. 214).

७ उप मा पेपिशत्तमः
कृष्णं व्यक्तमस्थित ।
उष ऋणेव यातय ॥

उप । मा । पेपिशत् । तमः ।
कृष्णम् । विऽअक्तम् । अस्थित ।
उषः । ऋणाऽइव । यातय ॥

7 **úpa mā pépiśat támaḥ,**	*The darkness, thickly painting,*
kr̥ṣṇám, víaktam asthita:	*black, palpable, has approached me:*
Úṣa r̥ṇéva yātaya.	*O Dawn, clear it off like debts.*

úpa asthita: 3. s. Ā. of root ao. of **sthā** *stand*. **pépiśat:** int. pr. pt. of **piś** *paint*, as if it were material. **úṣas:** Dawn, as a counterpart of Night, is invoked to exact = remove the darkness from Rātrī, as one exacts money owing. In hymns addressed to a particular deity, another who is cognate or in some way associated, is not infrequently introduced incidentally. **yātaya:** cs. of **yat**.

८ उप ते गा इवाकरं
वृणीष्व दुहितर्दिवः ।
रात्रि स्तोमं न जिग्युषे ॥

उप । ते । गाऽइव । आ । अकरम् ।
वृणीष्व । दुहितः । दिवः ।
रात्रि । स्तोमम् । न । जिग्युषे ॥

8 **úpa te gā́ ivā́karam,**	*Like kine I have delivered up to*
vr̥ṇīṣvá, duhitar divaḥ,	*thee* a hymn—*choose it O daughter*
Rā́tri, stómam ná jigyúṣe.	*of heaven, O Night—like a song of*
	praise to a victor.

úpa ā́ akaram (1. s. root ao. of **kr̥**): I have driven up for thee my song of praise, as a herdsman delivers up in the evening the cows which he has herded since the morning; cp. i. 114, 9, **úpa te stómān**

paśupā́ iva‿**ā́karam** *I have driven up songs of praise for thee like a herdsman.* **vṛṇīṣvá** : 2. s. ipv. Ā. from **vṛ** *choose.* b is parenthetical. **stómam** is to be supplied with **ā́karam**. **jigyúṣe** : dat. of pf. pt. of **ji** *conquer* (157 *b a*).

HYMN OF CREATION

In the following cosmogonic poem the origin of the world is explained as the evolution of the existent (sát) from the non-existent (ásat). Water thus came into being first; from it was evolved intelligence by heat. It is the starting-point of the natural philosophy which developed into the Sāṅkhya system.

x. 129. Metre: **Triṣṭubh.**

१ नासदासीन्नो सदासीत्तदानीं
नासीद्रजो नो व्योमा परो यत् ।
किमावरीवः कुह कस्य शर्मन्न्
अम्भः किमासीद्गहनं गभीरम् ॥

न । असत् । आसीत् । नो इति । सत् । आसीत् । तदानीम् ।
न । आसीत् । रजः । नो इति । विऽओम । परः । यत् ।
किम् । आ । अवरीवरिति । कुह । कस्य । शर्मन् ।
अम्भः । किम् । आसीत् । गहनम् । गभीरम् ॥

1 **nā́sad āsīn, nó sád āsīt tadā́nīṃ;**
nā́sīd rájo nó víomā paró yát.
kím ā́varīvaḥ? kúha? kásya śármann?
ámbhaḥ kím āsīd, gáhanaṃ gabhīrám?

There was not the non-existent nor the existent then; there was not the air nor the heaven which is beyond. What did it contain? Where? In whose protection? Was there water, unfathomable, profound?

Cf. ŚB. x. 5, 3, 1: **ná‿iva vā́ idám ágré'sad āsīd ná‿iva sád āsīt** *verily this* (universe) *was in the beginning neither non-existent nor existent as it were.* **tadā́nīm** : before the creation. **āsīt** : the usual form of the 3. s. ipf. of **as** *be*; the rarer form occurs in 3 b. **nó**: for **ná u** (24). **víomā**: the final vowel metrically lengthened (cp. p. 440, 4 B). **parás**: adv.; on the accent cp. note on ii. 35, 6 c. **ā́ avarīvar**: 3. s. ipf. int. of **vṛ** *cover* (cp. 173, 3); what did it *cover up* = *conceal* or *contain?* **kúha**: *where* was it? **kásya śárman**: who guarded it? **kím**: here as an inter. pcl. (p. 225). **ámbhas**: cp. 3 b, and TS., **ā́po vā́ idám ágre salilám āsīt** *this* (universe) *in the beginning* was *the waters, the ocean.*

२ न मृत्युरासीदमृतं न तर्हि
न रात्र्या अह्न आसीत्प्रकेतः ।
आनीदवातं स्वधया तदेकं
तस्माद्धान्यन्न परः किं चनास ॥

न । मृत्युः । आसीत् । अमृतम् । न । तर्हि ।
न । रात्र्याः । अह्नः । आसीत् । प्रऽकेतः ।
आनीत् । अवातम् । स्वधया । तत् । एकम् ।
तस्मात् । ह । अन्यत् । न । परः । किम् ।
चन । आस ॥

2 **ná mṛtyúr āsīd, amṛ́taṃ ná tárhi.**
ná rā́triā áhna āsīt praketáḥ.
ā́nīd avātáṃ svadháyā tád ékaṃ.
tásmād dhānyán ná paráḥ kíṃ canā́sa.

There was not death nor immortality then. There was not the beacon of night, nor *of day. That one breathed, windless, by its own power. Other than that there was not anything beyond.*

rā́tryās: gen. of **rā́trī** (p. 87). **áhnas**: gen. of **áhan** (91, 2). **ā́nīt**: 3. s. ipf. of **an** *breathe* (p. 143, 3 *a*). **tásmād**: governed by **anyád** (p. 317, 3). **dha** for **ha**: 54. **anyán ná**: 33. **parás**: cp. note on 1 b. **āsa**: pf. of **as** *be* (135, 2).

३ तम आसीत्तमसा गूळ्हमग्रे
ऽप्रकेतं सलिलं सर्वमा इदम् ।
तुच्छ्येनाभ्वपिहितं यदासीत्
तपसस्तन्महिनाजायतैकम् ॥

तमः । आसीत् । तमसा । गूळ्हम् । अग्रे ।
अप्रऽकेतम् । सलिलम् । सर्वम् । आः ।
इदम् ।
तुच्छ्येन । आभु । अपिऽहितम् । यत् ।
आसीत् ।
तपसः । तत् । महिना । अजायत । एकम् ॥

3 táma āsīt támasā gūḷhám ágre;
apraketám̐ salilám̐ sárvam ā idám.
tuchyénābhú ápihitam yád ā́sīt,
tápasas tán mahinā́jāyatáikam.

Darkness was in the beginning hidden by darkness; indistinguishable, this all was water. That which, coming into being, was covered with the void, that One arose through the power of heat.

gūḷhám: pp. of guh *hide* (69 *c*, cp. 3 *b* γ, p. 3 and 13). ās: 3. s. ipf. of as *be* (p. 142, 2 *b*); this form is also found twice (i. 85, 1. 7) alternating with āsīt. b is a Jagatī intruding in a Triṣṭubh stanza (cp. p. 445, f. n. 7). ābhú: the meaning of this word is illustrated by ā-babhū́va in 6 d and 7 a. mahinā́ = mahimnā́ (90, 2, p. 69).

४ कामस्तदग्रे समवर्तताधि
मनसो रेतः प्रथमं यदासीत् ।
सतो बन्धुमसति निरविन्दन्
हृदि प्रतीष्या कवयो मनीषा ॥

कामः । तत् । अग्रे । सम् । अवर्तत । अधि ।
मनसः । रेतः । प्रथमम् । यत् । आसीत् ।
सतः । बन्धुम् । असति । निः । अविन्दन् ।
हृदि । प्रतिऽइष्य । कवयः । मनीषा ॥

4 kā́mas tád ágre sám avartatā́dhi,
mánaso rétaḥ prathamám̐ yád ā́sīt.
sató bándhum ásati nír avindan
hṛdí pratī́ṣyā kaváyo manīṣā́.

Desire in the beginning came upon that, (desire) *that was the first seed of mind. Sages seeking* in their *hearts with wisdom found out the bond of the existent in the non-existent.*

ádhi sám avartata: 3. s. ipf. Ā. of vṛt *turn,* with sám *come into being*; ádhi *upon* makes the verb transitive = *come upon, take possession of.* tád *that* = tád ékam in 2 c, the unevolved universe. One of the two prps. here is placed after the vb. (cp. 191 *f*, and p. 468, 20 A *a*). yád: referring to kā́mas is attracted in gender to the predicate n. rétas. satás: they found the origin of the evolved world in the unevolved. prati-iṣyā: the gd. in ya has often a long final vowel (164, 1) which is always short in the Padapāṭha. manīṣā́: inst. of f. in ā (p. 77).

५ तिरश्चीनो विततो रश्मिरेषाम्
अधः स्विदासी३दुपरि स्विदा-
सी३त् ।
रेतोधा आसन्महिमान आसन्
स्वधा अवस्तात्प्रयतिः परस्तात् ॥

तिरश्चीनः । विऽततः । रश्मिः । एषाम् ।
अधः । स्वित् । आसी३त् । उपरि । स्वित् ।
आसी३त् ।
रेतःऽधाः । आसन् । महिमानः । आसन् ।
स्वधा । अवस्तात् । प्रऽयतिः । परस्तात् ॥

5 **tiraścī́no vítato raśmír eṣām:**
adháḥ svid āsī́3d, upári svid āsī3t?
retodhā́ āsan, mahimā́na āsan;
svadhā́ avástāt, práyatiḥ parástāt.

Their cord was extended across: was there below or was there above? There were impregnators, there were powers; there was energy below, there was impulse above.

raśmís: the meaning of this word here is uncertain, but it may be an explanation of **bándhu** in 4 c: the cord with which the sages (referred to by **eṣām**) in thought measured out the distance between the existent and non-existent, or between what was above and below; cp. viii. 25, 18, **pári yó raśmínā divó ántān mamé pṛthivyā́ḥ** *who with a cord has measured out the ends of heaven and earth*; cp. also the expression **sū́tram vítatam** (in AV. x. 8, 37) *the extended string* with reference to the earth. **āsīt**: accented because in an antithetical sentence (p. 468, 19 B β). The ī is prolated, and that syllable (and not ā) has the Udātta, as in the final syllable of a sentence in questions (Pāṇini viii. 2, 97); the second question **upári svid āsī3t** is quoted by Pāṇini (viii. 2, 102) as coming under this rule, but without accent. **retodhā́s** and **mahimā́nas** are contrasted as male and female cosmogonic principles, to which correspond respectively **práyatis** and **svadhā́**. In TS. iv. 3, 11, 1, mention is made of **tráyo mahimā́naḥ** connected with fertility. **svadhā́**: this is one of the five examples of a N. f. in **ā** left uncontracted with a following vowel: it is probable that the editors of the Saṃhitā text treated these forms as ending in **āḥ**, while the Padapāṭha gives them without Visarjanīya, doubtless owing to the greatly increasing prevalence of the nominatives in ā.

६ को अद्धा वेद क इह प्र वोचत्
कुत आजाता कुत इयं विसृष्टिः ।
अर्वाग्देवा अस्य विसर्जनेना-
था को वेद यत आबभूव ॥

कः । अद्धा । वेद । कः । इह । प्र । वोचत् ।
कुतः । आऽजाता । कुतः । इयम् । वि
ऽसृष्टिः ।
अर्वाक् । देवाः । अस्य । विऽसर्जनेन ।
अथ । कः । वेद । यतः । आऽबभूव ॥

6 **kó addhā́ veda? ká ihá prá vocat,**
kúta ā́jātā, kúta iyáṃ vísṛṣṭiḥ?
arvā́g devā́ asyá visárjanena:
áthā kó veda yáta ābabhū́va?

Who knows truly? Who shall here declare, whence it has been produced, whence is this creation? By the creation of this (universe) *the gods* (come) *afterwards: who then knows whence it has arisen?*

vocat: a ao. inj. of vac. **kutás**: b has one syllable too many (p. 441, 4 *a*). **arvā́k**: the sense is that the gods, being part of the creation, are later than the period preceding the creation, and therefore can know nothing of the origin of the universe. **áthā**: with metrically lengthened final vowel (p. 440, 4; cp. 179, 1).

७ इयं विसृष्टिर्यत आबभूव
यदि वा दधे यदि वा न ।
यो अस्याध्यक्षः परमे व्योमन्
सो अङ्ग वेद यदि वा न वेद ॥

इयम् । विऽसृष्टिः । यतः । आऽबभूव ।
यदि । वा । दधे । यदि । वा । न ।
यः । अस्य । अधिऽअक्षः । परमे । वि
ऽओमन् ।
सः । अङ्ग । वेद । यदि । वा । न । वेद ॥

7 **iyáṃ vísṛṣṭir yáta ābabhū́va;**
yádi vā dadhé yádi vā ná:
yó asyā́dhyakṣaḥ paramé vío-man
só aṅgá veda, yádi vā ná véda.

Whence this creation has arisen; whether he founded it or did not: he who in the highest heaven is its surveyor, he only knows, or else he knows not.

a and b are dependent on **veda** in d. **asya**: *of this* universe. b is defective by two syllables (p. 440, 4 *a*): possibly a metrical pause expressive of doubt may have been intended. **vyòman**: loc. (90, 2). **véda**: the accent is due to the formal influence of **yádi** (p. 246, 3 *a*).

YAMÁ

Three hymns are addressed to Yama, the chief of the blessed dead. There is also another (x. 10), which consists of a dialogue between him and his sister Yamī. He is associated with Varuṇa, Bṛhaspati, and especially Agni, the conductor of the dead, who is called his friend and his priest. He is not expressly designated a god, but only a being who rules the dead. He is associated with the departed Fathers, especially the Aṅgirases, with whom he comes to the sacrifice to drink Soma.

Yama dwells in the remote recess of the sky. In his abode, which is the home of the gods, he is surrounded by songs and the sound of the flute. Soma is pressed for Yama, ghee is offered to him, and he comes to seat himself at the sacrifice. He is invoked to lead his worshippers to the gods, and to prolong life.

His father is Vivasvant and his mother Saraṇyū. In her dialogue with him Yamī speaks of Yama as the 'only mortal', and elsewhere he is said to have chosen death and abandoned his body. He departed to the other world, having found out the path for many, to where the ancient Fathers passed away. Death is the path of Yama. His foot-fetter (páḍbīśa) is spoken of as parallel to the bond of Varuṇa. The owl (úlūka) and the pigeon (kapóta) are mentioned as his messengers, but the two four-eyed, broad-nosed, brindled dogs, sons of Saramā (sārameyáu) are his regular emissaries. They guard the path along which the dead man hastens to join the Fathers who rejoice with Yama. They watch men and wander about among the peoples as Yama's messengers. They are besought to grant continued enjoyment of the light of the sun.

As the first father of mankind and the first of those that died, Yama appears to have originally been regarded as a mortal who became the chief of the souls of the departed. He goes back to the Indo-Iranian period, for the primaeval twins, from whom the human race is descended, Yama and Yamī, are identical with the Yima and Yimeh of the Avesta. Yama himself may in that period have been regarded as a king of a golden age, for in the Avesta he is the ruler of an earthly, and in the RV. that of a heavenly paradise.

x. 135. Metre: **Anuṣṭubh.**

१ यस्मिन्वृक्षे सुपलाशे	यस्मिन् । वृक्षे । सुऽपलाशे ।
देवैः संपिबते यमः ।	देवैः । सम्ऽपिबते । यमः ।
अत्रा नो विश्पतिः पिता	अत्र । नः । विश्पतिः । पिता ।
पुराणाँ अनु वेनति ॥	पुराणान् । अनु । वेनति ॥

1 **yásmin vṛkṣé supalāśé**
deváiḥ saṃpíbate Yamáḥ,
átrā no viśpátiḥ pitā́
purāṇā́m̐ ánu venati.

Beside the fair-leaved tree under which Yama drinks together with the gods, there our father, master of the house, seeks the friendship of the men of old.

yásmin: the loc. is often used in the sense of *beside, near* (cp. 203, 2). **saṃpíbate:** *drinks* Soma *with.* **átrā:** with metrically long final vowel (cp. 433, 2 A). **nas:** *our* i. e. *of me* and the other members of the family. **pitā́:** my deceased *father.* **purāṇā́n:** ancient ancestors; Sandhi, 39. **ánu venati:** that is, associates with them.

२ पुराणाँ अनुवेनन्तं
चरन्तं पापयामुया ।
असूयन्नभ्यचाकशं
तस्मा अस्पृहयं पुनः ॥

पुराणान् । अनुऽवेनन्तम् ।
चरन्तम् । पापया । अमुया ।
असूयन् । अभि । अचाकशम् ।
तस्मै । अस्पृहयम् । पुनरिति ॥

2 **purāṇā́m̐ anuvénantam,**
cárantam pāpáyāmuyā́,
asūyánn abhy àcākaśam:
tásmā aspṛhayam púnaḥ.

Him seeking the friendship of the men of old, faring in this evil way, I looked upon displeased: for him I longed again.

In this and the preceding stanza a son speaks of his father who has gone to the world of Yama. **amuyā́:** inst. s. f. of the prn. ayám used adverbially with shift of accent (p. 109); with this is combined the inst. s. f. of the adj. **pāpá** similarly used, the two together meaning ***in this evil way,*** that is, going to the abode of the dead. **asūyán:** *being displeased,* that is, with him, opposed to aspṛhayam, *I longed for him,* that is, to see him again. **acākaśam:** ipf. int. of **kāś,** with shortening of the radical vowel (174).

३ यं कुमार नवं रथम्
अचक्रं मनसाकृणोः ।
एकेषं विश्वतः प्राञ्चम्
अपश्यन्नधि तिष्ठसि ॥

यम् । कुमार । नवम् । रथम् ।
अचक्रम् । मनसा । अकृणोः ।
एकऽईषम् । विश्वतः । प्राञ्चम्
अपश्यन् । अधि । तिष्ठसि ॥

3 yáṃ, kumāra, návaṃ rátham
acakráṃ mánasā́kṛṇoḥ,
ékeṣaṃ viśvátaḥ prā́ñcam,
ápaśyann ádhi tiṣṭhasi.

The new car, O boy, the wheelless, which thou didst make in mind, which has one pole, but faces in all directions, thou ascendest seeing it not.

In this stanza (and the next) the dead boy is addressed; he mounts the car which he imagines is to take him to the other world. **aca-krám**: perhaps because the dead are wafted to Yama by Agni. **éka** and **viśvátas** are opposed: though it has but one pole, it has a front on every side. **ápaśyan**: because dead.

४ यं कुमार प्रावर्तयो
रथं विप्रेभ्यस्परि ।
तं सामानु प्रावर्तत
समितो नाव्याहितम् ॥

यम् । कुमार । प्र । अवर्तयः ।
रथम् । विप्रेभ्यः । परि ।
तम् । साम । अनु । प्र । अवर्तत ।
सम् । इतः । नावि । आऽहितम् ॥

4 yáṃ, kumāra, prā́vartayo
ráthaṃ víprebhias pári,
táṃ sā́mā́nu prā́vartata,
sám itó nāví ā́hitam.

The car, O boy, that thou didst set rolling forth away from the priests, after that there rolled forth a chant placed from here upon a ship.

The departure of the dead is followed by a funeral chant. **pra-ávartayas**: 2. s. ipf. cs. of vṛt *turn*; accent, p. 464, 17, 1; p. 469, *β*; analysed by the Padapāṭha, as **prá ávartayas**; cp. note on viii. 48, 2 a. **ánu prá avartata**: 3. s. ipf. Ā. of vṛt: accent, p. 464, 17, 1; p. 466, 19; p. 468, 20 *a*. **víprebhyas**: the priests officiating at the funeral; abl. governed by **pári** (176, 1 *a*); Sandhi, 43, 2 *a*. **sám ā́-hitam**: accent, p. 462, 13 *b*. **nāví**: the funeral chant is placed on a boat as a vehicle to convey it from here (itás) to the other world.

५ कः कुमारमजनयद्
रथं को निरवर्तयत् ।
कः स्वित्तदद्य नो ब्रूयाद्
अनुदेयी यथाभवत् ॥

कः । कुमारम् । अजनयत् ।
रथम् । कः । निः । अवर्तयत् ।
कः । स्वित् । तत् । अद्य । नः । ब्रूयात् ।
अनुऽदेयी । यथा । अभवत ॥

5 káḥ kumārám ajanayad?
rátham kó nír avartayat?
káḥ svit tád adyá no brūyād,
anudéyī yáthā́bhavat?

Who generated the boy? Who rolled out his car? Who pray could tell us this to-day, how his *equipment* (?) *was?*

These questions seem to be asked by Yama on the deceased boy's arrival: Who was his father? Who performed his funeral? With what equipment was he provided for the journey? **nír avartayat:** cp. **yám prā́vartayo rátham** in 4 a b. **anudéyī:** this word occurs only in this and the following verse; it is a f. of **anu-déya,** which occurs in the sense of *to be handed over*; the exact sense is nevertheless uncertain. It not improbably means that with which the deceased was supplied for the journey to Yama's abode.

६ यथाभवदनुदेयी
ततो अग्रमजायत।
पुरस्ताद्बुध्न आततः
पश्चान्निरयणं कृतम्॥

यथा। अभवत्। अनुऽदेयी।
ततः। अग्रम्। अजायत।
पुरस्तात्। बुध्नः। आऽततः।
पश्चात्। निःऽअयनम्। कृतम्॥

6 yáthā́bhavad anudéyī,
tátŏ ágram ajāyata;
purástād budhná ā́tataḥ;
paścā́n niráyaṇam kṛtám.

As the equipment was, so the top arose; in front the bottom extended; behind the exit was made.

The sense of this stanza is obscure, chiefly because the object of which the details are here given is uncertain. The car on which the deceased is supposed to be conveyed may be meant. There is evidently correspondence between **yáthā** and **tátas, ágram** and **budhnás, purástād** and **paścā́d.** There is no doubt about the grammatical forms or the meaning of the individual words (except **anudéyī**). If the reference is to the car, the general sense of the stanza is: in proportion to the equipment is the height of the top, the space on the floor in front, and the size of the exit at the back.

७ इदं यमस्य सादनं
देवमानं यदुच्यते।

इदम्। यमस्य। सदनम्।
देवऽमानम्। यत्। उच्यते

इयमस्य धम्यते नाळीर्
अयं गीर्भिः परिष्कृतः ॥

इयम् । अस्य । धम्यते । नाळीः ।
अयम् । गीःऽभिः । परिऽकृतः ॥

7 idáṃ Yamásya sā́danaṃ
devamānā́ṃ yád ucyáte.
iyám asya dhamyate nāḷī́r.
ayáṃ gīrbhíḥ páriṣkṛtaḥ.

This is the seat of Yama that is called the abode of the gods. This is his flute that is blown. He it is that is *adorned with songs.*

The boy here arrives at the abode of Yama. **sā́danam**: note that the vowel of this word is always short in the Pada text, the compilers of which seem to have regarded it as a metrical lengthening; **sā́danam** occurs about a dozen times in the RV., beside the much commoner sádanam. **nāḷī́s**: with s in the nom. (100, I *a*). There is one syllable too many in c (cp. p. 428, 2 *a*). **ayám**: Yama. **pári-ṣkṛtas**: note that the Pada text removes the unoriginal s (p. 145, f. n. 1; cp. note on x. 127, 3 *a*). **gīrbhís**: dec. 82; accent, p. 458, *c* 1.

VĀ́TA

This god, as **Vā́ta**, the ordinary name of wind, is addressed in two short hymns. He is invoked in a more concrete way than his doublet **Vāyú**, who is celebrated in one whole hymn and in parts of others. Vāta's name is frequently connected with forms of the root vā, *blow*, from which it is derived. He is once associated with the god of the rain-storm in the dual form of Vātā-Parjanyā́, while Vāyu is often similarly linked with Indra as Índra-Vāyū́. Vāta is the breath of the gods. Like Rudra he wafts healing and prolongs life; for he has the treasure of immortality in his house. His activity is chiefly mentioned in connexion with the thunder-storm. He produces ruddy lights and makes the dawns to shine. His swiftness often supplies a comparison for the speed of the gods or of mythical steeds. His noise is also often mentioned.

x. 168. Metre: **Triṣṭubh.**

१ वातस्य नु महिमानं रथस्य
रुजन्नेति स्तनयन्नस्य घोषः ।
दिविस्पृग्यात्यरुणानि कृण्वन्न्
उतो एति पृथिव्या रेणुमस्यन् ॥

वातस्य । नु । महिमानम् । रथस्य ।
रुजन् । एति । स्तनयन् । अस्य । घोषः ।
दिविऽस्पृक् । याति । अरुणानि । कृण्वन् ।
उतो इति । एति । पृथिव्या । रेणुम् ।
अस्यन् ॥

1 Vā́tasya nú mahimā́nam ráthasya :
rujánn eti, stanáyann asya ghóṣaḥ.
divispŕ̥g yāti aruṇā́ni kr̥ṇvánn ;
utó eti pr̥thivyā́ reṇúm ásyan.

(I will) *now* (proclaim) *the greatness of Vāta's car : its sound goes shattering, thundering. Touching the sky it goes producing ruddy hues ; and it also goes along the earth scattering dust.*

mahimā́nam : the vb. can easily be supplied, the most obvious one being **prá vocam** according to the first verse of i. 32, **Índrasya nú vīryā̀ṇi prá vocam,** and of i. 154 **Víṣṇor nú kaṃ vīryā̀ṇi prá vocam. rujá́n :** similarly the Maruts are said to split the mountain with the felly of their cars (v. 52, 9), and their sound is thunder (i. 23, 11). **stanáyan :** used predicatively like a finite vb. (207) or **eti** may be supplied. **aruṇā́ni :** alluding to the ruddy hue of lightning, with which the Maruts are particularly associated. **asya :** accent, p. 452. **utó :** 24. **pr̥thivyā́ :** inst. expressing motion *over* (199, 4).

२ सं प्रेरते अनु वातस्य विष्ठा
ऐनं गच्छन्ति समनं न योषाः ।
ताभिः सयुक्सरथं देव ईयते
ऽस्य विश्वस्य भुवनस्य राजा ॥

सम् । प्र । ईरते । अनु । वातस्य । विऽस्थाः ।
आ । एनम् । गच्छन्ति । समनम् । न । योषाः ।
ताभिः । सऽयुक् । सऽरथम् । देवः । ईयते ।
अस्य । विश्वस्य । भुवनस्य । राजा ॥

2 sáṃ prérate ánu Vā́tasya viṣṭhā́ :
áinaṃ gachanti sámanaṃ ná yóṣāḥ.
tā́bhiḥ sayúk saráthaṃ devá īyate,
asyá víśvasya bhúvanasya rā́jā.

The hosts of Vāta speed on together after him : *they go to him as women to a festival. The god, the king of all this world, united with them, goes on the same car.*

sáṃ prá īrate : 3. pl. pr. Ā. of **īr** ; p. 468, 20 *a.* **viṣṭhā́s :** though the derivation is **vi-stha** (not analysed in the Pada text), the meaning is uncertain. It is probably the subject with which **yóṣās** are compared, the sense being: the rains follow the storm wind (**apā́ṃ sákhā** in 3 c), and accompany him on his course. **sarátham**: an adv. based on the cognate acc. (197, 4). **īyate**: from **ī** *go* according to the fourth class, from which the pr. forms **īyase, īyate, īyante,** and the pt. **ī́yamāna** occur; c is a Jagatī Pāda.

3 अन्तरिक्षे पथिभिरीयमानो
न नि विशते कतमच्चनाहः ।
अपां सखा प्रथमजा ऋतावा
क्व स्विज्जातः कुत आ बभूव ॥

अन्तरिक्षे । पथिऽभिः । ईयमानः ।
न । नि । विशते । कतमत् । चन । अहरिति ।
अपाम् । सखा । प्रथमऽजाः । ऋतऽवा ।
क्व । स्वित् । जातः । कुतः । आ । बभूव ॥

3 **antárikṣe pathíbhir ī́yamāno,**
ná ní viśate katamác canā́haḥ.
apā́ṃ sákhā prathamajā́ ṛtā́vā,
kua svij jātáḥ, kúta ā́ babhūva?

Going along his paths in the air he rests not any day. The friend of waters, the first-born, the holy, where pray being born, whence has he arisen?

pathíbhis: inst. in local sense (199, 4). **ī́yamānas**: see note on 2 c. **áhas**: acc. of duration of time (197, 2); cp. also **4** b and the Padapāṭha. **apā́ṃ sákhā**: as accompanied by rain (cp. note on 2 a). **prathama-jā́s**: 97, 2. **ṛtā́vā**: 15 *c*. **kvà**: = **kúa** (p. 448). **jātás**: as a finite verb (208); cp. x. 129, 6 b. **kúta ā́ babhūva** = what is his origin (cp. x. 129, 6 d); on the use of the pf. cp. 213 A *a*.

4 आत्मा देवानां भुवनस्य गर्भो
यथावशं चरति देव एषः ।
घोषा इदस्य शृण्विरे न रूपं
तस्मै वाताय हविषा विधेम ॥

आत्मा । देवानाम् । भुवनस्य । गर्भः ।
यथाऽवशम् । चरति । देवः । एषः ।
घोषाः । इत् । अस्य । शृण्विरे । न । रूपम् ।
तस्मै । वाताय । हविषा । विधेम ॥

4 **ātmā́ devā́nāṃ, bhúvanasya gárbho,**
yathāvaśáṃ carati devá eṣáḥ.

Breath of the gods, germ of the world, this god fares according to his will. His sounds are heard.

ghóṣā íd asya śṛṇvire, ná rūpam.	(but) *his form is not* (seen). *To*
tásmai Vā́tāya havíṣā vidhema.	*that Vāta we would pay worship with oblation.*

ātmā́: cp. x. 90, 13, where Vāyu is said to have been produced from the breath of Puruṣa; and x. 16, 3, where breath is allied to wind. **gárbhas**: Vāta is here called *germ of the world* as Agni is in x. 45, 6. **asya**: accent, p. 452. **ghóṣās**: cp. 1 b. **śṛṇvire**: 3. pl. Ā. pr. of śru with ps. sense (p. 145, γ). **ná rūpám**: the vb. dṛśyate is here easily supplied. **vidhema**: with dat. (200 A *f*).

VOCABULARY

Finite verbal forms are here given under the root from which they are derived, as also the prepositions with which they are compounded, even when separated from them. Nominal verbal forms (participles, gerunds, gerundives, infinitives), on the other hand, appear in their alphabetical order.

ABBREVIATIONS

a. = adjective. A. = accusative. Ā = Ātmanepada, middle voice. AA. = Aitareya Āraṇyaka. ab. = ablative. acc. = accusative. act. = active. adv. = adverb, adverbial. ao. = aorist. Arm. = Armenian. Av. = Avesta, Avestic. Bv. = Bahuvrīhi compound. cd. = compound. cj. = conjunction. cog. = cognate. corr. = correlative. cpv. = comparative. cs. = causative. D. = dative. dat. = dative. dec. = declension. dem. = demonstrative. den. = denominative. der. = derivative. Dv. = Dvandva compound. ds. = desiderative. du. = dual. emph. = emphatic, emphasizing. enc. = enclitic. Eng. = English. f. = feminine. ft. = future. G. = genitive. gd. = gerund. gdv. = gerundive. gen. = genitive. Gk. = Greek. Go. = Gothic. gov. = governing compound. I. = instrumental. ij. = interjection. ind. = indicative. indec. = indeclinable. inf. = infinitive. inj. = injunctive. inst. = instrumental. int. = intensive. inter. = interrogative. ipf. = imperfect. ipv. = imperative. irr. = irregular. itv. = iterative. K. = Karmadhāraya compound. m. = masculine. mid. = middle. L. = locative. Lat. = Latin. lc. = locative. Lith. = Lithuanian. N. = nominative. n. = neuter. neg. = negative. nm. = numeral. nom. = nominative. OG. = Old German. OI. = Old Irish. OP. = Old Persian. op. = optative. ord. = ordinal. OS. = Old Saxon. OSl. = Old Slavonic. P. = Parasmaipada, active voice. pcl. = particle. pf. = perfect. pl. = plural. poss. = possessive. pp. = past passive participle. ppf. = pluperfect. pr. = present. prn. = pronoun. proh. = prohibitive. prp. = preposition. prs. = person, personal. ps. = passive. pt. = participle. red. = reduplicated. ref. = reflexive. rel. = relative. rt. = root. s. = singular. sb. = subjunctive. sec. = secondary. sf. = suffix. Slav. = Slavonic. spv. = superlative. syn. = syntactical. Tp. = Tatpuruṣa compound. V. = vocative. vb. = verb, verbal. voc. = vocative. YV. = Yajurveda.

a, prn. root *that* in **á-tas, á-tra, á-tha, a-smái, a-syá.**

aṃś *attain*, v. **aśnóti, aśnuté** : see **aś.**

áṃh-as, n. *distress, trouble*, ii. 33, 2. 3 ; iii. 59, 2 ; vii. 71, 5.

ak-tú, m. *ointment* ; *beam of light* ; (clear) *night*, x. 14, 9 [añj *anoint*].

akṣ-á, m. *die* for playing, pl. *dice*, x. 34, 2. 4. 6. 7. 13 [perhaps *eye* = *spot*].

akṣ-án, n. *eye* (weak stem of **ákṣi**), x. 127, 1.
á-kṣīya-māṇa, pr. pt. ps. *unfailing*, i. 154, 4 [2. kṣi *destroy*].
akhkhalī-kŕtyā, gd. *having made a croak*, vii. 103, 3.
Ag-ní, m. *fire*, ii. 12, 3; iii. 59, 5; viii. 48, 6; x. 34, 11; *god of fire, Agni*, i. 1–7, 9; 35, 1; ii. 35, 15; v. 11, 1–6; vii. 49, 4; x. 15, 9. 12; 90, 13 [Lat. *ig-ni-s*, Slav. *og-nĭ*].
agni-dagdhá, Tp. cd. *burnt with fire*, x. 15, 14 [pp. of dah *burn*].
agní-dūta, a. (Bv.) *having Agni as a messenger*, x. 14, 13.
agni-ṣvāttá, cd. Tp. *consumed by fire*, x. 15, 11 [pp. of **svād** *taste well*].
ág-ra, n. *front; beginning; top*, x. 135, 6; lc. **ágre** *in the beginning*, x. 129, 3. 4.
agra-tás, adv. *in the beginning*, x. 90, 7.
a-ghn-yā́, f. *cow*, v. 83, 8 [gdv. *not to be slain*, from han *slay*].
aṅkuś-ín, a. *having a hook, hooked, attractive*, x. 34, 7 [aṅkuśá *hook*].
1. **áṅg-a**, n. *limb*, ii. 33, 9.
2. aṅgá, emphatic pcl. *just, only*, i. 1, 6; x. 129, 7 [180].
áṅgāra, m. *coal*, x. 34, 9.
Áṅgira, m. name of an ancient seer, iv. 51, 4.
Áṅgiras, m. pl. name of a group of ancestors, v. 11, 6; x. 14, 3. 4. 5. 6; s., as an epithet of Agni, i. 1, 6; v. 11, 6 [Gk. ἄγγελο-ς 'messenger'].
ac *bend*, I. P. ácati. úd-, *draw up*, v. 83, 8.
a-cakrá, a. (Bv.) *wheelless*, x. 135, 3.
á-cit, a. (K.) *unthinking, thoughtless*, vii. 86, 7.
a-cít-e, dat. inf. *not to know*, vii. 61, 5.
á-citti, f. (K.) *thoughtlessness*, vii. 86, 6.
a-citrá, n. *darkness, obscurity*, iv. 51, 3.
á-cyuta, pp. (K.) *not overthrown, unshakable*, i. 85, 4.
acyuta-cyút, a. (Tp.) *moving the immovable*, ii. 12, 9.
ácha, prp. with acc., *unto*, viii. 48, 6.
aj *drive*, I. P. ájati [Lat. *ago* 'lead', 'drive', Gk. ἄγω, 'lead'].
á- *drive up*, vi. 54, 10.
úd- *drive out*, ii. 12, 3; iv. 50, 5.
ajá-māyu, a. (Bv.) *bleating like a goat*, vii. 103, 6. 10 [māyú, m. *bleat*].
a-jára, a. (K.) *unaging*, i. 160, 4 [jṝ *waste away*].

á-jasra, a. (K.) *eternal*, ii. 35, 8 [*unfailing*: **jas** *be exhausted*].
ajāví, m. pl. Dv. cd. *goats and sheep*, x. 90, 10 [ajá + ávi].
a-jur-yá, a. *unaging*, iv. 51, 6 [jur *waste away*].
añj, VII. P. anákti *anoint*; Ā. aṅkté *anoint oneself*, viii. 29, 1.
áñjas-ā, adv. *straightway*, vi. 54, 1 [inst. of áñjas *ointment*: = with gliding motion].
añj-í, n. *ornament*, i. 85, 3; viii. 29, 1 [añj *anoint*].
á-tas, adv. *hence*, x. 14, 9; = ab. *from that*, iv. 50, 3; *than that*, x. 90, 3.
ati-rātrá, a. (celebrated) *overnight*, vii. 103, 7 [rā́trī *night*].
átka, m. *robe*, ii. 35, 14.
áty-etavái, dat. inf. *to pass over*, v. 83, 10 [áti + i *go beyond*].
á-tra, adv. *here*, i. 154, 6; ii. 35, 6.
á-trā, adv. *then*, vii. 103, 2; *there*, x. 135, 1.
Átri, m. an ancient sage, vii. 71, 5.
á-tha, adv. *then*; *so*, vi. 54, 7.
Áthar-van, m. pl. name of a group of ancient priests, x. 14, 6.
á-thā, adv. *then*, viii. 48, 6; x. 14, 10; 15, 4. 11; 129, 6; *so*, x. 127, 6.
átho, adv. *and also*, x. 90, 5 [átha + u].
ad, *eat*, II. P. átti, ii. 35, 7; x. 15, 8. 11. 12 [Lat. *edo*, Gk. ἔδω, Eng. *eat*].
á-dabdha, pp. (K.) *uninjured*, iv. 50, 2 [dabh *harm*].
Á-diti, f. name of a goddess, viii. 48, 2 [*unbinding, freedom*, from 3. dā *bind*].
ad-dhā́, adv. *truly*, x. 129, 6 [*in this manner*: a-d *this* + dhā].
a-dyá, adv. *to-day*, i. 35, 11; iv. 51, 3–4; x. 14, 12; 127, 4; 135, 5; *now*, x. 15, 2 [perhaps = **a-dyavi** *on this day*].
á-dri, m. *rock*, i. 85, 5 [*not splitting*: dṛ *pierce*].
ádri-dugdha, Tp. cd. *pressed out with stones*, iv. 50, 3 [pp. of duh *milk*].
ádha-ra, a. *lower*, ii. 12, 4.
adhás, adv. *below*, x. 129, 5.
ádhi, prp. with lc., *upon*, i. 85, 7; v. 83, 9; vii. 103, 5; with ab. *from*, x. 90, 5.
ádhy-akṣa, m. *eye-witness; surveyor*, x. 129, 7 [*having one's eye upon*].
adhvará, m. *sacrifice*, i. 1, 4. 8; iv. 51, 2.

adhvar-yú, m. *officiating priest*, vii. 103, 8.
a-dhvasmán, a. (Bv.) *undimmed*, ii. 35, 14 [*having no darkening*].
an *breathe*, II. P. **ániti**, x. 129, 2 [Go. *an-an* 'breathe'].
án-agni-dagdha, pp. (K.) *not burned with fire*, x. 15, 14.
án-abhi-mlāta-varṇa, a. (Bv.) *having an unfaded colour*, ii. 35, 13.
á-naṣṭa-vedas, a. (Bv.) *whose property is never lost*, vi. 54, 8.
an-amīvá, a. (Bv.) *diseaseless*, iii. 59, 3; n. *health*, x. 14, 11 [**ámīvā** *disease*].
án-āgas, a. (Bv.) *sinless*, v. 83, 2; vii. 86, 7 [**ā́gas** *sin*; Gk. ἀν-αγής 'innocent'].
an-idhmá, a. (Bv.) *having no fuel*, ii. 35, 4.
á-nimiṣ-am, (acc.) adv. *unwinkingly*, vii. 61, 3 [**ni-míṣ**, f. *wink*].
á-nimiṣ-ā, (inst.) adv. *with unwinking eye*, iii. 59, 1 [**ni-míṣ**, f *wink*].
á-niviśamāna, pr. pt. Ā. *unresting*, vii. 49, 1 [**ni + viś** *go to rest*].
án-irā, f. (K.) *languor*, *ailment*, vii. 71, 2; viii. 48, 4 [**írā**, f. *refreshment*].
án-īka, n. *face*, ii. 35, 11 [**an** *breathe*].
ánu, prp. with acc., *along*, x. 14, 1. 8; *among*, x. 14, 12.
anu-kāmám, (acc.) adv. *according to desire*, viii. 48, 8.
anu-déyī, f. *equipment* (?), x. 135, 5. 6 [f. gdv. of **anu-dā** *to be handed over*].
anu-paspaśāná, pf. pt. Ā. *having spied out*, x. 14, 1 [**spaś** *spy*].
anu-madyá-māna, pr. pt. ps. *being greeted with gladness*, vii. 63, 3.
anu-vénant, pr. pt. *seeking the friendship of* (acc.), x. 135, 2.
ánu-vrata, a. *devoted*, x. 34, 2 [*acting according to the will* (**vratá**) *of another*].
án-ṛta, n. (K.) *falsehood*, ii. 35, 6; vii. 61, 5; *misdeed*, *wrong*, 86, 6 [**ṛtá** *right*].
an-enás, a. (Bv.) *guiltless*, vii. 86, 4 [**énas** *guilt*].
ánta, m. *end*, iv. 50, 1; *edge*, *proximity*: lc. **ánte** *near*, x. 34, 16.
antár, prp. with lc., *within*, i. 35, 9; ii. 12, 3; 35, 7; iv. 51, 3; vii. 71, 5; 86, 2 (= *in communion with*); viii. 48, 2; *among*, viii. 29, 2. 3 [Lat. *inter*].
antári-kṣa, n. *air*, *atmosphere*, i. 35, 7. 11; ii. 12, 2; x. 90, 14; 168, 3 [*situated between* heaven and earth: **kṣa** = 1. **kṣi** *dwell*].
ánti-tas, adv. *from near*, iii. 59, 2 [**ánti** *in front*, *near*].
ándh-as, n. *Soma plant*; *juice*, i. 85, 6 [Gk. ἄνθ-ος 'blossom'].
án-na, n. *food*, ii. 35, 5. 7. 10. 11. 14; pl. 12; x. 90, 2 [pp. of **ad** *eat*].
anyá, prn. a. *other*, ii. 35, 3. 8. 13; x. 34, 4. 10. 11. 14; 129, 2; with ab. = *than*, ii. 33, 11; **anyó-anyá** *one-another*, vii. 103, 3. 4. 5; **anyé-anyé**, **anyā́ḥ-anyā́ḥ** *some-others*, x. 14, 3; ii. 35, 3 [cp. Lat. *aliu-s*, Gk. ἄλλο-ς 'other'].
áp, f. *water*, pl. N. **ā́pas**, ii. 35, 3. 4; vii. 49, 1. 2[2]. 3. 4; 103, 2; A. **apás**, v. 83, 6; inst. **adbhís**, x. 14, 9; G. **apā́m**, i. 85, 9; ii. 12, 7; 35, 1. 2. 3. 7. 9. 11. 13. 14; vii. 103, 4; x. 168, 3; L. **apsú**, ii. 35, 4. 5. 7. 8; vii. 103, 5 [Av. *ap* 'water'].
apa-dhā́, f. *unclosing*, ii. 12, 3.
ápa-bhartavái, dat. inf. *to take away*, x. 14, 2 [**bhṛ** *bear*].
apa-bhartṛ́, m. *remover*, ii. 33, 7 [**bhṛ** *bear*].
á-paśyant, pr. pt. (K.) *not seeing*, x. 135, 3.
ápas, n. *work*, i. 85, 9 [Lat. *opus* 'work'].
apás, a. *active*, i. 160, 4.
apás-tama, spv. a. *most active*, i. 160, 4.
Apā́ṃ nápāt, m. *son of waters*, name of a god, ii. 33, 13; 35, 1. 3. 7. 9.
ápi-hita, pp. *covered*, x. 129, 3 [**dhā** *put*].
apīc-yà, a. *secret*, ii. 35, 11 [**apīc** contraction of a presupposed **api-añc**].
a-praketá, a. (Bv.) *indistinguishable*, x. 129, 3 [**praketá** *perception*].
á-pratīta, pp. (K.) *irresistible*, iv. 50, 9 [**prati** + pp. of **i** *go*].
a-pramṛṣyá, gdv. *not to be forgotten*, ii. 35, 6 [**mṛś** *touch*].
á-budhya-māna, pr. pt. *unawakening*, iv. 51, 3 [**budh** *wake*].
abhi-kṣipánt, pr. pt. *lashing*, v. 83, 3.
abhí-tas, adv. *on all sides*, iv. 50, 3; with acc., *around*, vii. 103, 7.
abhimāt-ín, m. *adversary*, i. 85, 3 [**abhí-māti**, f. *hostility*].
abhí-vṛṣṭa, pp. *rained upon*, vii. 103, 4.
abhiṣṭí-dyumna, a. (Bv.) *splendid help*, iv. 51, 7 [**dyumná**, n. *splendour*].
abhíṣṭi-śavas, a. (Bv.) *strong to help*, iii. 59, 8 [**śávas**, n. *might*].

abhīti, f. *attack*, ii. 33, 5 [abhí + ití].
abhí-vṛta, pp. *adorned*, i. 35, 4 [1. vṛ *cover*].
á-bhv-a, a. *monstrous* ; n. *force*, ii. 33, 10 ; *monster*, iv. 51, 9 [*non-existent, monstrous* : -bhū *be*].
á-manya-māna, pr. pt. Ā. *not thinking* = *unexpecting*, ii. 12, 10 [man *think*].
á-martya, a. (K.) *immortal*, viii. 48, 12 ; f. ā, x. 127, 2.
a-mítra, m. (K.) *enemy*, ii. 12, 8 [mitrá *friend*].
ámīta-varṇa, a. (Bv.) *of unchanged colour*, iv. 51, 9.
ámī-vā, f. *disease*, i. 35, 9 ; ii. 33, 2 ; vii. 71, 2 ; viii. 48, 11 [am *harm*, 3. s. ámī-ti].
amu-y-á, inst. **adv.** *in this way, so*, x. 135, 2 [inst. f. of amú *this* used in the inflexion of ayám].
á-mūra, a. (K.) *wise*, vii. 61, 5 [*not foolish* : **mūrá**].
a-mṛ́ta, a. *immortal* ; m. *immortal being*, i. 35, 2 ; vii. 63, 5 ; viii. 48, 3[2] ; n. *what is immortal*, i. 35, 6 ; x. 90, 3 ; *immortality*, x. 129, 2 [*not dead*, **mṛtá**, pp. of mṛ *die* ; cp. Gk. ἄμβροτος 'immortal'].
amṛta-tvá, n. *immortality*, x. 90, 2.
ámbh-as, n. *water*, x. 129, 1.
á-vajvan, m. (K.) *non-sacrificer*, vii. 61, 4.
a-y-ám, dem. prn. **N.** s. m. *this*, iii. 59, 4 ; vii. 86, 3. 8 ; viii. 48, 10 ; x. 34, 13 (= *here*) ; *he*, i. 160, 4 : x. 135, 7.
a-yás, a. *nimble*, i. 154, 6 [*not exerting oneself* : **yās = yas** *heat oneself*].
a-rapás, a. (Bv.) *unscathed*, ii. 33, 6 ; x. 15, 4 [**rápas**, n. *infirmity, injury*].
áram-kṛta, pp. *well-prepared*, x. 14, 13 [*made ready*].
ár-am, **adv.** *in readiness* ; with **kṛ** *do service to* (dat.), vii. 86, 7.
á-rāti, f. *hostility*, ii. 35. 6 ; iv. 50, 11 ; viii. 48, 3 ; x. 34, 14 [*non-giving, niggardliness, enmity*].
a-rí, m. *niggard, enemy*, gen. **aryás**, ii. 12, 4. 5 ; iv. 50, 11 ; viii. 48, 8 [*having no wealth* : **ri = rai** ; 1. *indigent* ; 2. *niggardly*].
á-riṣṭa, pp. (K.) *uninjured*, vi. 54, 7 [**riṣ** *injure*].
ar-uṇá, a. f. **ī**, *ruddy*, x. 15, 7 ; n. *ruddy hue*, x. 168, 1.
ar-uṣá, a. *ruddy*, i. 85, 5 ; vii. 71, 1.
a-reṇú, a. (Bv.) *dustless*, i. 35, 11 [**reṇú** m. *dust*].
ark-á, m. *song*, i. 85, 2 ; x. 15, 9 [**arc** *sing*].
arc *sing, praise*, I. **árcati.** **sám-**, *praise universally*, pf. ānṛcé, i. 160, 4.
árc-ant, pr. pt., *singing*, i. 85, 2 ; viii. 29, 10.
arṇa-vá, a. *waving*, viii. 63, 2 ; m. *flood*, i. 85, 9.
ár-tha, n. *goal*, vii. 63, 4 [*what is gone for* : ṛ *go*].
arth-ín, a. *greedy*, x. 127, 5 [*having an object, needy*].
ar-páya, cs. of **ṛ** *go*. **úd-** *raise up*, ii. 33, 4.
aryá, a. *noble*, vii. 86, 7 ; x. 34, 13 ; m. *lord*, ii. 35, 2.
Arya-mán, m. name of one of the Ādityas, vii. 63, 6.
ár-vant, m. *steed*, ii. 33, 1 ; vii. 54, 5 [*speeding* : ṛ *go*].
arvák, adv. *hither*, x. 15, 4. 9 ; *afterwards*, x. 129, 6.
arváñc, a. *hitherward*, i. 35, 10 ; v. 83, 6.
árh-ant, pr. pt. *worthy*, ii. 33, 10[3].
av *help*, I. P. **ávati**, i. 85, 7 ; ii. 12, 14 ; 35, 15 ; iv. 50, 9. 11 ; vii. 49, 1-4 ; 61, 2 ; x. 15, 1. 5 ; *quicken*, v. 83, 4.
ava-tá, m. *well*, i. 85, 10 ; iv. 50, 3 [**áva** *down*].
a-vadyá, n. *blemish*, x. 14, 8 [gdv. *not to be praised, blameworthy*].
avá-ni, f. *river*, v. 11, 5 [áva *down*].
ava-páśyant, pr. pt. *looking down on* (acc.), vii. 49, 3.
ava-má, spv. a. *lowest* ; *nearest*, ii. 35, 12 ; *latest*, vii. 71, 3 [**áva** *down*].
ava-yātṛ́, m. *appeaser*, viii. 48, 2.
áva-ra, cpv. a. *lower*, x. 15, 1 ; *nearer*, ii. 12, 8 [áva *down*].
áv-as, n. *help*, i. 35, 1 ; 85, 11 ; ii. 12, 9 ; iii. 59, 6 ; x. 15, 4 [av *help*].
ava-sána, n. *resting place*, x. 14, 9 [*unbinding, giving rest* : **áva + sā = si** *tie*].
avás-tāt, adv. *below*, x. 129, 5.
avas-yú, a. *desiring help*, iv. 50, 9.
a-vātá, a. (Bv.) *windless*, x. 129, 2 [**váta** *wind*].
av-i-tṛ́, m. *helper*, ii. 12, 6.
a-vī́ra, a. (Bv.) *sonless*, vii. 61, 4 [**vīrá** *hero*].
a-vṛká, a. (K.) *friendly*, x. 15, 1 [*not harming* : **vṛ́ka** *wolf*].

a-vyathyá, gdv. *immovable*, ii. 35, 5 [**vyath** *waver*].

aś *reach, obtain*, V. **aśnóti, aśnuté**, i. 1, 3; 35, 2; ii. 33, 2. 6; iii. 59, 2; vii, 103, 9.

abhí- *attain to* (acc.), i. 154, 5.

áś-man, m. *rock*, ii. 12, 3 [Av. *asman* 'stone'; Gk. ἄκμων 'anvil'].

áś-va, m. *horse*, ii. 12, 7; 35, 6; iv. 51, 5; v. 83, 3. 6; vii. 71, 3. 5; x. 34, 3. 11; 90, 10 [Lat. *equu-s* 'horse', Gk. ἵππο-ς, OS. *ehu*].

áśva-magha, a. (Bv.) *rich in horses*, vii. 71, 1 [**maghá** *bounty*].

Aśv-ín, m. du. *horsemen*, name of the twin gods of dawn, vii. 71, 2. 3. 6.

aṣṭáu, nm. *eight*, i. 35, 8.

as *be*, II. P.: pr. 2. **ási**, i. 1, 4; ii. 12, 15; 33, 3; 3. **ásti**, ii. 12, 5; 33, 7. 10; vii. 71, 4; 86, 6; x. 34, 14; pl. 1. **smási**, vi. 54, 9; viii. 48, 9; 3. **sánti**, i. 35, 12; x. 90, 16; ipv. **ástu**, v. 11, 5; vii. 86, 8²; x. 15, 2; **sántu**, vii. 63, 5; op. **syā́ma**, iii. 59, 3; iv. 50, 6; 51, 10. 11; viii. 48, 12. 13; ipf. 3. **ā́s**, x. 129, 3; **āsīt**, x. 34, 2; 90, 6. 12. 14; 129, 1⁴. 2². 3². 4. 5²; **ā́san**, x. 90, 15. 16; 129, 5²; pf. **āsa**, vii. 86, 4; x. 129, 2; **ā́sur**, iv. 51, 7.

ápi- *be* or *remain in* (lc.); **syāma**, iii. 59, 4; x. 14, 6.

pári *be around, celebrate*, 2. pl. **stha**, vii. 103, 7.

prá- *be pre-eminent*, ipv. **astu**, iii. 59, 2.

ás-at, pr. pt. n. *the non-existent*, x. 129, 1. 4.

a-saścát, a. (Bv.) *inexhaustible*, i. 160, 2 [*having no second*, **saścát**: **sac** *follow*].

ás-ita, (pp.) a. *black*, iv. 51, 9.

á-sammṛṣṭa, pp. (K.) *uncleansed*, v. 11. 3 [**mṛj** *wipe*].

ás-u, m. *life*, x. 14, 12; 15, 1 [1. **as** *exist*].

asu-tṛ́p, a. (Tp.) *life-stealing*, x. 14, 12 [**tṛp** *delight in*].

ásu-nīti, f. *spirit-guidance*, x. 15, 14.

ásu-ra, m. *divine spirit*, i. 35, 7. 10; v. 83, 6 [Av. *ahura*].

asur-yà, n. *divine dominion*, ii. 33, 9; 35, 2.

asūyánt, pr. pt. *displeased, resentful*, x. 135, 2.

ás-ta, n. *home, abode*, x. 14, 8; 34, 10.

asmá, prn. stem of 1. prs. pl.; A. **asmā́n** *us*, viii. 48, 3. 11; x. 15, 5; D. **asmábhyam** *to us*, i. 35, 12; x. 14, 12; **asmé** *to us*, i. 160, 5; ii. 33, 12; Ab. **asmád** *from us*, ii. 33, 2; vii. 71, 1. 2; *than us*, ii. 33, 11; G. **asmā́kam** *of us*, vi. 54, 6; L. **asmé** *in* or *on us*, ii. 35, 4; iv. 50, 10. 11; viii. 48, 10; **asmā́su** *on us*, iv. 51, 10.

a-smín, L. of prn. root **a**, *in this*, ii. 35, 14; iv. 50, 10; x. 14, 5.

á-smera, a. (K.) *not smiling*, ii. 35, 4.

a-smái, D. of prn. root **a**, *to him*, ii. 35, 5. 12; *for him*, x. 14, 9; unaccented, **asmai** *to* or *for him*, ii. 12, 5. 13; 35, 2. 10; vi. 54, 4; vii. 63, 5; x. 14, 9. 11.

a-syá, G. of prn. root **a**, *of this*, ii. 33, 9; x. 129, 6; 168, 2; unaccented, **asya** *his, of him, its, of it*, i. 35, 7; 154, 5; 160, 3; ii. 12, 13; 35, 2. 6. 8. 11; iv. 50, 2; vi. 54, 3; vii. 86, 1; viii. 48, 12; x. 34, 4. 6; 90, 3³. 4. 6. 12². 15; 129, 7; 135, 7; 168, 1.

ás-yant, pr. pt. *scattering*, x. 168, 1 [**as** *throw*].

a-syái, D. f. of prn. root **a**, *to that*, ii. 33, 5.

ah *say*: pf. 3. pl. **āhur**, ii. 12, 5; v. 11, 6; vii. 86, 3; x. 34, 4.

áha, emphasizing pcl., *indeed*, i. 154, 6; v. 83, 3; vii. 103, 2.

áhan, n. *day*, viii. 48, 7; x. 129, 2.

ahám, prs. prn., *I*, viii. 86, 7; x. 15, 3; 34, 2. 3. 12.

áhar, n. *day*, vii. 103, 7.

áhas, n. *day*, x. 168, 3.

a-hastá, a. (Bv.) *handless*, x. 34, 9.

áh-i, m. *serpent*, ii. 12, 3. 11 [Av. *aži*, Gk. ἔχι-ς 'viper', Lat. *angui-s*].

á-hṛṇāna, pr. pt. Ā. *free from wrath* [**hṛ** *be angry*].

Ā, prp. with ab. *from*, ii. 35, 2; iv. 50, 3; 51, 10; with L., *in*, i. 35, 4; ii. 35, 7. 8; iii. 59, 3; viii. 48, 6.

ā́, pcl. *quite, very*, ii. 12, 15; with D., viii. 48, 4.

ā́-gata, pp. *come*, vii. 103, 3. 9 [**gam** *go*].

ā́-gam-iṣṭha, a. spv. *coming most gladly*, x. 15, 3.

ā́g-as, n. *sin*, vii. 86, 4; x. 15, 6 [cp Gk. ἄγος 'guilt'].

ā́c-ya, gd. *bending*, x. 15, 6 [**ā́**+**ac** *bend*].

ā́-jāta, pp. *produced*, x. 129, 6 [**jan** *generate*].

áj-ya, n. *melted butter*, x. 90, 6 [**á-añj** *anoint*].
āṇí, m. *axle-end*, i. 35, 6.
á-tata, pp. *extended*, x. 135, 6 [tan *stretch*].
ā-tasthivā́ms, red. pf. pt. *having mounted*, ii. 12, 8 [**á** + sthā *stand*].
āt-mán, m. *breath*, x. 168, 4 [Old Saxon *āthom* 'breath'].
Ādityá, m. *son of Aditi*, iii. 59, 2. 3. 5.
āp *obtain*, V. P. āpnóti ; pf. āpa, iv. 51, 7 [Lat. *ap-iscor* 'reach', *ap-ere* 'seize'].
ā-bhis, I. pl. f. of prn. root **a**, *with these*, v. 83, 1.
ā-bhú, a. *coming into being*, x. 129, 3.
āmá, a. *raw, unbaked*, ii. 35, 6 [Gk. ὠμό-ς 'raw'].
ā-yat-í, pr. pt. f. *coming*, x. 127, 1. 3 [**á** + i *go*].
āyas-á, a. f. **í**, *made of iron*, viii. 29, 3 [áyas *iron*].
āy-ú, a. *active* ; m. *living being, mortal*, iii. 59, 9 [i *go*].
á-yudh-a, n. *weapon*, viii. 29, 5 [**á** + yudh *fight*].
áy-us, n. *span of life*, vii. 103, 10 ; viii. 48, 4. 7. 10. 11 ; x. 14, 14 [*activity* : i *go*].
āraṇyá, a. *belonging to the forest*, x. 90, 8 [áraṇya].
ā-róhant, pr. pt. *scaling*, ii. 12, 12 [ruh *mount*].
āvís, adv. *in view*, with **kṛ**, *make manifest*, v. 83, 3.
āś-ú, a. *swift*, vii. 71, 5 [Gk. ὠκύ-ς].
āśu-héman, a. (Bv.), *of swift impulse*, ii. 35, 1.
ā-sām, gen. pl. f. of the prn. root **a**, *of them*, iv. 51, 6.
ā́s-īna, irr. pr. pt. Ā., *sitting*, x. 15, 7 [ās *sit*].
á-hita, pp. *placed in* (lc.), viii. 29, 4 ; x. 14, 16 ; with sám *placed upon* (lc.), x. 135, 4 [dhā *put*].
á-huta, pp. *to whom offering is made*, v. 11, 3.

I *go*, II. P. émi, x. 34, 5 ; éti, iv. 50, 8 ; x. 34, 6 ; 168, 1[2] ; yánti, vii. 49, 1 ; *approach* (acc.), viii. 48, 10 ; áyan, pr. sb. *pass*, vii. 61, 4 ; *attain*, vii. 63, 4 ; pf. īyúr, x. 15. 1. 2.
 ánu- *go after*, vi. 54, 5 ; *follow* (acc.), viii. 63, 5.
 ápa- *go away*, x. 14, 9.
 abhí- *come upon*, ipf. áyan, vii. 103, 2.
 áva- *appease* : op. iyām, vii. 86, 4.
 á- *come*, ii. 33, 1 ; v. 83, 6 ; *go to*, x. 14, 8.
 úpa á- *come to* (acc.), i. 1, 7.
 úd- *rise*, vii. 61, 1 ; 63, 1–4 ; ipf. **ait**, x. 90, 4.
 úpa- *approach*, vii. 86, 3 ; 103, 3 ; x. 14, 10 ; 34, 10 ; *flow to*, ii. 35, 3.
 párā- *pass away*, pf. īyúr, x. 14, 2. 7.
 pári- *surround*, ii. 35, 4. 9.
 prá- *go forth*, i. 154, 3 ; x. 14, 7.
 ánu prá- *go forth after*, vi. 54, 6.
 ví- *disperse*, x. 14, 9.
 sám- *flow together*, ii. 35, 3 ; *unite*, vii, 103, 2.
ichá-māna, pr. pt. Ā. *desiring*, x. 34, 10 [iṣ *wish*].
i-tás, adv. *from here*, x. 135, 4.
í-ti, pcl. *thus*, ii. 12, 5[2] ; vi. 54, 1. 2 ; x. 34, 6 [180].
it-thā́, adv. *thus*, ii. 35, 11 ; *truly*, i. 154, 5 [id + thā ; 180].
í-d, emphasizing pcl. *just, even*, i. 1, 4. 6 ; 85, 8 ; 154, 3 ; ii. 35, 8. 10 ; iv. 50, 7. 8 ; 51, 9 ; vii. 86, 3. 6 ; x. 14, 16 ; 34, 5. 7. 8. 13 ; 127, 3 [Lat. *id* : 180].
i-d-ám, dem. prn. n. *this*, i. 154, 3 ; ii. 12, 14 ; 33, 10 ; iv. 51, 1 ; v. 11, 5 ; x. 14, 15 ; 15, 2 ; 90, 2 ; 129, 3 ; 135, 7 ; *this world*, v. 83, 9 ; = *here*, vi. 54, 1 [111].
i-dā́nīm, adv. *now*, i. 35, 7.
idh *kindle*, VII. Ā. inddhé.
 sám- *kindle*, 3. pl. indhate, ii. 35, 11 ; pf. īdhiré, v. 11, 2.
idh-má, m. *fuel*, x. 90, 6 [idh *kindle*].
índ-u, m. *drop, Soma*, viii. 48, 2. 4. 8. 12. 13. 15 ; pl. iv. 50, 10 ; viii. 48, 5.
Índra, m. name of a god, i. 85, 9 ; ii. 12, 1–15 ; iv. 50, 10. 11 ; v. 11, 2 ; vii. 49, 1 ; viii. 48, 2. 10 ; x. 15, 10 ; 90, 13.
indr-iyá, n. *might of Indra*, i. 85, 2 [Índra].
i-nv *go*, I. P. ínvati [secondary root from i *go* according to class v.: i-nu].
 sam- *bring*, i. 160, 5.
imá, dem. prn. stem, *this*, A. m. **imám**, ii. 35, 2 ; x. 14. 4 ; 15, 6 ; N. m. pl. imé, vi. 54, 2 ; viii. 48, 5 ; n. **imā́**, ii. 12, 3 ; x. 15, 4 ; **imā́ni**, vii. 61, 6 ; 71, 6 [111].

i-y-ám, dem. prn. f. *this*, v. 11, 5; vii. 61, 7; 71, 6²; x. 129, 6. 7 [111].
írā, f. *nurture*, v. 83, 4.
ír-iṇa, n. *dice-board*, x. 34, 1. 9.
ír-ya, a. *watchful*, vi. 54, 8.
i-va, enc. pcl. *like*, i. 1, 9; 85, 5. 8²; ii. 12, 4. 5; 33, 6; 35, 5. 13; iv. 51, 2; v. 11, 5; 83, 3; vii. 63, 1; 103, 5²; viii. 29, 8; 48, 4². 6. 7²; x. 34, 1. 3. 5. 8; 127, 7. 8 [180].
iṣ-irá, a. *devoted*, viii. 48, 7.
iṣṭá-vrata, a. (Bv.) *accordant with desired ordinances*, iii. 59, 9.
iṣṭā-pūrtá, n. (Dv.) *sacrifice and good works*, x. 14, 8 [**iṣ-ṭā**, pp. du. of **yaj** *sacrifice* + **pūrtá**, pp. of **pṝ** *fill*, *bestowed*].
i-há, adv. *here*, i. 1, 2; 35, 1. 6; ii. 35, 13. 15; vi. 54, 9; vii. 49, 1. 2. 3. 4; x. 14, 5. 12; 15, 3. 5. 7. 11. 13²; 90, 4; 129, 6.
íḷā, f. *consecrated food*, iv. 50, 8.

ī *go*, IV. Ā. **íyate**, x. 168, 2; *approach*, **īmahe**, vi. 54, 8.
antár- *go between* (acc.), i. 35, 9; 160, 1.
īj-āná, pf. pt. Ā. (of **yaj**), *sacrificer*, iv. 51, 7.
īḍ *praise*, II. Ā., **íḷe**, i. 1, 1.
íḍ-ya, gdv. *praiseworthy*, i. 1, 2 [**īḍ** *praise*].
īm, enc. pcl. (acc. of prn. **i**), i. 85, 11; ii. 12, 5; 33, 13²; 35, 1; vii. 103, 3 [180].
íya-māna, pr. pt. Ā. *going*, x. 168, 3 [**ī** *go*].
īr *stir*, *set in motion*, II. Ā. **írte**.
ánu sáṃ prá- *speed on together after*, x. 168, 2.
úd- *arise*, x. 15, 1; v. 83. 3.
prá-, cs. **īráya**, *utter forth*, ii. 33. 8.
īś *be master of*, *overpower*, II. Ā. **íṣṭe**, with gen., viii. 48, 14.
íś-āna, pr. pt. Ā. *ruling over*, *disposing of* (gen.), vi. 54, 8; x. 90, 2; m. *ruler*, ii. 33, 9.
īṣ *move*, I. **íṣati**, -te, from (ab.), v. 83, 2.
īḷ-itá, pp. *implored*, x. 15, 12 [**īḍ** *praise*].

u, enc. pcl. *now*, *also*, i. 35, 6; 154, 4; ii. 33, 9; 35, 10. 15; iv. 51, 1. 2; v. 83, 10²; vi. 54, 3; vii. 61, 6; 63, 1. 2; 86, 3. 8; viii. 48, 3; x. 14, 2; 15, 3; 127, 3²; 129. 1² [180].

uk-thá, n. *recitation*, iv. 51, 7 [**vac** *speak*].
1. **ukṣ** *sprinkle*, VI. **ukṣáti, -te**, x. 90, 7.
pra- *besprinkle*, x. 90, 7.
2. **ukṣ** *grow*.
ukṣ-itá, pp. *grown strong*, i. 85, 2 [2. **ukṣ** = **vakṣ** *grow*].
ug-rá, a. *mighty*, ii. 33, 9; x. 34, 8; *fierce*, *terrible*, ii. 33, 11; viii. 29, 5.
uchánt, pr. pt. *shining*, iv. 51, 2 [1. **vas** *shine*].
u-tá, pcl. *and*, i. 85, 5; 154, 4; ii. 12, 5; 35, 11; iii. 59, 1; iv. 50, 9; v. 83, 2². 10; vi. 54, 6; vii. 63, 5; 86, 2; viii. 48, 1. 5. 8. 14; x. 34, 2; 90, 2; **utá vā**, vii. 49, 2²; = *and*, viii. 48, 15 [180].
utó, pcl. *and also*, x. 168, 1 [**utá** + **u**].
út-tara, cpv. a. *upper*, i. 154, 1 [**úd** *up*].
út-sa, m. *spring*, i. 85, 11; 154, 5 [**ud** *wet*].
ud *wet*, VII. P. **unátti, undánti** [cp. Lat. *und-a* 'wave'].
ví- *moisten*, *drench*, i. 85, 5; v. 83, 8.
ud-án, n. *water*, i. 85, 5 [Go. *watō* 'water'].
udan-vánt, a. *water-laden*, v. 83, 7.
úd-ita, pp. *risen*, vii. 63, 5 [**i** *go*].
udumbalá, a. *brown* (?), x. 14, 12.
ud-vát, f. *upward path*, i. 35, 3; *height*, v. 83, 7; x. 127, 2 [**úd** *up* + sf. **vat**].
upa-kṣiyánt, pr. pt. *abiding by* (acc.), iii. 59, 3 [**kṣi** *dwell*].
upa-má, spv. a. *highest*, viii. 29, 9.
upa-yánt, pr. pt. *approaching*, ii. 33, 12 [**i** *go*].
úpa-ra, cpv. a. *later*, x. 15, 2 [Av. *upara* 'upper', Gk. ὕπερο-ς 'pestle', Lat. *s-uperu-s* 'upper'].
upári, adv. *upward*, x. 34, 9; *above*, x. 129, 5 [Gk. ὑπέρ, ὑπείρ = ὑπέρι, Lat. *s-uper*, Old High German *ubir* 'over'].
úpa-śrita, pp. impressed on (lc.), vii. 86, 8 [**śri** *resort*].
upa-sádya, gdv. *to be approached*, iii. 59, 5 [**sád** *sit*].
upá-stha, m. *lap*, i. 35, 5. 6; vii. 63, 3; x. 15, 7.
upa-hatnú, a. *slaying*, ii. 33, 11 [**ha-tnu** from **han** *slay*].
úpa-hūta, pp. *invited*, x. 15, 5 [**hū** *call*].
upārá, m. *offence*, vii. 86, 6 [**upa** + **ara** from **ṛ** *go*: *striking upon*, *offence*].

ubj *force*, VI. P., **ubjáti.**
nir- *drive out*, i. 85, 9.
ubhá, a. *both*, i. 35, 9; x. 14, 7 [cp. Lat. *am-bo*, Gk. *ἄμ-φω* 'both', Eng. *bo-th*].
ubhá-ya, a. pl. *both*, ii. 12, 8.
ubhayā́-dat, a. *having teeth on both jaws*, x. 90, 10.
ur-ú, a., f. **urv-ī́**, *wide*, i. 85, 6. 7; 154, 2; vii. 61, 2; 86, 1; x. 127, 2 [Av. *vouru*, Gk. *εὐρύ-ς*].
uru-kramá, a. (Bv.) *wide-striding*, i. 154, 5 [**kráma**, m. *stride*].
uru-gāyá, a. (Bv.) *wide-paced*, i. 154, 1. 3. 6; viii. 29, 7 [**-gāya** *gait* from **gā** *go*].
uru-cákṣas, a. (Bv.) *far-seeing*, vii. 63, 4 [**cákṣas**, n. *sight*].
uru-vyácas, a. (Bv.) *far-extending*, i. 160, 2 [**vyácas**, n. *extent*].
uru-śáṃsa, a. (Bv.) *far-famed*, viii. 48, 4 [**śáṃsa**, m. *praise*].
uru-ṣyú, a. *freedom-giving*, viii. 48, 5 [from den. **uru-ṣya** *put in wide space, rescue*].
urū-ṇasá, a. (Bv.) *broad-nosed*, x. 14, 12 [**urú** + **nás** *nose*].
urviyā́, adv. *widely*, ii. 35, 8 [inst. f. of **urvī́** *wide*].
urv-ī́, f. *earth*, x. 14, 16 [**urú** *wide*].
uś-ánt, pr. pt. *eager*, vii. 103, 3; x. 15, 8[3] [**vaś** *desire*].
Uṣ-ás, f. *Dawn*, ii. 12, 7; vii. 63, 3; 71, 1; x. 127, 3. 7; pl. iv. 51, 1–9; 11 [1. **vas** *shine*; cp. Gk. *ἠώς* (for *āus-ōs*), Lat. *aur-or-a*].
usrá-yāman, a. (Bv.) *faring at daybreak*, vii. 71, 4 [**usrá** *matutinal*, **yā́man**, n. *course*].
usr-íyā, f. *cow*, iv. 50, 5 [f. of **usr-íya** *ruddy* from **us-rá** *red*].

Ū, enc. pcl., ii. 35, 3; iv. 51, 2 [metrically lengthened for u].
ū-tí, f. *help*, i. 35, 1; viii. 48, 15; x. 15, 4 [**av** *favour*].
ūrú, m. du. *thigh*, x. 90, 11. 12.
ū́rj, f. *vigour, strength*, vii. 49, 4; x. 15, 7.
ūrjáyant, den. pr. pt. *gathering strength*, ii. 35, 7.
ūrdh-vá, a. *upright*, ii. 35, 9; *upward*, x. 90, 4 [Gk. *ὀρθό-ς* for *ὀρθ-Fό-ς*; Lat. *arduu-s* 'lofty'].
ūrdhvám, acc. adv. *upwards*, i. 85, 10.
ū́rmyā, f. *night*, x. 127, 6.
ūr-vá, n. *receptacle*, ii. 35, 3; *fold, herd*, iv. 50, 2 [1. **vṛ** *cover*].

Ṛ *go*, V. P. **ṛṇóti**, int. **álarti** *arise*, viii. 48, 8 [Gk. *ὄρ-νῡ-μι* 'stir up'].
abhí- *penetrate to* (acc.), i. 35, 9.
prá- *send forth*, III. **íyarti**, vii. 61, 2.
ṛ́k-van, m. pl. name of a group of ancestors, x. 14, 3 [*singing* from **arc** *sing*].
ṛ́k-vant, a. *singing, jubilant*, iv. 50, 5 [**arc** *sing*].
ṛ́c, f. *stanza*, ii. 35, 12; *collection of hymns, Ṛgveda*, x. 90, 9 [**arc** *sing, praise*].
ṛcás-e, dat. inf. with **prá**, *to praise*, vi. 61, 6 [**arc** *praise*].
ṛ-ṇá, n. *debt*, x. 127, 7.
ṛṇā-ván, a. *indebted*, x. 34, 10 [**ṛṇá** *debt*].
ṛ-tá, n. *settled order*, i. 1, 8; iv. 51, 8; *truth*, x. 34, 12 [pp. of **ṛ** *go*, *settled*].
ṛtá-jāta-satya, a. *punctually true*, iv. 51, 7 [*true as produced by established order*].
ṛta-jñá, a. *knowing right*, x. 15, 1.
ṛta-yúj, a. *yoked in due time*, iv. 51, 5; vii. 71, 3.
ṛta-spṛ́ś, a. *cherishing the rite*, iv. 50, 3.
ṛtā́-van, a. *holy*, ii. 35, 8; x. 168, 3; *pious*, vii. 61, 2; f. **-varī** *observing order*, i. 160, 1.
ṛ-tú, m. *season*, vii. 103, 9 [*fixed time*: from **ṛ** *go*].
ṛ-té, adv. prp. with ab., *without*, ii. 12, 9 [loc. of **ṛtá**].
ṛtv-íj, m. *ministrant*, i. 1, 1 [**ṛtú** + **ij** = **yaj** *sacrificing in season*].
ṛdūdára, a. *compassionate*, ii. 33, 5; *wholesome*, viii. 48, 10.
ṛdh *thrive*, V. P. **ṛdhnóti.**
ánu- *bring forward*, op. 2. s. **ṛdhyās**, viii. 48, 2.
ṛ́dhak, adv. *separately*, vii. 61, 3.
Ṛbh-ú, m. pl. name of three divine artificers, iv. 51, 6 [*skilful*, from **rabh** *take in hand*].
ṛ́ṣ-i, m. *seer*, i. 1, 2; iv. 50, 1; x. 14, 15; 90, 7.
ṛṣ-tí, f. *spear*, i. 85, 4 [**ṛṣ** *thrust*].
ṛṣ-vá, a. *high, lofty*, vii. 61, 3; 86, 1.

É-ka, nm. *one*, i. 35, 6; 154, 3. 4; vii. 103, 6[4]; viii. 29, 1–8. 10; x. 14, 16; 129, 2. 3 [prn. root **e**].
eka-pará, a. *too high by one*, x. 34, 2.
ékeṣa, a. *having one pole*, x. 135, 3 [**īṣā** + *pole* of a car].
e-tá, dem. prn. stem, *this*: n. **etád**, iii. 59, 5; acc. m. **etám** *this*, x. 14, 9; *him*,

x. 34, 4 ; inst. **eténa**, v. 83, 6 ; n. pl. **etā́**, x. 15, 14 ; m. pl. **eté** *these*, vii. 103, 9 [prn. root e + **tá** *this*].
éta-śa, m. steed of the Sun, vii. 63, 2 [**éta** *speeding*, from i *go*].
etā́-vant, a. *such*, x. 90, 3 [prn. **etá** *this* + sf. **vant**].
e-na, enc. prn. stem of 3. prs. *he*, *she*, *it* : acc. **enam** *him*, ii. 12, 5 ; iii. 59. 8 ; vii. 103, 2 ; x. 14, 11 ; 34, 4 ; 168, 2 ; acc. pl. **enān** *them*, vii. 103, 3 ; gen. du. **enos** *of them two*, vii. 103, 4 [prn. root e].
én-as, n., ii. 12, 10 ; vii. 71, 4 ; 86, 3.
enā́, inst. *by it*, x. 14, 4 ; adv. *thither*, x. 14, 2 [inst. of prn. root a].
e-bhis, I. pl. *with them*, x. 34, 5 [prn. root a].
e-bhyas, D. pl. *to them*, x. 34, 8 [prn. root a].
e-vá, pcl. *thus*, *just*, i. 1, 3 ; ii. 12, 1 ; iv. 51, 9 ; vi. 54, 1. 2 ; x. 90, 2 [prn. root e ; cp. 180].
e-vā́ (= **evá**), adv. *thus*, *just*, ii. 33, 15 ; iv. 50, 8 [prn. root e].
e-ṣá, dem. prn. : N. s. m. **eṣáḥ** *this*, x. 168, 4 ; *he*, ii. 12, 15 ; vii. 63, 3 ; viii. 29, 6 ; f. **eṣā́** *this*, x. 14, 2 ; *she*, x. 34, 2 [from prn. root e + **sa**].
e-ṣām, G. pl. m. *of them*, i. 85, 3 ; vii. 103, 5². 6 ; x. 34, 5. 8 ; 129, 5 [prn. root a].

Ók-as, n. *abode*, iv. 50, 8 [*wonted place* : uc *be wont*].
ój-as, n. *might*, i. 85, 4. 10 ; 160, 5 [uj = vaj ; cp. Lat. *augus-tu-s* ' mighty ', ' august '].
ojā-yámāna, den. pr. pt. Ā. *showing one's strength*, ii. 12, 11 [**ójas**].
ój-īyāṃs, cpv. a. *mightier*, ii. 33, 10.
óṣa-dhī, f. *plant*, v. 83, 1. 4. 5. 10 ; vii. 61, 3 [**áv(a)s-a** *nurture* (av *further*) + **dhī** *holding*, from dhā *hold*].

Ká, inter. prn. *who?* i. 35, 7 ; x. 129, 6 ; 135, 5³ ; G. **kásya**, x. 129, 1 ; du. **káu**, x. 90, 11² ; with cid : I. **kéna** cid *by any*, x. 15, 6 ; pl. N. **ké** cid *some*, viii. 103, 8.
ka-kúbh, f. *peak*, i. 35, 8.
ka-tamá, inter. prn. *which* (*of many*)? i. 35, 7 ; iv. 51, 6 ; with **caná** *any*, x. 168, 3 [Lat. *quo-tumu-s*].
kati-dhā́, adv. *into how many parts?* x. 90, 11 [**ká-ti** *how many?* Lat. *quot*].
ka-dā, inter. adv. *when?* vii. 86, 2 ; with **caná**, *ever*, vi. 54, 9 [**ká** *who?*].
kánikradat, int. pr. pt. *bellowing*, iv. 50, 5 ; v. 83, 1. 9 [**krand** *roar*].
kán-īyāṃs, cpv. *younger*, vii. 86, 6 [cp. **kan-yā̀**, f. *girl* ; Gk. *καινό-ς* ' new ' for *καν̯ιό-ς*].
kam, pcl., i. 154, 1 [*gladly* : cp. p. 225, 2].
kár-tave, dat. inf. of kṛ *do*, i. 85, 9.
kalmalik-ín, a. *radiant*, ii. 33, 8.
kav-í, m. *sage*, v. 11, 3 ; vii. 86, 3 ; x. 129, 4 [Av. *kavi* ' king '].
kaví-kratu, a. (Bv.) *having the intelligence of a sage*, i. 1, 5 ; v. 11, 4.
kaví-tara, cpv. a. *wiser*, vii. 86, 7.
kavi-śastá, pp. (Tp.) *recited by the sages*, x. 14, 4.
kav-yá, a. *wise*, x. 15, 9 ; m. pl. name of a group of Fathers, x. 14, 3.
kaśā́, f. *whip*, v. 83, 3.
kā́m-a, m. *desire*, i. 85, 11 ; x. 34, 6 ; 129, 4 [**kam** *desire*].
kāś *appear*, int. **cākaśīti**.
abhi- *look upon*, x. 135, 2.
kitavá, m. *gambler*, x. 34, 3. 6. 7. 10. 11. 13.
kí-m, inter. prn. *what?* vii. 86, 2. 4 ; viii. 48, 3² ; x. 90, 11 ; 129, 1² ; with **caná** *anything*, x. 129, 2 [Lat. *qui-s*, *qui-d*].
kíla, adv. emphasizing preceding word, *indeed*, ii. 12, 15 [180].
kīr-í, m. *singer*, ii. 12, 6 [2. kṛ *commemorate*].
ku-cará, a. *wandering at will*, i. 154, 2 [**ku**, inter. prn. root *where?* = *anywhere* + **cara** from **car** *fare*].
ku-tás, inter. adv. *whence?* x. 129, 6² ; 168, 3 [prn. root *where?*].
ku-mārá, m. *boy*, x. 135, 3. 4. 5 ; = *son*, ii. 33, 12.
kumārá-deṣṇa, a. (Bv.) *presenting gifts like boys*, x. 34, 7 [**deṣṇá**, n. *gift* from dā *give*].
kul-yā́, f. *stream*, v. 83, 8.
kuv-íd, inter. pcl. *whether?* ii. 35, 1. 2 ; iv. 51, 4 [**ku** + **íd** : cp. p. 226].
kú-ha, inter. adv. *where?* ii. 12, 5 ; x. 129, 1 [**ku** + sf. **ha** = **dhā** : cp. p. 212].
kṛ *make*, V. **kṛṇóti**, **kṛṇuté**, iv. 50, 9 ; v. 83, 3 ; = *hold*, x. 34, 12 ; = *raise*

(voice), 8; pr. sb. 3. s. kṛṇávat, viii. 48, 3; 3. pl. kṛṇávan, iv. 51, 1; vii. 63, 4; 2. pl. Ā. kṛṇúdhvam, x. 34, 14; ipv. kṛṇuhí, x. 135, 3; pf. cakrmá, vii. 86, 5; x. 15, 4; cakrúr, vii. 63, 5; Ā. cakré, x. 90, 8; cakrā́te, viii. 29, 9; cakriré, i. 85, 1. 2. 7. 10; ft. kariṣyási, i. 1, 6; root ao. ákar, ii. 12, 4; iii. 59. 9; v. 83, 10; ákran, x. 14, 9; 3. pl. Ā. ákrata, vii. 103, 8; x. 34, 5; sb. kárati, ii. 35, 1; kárāma, x. 15, 6; ao. ps. ákāri, vii. 61, 7 [cp. Gk. κραίνω 'accomplish', Lat. creō 'create'].

úpa á- *drive up for*: rt. ao. ákaram, x. 127, 8.

āvís- *make manifest*, v. 83, 3.

nís- *turn out*: rt. ao. askṛta, x. 127, 3.

kṛṇv-ánt, pr. pt. *making* = *offering*, vii. 103, 8; x. 168, 1 [kṛ *make*].

kṛ-tá, pp. *made*, i. 85, 6; ii. 12, 4; vii. 61, 6 (= *offered*); x. 90, 12. 15; 135, 6; n. *lucky throw*, x. 34, 6 [Av. *kereta*, Old Persian *karta* 'made'].

kṛ́tā, f. *breast*(?), ii. 35, 5.

kṛ-tví, gd. *having made*, x. 15, 12.

kṛś-á, a. *poor*, ii. 12, 6 [kṛś *grow lean*].

kṛ́śana, n. *pearl*, i. 35, 4.

kṛṣ *draw*, I. P. kárṣati, v. 83, 7; VI. P. kṛṣá-ti *till*, x. 34, 13.

kṛṣ-í, f. *field*, x. 34, 13 [kṛṣ *till*].

kṛṣ-ṭí, f. pl. *people*, i. 160, 5; iii. 59, 1 [*tillage*, *settlement*: kṛṣ *till*].

kṛṣ-ṇá, a. *black*, i. 35, 2. 4. 9; x. 127, 7; f. í, vii. 71, 1.

kḷp *be fit*, I. kálpati, cs. kalpáyati, -te *arrange*, x. 15, 14.

ví- *dispose*, x. 90, 11. 14.

ket-ú, m. *banner*, v. 11, 2. 3; vii. 63, 2 [cit *appear*; Go. *haidu-s* 'manner'].

kévaṭa, m. *pit*, vi. 54, 7.

kóśa, m. *bucket*, v. 83, 8; *well* (of a car), vi. 54, 3.

kr-á-tu, m. *power*, ii. 12, 1; *wisdom*, vii. 61, 2 [kṛ *do*].

krand *bellow*, I. P. krándati.

abhí- *bellow towards*, v. 83, 7.

kránd-as, n. *battle array*, ii. 12, 8 [*battle cry*: krand *shout*].

kram *stride*, I. P. krámati, Ā. krámate.

ví- *stride out*, pf. cakrame, viii. 29, 7.

abhí ví- *spread asunder*, *develop into*: ipf. ákrāmat, x. 90, 4.

krīḍ *play*, I. krīḷa, x. 34, 8

krudh *be angry*, IV. P. krúdhyati; red. ao. inj. cukrudhāma, ii. 33, 4.

kvà, inter. adv. *where?* i. 35, 7; ii. 33, 7; iv. 51, 6; x. 168, 3; with svid *who knows where*, x. 34, 10 [pronounced kúa].

kṣa-trá, n. *dominion*, i. 160, 5 [kṣa = kṣi *rule*].

kṣam *forbear*, I. Ā. kṣámate.

abhí- *be merciful to* (acc.), ii. 33, 1. 7.

kṣi *dwell*, II. P. kṣéti, iv. 50, 8.

ádhi- *dwell in* (lc.), i. 154, 2.

kṣiy-ánt, pr. pt. *dwelling*, ii. 12, 11 [kṣí *dwell*].

kṣé-ma, m. *possession*, viii. 86, 8 [kṣi: kṣáyati *possess*].

Khan-í-trima, a. *produced by digging*, vii. 49, 2 [khan *dig*].

khálu, adv. *indeed*, x. 34, 14 [p. 227].

khā-tá, pp. *dug*, iv. 50, 3 [khan *dig*].

khyā *see*: no present; a ao. ákhyat.

abhí- *perceive*, vii. 86, 2.

ví- *survey*, i. 35, 5. 7. 8; x. 127, 1.

Gaṇ-á, m. *throng*, iv. 50, 5; x. 34, 12.

gabh-īrá, a. *profound*, x. 129, 1 [gabh = gāh *plunge*].

gabhīrá-vepas, a. (Bv.) *of deep inspiration*, i. 35, 7.

gam *go*, I. gáchati, -te *to* (acc.), i. 1, 4; x. 14, 13; root ao. 3. pl. ágman, vii. 71, 6; 1. pl. áganma, viii. 48, 3. 11 [Gk. βαίνω, Lat. venio, Eng. *come*].

á- *come*, i. 1, 5; 85, 11; root ao. ipv. gahí, vi. 54, 7; x. 14, 5; 2. pl. gatá, x. 15, 4; 3. gámantu, x. 15, 5[2]. 11; *go to* (acc.), x. 168, 2.

sám- *go with* (inst.), a ao. op., vi. 54, 2; *unite with* (inst.), x. 14, 8.

gám-a-dhyai, dat. inf. (of gam) *to go*, i. 154, 6.

garta-sád, a. (Tp.) *sitting on a car-seat*, ii. 33, 11.

gárbh-a, m. *germ*, ii. 33, 13; v. 83, 1. 7; x. 168, 4 [gṛbh *receive*].

gáv-y-ūti, f. *pasturage*, x. 14, 2 [Bv. *having nurture for cows*: go].

gáh-ana, a. *unfathomable*, x. 129, 1 [gāh *plunge*].

gā *go*, III. P. jígāti.

abhí- *approach*, vii. 71, 4.

á- *come*: rt. ao. agāt, i. 35, 8.

pári- *go by* (acc.): root ao. inj. gāt, ii. 33, 14.

prá- *go forward*, ipv. **jigāta**, i. 85, 6; *enter*, root ao., viii. 48, 2.
gā-tú, m. *path, way*, iv. 51, 1; vii. 63, 5; x. 14, 2 [**gā** *go*].
gātre-gātre, lc. itv. cd., *in every limb*, viii. 48, 2 [**gā** *go*].
gāya-trī́, f. a metre, x. 14, 16 [*song*: **gā** *sing*].
gír, f. *song*, ii. 35, 1; v. 11, 5; 83, 1; vii. 71, 6; x. 135, 7 [**gṛ** *sing*].
giri-kṣí-t, a. *mountain-dwelling*, i. 154, 3 [**kṣi** *dwell*].
giri-ṣṭhā́, a. *mountain-haunting*, i. 154, 2 [**sthā** *stand*].
gup *guard*: pf. **jugupur**, vii. 103, 9 [secondary root from the den. **go-pā-ya**].
gúhā, adv. *in hiding*, v. 11, 6; with **kṛ**, *cause to disappear*, ii. 12, 4 [from **guh-ā́**, inst. of **gúh** *concealment*, w. adverbial shift of accent].
gúh-ya, gdv. *to be hidden*, vii. 103, 8 [**guh** *hide*].
gū́h-ant, pr. pt. *hiding*, iv. 51, 9 [**guh** *hide*].
gūḷhá, pp. *hidden*, x. 129, 3 [**guh** *hide*].
1. **gṛ** *sing*, IX. **gṛṇā́ti**, **gṛṇīté**, ii. 33, 8. 12.
abhí- *greet favourably*, x. 15, 6.
2. **gṛ** *waken*: red. ao. 2. du. ipv. **jigṛtam**, iv. 50, 11.
gṛṇ-ánt, pr. pt. *singing*; m. *singer*, iii. 59, 5 [**gṛ** *sing*].
gṛṇ-āná, pr. pt. Ā. *singing, praising*, i. 35, 10; 160, 5 [**gṛ** *sing*].
gṛ́t-sa, a. *experienced*, vii. 86, 7.
gṛdh *be greedy*, IV. P. **gṛ́dhyati**; a ao. **ágṛdhat**, x. 34, 4.
gṛbh-āyá, den. P. *grasp*.
úd- *hold up, cease*, v. 83, 10.
gṛh-á, m. *house*, pl., vi. 54, 2 [**grah** *receive, contain*].
gṛhé-gṛhe, lc. itv. cd., *in every house*, v. 11, 4.
gó, f. *cow*, pl. N. **gā́vas**, i. 154, 6; ii. 12, 7; viii. 48, 5 (= *straps*); x. 34, 13; 90, 10; A. **gā́s**, ii. 12, 3; vi. 54, 5. 6; 127, 8; G. **gávām**, iv. 51, 8; vii. 103, 2. 10 [Av. N. *gau-s*, Gk. *βοῦ-ς*, Lat. *bo-s* (*bov-*), OI. *bō*, Eng. *cow*].
Gó-tama, m. name of a seer, i. 85, 11 [spv. of **go** *cow*].
go-pā́, m. Tp. (*cow-protector*), *guardian*, i. 1, 8; v. 11, 1; viii. 48, 9 [**gó** *cow* + **pā** *protect*].
gó-magha, a. (Bv.) *rich in cows*, vii. 71, 1 [*having abundance of cows*].
gó-mātṛ, a. (Bv.) *having a cow for a mother*, i. 85, 3.
gó-māyu, a. (Bv.) *lowing like a cow*, vii. 103, 6. 10 [**māyú**, m. *lowing*].
grabh *seize*, IX. **gṛbhṇā́ti**, **gṛbhṇīté**, vii. 103, 4.
ánu- *greet*, vii. 103, 4.
grā́ma, m. *village*, x. 127, 5; pl. = *clans*, ii. 12, 7.
grām-yá, a. *belonging to the village*, x. 90, 8 [**grā́ma**].
grīṣmá, m. *summer*, x. 90, 6.

Ghar-má, m. *hot milk offering*, vii. 103, 9 [Av. *garᵉma*, Lat. *formu-s*, Gk. *θερμό-ς* 'warm', Eng. *warm*].
gharma-sád, a. (Tp.) *sitting at the heating vessel*, x. 15, 9. 10 [**sad** *sit*].
gharm-ín, a. *heated*, vii. 103, 8.
ghas *eat*: root ao. 3. pl. **ákṣan**, x. 15, 12 [= **á-gh(a)s-an**].
ghā, enc. emphasizing pcl., iv. 51, 7 [180].
ghṛ́-ṇi, f. *heat*, ii. 33, 6 [**ghṛ** = **hṛ** *be hot*].
ghṛ-tá, (pp.) n. *clarified butter, ghee*, i. 85, 8; ii. 33, 11. 14; v. 11, 3; 83, 8 [**ghṛ** *be hot*].
ghṛtá-nirṇij, a. (Bv.) *having a garment of ghee*, ii. 35, 4 [**nir-ṇíj**, f. *splendour* from **nís** *out* + **nij** *wash*].
ghṛtá-pratīka, a. (Bv.) *butter-faced*, v. 11, 1 [**prátīka**, n. *front* from **pratyáñc** *turned towards*].
ghṛtá-vant, a. *accompanied with ghee*, iii. 59, 1; *abounding in ghee*, x. 14, 14.
ghṛ́ṣ-vi, a. *impetuous*, i. 85, 1 [**ghṛṣ** = **hṛṣ** *be excited*].
gho-rá, a. *terrible*; n. *magic power*, v. 34, 14.
ghóṣ-a, m. *sound*, x. 168, 1. 4 [**ghuṣ** *make a noise*].

Ca, enc. pcl. *and*, i. 160, 2. 3; ii. 33, 13²; 35, 6. 8; iv. 50, 10; v. 11, 5; vii. 86, 1; x. 14, 7. 9. 14; 34, 11; 90, 2. 3. 7. 8. 10; *if*, viii. 48, 2; x. 34, 5; **ca-ca**, i. 35, 11; iv. 51, 11; x. 14, 3. 11; 15, 3. 13²; 90, 13 [Av. *ca*, Lat. *que* 'and'; cp. 180].
cakr-á, n. *wheel*, vi. 54, 3; vii. 63, 2 [Gk. *κύκλο-ς*, Anglo-Saxon *hweowol*].
cakṣ, *see* II. **cáṣṭe** [reduplicated form of **kas** = **kāś** *shine*: = **ca-k(a)s**].

abhí- *regard*, iii. 59, 1; vii. 61, 1.
prá-, cs. cakṣáya *illumine*, viii. 48, 6.
ví- *reveal*, x. 34, 13.
cákṣ-u, n. *eye*, x. 90, 13 [cakṣ *see*].
cákṣ-us, n. *eye*, vii. 61, 1; 63, 1 [cakṣ *see*].
cat *hide* (intr.), I. P. cátati; cs. cātáya *drive away*, ii. 33, 2.
catur-akṣá, a. (Bv.) *four-eyed*, x. 14, 10. 11 [akṣá = ákṣi *eye*].
catuṣ-pád, a. (Bv.) *four-footed*, iv. 51, 5 [catúr *four*, Lat. *quattuor*, Go. *fidwōr*].
catvāriṃśá, ord., f. í, *fortieth*, ii. 12, 11.
ca-ná, pcl. *and not*, vii. 86, 6.
candrá-mās, m. *moon*, x. 90, 13 [K. cd. *bright* (candrá) *moon* (mā́s)].
car *fare*, I. cárati, -te, iv. 51, 6. 9; viii. 29, 8; x. 14, 12; 168, 4.
abhí- *bewitch*, x. 34, 14.
ā́- *approach*, iv. 51, 8.
prá- *go forward, enter*, viii. 48, 6.
abhí sám- *come together*, viii. 48, 1.
cará-tha, n. *motion, activity*, iv. 51, 5 [car *fare*].
cár-ant, pr. pt. *wandering*, x. 34, 10; *faring*, x. 135, 2.
car-í-tra, n. *leg*, viii. 48, 5 [car *move*].
cár-man, n. *skin, hide*, i. 85, 5; vii. 63, 1.
carṣaṇī-dhṛ́-t, a. (Tp.) *supporting the folk*, iii. 59, 6 [carṣaṇí, a. *active*, f. *folk* + dhṛ-t *supporting*].
cā́-ru, a. *dear*, ii. 35, 11 [can *gladden*; Lat. *cā-ru-s* 'dear'].
ci-kit-vā́ṃs, red. pf. *wise*, vii. 86, 3 [cit *think*].
cit *perceive*, I. cétati, -te; pf. cikéta, i. 35, 7; sb. cíketat, i. 35, 6; cs. citáya *stimulate*, iv. 51, 3; cetáya *cause to think*, vii. 86, 7.
ā́- *observe*: pf. ciketa, vii. 61, 1.
cit-rá, a. *brilliant*, iv. 51, 2; n. *marvel*, vii. 61, 5.
citrá-bhānu, a. (Bv.) *of brilliant splendour*, i. 35, 4; 85, 11.
citrá-śravas, a. (Bv.) *having brilliant fame*; spv. -tama *of most brilliant fame*, i. 1, 5; *bringing most brilliant fame*, iii. 59, 6.
cid, enc. pcl. *just, even*, i. 85, 4. 10; ii. 12, 8. 13. 15; 33, 12; vii. 86, 1. 3. 8; x. 34, 8²; 127, 5 [Lat. *quid*].
cekit-āna, int. pr. pt. *famous*, ii. 33, 15 [cit *perceive*].

cod-i-tṛ́, m. *furtherer*, ii. 12, 6 [cud *impel*].
cyáv-ana, a. *unstable*, ii. 12, 4 [cyu *move*].
cyáv-āna, m. name of a seer, vii. 71, 5 [pr. pt. of cyu *move*].
cyu *waver, fall*, I. cyávate.
prá-, cs. cyāváya *overthrow*, i. 85, 4.

Chand *seem*, II. P. chántti; pf. cachánda, vii. 63, 3; *seem good, please*, 3. s. s ao. áchān, x. 34, 1.
chánd-as, n. *metre*, x. 14, 16; 90, 9.
chāyā́, f. *shade*, ii. 33, 6 [Gk. σκιά].

Jágat, n. *world*, i. 35, 1 [pr. pt. of gā *go*].
jágm-i, a. *nimble, speeding*, i. 85, 8 [from red. stem jag(a)m of gam *go*].
jajñ-āná, pf. pt. Ā. *having been born*, x. 14, 2 [jan *generate*].
jan *generate, create*, I. jánati; pf. jajā́na, i. 160, 4; ii. 12, 3. 7; 35, 2; jajñiré *were born*, x. 90, 9². 10; iṣ ao. ájaniṣṭa *has been born*, iii. 59, 4; v. 11, 1; red. ao. ájījanas *hast caused to grow*, v. 83, 10; cs. janáya *generate*, ii. 35, 13; x. 135, 5 [Old Lat. *gen-ō* 'generate'; Gk. ao. ἐ-γεν-ό-μην].
prá- *be prolific*, IV. Ā. jāya, ii. 33, 1; 35, 8.
ján-a, m. *mankind*, ii. 35, 15; iii. 59, 9; iv. 51, 1; v. 11, 1; pl. *men, people*, i. 35, 5; ii. 12, 1–14; iii. 59, 1. 8; iv. 51, 11; vii. 49, 3; 61, 5; 63, 2. 4; x. 14, 1 [jan *generate*; cp. Lat. *gen-us*, Gk. γέν-ος, Eng. *kin*].
janáy-ant, cs. pr. pt. *generating*, i. 85, 2.
ján-i, f. *woman*, i. 85, 1.
ján-i-man, n. *birth*, ii. 35, 6.
jan-ús, n. *generation*, vii. 86, 1 [jan *generate*].
jáy-ant, pr. pt. *conquering*; m. *victor*, x. 34, 7 [ji *conquer*].
jár-ant, pr. pt. *aging, old*, x. 34, 3 [jṝ *waste away*; Gk. γέρ-οντ- 'old man'].
jar-ás, m. *old age*, vii. 71, 5 [jṝ *waste away*; cp. Gk. γῆρας 'old age'].
jar-i-tṛ́, m. *singer*, ii. 33, 11 [jṛ *sing*].
jálāṣa, a. *cooling*, ii. 33, 7.
jálāṣa-bheṣaja, a. (Bv.) *having cooling remedies*, viii. 29, 5 [bheṣajá, n. *remedy*].
jálp-i, f. *idle talk, chatter*, viii. 48, 14 [jalp *chatter*].
jas *be exhausted*, I. jása; pf. ipv. jajastám *weaken*, iv. 50, 11.

áva- *slacken* (Ā.), ii. 33, 14.
á- *extend to* (acc.), i. 85, 7.
ánu á- *extend over*, viii. 48, 13.
tán-aya, n. *descendant*, ii. 33, 14 [tan *extend*].
tan-ū́, f. *body*, i. 85, 3; ii. 35, 13; iv. 51, 9; viii. 48, 9; x. 14, 8; 15, 14; 34, 6; *self*, vii. 86, 2. ŏ (pl.) [tan *stretch*: cp. Lat. *ten-u-i-s*, Gk. ταν-ύ-, Eng. *thin*].
tanv-āná, pr. pt. Ā. *performing*, x. 90, 15 [tan *extend*].
tap *burn*, I. tápa; pf. tatā́pa = *it pains*, x. 34, 11; ps. tapyáte, *is distressed*, x. 34, 10 [cp. Lat. *tep-ēre* 'be warm'].
táp-ana, a. *burning*, x. 34, 7 [tap *burn*].
táp-as, n. *heat*, x. 129, 3 [Lat. *tep-or*].
tap-tá, pp. *heated*, vii. 103, 9 [tap *burn*].
tám-as, n. *darkness*, iv. 50, 4; 51, 1. 2. 3; vii. 63, 1; 71, 5; 127, 2. 3. 7; 129, 3[2] [tam *faint*].
támiṣ-ī́c-ī, f. *power of darkness*, viii. 48, 11 [tamis = támas + īc = i-añc].
tar-áṇi, a. *speeding onward*, vii. 63, 4 [tṝ *cross*].
tá-rhi, adv. *then*, x. 129, 2 [prn. root tá].
táva, gen. (of. tvám) *of thee*, i. 1, 6; vi. 54, 9; viii. 48, 8 [Av. *tava*, Lith. *tavè*].
tav-ás, a. *mighty*, ii. 33, 3; v. 83, 1 [tu *be strong*].
tavás-tama, spv. *mightiest*, ii. 33, 3.
táv-iṣ-ī, f. *might*, i. 35, 4 [távis = táv-as, n. *might*].
táskara, m. *thief*, viii. 29, 6.
tasthi-vā́ṃs, pf. pt. act. *having stood*, ii. 35, 14 [sthā *stand*].
tāpay-iṣṇú, a. *causing to burn*, x. 34, 7 [from cs. of tap *burn*].
tāy-ú, m. *thief*, vii. 86, 5 [= stāyú; cp. ste-ná *thief*].
tig-má, a. *sharp*, viii. 29, 5 [tij *be sharp*].
tiraśc-ī́na, a. *across*, x. 129, 5 [tirás].
tir-ás, prp. *across*, vii. 61, 7 [tṝ *cross*; Av. *tarō*; cp. Lat. *trans* = 'crossing', N. pr. pt.].
tisṛ́, nm. f. of trí *three*, N. tisrás, i. 35, 6; ii. 35, 5.
tú, pcl. *indeed*, vii. 86, 1 [prn. root tu in tu-ám].
tuch-yá, n. *void*, x. 129, 3.
túbhya, D. (of tvám) *to thee*, v. 11, 5 [cp. Lat. *tibi*].
túbhyam, D. (of tvám) *for thee*, iv. 50, 3; v. 11, 5; (angry) *with thee*, vii. 86, 3; = *by thee*, vii. 86, 8.
tur-á, a. *eager*, vii. 86, 4 [tur = tvar *speed*].
tuvi-jātá, pp. *high-born*, iv. 50, 4 [tuvi from tu *be strong*].
túviṣ-mant, a. *mighty*, ii. 12, 12 [tuv-is, n. *might* from tu *be strong*].
tṛp *be pleased*, IV. P. tṛpṇoti; cs. tarpáya *satisfy*, i. 85, 11 [cp. Gk. τέρπω].
tṛṣ *thirst*, IV. tṛṣya; pf. tātṛṣúr, x. 15, 9 [cp. Gk. τέρσομαι 'become dry', Lat. *torreo* 'scorch', Eng. *thirst*].
tṛṣ-ṇáj, a. *thirsty*, i. 85, 11.
tṛṣyā́-vant, a. *thirsty*, vii. 103, 3 [tṛṣyā *thirst*].
tṝ *cross*, VI. tirá.
prá- *extend, increase* (family), vii. 61, 4; *prolong* (life), 103, 10; iṣ ao., viii. 48, 4. 7. 11.
ví- *run counter to* (acc.), x. 34, 6.
te, enc. dat. (of tvám), *to thee*, ii. 33, 1; iii. 59, 2; viii. 48, 13; x. 127, 8; *for thee*, iv. 50, 3; gen. *of thee*, i. 35, 11; ii. 12, 15; 33, 7. 11; v. 11. 3; vi. 54, 9; viii. 48, 6. 7. 9; x. 14, 5. 11; 127, 4 [Av. *tōi*, Gk. τοί].
tok-á, m. *offspring, children*, ii. 33, 14; vii. 63, 6.
tmán, *self*, vii. 63, 6 [cp. ātmán].
tyá, dem. prn., n. tyád *that*, iv. 51, 1; pl. tyā́ *those*, viii. 48, 11.
tras *tremble*, I. trasa [Gk. τρέω, Lat. *terreo* 'frighten'].
nís- *speed away*, viii. 48, 11.
trā́ *protect*, IV. Ā. trā́yate; s ao. op., vii. 71, 2.
trā́-tṛ, a. *protecting*, viii. 48, 14 [trā *protect*].
trí, nm. *three*, i. 35, 8; 154, 2. 3. 4; viii. 29, 7 [Gk. τρι-, Lat. *tri-*, OI. *trī*, Eng. *three*].
trí-kadruka, m. pl. *three Soma vats*, x. 14, 16 [kadrū́, f. *Soma vessel*].
tri-dhā́tu, a. (Bv.) *having three parts, threefold*, i. 85, 12; 154, 4.
tri-pañcāśá, a. *consisting of three fifties*, x. 34, 8.
tri-pā́d, a. (Bv.) *consisting of three-fourths*, x. 90, 4; m. *three-fourths*, x. 90, 3.
tri-vandhurá, a. *three-seated*, vii. 71, 4.
tri-ṣadhasthá, a. (Bv.) *occupying three seats*, iv. 50, 1; n. *threefold abode*, v. 11, 2 [sadhá-stha, n. *gathering-place*].

jā *be born*, IV. Ā. **jā́yate** *is born*, v. 11, 3; 88, 4; x. 90, 5; **jā́yase** *art born*, v. 11, 6; ipf. **ájāyata** *was born*, x. 90, 9. 12. 13² ; 129, 3; 135, 6; **ájāyanta**, x. 90. 10.

jā́gr-vi, a. *watchful*, v. 11, 1 ; *stimulating*, x. 34, 1 [from red. stem of 2. **gr** *wake*].

jā-tá, pp. *born*, ii. 12, 1; x. 90, 5. 7; 168, 3; = finite vb., *were born*, x. 90. 10. 13; n. *what is born*, ii. 33, 3 [jā *be born*].

jātá-vedas, a. (Bv.) *having a knowledge of beings*, x 15, 12. 13 [véd-as, n. *knowledge* from vid *know*].

jā́n-u, n. *knee*, x. 15, 6 [Gk. γόν-υ, Lat. genu, Go. kniu, Eng. *knee*].

jā́ya-māna, pr. pt. *being born*, iv. 50, 4 [jā *be born*].

jā-yā́, f. *wife*, x. 34, 2. 4. 10. 11. 13 [jā *be born*].

jār-íṇ-ī, f. *courtesan*, x. 34, 5 [*having paramours*: jārá].

Jāhuṣ-á, m. name of a protégé of the Aśvins, vii. 71, 5.

ji *conquer*, I. **jáyati** ; ft. **jeṣyā́mi**, x. 34, 6; ps. **jīyate**, iii. 59, 2 [when accented this form appears in the RV. as jíyate, i. e. it is then pr. Ā. of jyā *overpower*].

  ví- *conquer*, ii. 12, 9.

  sám- *win*, iv. 50, 9.

jigī-vā́ṃs, red. pf. pt. *having conquered*, ii. 12, 4; x. 127, 8 [ji *conquer*].

jihmá, a. *transverse* = *athwart*, i. 85, 11 : *prone*, ii. 35, 9.

jirá-dānu, a. (Bv.) *having quickening gifts*, v. 83, 1.

jīv-á, n. *living world*, iv. 51, 5 [Lat. vīv-o-s].

jīvás-e, dat. inf. *to live*, viii. 48, 4 ; with **prá** *to live on*, x. 14, 14.

juṣ *enjoy*, VI. **juṣá**, vii. 71, 6 ; 86, 2 ; x. 15, 4. 13; pf. sb. **jújuṣan**, vii. 61, 6 ; is ao. sb. **jóṣiṣat**, ii. 35, 1 [cp. Gk. γεύω, Lat. gus-tus, Go. kiusan, Eng. *choose*].

juṣ-āṇá, pr. pt. Ā. *enjoying*, viii. 48, 2.

júṣ-ṭa, pp. (with shifted accent) *acceptable*, iii. 59, 5 [juṣ *enjoy*].

jū, IX. P. **junā́ti** *speed*, vii. 86, 7.

jṛ, I. Ā. **jára** *awake, be active*, iv. 51, 8.

jéha-māna, pr. pt. Ā. *gasping*, x. 15, 9 [jeh *gasp*].

jñā *know*, IX. **jānā́ti**, x. 34, 4 [cp. Gk. ǵ-γνω-ν, Lat. co-gno-sco, Eng. *know*].

ví-, ps. **jñāyáte** *be distinguished*, iv. 51, 6.

jmā́, f. *earth*, gen. **jmás**, iv. 50, 1.

jyā́-yāms, cpv. *more*, x. 90, 3 ; *elder*, vii. 86, 6 [jyā *overpower* ; Gk. βία 'force'].

jyé-ṣṭha, spv. *highest*, ii. 35, 9 ; *chief*, vii. 86, 4 [spv. of jyā].

jyót-iṣ, n. *light*, iv. 50, 4 ; 51, 1 ; viii. 48, 3 ; x. 127, 2 [jyut = dyut *shine*].

Tá, dem. prn., *that* ; *he, she, it* ; n. **tád** *that*, i. 1, 6 ; 35, 6 ; 154, 2. 5. 6 ; ii. 35, 11. 15 ; iv. 51, 10. 11 ; vii. 86, 2. 3. 4 ; 103, 5. 7 ; x. 34, 12. 13 ; 90, 12 ; 129, 2. 3. 4 ; 135, 5 ; m. A. **tám** *him*, ii. 33, 13 ; 35, 3. 4 ; iv. 50, 1. 9 ; vi. 54, 4 ; *that*, x. 90, 7 ; 135, 4 ; I. **téna** *with it*, viii. 29, 4. 10 ; *with him*, x. 90, 7 ; I. f. **táyā** *with that*, i. 85, 11 ; D. **tásmai** *to him*, iii. 59, 5 ; iv. 50, 8² ; x. 34, 12 ; *for him*, x. 135, 2 ; *to that*, viii. 48, 12. 13 (= *as such*) ; x. 168, 4 ; *for that*, viii. 48, 10 ; ab. **tásmād** *from him*, x. 90, 5. 8. 9³. 10⁵ ; *than that*, x. 129, 2 ; G. **tásya** *of him*, ii. 35, 9 ; iii. 59, 4 ; *of that*, viii. 48, 8 ; x. 15, 7 ; du. m. **táu** *these two*, x. 14, 12 ; f. **té** *these two*, i. 160, 1. 5 ; D. **tā́bhyām** *to those two*, x. 14, 11 ; pl. N. m. **té** *they*, i. 85, 2. 7. 10 ; viii. 48, 5 ; x. 15, 3. 5³. 12. 13 ; *those*, x. 15, 1 ; 90, 16 ; = *as such*, x. 15, 4. 7 ; f. **tā́s** *they*, iv. 51, 8 ; *those*, iv. 51, 7². 9 ; vii. 49, 1. 2. 3. 4 ; n. **tā́** *those*, i. 154, 6 ; ii. 33, 13 ; x. 14, 16 ; **tā́ni** *those*, i. 85, 12 ; x. 90, 16 ; A. **tā́n** *those* = *that*, x. 90, 8 ; I. **tébhis** *with them*, i. 35, 11 ; x. 15, 8. 14 ; f. **tā́bhis** *with them*, x. 168, 2 ; G. **téṣām** *of them*, x. 14, 6 ; L. **tā́su** *in them*, ii. 33, 13.

tams *shake*.

  abhí- *attack*: pf. **tatasré**, iv. 50, 2.

tatan-vā́ṃs, pf. pt. *having spread*, vii. 61, 1 [tan *stretch*].

tá-tas, adv. *thence*, x. 90, 4 ; *so*, x. 135, 6 [prn. root tá].

tá-tra, adv. *there*, x. 34, 13 [prn. root tá].

tá-thā, adv. *thus*, x. 90, 14 [prn. root tá].

ta-dā́nīm, adv. *then*, x. 129, 1 [prn. root tá].

tan *extend* = *perform*, VIII. **tanóti** ; ipf. **átanvata**, x. 90, 6 [cp. Gk. τάννμαι 'stretch', Lat. tendo 'stretch'].

  abhí- *extend over*: red. pf. sb., i. 160, 5.

tri-ṣṭúbh, f. name of a metre, x. 14, 16.
trí-s, adv. *thrice*, x. 90, 11 [Gk. τρίς].
tre-dhā́, adv. *in three ways*, i. 154, 1.
tvákṣ-īyāṃs, cpv. *most vigorous*, ii. 33, 6.
tvád, ab. (of **tvám**) *than thee*, ii. 33, 10.
tvám, prs. prn. *thou*, i. 1, 6; 35, 8; ii. 33, 12; viii. 48, 9. 13. 15³; x. 15, 12². 13.
Tváṣ-ṭṛ, m. name of the artificer god, i. 85, 9; cp. viii. 29, 3 [**tvakṣ = takṣ** *fashion*].
tvā, enc. A. (of tvám) *thee*, i. 1, 7; ii. 33, 4; v. 11, 3; vii. 86, 4; x. 14, 4.
tvā́-datta, pp. (Tp. cd.) *given by thee*, ii. 33, 2.
tvā́m, prs. prn. A. (of **tvám**) *thee*, v. 11, 5. 6².
tveṣ-á, a. *terrible*, ii. 33, 8. 14 [**tviṣ** *be agitated*].
tveṣá-saṃdṛś, a. (Bv.) *of terrible aspect*, i. 85, 8.
tvóta, pp. (Tp.) *aided by thee*, iii. 59, 2 [**tvā** inst. + **ūta**, pp. of **av** *favour*].

Dákṣ-a, m. *will*, vii. 86, 6; *might*, viii. 48, 8 [**dakṣ** *be able*].
dákṣ-iṇa, a. *right*, vi. 54, 10 [cp. Gk. δεξιό-ς, Lat. *dexter*].
dakṣiṇa-tás, adv. *to the south*, x. 15, 6.
dád-at, pr. pt. *giving*, vii. 103, 10 [**dā** *give*].
dádhat, pr. pt. *bestowing*, i. 35, 8; with **ā́** (following), x. 34, 6 [**dhā** *put*].
dádh-āna, pr. pt. Ā. *committing, assuming*, i. 35, 4; ii. 12, 10; = *going*, x. 15, 10 [**dhā** *put*].
dám-a, m. *house*, i. 1, 8; ii. 35, 7 [Gk. δόμο-ς, Lat. *domu-s*].
dáśa, nm. *ten*, x. 34, 12 [Gk. δέκα, Lat. *decem*, Eng. *ten*].
daśāṅgulá, *length of ten fingers*, x. 90, 1 [dáśa + **aṅgúli** *finger*].
Dáśa-gv-a, m. an ancient priest, iv. 51, 4 [*having ten cows*: **gu = go**].
dás-yu, m. *non-Aryan*, ii. 12, 10 [**das** *lay waste*].
dah *burn*, I. **dáha.**
  nís- *burn up*, x. 34, 9.
1. dā *give*, III. **dadā́ti,** ii. 35, 10; x. 14, 9; ao. **ádāt,** vii. 103, 10³; ipv. 3. du. **dātām,** x. 14, 12; **s** ao. op. **diṣiya,** ii. 33, 5 [cp. Gk. δίδωμι, Lat. *dă-re*].
  ánu- *forgive*, ii. 12, 10.
  ā́- *take*, ii. 12, 4.
  párā- *abandon*: ao. inj., viii. 48, 8.
  pári- *give over to*: ipv. **dehi,** x. 14, 11.
  prá- *present*: root ao. **ádās,** x. 15, 12.
2. dā *divide*, IV. **dáya**; *wield*, ii. 33, 10.
dādṛhāṇá, pf. pt. Ā. *steadfast*, i. 85, 10 [**dṛh** *make firm*].
dā-tṛ́, m. *giver*, ii. 33, 12.
Dā́nu, m. *son of Dānu*, a demon, ii. 12, 11.
dā́-man, n. *rope*, viii. 86, 5 [3. **dā** *bind*].
dāś-vā́ṃs, pf. pt. *worshipping*, m. *worshipper*, i. 1, 6; 85, 12; vii. 71, 2; x. 15, 7 [**dāś** *honour*].
dā́s-a, a. *non-Aryan*, ii. 12, 4 [**dās** *be hostile*].
dās-á, m. *slave*, vii. 86, 7.
didṛ́k-ṣu, adv. *with a desire to see* = *find out*, vii. 86, 3 [from ds. of **dṛś** *see*].
div, m. *sky*, A. **dívam,** iii. 59, 7; G. **divás,** iv. 51, 1. 10. 11; v. 83, 6; vii. 61, 3; 63, 4; x. 15, 14; 127, 8; L. **diví,** i. 85, 2; v. 11, 3; viii. 29, 9; x. 90, 3 [Gk. Δίϝα, Διϝός, Διϝί].
div *play*, IV. **dī́vya,** x. 34, 13.
dív-ā, adv. *by day*, vii. 71, 1. 2 [w. shift of accent for **div-ā́**].
divi-spṛ́ś, a. *touching the sky*, v. 11, 1; x. 168, 1 [**diví** L. of **div** + **spṛś** *touch*].
divé-dive, lc. itv. cd. *every day*, i. 1, 3. 7 [L. of **divá** *day*].
div-yá, a. *coming from heaven, divine*, vii. 49, 1; 103, 2; x. 34, 9 [**dív** *heaven*].
díś, f. *quarter* (of the sky), i. 85, 11; x. 90, 14 [**diś** *point*].
1. dī *fly*, IV. **dī́ya.**
  pári- *fly around*, ii. 35, 14; v. 83, 7.
2. dī *shine*: pf. **dīdā́ya,** ii. 33, 4.
dīdi-vā́ṃs, pf. pt. *shining*, ii. 35, 3. 14 [**dī** *shine*].
dī́divi, a. *shining*, i. 1, 8 [**dī** *shine*].
dī́dhy-āna, pr. pt. Ā. *pondering*, iv. 50, 1 [**dhī** *think*].
dīp *shine*, IV. Ā. **dī́pya.**
  sám- *inflame*: red. ao. inj. **didīpas,** viii. 48, 6 [cp. **dī** *shine*].
dī́y-ant, pr. pt. *flying*, vii. 63, 5 [**dī** *fly*].
dīrghá, a. *long*, i. 154, 3; x. 14, 14 [Gk. δολιχό-ς].
dīrgha-śrú-t, a. *heard afar*, vii. 61, 2 [**śru** *hear* + **t**].
du *go*: **iṣ** ao. sb. **daviṣāni,** x. 34, 5.
dudhrá, a. *fierce*, ii. 12, 15.
dur-i-tá, (pp.) n. *faring ill, hardship*, i. 35, 3 [**dus** *ill* + pp. of **i** *go*].

dur-gá, n. *hardship*, vii. 61, 7 [**dus** + **ga** = **gam** *go*].
dur-matí, f. *ill-will*, ii. 33, 14 [**dus** *ill* + **matí** *thought*].
duvas-ya, den. *present with* (inst.), x. 14, 1 [**dúvas**, n. *gift*].
duṣ-kṛ́t, m. *evil-doer*, v. 83, 2. 9 [**dus** + **kṛ** *do* + **t**].
dú-ṣṭuti, f. *ill praise*, ii. 33, 4 [**dus** *ill* + **stutí** *praise*].
duh *milk*, II. P. **dógdhi**; **s** ao. **dukṣata**, with two acc., i. 160. 3.
duh-i-tṛ́, f. *daughter*, iv. 51, 1. 10. 11; x. 127, 8 [Gk. θυγάτηρ, Go. *dauhtar*].
dū-ḍábha, a. (Bv.) *hard to deceive*, vii. 86, 4 [**dus** + **dábha** *deception*].
dū-tá, m. *messenger*, v. 11, 4; 83, 3; x. 14, 12.
dūrā́d, ab. adv. *from far*, iii. 59, 2; v. 83, 3 [**dū-rá**, a. *far*].
dūré-artha, a. (Bv.) *whose goal is distant*, vii. 63, 4.
dṛ *pierce*, int. **dardarṣi**, ii. 12, 15.
dṛ́-ti, m. *water-skin*, v. 83, 7; vii. 103, 2 [**dṛ** *split*; cp. Gk. δέρω, Eng. *tear*].
dṛś *see*: pf. **dádṛśe** *is seen*, vii. 61, 5.
dṛśáye, dat. inf. *to see*, x. 14, 12.
dṛṣ-ṭvā́ya, gd. *having seen*, x. 34, 11.
dṛh *make firm*, I. P. **dṛ́ṃha**; ipf. **ádṛṃhat**, ii. 12, 2.
dev-á, m. *god*, i. 1, 1. 2. 4. 5; 35, 1. 2. 3². 8. 10. 11; 160, 1. 4; ii. 12, 1²; 33, 15; 35, 5. 15; iii. 59, 6. 8. 9; iv. 50, 9; v. 11, 2; vii. 61, 1. 7; 63, 1. 3; 86, 7²; viii. 29, 2. 3. 7; 48, 3. 9. 14; x. 14, 3². 7. 14; 15, 10. 12; 34, 8; 90, 6. 7. 15. 16°, 129, 6; 135, 1; 168, 2. 4² [*celestial* from **dív** *heaven*].
deva-trā́, adv. *among the gods*, x. 15, 9.
deva-mānā́, n. *abode of the gods*, x. 135, 7.
deva-yú, a. *devoted to the gods*, i. 154, 5.
deva-vandá, a. *god-praising*, x. 15, 10 [**vand** *greet*].
devá-hiti, f. *divine order*, viii. 103, 9 [**devá** *god* + **hi-tí**, f. *impulse* from **hi** *impel*].
dev-ī́, f. *goddess*, i. 160, 1; ii. 35, 5; iv. 51, 4. 5. 8. 11; vii. 49, 1. 2. 3. 4; x. 127, 1. 2. 3 [f. of **dev-á** *god*].
doṣā́-vastṛ, m. (Tp.) *illuminer of gloom*, i. 1, 7 [**doṣā́** *evening* + **vas-tṛ** from **vas** *shine*].
dáiv-ya, a. *divine*, i. 35, 5; viii. 48, 2; *coming from the gods*, ii. 33, 7; n. *divinity*, ii. 35, 8 [from **devá** *god*].
Dyā́vā-pṛthivī́, du. (Dv.) *Heaven and Earth*, i. 35, 9; 160, 1. 5; v. 83, 8; viii. 48, 13; the parts of the cd. separated, ii. 12, 13.
dyu-mát, adv. *brilliantly*, v. 11, 1 [n. of **dyu-mánt**, a. *bright*].
dyu-mná, n. *wealth*, iii. 59, 6.
dyó, m. *heaven*, N. **dyáus**, iv. 51, 11; x. 90, 14; acc. **dyā́m**, i. 35, 7. 9; 154, 4; ii. 12, 2. 12; iii. 59, 1; N. pl. f. **dyā́vas**, i. 35, 6 [Gk. Ζεύς, Ζῆν, Lat. *diem*].
dyót-ana, a. *shining*, viii. 29, 2 [**dyut** *shine*].
drávˑiṇa, n. *wealth*, iv. 51, 7 [*movable* property, from **dru** *run*].
dru *run*, I, **dráva**.
  áti- *run past* (acc.), x. 14, 10.
drug-dhá, n. *misdeed*, vii. 86, 5 [pp. of **druh** *be hostile*].
drúh, f. *malice*, ii. 35, 6; m. *avenger*, vii. 61, 5.
dvá, nm. *two*, i. 35, 6; viii. 29, 8. 9 [Gk. δύω, Lat. *duo*, Lith. *dù*, Eng. *two*].
dvādaśá, a. *consisting of twelve*, m. *twelvemonth*, vii. 103, 9.
dvā́r, f. du. *door*, iv. 51, 2 [cf. Gk. θύρα, Lat. *fores*, Eng. *door*; perhaps from **dhvṛ** *close* with loss of aspirate through influence of **dvá** *two*, as having two folds].
dvi-tā́, (inst.) adv. (*doubly*) *as well*, vii. 86, 1 [**dvi** *two*].
dvi-pā́d, a. (Bv.) *two-footed*, iv. 51, 5 [Gk. δί-ποδ-, Lat. *bi-ped-*].
dviṣ *hate*, II. **dvéṣṭi**, x. 34, 3.
dvéṣ-as, n. *hatred*, ii. 33, 2 [**dviṣ** *hate*].

Dhán-a, n. *wealth*, *money*, iv. 50, 9; x. 34, 10. 12.
1. **dhán-van**, n. *waste land*, i. 35, 8; *desert*, v, 83, 10.
2. **dhán-van**, n. *bow*, ii. 33, 10.
dham *blow*, I. P. **dhámati**, ps. **dhamyéte**, x. 135, 7.
  ví- *blow asunder*, iv, 50, 4.
dhám-ant, pr. pt. *blowing*, i. 85, 10.
dhár-man, n. *ordinance*, *law*, i. 160, 1; x. 90, 16 [that which holds or is established: **dhṛ** *hold*].
1. **dhā** *put*, III. **dádhāti**, v. 83, 1; *supply with* (inst.), ii. 35, 12; *bestow*, ipv. **dhehí**, x. 14, 11; **dhattá**, i. 85, 12; ii. 12, 5; x. 15, 7; **dadhāta**, x. 15, 4.

7 ; **dadhātana**, x. 15, 11 ; **dhattā́m**, iv. 51, 11 ; **dadhantu**, vii. 63, 6 ; *perform*, ipf. **dhatta**, i. 85, 9 ; *bestow*, s ao. sb. **dhāsathas**, i. 160, 5 ; *establish*, pf. **dadhé**, x. 129, 7 ; ds. *desire to bestow*, **didhiṣanti**, ii. 35, 5 ; *support*, **dídhiṣāmi**, ii. 35, 12 [Gk. τίθημι].
ádhi- *put on* (acc.) : pf. **dadhire**, i. 85, 2 ; ao. **ádhita**, x. 127, 1.
ā́- *deposit*, root ao. sb. **dhās**, v. 83, 7.
ní- *deposit*, root ao. **dhātam**, vii. 71, 5 ; ps. ao. **ádhāyi**, viii. 48, 10.
pári- *put around*, vi. 54, 10.
prá- *put from* (ab.) *into* (lc.), vii. 61, 3.
ví- *impose* : pf. **dadhur**, iv. 51, 6 ; *divide*, ipf. **ádadhur**, x. 90, 11.
canas- *accept gladly*, ii. 35, 1.
purás- *place at the head, appoint Purohita* : pf. **dadhire**, iv. 50, 1.
2. **dhā** *suck*, IV. P. **dháya**, ii. 33, 13 ; 35, 5.
dhā́-man, n. *power*, i. 85, 11 ; *ordinance*, vii. 61, 4 ; 63, 3 [dhā *put, establish*].
dhārayát-kavi, a. (gov.) *supporting the sage*, i. 160, 1 [dhāráyat, pr. pt. cs. of dhṛ *hold*].
dhā́-rā, f. *stream*, i. 85, 5 ; v. 83, 6 [dhāv *run*].
dhiṣáṇā, f. *bowl*, i. 160, 1.
dhī́, f. *thought*, i. 1, 7 ; iv. 50, 11.
dhī *think*, III. **dī́dhye**.
ā́- *think to oneself*, ā- **dī́dhye**, x. 34, 5.
dhī́-ra, a. *thoughtful*, viii. 48, 4 ; *wise*, i. 160, 3 ; *intelligent*, vii. 86, 1 [dhī *think*].
dhunéti, a. (Bv.) *having a resounding gait*, iv. 50, 2 [dhuna + íti].
dhúr, f. *pole* (of a car), vii. 63, 2 ; viii. 48, 2.
dhū-má, m. *smoke*, v. 11, 3 [dhū *agitate* ; Gk. θυμό-ς, Lat. *fumu-s*].
dhūr-tí, f. *malice*, viii. 48, 3 [dhvṛ *injure*].
dhṛ *support, fix firmly* : pf. **dādhā́ra**, i. 154, 4 ; iii. 59, 1.
dhṛṣ-ṇú, n. adv. *forcibly*, x. 34, 14 [dhṛṣ *be bold, dare*].
dhe-nú, f. *cow*, i. 160, 3 ; ii. 35, 7 [*yielding milk* : dhe = dhā *suck*].
dhrú-ti, f. *seduction*, vii. 86, 6 [dhru = dhvṛ *injure*].

1. **Ná**, pcl. *as, like*, i. 35, 6 ; 85, 1. 7. 8² ; 154, 2 ; ii. 33, 11 ; iv. 51, 8 ; vii. 61, 2 ; 63, 5 ; 86, 5². 7 ; 103, 2². 3. 7 ; viii. 48, 5. 6 ; x. 127, 4. 8 ; 168, 2 [180].
2. **ná**, neg. pcl. *not*, ii. 12, 5. 9. 10 ; 33, 9. 10. 15² ; 35, 6² ; iii. 59, 2⁴ ; iv. 51, 6 ; vi. 54, 3². 4. 9 ; vii. 61, 5³ ; 63, 3 ; 86, 6 ; 103, 8 ; viii. 48, 10 ; x. 14, 2 ; 15, 13² ; 34, 2–5. 12 ; 129, 1⁴. 2. 7² ; 168, 3. 4 [180].
nákt-am, acc. adv. *by night*, vii. 71, 1. 2 ; x. 34, 10 [stem nakt, cp. Lat. *nox* = *noct-s*].
ná-kṣatra, n. *star* ; *day-star*, vii. 86, 1 [nák *night* + kṣatrá *dominion* = *ruling over night*].
nad-ī́, f. *stream*, ii. 35, 3 [nad *roar*].
ná-pāt, m. *son*, ii. 35, 1. 2. 3. 7. 10. 13 ; *grandson*, x. 15, 3 [Lat. *nepōt-* 'nephew'].
náptṛ, m. (weak stem of **nápāt**) *son* : gen. **náptur**, ii. 35, 11 ; dat. **náptre**, ii. 35, 14 [ná-pitṛ *having no father* = 'nephew', 'grandson'].
nábh-as, n. *sky*, v. 83, 3 [Gk. νέφος, OSl. *nebo*].
nam *bend*, I. **náma** ; Ā : ii. 12, 13 ; iv. 50, 8 ; *before* (dat.), x. 34, 8 ; int. **nánnamīti** *bend low*, v. 83, 5.
práti- *bend towards* : pf. **nānāma**, ii. 33, 12.
nám-as, n. *homage*, i. 1, 7 ; ii. 33, 4. 8 ; 35, 12 ; iii. 59, 5 ; iv. 50, 6 ; v. 83, 1 ; vii. 61, 6 ; 63, 5 ; 86, 4 ; x. 14, 15 ; 15, 2 ; 34, 8 [nam *bend*].
namas-yá, den. *adore*, ii. 33, 8 [námas *homage*].
namas-yà, a. *adorable*, iii. 59, 4.
nár-ya, a. *manly*, i. 85, 9.
náv-a, a. *new*, iv. 51, 4 ; vii. 61, 6 ; x. 135, 3 [Gk. νέο-ς, Lat. *novu-s*, OSl. *novu*, Eng. *new*].
Náva-gv-a, m. an ancient priest, iv. 51, 4 ; pl. a family of ancient priests, x. 14, 6 [*having nine cows* : gu = gó].
náv-yas, cpv. a. *renewed*, v. 11, 1 [Lat. *nov-ior*].
1. **naś** *be lost*, IV. P. **náśya** ; ao. **neśat**, vi. 54, 7.
2. **naś** *reach*, I. **náśa**.
ví- *reach*, ii. 35, 6.
náś, f. *night*, vii. 71, 1.
naṣ-ṭá, pp. *lost*, vi. 54, 10 [naś *be lost*].
nas, prs. prn., A. *us*, i. 1, 9 ; 35, 11² ; ii. 33, 1. 2. 3. 5. 14 ; iv. 50, 11 ; vii. 61, 7² ; 63, 6 ; 71, 2. 4. 6 ; 86, 8 ; viii. 48, 6. 8. 15 c ; x. 14, 14 ; 15, 1. 6 ; 34,

14; *to us*, x. 127, 4, D., i. 1, 9a; 85, 12; 160, 5; ii. 33, 15; iv. 50, 2; v. 83, 5. 6; vi. 54, 5. 10; vii. 63, 6²; vii. 86, 8; 10, 10; viii. 48, 8. 9. 12. 14. 15a; x. 14, 2, 15, 4; 34, 14; 127, 6; 135, 5; G. *of us*, ii. 33, 4. 13; v. 11, 4; 83, 6; vi. 54, 5; 86, 5; viii. 48, 4². 7. 9; x. 14, 2. 6. 7; 15, 8; 135, 1.

nah *bind*, IV. **náhya**.
 sám- *knit together*: irr. pf. 2. pl. **anāha**, viii. 48, 5.

nā́ = ná *not*, x. 34, 8.

nā́ka, n. *firmament*, i. 85, 7; vii. 86, 1; x. 90, 16.

nāḷī́, f. *flute*, x. 135, 7.

nāth-itá, pp. *distressed*, x. 34, 3 [**nāth** *seek aid*].

nādyá, m. *son of streams*, ii. 35, 1.

nā́dh-amāna, pr. pt. Ā. *seeking aid, suppliant*, ii. 12, 6; 33, 6.

nā́nā, adv. *separately*, ii. 12, 8.

nā́bhi, f. *navel*, x. 90, 14.

nā́-man, n. *name*, ii. 33, 8; 35, 11; vii. 103, 6 [Gk. ὄνομα, Lat. *nōmen*, Go. *namō*, Eng. *name*].

nā́rī, f. *woman*, ii. 33, 5 [from **nár** *man*].

nā́satya, m. du. epithet of the **Aśvins**, vii. 71, 4 [**ná** + **asatyá** *not untrue*].

ni-kṛ́t-van, a. *deceitful*, x. 34, 7 [**ní** *down* + **kṛ** *do*].

ni-citá, pp. *known*, ii. 12, 13 [**ni** + **ci** *note*].

niṇyá, n. *secret*, vii. 61, 5.

ni-todín, a. *piercing*, x. 34, 7.

ni-drā́, f. *sleep*, viii. 48, 14 [**ní** + **drā** *sleep*; cp. Gk. δαρ-θάνω, Lat. *dor-mio*].

ni-dhí, m. *treasure*, viii. 29, 6; *deposit*, x. 15, 5 [**ní** *down* + **dhi** = **dhā** *put*].

ní-dhruvi, a. *persevering*, viii. 29, 3 [**ní** + **dhrúvi** *firm*].

ni-pādá, m. *valley*, v. 83, 7 [**ní** *down* + **pā́da**, m. *foot*].

nir-áyaṇa, n. *exit*, x. 135, 6 [**nís** *out* + **áy-ana** *going*: **i** *go*].

ni-vát, f. *depth*, x. 127, 2 [**ní** *down*].

ni-véśanī, a. *causing to rest*, i. 35, 1 [from cs. of **ní** + **viś** *cause to turn in*].

ní-ṣatta, pp. with **ā**, *having sat down in* (lc.), x. 15, 2 [**ní** + **sad** *sit down*].

ni-ṣád-yā, gd. *having sat down*, ii. 35, 10; x. 15, 6; with **ā́**, x. 14, 5.

ni-siñc-ánt, pr. pt. *pouring down*, v. 83, 6 [**sic** *sprinkle*].

niṣká, m. *necklace*, ii. 33, 10.

niṣ-kṛtá, n. *appointed place*, x. 34, 5 [pp. *arranged*: **nís** *out* + **kṛ** *make*].

nī *lead*, I. **náya**; 2. pl. ipv., x. 34, 4.
 sám- *conjoin with* (inst.), vi. 54, 1.

nīc-ā́, adv. *down*, x. 34, 9 [inst. of **nyàñc** *downward*].

nú, adv. *now*, i. 154, 1; ii. 33, 7; iv. 51, 9; x. 34, 14²; 168, 1; = inter. pcl. *pray?* vii. 86, 2 [Gk. νύ, OI. *nu*, OG. *nu*].

nud *push*, VI. **nudá**; pf. 3. pl. Ā. **nunudre**, i. 85, 10. 11.
 prá- *push away*: pf. vii. 86, 1.

nū́, adv. = **nú** *now*, vii. 63, 6 [OG. *nū*].

nū́-tana, a. *present*, i. 1, 2 [**nū́** *now*].

nū-nám, adv. *now*, iv. 51, 1; vii. 63, 4; viii. 48, 3; x. 15, 2 [**nū́** *now*].

nṛ́, m. *man*, pl. N. **náras**, i. 85, 8; 154, 5; v. 11, 2. 4; vii. 103, 9 [Gk. ἀνήρ, ἀνδρός].

nṛ-cákṣas, a. (Bv.) *observer of men*, viii, 48, 9. 15; x. 14, 11 [**nṛ** *man* + **cákṣas** *look*].

nṛ-páti, m. *lord of men*, vii. 71, 4.

nṛ-mṇá, a. *manliness, valour*, ii. 12, 1 [cp. **nṛ-máṇas** *manly*].

ne-tṛ́, m. *guide*, ii. 12, 7 [**nī** *lead*].

nó = **ná** + **u** *also not*, vi. 54, 3.

náu, f. *ship*, x. 135, 4 [Gk. ναῦ-ς, Lat. *nāv-i-s*].

ny-àñc, a. *downward*, v. 83, 7 [**ní-** *down* + **-añc** *-ward*].

ny-ùpta, pp. *thrown down*, x. 34, 5. 9 [**ní** + **vap** *strew*].

Pakṣ-ín, a. *winged*, x. 127, 5 [**pakṣá**, m. *wing*].

pác-ant, pr. pt. *cooking*, ii. 12, 14. 15 [**pac** *cook*, Lat. *coquo* for *pequo*, OSl. 3. s. *pečetŭ*].

páñca, nm. *five*, iii. 59, 8 [Av. *panca*, Gk. πέντε, Lat. *quinque*].

páṇ-i, m. *niggard*, iv. 51, 3 [**paṇ** *bargain*].

pat *fly*, I. **páta**, x. 14, 16; cs. **patáya** *fall*, v. 83, 4 [Gk. πέτ-ε-ται *flies*, Lat. *pet-o*].

pát-i, m. *lord*, pl. N. **pátayas**, iv. 50, 6; 51, 10; viii. 48, 13 [Gk. πόσι-ς].

páth, m. *path*, viii. 29, 6; x. 14, 10 [cp. Gk. πάτο-ς].

path-í, m. *path*, i. 35, 11; x. 14, 7; 168, 3.

pathi-kṛ́t, m. *path-maker*, x. 14, 15 [**kṛ-t** *making*: **kṛ** + determinative **t**].

pathi-rákṣi, a. (Tp.) *watching the path*, x. 14, 11.

path-yā̀, f. *path*, x. 14, 2.

pad *fall*, IV. Ā. **pádya**; pp. **papā̆da**, x. 34, 11.

áva- *fall down*, vi. 54, 3.

pád, *foot*, du. ab. **padbhyā́m**, x. 90, 12. 14 [Gk. ποδ-, Lat. *ped-*, Eng. *foot*].

pad-á, n. *step*, i. 154, 3. 4. 5. 6; ii. 35, 14 [**pad** *walk*; Gk. πέδ-ο-ν 'ground'].

pad-vánt, a. *having feet*, x. 127, 5.

pan-áyya, gdv. *praiseworthy*, i. 160, 5 [**pan** *admire*].

pánthā, m. *path*, i. 35, 11; vii. 71, 1; x. 14, 1 [cp. Gk. πόντο-ς].

pánya-tama, spv. gdv. *most highly to be praised*, iii. 59, 5 [**pánya**, gdv. *praiseworthy*: **pan** *admire*].

paprath-āná, pf. pt. Ā. *spreading oneself*, iv. 51, 8 [**prath** *spread*].

páy-as, n. *milk, moisture*, i. 160, 3 [**pī** *swell*].

pár-a, a. *farther*, ii. 12, 8; *higher*, x. 15, 1; *remote*, x. 15, 10 [**pṛ** *pass*].

para-má, spv. a. *farthest*, iv. 50, 3; x. 14, 8; 129, 7; *highest*, i. 154, 5. 6; ii. 35, 14; iv. 50, 4.

par-ás, adv. *far away*, ii. 35, 6; *beyond*, x. 129, 1. 2.

parás-tād, adv. *from afar*, vi. 54, 9; *above*, x. 129, 5.

parā-yánt, pr. pt. *departing*, x. 34, 5 [**párā** *away*, Gk. πέρα *beyond*, + **i** *go*].

parā-vát, f. *distance*, i. 35, 3; iv. 50, 3.

pári, prp. *round*; with ab. *from*, ii. 35, 10; x. 135, 4 [Av. *pairi*, Gk. πέρι].

pari-dhí, m. pl. *sticks enclosing* the altar, x. 90, 15 [**pári** *round* + **dhi** reduced form of **dhā** *put*].

pari-bhū́, a. *being around, encompassing* (acc.), i. 1, 4 [**bhū** *be*].

parivatsar-ī́ṇa, a. *yearly*, vii. 10, 8 [**pári-** + **vatsará**, m. *complete year*].

pári-ṣkṛta, pp. *adorned*, x. 135, 7 [**pári** *round* + **skṛ** = **kṛ** *make* = *put*].

pareyi-vā́ṃs, red. pf. pt. *having passed away*, x. 14, 1 [**párā** *away* + **īy-i-vā́ṃs**: from **i** *go*].

Parjánya, m. a god of rain, v. 83, 1–5. 9.

Parjánya-jinvita, pp. *quickened by Parjanya*, vii. 103, 1 [**jinv** sec. root = **ji-nu** from **ji** *quicken*].

pary-ā-vívṛtsant, pr. pt. ds. *wishing to revolve hither* (acc.), vii. 63, 2 [**vṛt** *turn*].

párva-ta, m. i. 35, 10; ii. 12, 2. 11. 13 [*jointed*; Lesbian Gk. πέρρατα 'limits'].

pár-van, n. *joint, section*, vii. 103, 5; viii. 48, 5 [cp. Gk. πέρϝαρ in περαίνω 'finish' for περϝανιω].

pav-í, m. *felly*, vi. 54, 3.

pavítra-vant, a. *purifying*, i. 160, 3 [**pavítra**, n. *means of purification*; root **pū** *purify*].

paś = **spaś** *see*, i. 35, 2; x. 14, 7 [Av. *spas*, Lat. *spec-iō*].

paś-ú, m. *beast*, x. 90, 8; *victim*, x. 90, 15 [Av. *pasu-*, Lat. *pecu-s*, Go. *faihu*].

paśu-tṛ́p, a. *cattle-stealing*, vii. 86, 5 [**tṛp** *be pleased with*].

paścā́-tād, adv. *behind*, viii. 48, 15 [**paścā́** inst. adv. Av. *pasca* 'behind'].

paścā́d, (ab.) adv. *behind*, x. 90, 5; *afterwards*, x. 135, 6.

1\. **pā** *drink*, I. **píba**, iv. 50, 10; root ao. **ápāma**, viii. 48, 3 [cp. Lat. *bibo* 'drink'].

sám- *drink together*, x. 135, 1.

2\. **pā** *protect*, II. **pā́ti**, *from* (ab.), ii. 35, 6; vii. 61, 7; 63, 6; 71, 6; 86, 8; viii. 48, 15.

pā́th-as, n. *path*, vii. 63, 5; *domain*, i. 154, 5 [related to **páth**, m. *path*].

pā́d-a, m. *foot*, x. 90, 11; *one-fourth*, x. 90, 3. 4 [sec. stem formed from acc. **pā́d-am** of **pád** *foot*].

pāpáyā, inst. f. adv. *evilly*, x. 135, 2 [**pāpá**, a. *bad*].

pār-á, m. *farther shore*, ii. 33, 3 [**pṛ** *pass* = *crossing*; Gk. πόρο-ς 'passage'].

pā́rthiva, a. *earthly*, i. 154, 1; x. 15, 2 [a. from **pṛthivī́** *earth*].

pāv-aká, a. *purifying*, iv. 51, 2; vii. 49, 2. 3 [**pū** *purify*].

pi *swell*, I. **páyate**; pf. **pīpā́ya**, ii. 35, 7; viii. 29, 6.

pi-tú, m. *drink*, x. 15, 3 [**pā** *drink*].

pi-tṛ́, m. *father*, i. 1, 9; 160, 2^2. 3; ii. 33, 1. 12. 13; iv. 50, 6; v. 83, 6; vii. 103, 3; viii. 48, 4; x. 14, 5. 6; 34, 4; 135, 1; pl. *fathers, ancestors*, viii. 48, 12. 13; x. 14, 2. 4. 7. 8. 9; 15, 1–13 [Gk. πατήρ, Lat. *pater*, Go. *fadar*].

pítr-ya, a. *paternal*, vii. 86, 5; viii. 48, 7 [**pitṛ́** *father*].

pinv *yield abundance*, I. **pínva**, iv. 50, 8; *overflow*, v. 83, 4 [sec. root = **pi-nu** from **pī** *swell*].

prá- *pour forth*, v. 83, 6

piś *adorn*, VI. **piṃśá**: pf. **pipiśúr**, vii. 103, 6; Ā. pipiśe, ii. 33, 9.
pī-tá, pp. *drunk*, viii. 48, 4. 5. 10. 12.
pīyū́ṣa, m. n. *milk*, ii. 35, 5 [pī *swell*].
putrá, m. *son*, i. 160, 3; v. 11, 6; vii. 103, 3; x. 15, 7; 34, 10.
púnar, adv. *again*, vi. 54, 10; x. 14, 8; 90, 4; 135, 2; *back*, x. 14, 12.
punar-hán, a. *striking back*, x. 34, 7.
punāná, pr. pt. *purifying*, vii. 49, 1 [pū *purify*].
púr, f. *citadel*, ii. 35, 6 [pṛ *fill*].
púraṃ-dhi, f. *reward*, iv. 50, 11 [a. dhi *bestowing* (reduced form of dhā) *abundance*, púr-am acc.].
purás-tād, adv. *in the east*, iv. 51, 1. 2. 3; *forward*, v. 83, 8; *before*, viii. 48, 15; *in front*, x. 135, 6.
purā́, adv. *formerly*, iv. 51, 7.
purā-ṇá, a., f. ī́, *ancient*, iv. 51, 6; m. pl. *ancients*, x. 135, 1. 2 [purā́ *formerly*].
puru-táma, a. spv. *most frequent*, iv. 51, 1 [purú, Gk. πολύ-ς].
puru-trā́, adv. *in many places*, x. 127, 1; *in many ways*, vii. 103, 6.
puru-rū́pa, a. (Bv.) *having many forms*, ii. 33, 9.
Púru-ṣa, m. *the primaeval Male*, x. 90, 1. 2. 4. 6. 7. 11. 15.
puruṣá-tā, f. *human frailty*, x. 15, 6.
puró-hita, pp. *placed in front*, m. *domestic priest*, i. 1, 1; v. 11, 2 [purás + hitá, pp. of dhā *put*].
puró-hiti, f. *priestly service*, vii. 61, 7.
puṣ-ṭá, n. (pl.) *earnings*, ii. 12, 4 [pp. of puṣ *thrive*].
puṣ-ṭí, f. *earnings*, ii. 12, 5; *prosperity*, viii. 48, 6.
pū *purify*, IX. punā́ti, i. 160, 3.
pūr-ṇá, pp. *full*, i. 154, 4; vii. 103, 7 [pṝ *fill*: cp. Gk. πολλοί 'many', Eng. *full*].
pū́ruṣa, m. metrical for púruṣa, x. 90, 3. 5.
pū́r-va, a. *former*, i. 1, 2; *being in front*, iv. 50, 8; *early*, *ancient*, x. 14, 2. 7. 15; 15, 2. 8. 10; 90, 16.
pūrva-já, a. *born of old*, x. 14, 15 [jā *be born*].
pūrva-bhā́j, a. *receiving the preference*, iv. 50, 7 [bhaj *share*].
pūrva-sū́, a. *bringing forth first*, ii. 35, 5.
pūrvāhṇ-á, m. *morning*, x. 34, 11 [pūrvá *early* + ahna = áhan *day*].
pūrv-yá, a. *ancient*, i. 35, 11; x. 14, 7.

Pūṣ-án, m. *a solar deity*, vi. 54, 1–6. 8–10 *prosperer* [puṣ *thrive*].
pṛ *take across*, III. P. píparti; ipv. **pi-pṛtám**, vii. 61, 7; II. P. párṣi = ipv., ii. 33, 3.
pṛc *mix*, VII. **pṛnákti**.
sám-, Ā. **pṛṅkté**, *mingle*, vii. 103, 4.
pṛchá-māna, pr. pt. Ā. *asking oneself*, x. 34, 6 [prach *ask*].
pṛ́t-anā, f. *battle*, i. 85, 8.
pṛthiv-ī́, f. *earth*, i. 35, 8; 154, 4; ii. 12, 2; iii. 59, 1. 3. 7; iv. 51, 11; v. 83, 4. 5. 9; vii. 61, 3; x. 168, 1 [*the broad one* = **pṛthvī́**, f. of pṛthú from **prath** *spread*].
pṛ́ś-ni, a. *speckled*, i. 160, 3; vii. 103, 4. 6. 10.
Pṛ́śni-mātṛ, a. (Bv.) *having Pṛśni as a mother*, i. 85, 2.
pṛ́ṣat-ī, (pr. pt.) f. *spotted mare*, i. 85, 4. 5.
pṛṣad-ājyá, n. *clotted butter*, x. 90, 8.
pṛ́ṣ-ant, (pr. pt.) a. *variegated*, iv. 50, 2.
pṝ *fill*, IX. **pṛṇā́ti**, ii. 35, 3.
ā́- *fill up*, v. 11, 5; vii. 61, 2.
pépiś-at, pr. pt. int. *thickly painting*, x. 127, 7 [piś *paint*].
póṣ-a, m. *prosperity*, i. 1, 3 [puṣ *thrive*].
pra-ketá, m. *beacon*, x. 129, 2 [prá + cit *appear*].
prach *ask*, VI. **pṛchá**, ii. 12, 5; vii. 86, 3 [sec. root: praś + cha; cp. Lat. *posco* = *porc-sco* and *prec-or*, OG. *forsc-ōn*].
pra-jā́, f. *offspring*, ii. 33, 1; pl. *progeny*, ii. 35, 8; = *men*, v. 83, 10 [cp. Lat. *pro-gen-ies*].
prajā́-vant, a. *accompanied by offspring*, iv. 51, 10.
prati-kāmám, adv. *at pleasure*, x. 15, 8 [kā́ma *desire*].
prátijan-ya, a. *belonging to adversaries*, iv. 50, 9; n. *hostile force*, iv. 50, 7 [prati-janá, m. *adversary*].
prati-dī́van, m. *adversary at play*, x. 34, 6 [div *play*].
prati-doṣám, adv. *towards eventide*, i. 35, 10 [doṣā́ *evening*].
prati-búdhyamāna, pr. pt. *awaking towards* (acc.), iv. 51, 10.
prati-mā́na, n. *match*, ii. 12, 9 [*counter-measure*: mā *measure*].
prá-tir-am, acc. inf. *to prolong*, viii. 48, 10 [tṛ *cross*].
pra-tná, a. *ancient*, iv. 50, 1 [prá *before*].

prath *spread out*, I. Ā. **prátha** : ppf. **paprāthat**, vii. 86, 1.
pra-thamá, ord. *first*, i. 35, 1[4] ; v. 11, 2 ; vi. 54, 4 ; x. 14, 2 ; 34, 12 ; 90, 16 ; 129, 4 ; *chief*, ii. 12, 1 [= **pra-tamá** *foremost* ; OP. *fra-tama*].
prathama-jā́, a. *first-born*, x. 168, 3 [jā = jan].
prathamá-m, adv. *first*, iv. 50, 4.
pra-díś, f. *control*, ii. 12, 7 [diś *point*].
pra-bodháyant, cs. pr. pt. *awakening*, iv. 51, 5 [budh *wake*].
prá-yata, pp. *extended*, i. 154, 3 ; *offered*, x. 15, 11. 12 [yam *stretch out*].
prá-yati, f. *impulse*, x. 129, 5 [yam *extend*].
práyas-vant, a. *offering oblations*, iii. 59, 2 [práy-as *enjoyment* from prī *please*].
pra-yotṛ́, m. *warder off*, vii. 86, 6 [2. yu *separate*].
pra-vát, f. *slope, downward path*, i. 35, 3 ; *height*, x. 14, 1 [prá *forward*].
pravāte-já, a. *born in a windy place*, x. 34, 1 [pra-vātá + ja = jan].
pra-vāsá, m. *traveller*, viii. 29, 8 [prá + vas *dwell away* from home].
prá-viṣṭa, pp. *having entered*, vii. 49, 4 [viś *enter*].
pra-sargá, m. *discharge*, vii. 103, 4 [sṛj *emit*]
pra-savītṛ́, m. *rouser*, vii. 63, 2 [sū *stimulate*].
prá-siti, f. *toils*, x. 34, 15 [si *bind*].
prá-sūta, pp. *aroused*, vii. 63, 4 [sū *impel*].
pra-stará, m. *strewn grass*, x. 14, 4 [stṛ *strew*].
prā *fill* [extended form, pr-ā, of pṝ *fill*].
  ā́- *pervade*, s ao. **áprās**, x. 127, 2.
prā́ñc, a., f. **prāc-ī́**, *forward*, x. 34, 12 ; *facing*, x. 135, 3 [prá + añc].
prāṇá, m. *breath*, x. 90, 13 [prá + an *breathe*].
prā-vṛ́ṣ, f. *rainy season*, vii. 103, 3. 9 [vṛṣ *rain*].
prāvṛṣ-á, a., f. **ī́**, *belonging to the rains*, vii. 103, 7.
prā-vep-á, a. *dangling*, x. 34, 1 [prá + vip *tremble*].
priy-á, a. *dear*, i. 85, 7 ; 154, 5 ; ii. 12, 15 ; viii. 48, 14 ; x. 15, 5 [prī *please*].

Phaligá, *cave*, iv, 50, 5.

Bad-dhá, pp. *bound*, x. 34, 4 [bandh *bind*].

bandh *bind*, ix. **badhnā́ti** : ipf. **ábadhnan**, x. 90, 15.
bándh-u, a. *akin*, i. 154, 5 ; m. *bond*, x. 129, 4 [bandh *bind*].
babhrú, a. (*ruddy*) *brown*, ii. 33, 5. 8. 9. 15 ; vii. 103, 10 ; viii. 29, 1 ; x. 34, 5. 11. 14.
barh-áṇa *magic power*, x. 34, 7 [bṛh *make big*].
barhi-ṣád, a. (Tp.) *sitting on the sacrificial grass*, x. 15, 3. 4 [for barhiḥ-ṣád : sad *sit*].
barhiṣ-yà, a. *placed on the sacrificial grass*, x. 15, 5 [barhís].
barh-ís, n. *sacrificial grass*, i. 85, 6. 7 ; v. 11, 2 ; x. 14, 5 ; 15, 11 ; 90, 7.
bah-ú, a. *many*, ii. 35, 12 ; x. 14, 1 ; 34, 13.
bādh *drive away*, I. Ā. **bā́dhate**, x. 127, 2 ; int. **badbadhe** *press apart*, vii. 61, 4.
  ápa- *drive away*, i. 35, 3. 9 ; 85, 3.
bāh-ú, m. *arm*, i. 85, 6 ; du. x. 90, 11. 12 [Av. *bāzu*, Gk. *πῆχυ-ς*, OG. *buog*].
bíbhy-at, pr. pt. *fearing*, x. 34, 10 [bhī *fear*].
bíbhr-at, pr. pt. *bearing*, vii. 103, 6 [bhṛ *bear*].
bíl-ma, n. *shavings*, ii. 35, 12.
budh-āná, ao. pt. Ā. *waking*, iv. 51, 3.
budh-ná, m. n. *bottom*, x. 135, 6 [Lat. *fundu-s*].
bṛh-át, (pr. pt.) adv. *aloud*, ii. 33, 15 ; 35, 15.
bṛh-ánt, a. *lofty*, i. 35, 4 ; v. 11, 1 ; vii. 61, 3 ; 86, 1 ; x. 34, 1 ; *ample*, i. 160, 5 ; n. *the great world*, x. 14, 16 [pr. pt. of bṛh *make big*].
Bṛ́has-páti, m. *Lord of prayer*, name of a god, iv. 50, 1. 2. 3. 4. 5. 6. 7. 10. 11 ; x. 14, 3 [bṛ́h-as prob. gen. = **bṛhás** ; cp. bráhmaṇas páti].
bodhi, 2. s. ipv. ao. of bhū *be*, ii. 33, 15 [for bhū-dhí].
bráh-man, n. *prayer*, ii. 12, 14 ; vii. 61, 2. 6 ; 71, 6 ; 103, 8 [bṛh *swell*].
brah-mán, m. *priest*, iv. 50, 8. 9 ; *Brahmin*, ii. 12, 6 [bṛh *swell*].
brāhmaṇá, m. *Brahmin*, vii. 103, 1. 7. 8 ; 90, 12.
bruv-ánt, pr. pt. *calling* (acc.), viii. 48, 1 [brū *speak*].
bruv-āṇá, pr. pt. *speaking*, iii. 59, 1 [brū *speak*].
brū *speak*, II. **bravīti**, i. 35, 6 ; sb. **bravat**, vi. 54, 1. 2 ; *tell*, op. x. 135, 5.

ádhi- *speak for* (acc.), i. 85, 11; x. 15, 5.
úpa-, Ā. *implore*, iv. 51, 11.

Bhakṣ-á, m. *draught*, x. 34, 1 [bhak-ṣ, sec. root *consume* from bhaj *partake of*].
bhaj *partake of* (gen.), x. 15, 3; s ao., viii. 48, 1. 7.
bhad-rá, a. *auspicious*, i. 1, 6; ii. 35, 15; iii. 59, 4; iv. 51, 7; x. 14, 6. 12 [*praiseworthy*: bhand *be praised*].
Bhar-atá, m. pl. name of a tribe, v. 11, 1.
bhár-ant, pr. pt. *bearing*, i 1, 7 [bhṛ *bear*].
bháv-ya, a. *that will be, future*, x. 90, 2 [gdv. of bhū *be*].
bhā *shine*, II. P. bhā́ti.
áva- *shine down*, i. 154, 6.
ví- *shine forth*, ii. 35, 7. 8; v. 11, 1.
bhid *split*, VII. bhinátti [Lat. *find-o*].
ví- *split open*, i. 85, 10.
bhiṣák-tama, m. spv. *best healer*, ii. 33, 4 [bhiṣáj *healing*].
bhiṣáj, m. *physician*, ii. 33, 4.
bhī *fear*, I. Ā. bháyate, i. 85, 8; ii. 12, 13; pf. bibhā́ya, v. 83, 2; s ao. ábhaiṣur, viii. 48, 11.
bhī-má, a. *terrible*, i. 154, 2; ii. 33, 11 [bhī *fear*].
bhur *quiver*, int. járbhurīti, v. 83, 5.
bhúv-ana, n. *creature*, i. 35, 2. 5. 6; 85, 8; 154, 2. 4; 160, 2. 3; ii. 35, 2. 8; vii. 61, 1; *world*, ii. 33, 9; v. 83, 2. 4; iv. 51, 5; x. 168, 2. 4 [bhū *be*].
bhū *become, be*, I. bháva, i. 1, 9; v. 83, 7. 8; ipv., x. 127, 6; pr. sb., viii. 48, 2; ipf. ábhavat, v. 11, 3. 4; x. 135, 5. 6; *come into being*, x. 90, 4; pf. babhū́va, ii. 12, 9; vii. 103, 7; x. 34, 12; pf. op. babhūyā́t, iv. 51, 4; root ao., viii. 48, 3; ábhūvan, vii. 61, 5; root ao. sb. bhuvāni, vii. 86, 2; ipv. bhū́tu, iv. 50, 11 [cp. Gk. φύ-ω, Lat. *fu-i-t*].
abhí- *be superior to* (acc.), iii. 59, 7.
ā́- *arise*, pf., x. 129, 6. 7; 168, 3.
āvís- *appear*, vii. 103, 8.
sám- *do good to* (dat.), viii. 48, 4.
bhū-tá, pp. *been*, x. 90, 2; n. *being*, x. 90, 3.
bhū́-man, n. *earth*, i. 85, 5; vii. 86, 1; x. 90, 1. 14 [cp. Gk. φῦ-μα 'growth'].
bhū́-ri, a. *great*, ii. 33, 9; *much*, ii. 33, 12; adv. *greatly*, i. 154, 6.
bhū́ri-śṛṅga, a. (Bv.) *many-horned*, i. 154, 6.
bhū́r-ṇi, a. *angry*, vii. 86, 7.
bhūṣ *strive*, I. P. bhū́ṣati [extended form of bhū *be*].
pári- *surpass*, ii. 12, 1.
bhṛ *bear*, III. bíbharti, ii. 33, 10; iii. 59, 8; *hold*, iv. 50, 7; viii. 29, 3. 4. 5 [Gk. φέρω, Lat. *ferō*, Arm. *berem*, OI. *berim*, Go. *baira*].
ví-, I. bhara, *carry hither and thither*, v. 11, 4.
Bhṛ́g-u, m. pl. a family of ancient priests, x. 14, 6.
bheṣaj-á, a. *healing*, ii. 33, 7; n. *medicine, remedy*, ii. 33, 2. 4. 12. 13 [bhiṣáj *healing*].
bhóg-a, m. *use*, x. 34, 3 [bhuj *enjoy*].
bhoj-á, m. *liberal man*, iv. 51, 3.
bhój-ana, n. *food*, v. 83, 10 [bhuj *enjoy*].
bhyas = bhī *fear*, I. Ā. bhyásate, ii. 12, 1.
bhrāj *shine*, I. Ā. bhrā́jate.
ví- *shine forth*, i. 85, 4.
bhrā́ja-māna, pr. pt. Ā. *shining*, vii. 63, 4.
bhrā́-tṛ, m. *brother*, x. 34, 4 [Gk. φράτωρ, Lat. *frāter*, OI. *brāthir*, Go. *brōthar*, OSl. *bratrŭ*].

Mah, máṃh *be great*, máṃhate and máhe (3. s.).
sám- *consecrate*, vii. 61, 6.
maghá-vant, m. *liberal patron*, ii. 33, 14; 35, 15 [magh-á *bounty*: mah *be great*].
maghónī, a. f. *bounteous*, iv. 51, 3 [f. of maghávan].
maṇḍū́ka, m. *frog*, vii. 103, 1. 2. 4. 7. 10.
math-itá, pp. *kindled by friction*, viii. 48, 6.
math-yá-māna, pr. pt. ps. *being rubbed*, v. 11, 6.
mad *rejoice*, I. máda, *in* (lc.), i. 85, 1; 154, 5; *in* (inst.), 154, 4; x. 14, 3. 7; *with* (inst.), x. 14, 10; *be exhilarated*, viii. 29, 7; *drink with exhilaration*, vii. 49, 4; cs. mādaya, Ā. *rejoice*, x. 15, 14; *in* (inst.), x. 14, 14; (gen.), i. 85, 6; *with* (inst.), x. 14, 5; *gladden*, x. 34, 1 [Gk. μαδάω, Lat. *madeō* 'drip'].
mád-a, m. *intoxication*, i. 85, 10; viii. 48, 6.
mada-cyút, a. *reeling with intoxication*, i. 85, 7 [cyu *move*].

mád-ant, pr. pt. *rejoicing*, iv. 50, 2; *delighting in* (inst.), iii. 59, 3.
mádh-u, n. *honey*, *mead*, i. 154, 4. 5; iv. 50, 3; viii. 48, 1; x. 34, 7; a. *sweet*, i. 85, 6 [Gk. *μέθυ*, Lith. *medù-s*, OSl. *medŭ*, Eng. *mead*].
mádhu-mat-tama, spv. a. *most honied*, v. 11, 5; x. 14, 15.
madhu-ścút, a. (Tp.) *dripping with honey*, *distilling sweetness*, vii. 49, 3 [ścut *drip*].
mádhya, a. *middle*, vii. 49, 1. 3; x. 15, 14 [Lat. *mediu-s*].
madhya-má, spv. a. *middlemost*, x. 15, 1.
man *think*, VIII. Ā. manute, viii. 29, 10; IV. Ā. **mányate**, viii. 48, 6; x. 34, 13.
mán-as, n. *mind*, x. 90, 13; 129, 4; 135, 3 [Av. *manō*, Gk. *μένος*].
mánas-vant, a. *wise*, ii. 12, 1.
man-ā́, f. *jealousy*, ii. 33, 5 [**man** *think*].
man-īṣā́, f. *thought*, vii. 71, 6; *wisdom*, x. 129, 4: *prayer*, v. 11, 5; *hymn of praise*, v. 83, 10 [man *think*].
Mán-u, m. an ancient sage, ii. 33, 13.
mano-jū́, a. *swift as thought*, i. 85, 4 [**mánas** *mind* + jū *to speed*].
mán-tra, m. *hymn*, ii. 35, 2; *spell*, x. 14, 4.
mand *exhilarate*, I. mánda: iṣ ao. Ā. ámandiṣātām, vii. 103, 4.
  úd- *gladden*, pf. mamanda, ii. 33, 6 [= mad *rejoice*].
mand-as-āná, ao. pt. *rejoicing*, iv. 50, 10 [mand = mad *rejoice*].
mand-rá, a. *gladdening*, v. 11, 3 [mand *exhilarate*].
mandrá-jihva, a. (Bv.) *pleasant-tongued*, iv. 50, 1.
mán-man, n. *thought*, vii. 61, 6; *hymn*, i. 154, 3; vii. 61, 2 [man *think*].
man-yú, m. *intention*, vii. 61, 1; *wrath*, vii. 86, 6; viii. 48, 8; x. 34, 8. 14 [man *think*].
mayo-bhú, a. *beniflcent*, ii. 33, 13 [máy-as *gladness* + bhu = bhū *being for* = *conducing to*].
Mar-út, m. pl. the storm gods, i. 85, 1. 4–6. 8. 10. 12; ii. 33, 1. 13; v. 83, 6.
marút-vant, a. *accompanied by the Maruts*, ii. 33, 6.
marḍ-i-tṛ́, m. *one who pities*, x. 34, 3 [mṛḍ *be gracious*].
már-ta, m. *mortal*, iii. 59, 2 [Gk. *μορ-τό-ς*, *βρο-τό-ς* 'mortal', Lat. *mor-ta* 'goddess of death'].
márt-ya, a. *mortal*; m. *mortal man*, i. 35, 2; vii. 61, 1; 71, 2; viii. 48, 1. 3. 12; x. 15, 7.
marmṛjyá-māna, pr. pt. int. *making bright*, ii. 35, 4 [mṛj *wipe*].
máh, a. *great*, ii. 33, 8; G. **mahás**, iv. 50, 4; f. **-í**, v. 11, 5 [Av. *maz* 'great'; from **mah** *be great*].
mah-án, m. *greatness*, ii. 12, 1; 35, 2 [mah *be great*].
mah-ánt, a. *great*, iii. 59, 5; v. 11, 6; 83, 8; vii. 63, 2; x. 34, 12 [pr. pt. of **mah** *be great*].
mahā́-vadha, a. (Bv.) *having a mighty weapon*, v. 83, 2.
máh-i, a. *great*, i. 160, 5; ii. 12, 10; v. 83, 5; viii. 29, 10 [**mah** *be great*].
mahi-tvá, n. *greatness*, vii. 61, 4.
mahi-tvaná, n. *greatness*, i. 85, 7.
mah-ín, a., f. -ī, *great*, i. 160, 2. 5.
mah-i-mán, m. *greatness*. i. 85, 2; ii. 35, 9; iii. 59, 7; vii. 86, 1; x. 90, 3. 16; 168, 1; *power*, x. 129, 3; pl. *powers*, x. 129, 5.
mah-ī́, a. f. *great*, ii. 33, 8. 14; x. 14, 1 [**mah** *be great*].
má-hyam, prs. prn. D. *to me*, x. 34, 1. 2 [cp. Lat. *mihi*].
mā *measure*, III. Ā. mímīte.
  vi- *measure out*: pf. vi-mamé, i. 154, 1. 3; 160, 4; ii. 12, 2.
mā, enc. prs. prn. A. *me*, ii. 33, 6. 7; viii. 48, 5³. 6. 10; x. 34, 1. 2; 127, 7 [Lat. *mē*, Eng. *me*].
mā́, proh. pcl. *not*, ii. 33, 1. 4³. 5; viii. 48, 8. 14²; x. 15, 6; 34, 13. 14 [Gk. *μή* 'not'].
mā́-kis, proh. prn. pcl. *not any one*, vi. 54, 7 [Gk. *μή-τις* 'no one'].
mā́-kīm, proh. prn. pcl. *no one*, vi. 54, 7².
Mā́talī, m. a divine being, x. 14, 3.
mā-tṛ́, f. *mother*, i. 160, 2; v. 11, 3; x. 34, 4. 10 [Gk. *μήτηρ*, Lat. *māter*, OI. *māthir*, Eng. *mother*].
mādhvī, m. du. *lovers of honey*, vii. 71, 2 [**mádhu** *honey*].
mā́nuṣa, a. *human*; m. *man*, vii. 63, 1 [mánus *man*].
mā́m, prs. prn. A. *me*, vii. 49, 1–4.
mā-yā́, f. *mysterious power*, i. 160, 3 [mā *make*].
mā-yú, a. *lowing*, vii. 103, 2 [**mā** *bellow*].
mā́s-a, m. *month*, vii. 61, 4 [**mā́s** *moon*].

mi-tá, pp. *set up*, iv. 51. 2 [**mi** *set up*].

mitá-jñu, a. (Bv.) *firm-kneed*, iii. 59, 3.

Mi-trá, m. a sun god, iii. 59, 1–9 ; vii. 61, 4 ; 63, 1. 6 ; n. *friendship*, x. 34, 14.

Mitrā́-Váruṇā, du. cd. *Mitra and Varuṇa*, i. 35, 1 ; vii. 61, 2. 3. 6. 7 ; 63, 5.

mī *damage*, IX. **minā́ti** [cp. **Gk.** *μι-νύ-ω*, Lat. *mi-nu-o*].
ā́- *diminish*, ii. 12, 5.
prá- *infringe*, vii. 63, 3 ; 103, 9 ; viii. 48, 9.

mīḍh-vā́ṃs, a. *bounteous*, ii. 33, 14 ; vii. 86, 7 [unred. pf. pt., probably from **mih** *rain*].

múkha, n. *mouth*, x. 90, 11–13.

muc *release*, VI. **muñcá** : ppf. **ámumuktam**, vii. 71, 5.

mud *be merry*, I. Ā. **móda**.
práti- *exult*, v. 83, 9.

mṛg-á, m. *beast*, i. 154, 2 ; ii. 33, 11.

mṛj *wipe*, II. **mā́rjmi**.
sám- *rub bright*, ii. 35, 12.

mṛḍ *be gracious*, VI. **mṛḷá**, ii. 33, 11. 14 ; viii. 48, 9 ; x. 34, 14 ; cs. **mṛḷáya**, *id.*, viii. 48, 8.

mṛḷay-ā́ku, a. *merciful*, ii. 33, 7 [**mṛḍ** *be gracious*].

mṛḷ-īká, n. *mercy*, vii. 86, 2 ; viii. 48, 12 [**mṛḍ** *be gracious*].

mṛ-tyú, m. *death*, x. 129, 2 [**mṛ** *die*].

mṛś *touch*, VI. **mṛśá**.
pári- *embrace*, x. 34, 4.

mṛṣ *be heedless*, IV. **mṛ́ṣya**.
ápi- *forget*, vi. 54, 4.

me, enc. prs. prn. D. *to me*, vii. 63, 3 ; 86, 3. 4 ; x. 34, 13 ; G. *of me*, ii. 35, 1 ; vii. 86, 2 ; viii. 29, 2 [Gk. *μοι*].

maujavatá, a. *coming from Mūjavant*, x. 34, 1.

Yá, rel. prn. *who, which, that* : N. **yás**, i. 35, 6 ; 154, 1^{2}. 3. 4 ; 160, 4 ; ii. 12, 1–7. 9–15 ; 33, 5. 7 ; iii. 59, 2. 7 ; iv. 50, 1. 7. 9 ; vi. 54, 1. 2. 4 ; vii. 61, 1 ; 63, 1. 3 ; vii. 71, 4 ; 86, 1 ; viii. 48, 10^{2}. 12 ; x. 14, 5 ; 34, 12 ; 129, 7 : f. **yā́**, iv. 50, 3 ; n. **yád**, i. 1, 6 ; ii. 35, 15 ; vii. 61, 2 ; 63, 2 ; 103, 5. 7 ; x. 15. 6 ; 90, 2^{3}. 12 ; 129, 1. 3. 4 ; 135, 7 ; *with* **kím ca** *whatever*, v. 83, 9 ; A. **yám**, i. 1, 4 ; ii. 12, 5. 7. 9 ; 35, 11 ; viii. 48, 1 ; x. 135, 3. 4 ; I. **yéna**, i. 160, 5 ; ii. 12, 4 ; iv. 51, 4 ; f. **yáyā**, iv. 51, 6 ; Ab. **yásmād**, ii. 12, 9 ; G. **yásya**, i. 154, 2 ; ii. 12, 1. 7^{4}. 14^{2} ; 35, 7 ; v. 83, 4^{3} ; vii. 61, 2 ; x. 34, 4 ; f. **yásyās**, x. 127, 4 ; L. **yásmin**, iv. 50, 8 ; x. 135. 1 ; du. **yáu**, x. 14, 11 ; pl. N. **yé**, i. 35, 11 ; 85, 1. 4 ; iv. 50, 2 ; x. 14, 3. 10 ; 15, 1–4. 8–10. 13^{2}. 14^{2} ; 90, 7. 8 ; with **ké** *whatever*, x. 90, 10 ; f. **yā́s**, vii. 49, 1. 2. 3 ; n. **yā́ni**, ii. 33, 13 ; **yā́**, i. 85, 12 ; ii. 33, 13^{3} ; iv. 50, 9 ; vii. 86, 5 ; A. m. **yā́n**, x. 14, 3 ; 15, 13^{2} ; G. f. **yā́sām**, vii. 49, 3 ; L. f. **yā́su**, iv. 51, 7 ; vii. 49, 4^{4} ; 61, 5.

yakṣ-á, n. *mystery*, vii. 61, 5.

yaj *sacrifice*, I. **yája** ; ipf. **áyajanta**, x. 90, 7. 16.

yaj-atá, a. *adorable*, i. 35, 3. 4 ; ii. 33, 10 [Av. *yazata* ; from **yaj** *worship*].

yaj-átha, m. *sacrifice*, v. 11, 2 [**yaj** *worship*].

yája-māna, m. *sacrificer*, vi. 54, 6 [pr. pt. Ā. of **yaj** *worship*].

yáj-us, n. *sacrificial formula*, x. 90, 9 [**yaj** *worship*].

yaj-ñá, m. *worship, sacrifice*, i. 1, 1. 4 ; ii. 35, 12 ; iv. 50, 6. 10 ; v. 11, 2. 4 ; vii. 61, 6. 7 ; x. 14, 5. 13 ; 15, 6. 13 ; 90, 7–9. 15.16^{2} [Av. *yasna*, Gk. *ἁγνό-ς*].

yajñá-ketu, a. (Bv.) *whose token is sacrifice*, iv. 51, 11.

yajdá-manman, a. (Bv.) *whose heart is set on sacrifice*, vii. 61, 4.

yajñ-íya, a. *worthy of worship, holy*, iii. 59, 4 ; *adorable*, x. 14, 5. 6 [**yajñá** *worship*].

yat *array oneself*, I. **yáta** : pf. i. 85, 8 ; cs. **yātáya** *marshal, stir*, iii. 59, 1 ; *clear off*, x. 127, 7.

yá-tas, adv. *whence*, x. 129, 6. 7 [prn. root **yá**].

yá-ti, prn. *how many*, x. 15, 13 [prn. root **yá**].

yá-tra, rel. adv. *where*, i. 154, 5. 6 ; vii. 63, 5 ; viii. 29, 7 ; 48, 11 ; x. 14, 2. 7 ; 90, 16 [prn. root **yá**].

yá-thā, rel. adv. *how*, x. 135, 5. 6 ; *so that*, ii. 33, 15 ; unaccented = **iva** *like*, viii. 29, 6 [prn. root **yá**].

yathā-vaśám, adv. *according to* (thy, his) *will*, x. 15, 14 ; 168, 4 [**váśa**, m. *will*].

yá-d, cj. *when*, i. 85, 3. 4. 5. 7. 9 ; iv. 51, 6 ; v. 83, 2–4. 9 ; vii. 103, 2–5 ; x. 34, 5 ; 90, 6. 11. 15 ; *in order that*, vii. 71, 4 ; *so that*, vii. 86, 4 ; *since*, i. 160, 2 ; *if*, viii. 48, 9 [n. of rel. **yá**].

yád-i vā, cj. *whether*, x. 129, 7; *or, or else*, *ibid.* [yá-d-i *if*, rel. adv. + vā *or*].
y-ánt, pr. pt. *going*, vii. 61, 3 [i *go*].
yam *extend, bestow*, I. yácha, iv. 51, 10; v. 83, 5; pf. Ā. yemire *submit to* (dat.), iii. 59, 8; s ao. *bestow on* (dat.), ii. 35, 15[2].
ádhi- *extend to* (dat.), i. 85, 12.
á- *guide to* (lc.), root ao. inj. yamat, x. 14, 14.
ni- *bestow*, iv. 50, 10.
prá- *present a share of* (gen.), x. 15, 7.
ví- *extend to*, i. 85, 12.
Yam-á, m. god of the dead, i. 35, 6; x. 14, 1-5. 7-16; 15, 8; 135, 1. 7.
yaś-ás, a. *glorious*, i. 1, 3; iv. 51, 11; viii. 48, 5.
yahví, f. *swift one*, ii. 33, 9; 35, 14.
yā *go*, II. yāti, i. 35, 3[3]. 10; vii. 49, 3; x. 168, 1.
á- *come*, i. 35, 2; x. 15, 9.
úpa á- *come hither*, vii. 71, 2.
á úpa *come hither to*, vii. 71, 4.
pári prá- *proceed around*, iv. 51, 5.
yātayáj-jana, a. (gov. cd.) *stirring men*, iii. 59, 5 [yātáyant, pr. pt. cs. of yat *array oneself* + jána *man*].
yātu-dhána, m. *sorcerer*, i. 35, 10 [yātú, m. *sorcery* + dhāna *practising* from dhā *put, do*].
yá-ma, m. *course*, iv. 51, 4 [yā *go*].
yá-man, n. *course*, i. 85, 1; *approach*, x. 127, 4 [yā *go*].
yu *separate*, III. yuyóti, ii. 33, 1. 3; vii. 71, 1. 2; s ao. *depart from* (ab.), ii. 33. 9; cs. yaváya *save from*, viii. 48, 5; yāváya *ward off*, x. 127, 6[2].
yuk-tá, pp. *yoked*, vii. 63, 2 [yuj *yoke*, Gk. ζευκτό-ς, Lat. *iunctu-s*, Lith. *jùnkta-s*].
yuktá-grāvan, a. (Bv.) *who has to work the stones*, ii. 12, 6.
yuj *yoke*, VII. yunákti: pf. yuyujé, x. 34, 11; rt. ao. áyugdhvam, i. 85, 4.
prá- *yoke in front*, i. 85, 5.
yúdhya-māna, pr. pt. Ā. *fighting*; m. *fighter*, ii. 12, 9 [yudh *fight*].
yúyudh-i, m. *warrior*, i. 85, 8 [from red. stem of yudh *fight*].
yuva-tí, f. *young maiden*, ii. 35, 4. 11 [f. of yúvan *youth*].
yúv-an, a. *young*, ii. 33, 11; m. *youth*, ii. 35, 4 [Lat. *iuven-i-s*].
yuv-ám, prs. prn. N. *you two*, vii. 71, 5; dat. yuvábhyām *to you two*, vii. 61, 7 [= yū- + am].
yuva-yú, a. *addressed to you*, vii. 71, 7.
yūy-ám, prs. prn. pl. N. *you*, iv. 51, 5; vii. 61, 7; 63, 6; 71, 6; 86, 8 [for yūṣ-ám, Av. *yūš*, *yūšem*, Go. *yus*].
yóg-a, m. *acquisition*, vii. 86, 8 [yuj *yoke*].
yój-ana, n. *league*, i. 35, 8 [*yoking* from yuj *yoke*].
yó-ni, m. *womb*, ii. 35, 10; *abode*, iv. 50, 2; x. 34, 11; *receptacle*, viii. 29, 2 [*holder* from yu *hold*].
yóṣ-á, f. *woman*, x. 168, 2.
yós, n. *blessing*, ii. 33, 13; x. 15, 4

Raṃh *hasten*, I. ráṃha; cs. raṃháya *cause to speed*, i. 85, 5.
rakṣ *protect*, I. rákṣa, i. 35. 11; 160, 2; iv. 50, 2; vi. 54, 5; viii. 48, 5 [Gk. ἀλέξω 'ward off'].
rákṣa-māṇa, pr. pt. Ā. *protecting*, vii. 61, 3 [rakṣ *protect*].
rakṣ-ás, m. *demon*, i. 35. 10; v. 83, 2.
rakṣ-i-tṛ́, m. *guardian*, x. 14, 11 [rakṣ *protect*].
raghu-pátvan, a. (Tp.) *flying swiftly*, i. 85, 6 [raghú *swift*: Gk. ἐλαχύ-ς].
raghu-ṣyád, a. *swift-gliding*, i. 85, 6 [raghú *swift* + syand *run*].
ráj-as, n. *space, air*, i. 35, 4. 9; 154, 1; 160, 1. 4; x. 15, 2; 129, 1 [Gk. ἔρεβος, Go. *riqiz-a*].
rán-ya, a. *glorious*, i. 85. 10 [ran *rejoice*].
rá-tna, n. *gift, treasure*. i. 35, 8 [rā *give*].
ratna-dhá, a. (Tp.) *bestowing treasure*, i. 1, 1.
rá-tha, m. *car*, i. 35, 2. 4. 5; 85, 4. 5; ii. 12, 7. 8; v. 83, 3. 7; vii. 71, 2-4; viii. 48, 5; x. 135, 3-5; 168, 1 [ṛ *go*].
ráth-ya, a. *belonging to a car*, i. 35. 6.
rad *dig*, I. ráda: pf raráda, vii. 49, 1.
radh-rá, a. *rich*, ii. 12, 6 [rādh *succeed*].
randh *make subject*, IV. P. rádhya: red. ao., ii. 33, 5.
ráp-as, n. *bodily injury*, ii. 33, 3. 7.
ram *set at rest*, IX. ramṇáti: ipf. ii. 12, 2; I. Ā. ráma *rejoice in* (lc.), x. 34, 13.
ray-í, m. *wealth*, i. 1, 3; 85, 12; iv. 50, 6. 10; 51, 10; viii. 48, 13; x. 15, 7. 11 [probably from ri = reduced form of rā *give*].
ráv-a, m. *roar*, iv. 50, 1. 4. 5 [ru *cry*].
raś-mí, m. *ray*, i. 35, 7; *cord*, x. 129, 5.
rā *give*, II. ráti; 2. ind. rāsi = ipv., ii

33, 12; III. ipv. 2. pl. rarīdhvam, v. 83, 6.
rāj *rule, over* (gen.), I. P. rā́jati, i. 1, 8.
rā́j-an, m. *king*, i. 85, 8; iii. 59, 4; iv. 50, 7. 9; vii. 49, 3. 4; 86, 5; viii. 48, 7. 8; x. 14, 1. 4. 7. 11. 15; 34, 8. 12; 168, 2 [rāj *rule*, Lat. *reg-ō*].
rā́j-ant, pr. pt. *ruling over* (gen.), i. 1, 8 [rāj *rule*].
rājan-yà, a. *royal*; m. *warrior* (earliest name of the second caste), x. 90, 12.
rā́trī, f. *night*, i. 35, 1; x. 127, 1. 8; 129, 2.
rā́dh-as, n. *gift*, *blessing*, ii. 12, 14 [rādh *gratify*].
rādho-déya, n. *bestowal of wealth*, iv. 51, 8 [déya, gdv. *to be given* from dā *give*].
ri *release*, IX. riṇā́ti, ii. 12, 3.
ánu- *flow along*, i. 85, 3.
ric *leave*, VII. P. rinákti, vii. 71, 1 [Gk. λείπω, Lat. *linquo*].
áti- *extend beyond*: ps. ipf. áricyata, x. 90, 5.
ríṣ, f. *injury*, ii. 35, 6.
riṣ *be hurt*, IV. ríṣyati, vi. 54, 8; a ao. inj., vi. 54, 7. 9; *injure*, viii. 48, 10.
rih *kiss*, II. réḍhi, ii. 33, 13.
ruk-má, m. *golden gem*, vii. 63, 4 [ruc *shine*].
ruc *shine*, I. róca; cs. rocáya *cause to shine*, viii. 29, 10.
ruc-āná, rt. ao. pt. Ā. *beaming*, iv. 51, 9.
ruj *burst*, VI. P. rujá: pf. rurója, iv. 50, 5.
ruj-ánt, pr. pt. *shattering*, x. 168, 1.
Rud-rá, m. name of a god, i. 85, 1; ii. 33, 1-9. 11-13. 15; pl. = *sons of Rudra, the Maruts*, i. 85, 2 [rud *cry, howl*].
rudh *obstruct*, VII. ruṇaddhi, runddhé, x. 34, 3.
ápa- *drive away*: rt. ao. arodham, x. 34, 3.
rúś-ant, pr. pt. *gleaming*, iv. 51, 9.
ruh *grow*, I. róhati, róhate.
áti- *grow beyond* (acc.), x. 90, 2.
ā́- *rise up in* (acc.), viii. 48, 11.
rūpá, n. *form*, x. 168, 4; *beauty*, i. 160, 2.
re-ṇú, m. *dust*, x. 168, 1 [perhaps from ri *run* = *disperse*].
ré-tas, n. *seed*, v. 83, 1. 4; x. 129, 4 [ri *flow*].
reto-dhā́, m. *impregnator*, x. 129, 5 [rétas *seed* + dhā *placing*].
rebh-á, m. *singer*, vii. 63, 3 [ribh *sing*].
revát, adv. *bountifully*, ii. 35, 4 [n. of revánt].
re-vát-ī, f. *wealthy*, iv. 51, 4 [f. of revánt].
re-vánt, a. *wealthy*, viii. 48, 6 [re = rai *wealth*].
ródas-ī, f. du. *the two worlds* (= heaven and earth), i. 85, 1; 160, 2. 4; ii. 12, 1; vii. 64, 4; 86, 1.
rái, m. *wealth*, vi. 54, 8; vii. 86, 7; viii. 48, 2; G. rāyás, viii. 48, 7 [*bestowal* from rā *give*; Lat. *rē-s*].
Rauhiṇá, m. name of a demon, ii. 12, 12 [metronymic: *son of Róhiṇī*].

Lak-ṣá, n. *stake* (at play), ii. 12, 4 [*token, mark*: lag *attach*].
lok-á, m. *place*, x. 14, 9; *world*, x. 90, 14 [*bright space* = rok-á *light*; cp. Gk. λευκό-ς 'white', Lat. *lux*, *lūc-is*].

Vag-nú, m. *sound*, vii. 103, 2 [vac *speak*].
vac *utter*, III. P. vívakti; ao. op., ii. 35, 2; *speak*, ps. ucyáte, x. 90, 11; 135, 7 [Lat. *voc-āre* 'call'].
ádhi- *speak for* (dat.), viii. 48, 14.
prá- *proclaim*, i. 154, 1; vii. 86, 4; *declare*, x. 129, 6.
vác-as, n. *speech*, v. 11, 5 [vac *speak*; Gk. ἔπος].
vacas-yā́, f. *eloquence*, ii. 35, 1.
vá́j-ra, m. *thunderbolt*, i. 85, 9; viii. 29, 4 [vaj *be strong*; Av. *vazra* 'club'].
vájra-bāhu, a. (Bv.) *bearing a bolt in his arm*, ii. 12, 12. 13; 33, 3.
vájra-hasta, a. (Bv.) *having a bolt in his hand*, ii. 12, 13.
vajr-ín, m. *bearer of the bolt*, vii 49, 1.
vatsá, m. *calf*, vii. 86, 5 [*yearling* from *vatas, Gk. ϝέτος *year*, Lat. *vetus* in *vetus-tas* 'age'].
vats-ín, a., f. -ī, *accompanied by calves*, vii. 103, 2.
vad *speak*, I. váda, ii. 33, 15; op. ii. 35, 15; vii. 103, 5[a]; x. 34, 12.
áchā- *invoke*, v. 83, 1.
ā́- *utter*, ii. 12, 15; viii. 48, 14.
prá- *utter forth*, iṣ ao., avādiṣur, vii. 103, 1.
sám- *converse about* (acc.) *with* (inst.), vii. 86, 2.
vád-ant, pr. pt. *speaking*, vii. 103, 3. 6. 7.

van *win*, VIII. **vanóti** *win* [Eng. *win*; cp. Lat. *ven-ia* 'favour'].
á-, ds. **vivāsa** *seek to win*, ii. 33, 6; v. 83, 1.
van-ús, m. *enemy*, iv. 50, 11 [*eager, rival*: **van** *win*].
váne-vane, lc. itv. cd. *in every wood*, v. 11, 6.
vand *praise*, I. Ā. **vándate**, iv. 50, 7 [nasalized form of **vad**].
pári- *extol*, *with* (inst.), ii. 33, 12.
vánda-māna, pr. pt. Ā. *approving*, ii. 33. 12.
vap *strew*, I. **vápati**, **vápate**.
ní- *lay low*, ii. 33, 11.
vapuṣ-yà, a. *fair*, i. 160, 2 [**vápus**, n. *beautiful appearance*].
vay-ám, prs. prn. N. pl. *we*, i. 1, 7; ii. 12, 15; iii, 59, 3. 4; iv. 50, 6; 51, 11; vi. 54, 8. 9; vii. 86, 5; viii. 48, 9. 13. 14; x. 14, 6; 127, 4 [Av. *vaem*, Go. *wais*, Eng. *we*].
váy-as, n. *force*, ii. 33, 6; viii. 48, 1 [*food, strength*: **vī** *enjoy*].
vay-á, f. *offshoot*, ii. 35, 8.
vayúnā-vat, a. *clear*, iv. 51, 1 [**vayúnā**].
vayo-dhā́, m. *bestower of strength*, viii. 48, 15 [**váyas** *force* + **dhā** *bestowing*].
vár-i-man, n. *expanse*, iii. 59, 3 [**vṛ** *cover*].
vár-i-vas, n. *wide space*, vii. 63, 6; *prosperity*, iv. 50, 9 [*breadth, freedom*: **vṛ** *cover*].
varivo-vít-tara, cpv. m. *best finder of relief, best banisher of care*, viii. 48, 1 [**várivas** + **vid** *find*].
vár-īyas, cpv. a. *wider*, ii. 12, 2 [**urú** *wide*].
Vár-uṇa, m. vii. 49, 3. 4; 61, 1. 4; 63, 1. 6; 86, 2. 3². 4. 6. 8; x. 14, 7 [Gk. οὐρανό-ς 'heaven'; **vṛ** *cover, encompass*].
vár-ṇa, m. *colour*, ii. 12, 4 [*coating*: **vṛ** *cover*].
várta-māna, pr. pt. Ā., with **á** *rolling hither*, i. 35, 2 [**vṛt** *turn*].
várt-man, n. *track*, i. 85, 3 [**vṛt** *turn*].
várdh-ana, n. *strengthening*, ii. 12, 14 [**vṛdh** *increase*].
várdha-māna, pr. pt. Ā. *growing*, i. 1, 8 [**vṛdh** *grow*].
várvṛt-āna, pr. pt. Ā. int. *rolling about*, x. 34, 1 [**vṛt** *turn*].
varṣ-á, n. *rain*, v. 83, 10 [**vṛṣ** *rain*].
varṣ-yà, a. *rainy*, v. 83, 8².
val-á, m. *enclosure*, *cave*, iv. 50, 5 [**vṛ** *cover*].
valgū-yá, den. *honour*, iv. 50, 7.
vaś *desire*, II. **váṣṭi**, s. 1. **váśmi**, ii. 33, 13; pl. 1. **uśmasi**, i. 154, 6.
1. **vas** *shine*, VI. P. **ucháti**: pf. pl. 3. **ūsa**, iv. 51, 4 [Av. *usaiti* 'shines'].
2. **vas** *wear*, II. Ā. **váste** [cp. Gk. ἕννυμι = ϝέσνυμι, AS. *werian*, Eng. *wear*].
abhí-, cs. *clothe*, i. 160, 2.
3. **vas** *dwell*, I. P. **vásati** [AS. *wesan* 'be', Eng. *was*; in Gk. ἄστυ = ϝάστυ].
prá- *go on journeys*, viii. 29, 8.
vas, enc. prs. prn. A. *you*, i. 85, 6; iv. 51, 10. 11; D. *to* or *for you*, i. 85, 6. 12; iv. 51, 4; x. 15, 4. 6; G. *of you*, ii. 33, 13; x. 34, 12. 14 [Av. *vō*, Lat. *vōs*].
vas-atí, f. *abode*, *nest*, x. 127, 4 [**vas** *dwell*].
vas-ant-á, m. *spring*, x. 90, 6 [**vas** *shine*].
vás-āna, pr. pt. Ā. *clothing oneself in* (acc.), ii. 35, 9 [2. **vas** *wear*].
vás-iṣṭha, spv. a. *best*; m. name of a seer, vii. 86, 5; pl. a family of ancient seers, x. 15, 8 [**vas** *shine*].
vás-u, n. *wealth*, vi. 54, 4; vii. 103, 10; x. 15, 7 [**vas** *shine*].
vasu-déya, n. *granting of wealth*, ii. 33, 7.
vásu-mant, a. *laden with wealth*, vii. 71, 3. 4.
vásn-ya, a. *for sale*, x. 34, 3 [**vasná**, n. *price*, Gk. ὦνο-ς = ϝῶσ-νο-ς 'purchase price', Lat. *vēnu-m* = *ves-num*].
vás-yas, acc. adv. *for greater welfare*, viii. 48, 9 [cpv. of **vásu** *good*].
vás-yāṃs, cpv. a. *wealthier*, viii. 48, 6 [cpv. of **vás-u**].
vah *carry, draw, drive*, I. **váha**, vii. 63, 2; s ao. **ávāṭ**, x. 15, 12 [Lat. *veh-ere*, Eng. *weigh*].
ánu- *drive after*: pf. **anūhiré**, x. 15, 8.
á- *bring*, i. 1, 2; 85, 6; vii. 71, 3; x. 14, 4.
ní- *bring*: pf. **ūhathur**, vii. 71, 5.
váh-ant, pr. pt. *carrying*, i. 85, 5; *bearing*, ii. 35, 9; *bringing*, vii. 71, 2.
váh-ant-ī, pr. pt. f. *bringing*, ii. 35, 14.
váh-ni, m. *driver*, i. 160, 3 [**vah** *drive*].
vā *blow*, II. P. **vā́ti** [Av. *vaiti*, Gk. ἄησι = ἄ-ϝη-σι; cf. Go. *waian*, German *wehen* 'blow'].
prá- *blow forth*, v. 83, 4.
vā, enc. cj. *or*, iv. 51, 4; x. 15, 2 [Lat. *ve*].

vā́c, f. *voice*, vii. 103, 1. 4. 5. 6. 8 ; x. 34, 5 [**vac** *speak* ; Lat. *vōx* = *vōc-s*].
vā́j-a, m. *conflict*, i. 85, 5 ; *booty*, ii. 12, 15 ; vi. 54, 5 [**vaj** *be strong*].
vāja-yú, a. *desirous of gain*, ii. 35, 1.
vāj-ín, a. *victorious*, x. 34, 4 [**vā́ja**].
vāṇá, m. *pipe*, i. 85, 10.
vā́-ta, m. *wind*, v. 83, 4 ; x. 168, 1. 2. 4 [**vā** *blow* ; cp. Lat. *ven-tu-s*, Gk. ἀήτη-ς].
vām, enc. prs. prn. du. A. *you two*, iv. 50, 10 ; vii. 61, 6³ ; 63, 5 ; 71, 1 ; D. *for you two*, vii. 61, 2. 5² ; vii. 71, 4 ; G. *of you two*, i. 154, 6 ; iv. 50, 11 ; vii. 61, 1 ; 71, 3. 4.
vā-má, n. *wealth*, vii. 71, 2 [**vā** = **van** *win*].
vāyav-yà, a. *relating to the wind*, *aërial*, x. 90, 8 [**vāyú**].
vā-yú, m. *wind*, x. 90, 13 [**vā** *blow*].
vā́r-ya, gdv. *desirable*, i. 35, 8 [**vṛ** *choose*].
vā́vaś-at, pr. pt. int. *lowing*, iv. 50, 5 [**vāś** *low*].
vāvṛdh-āná, pr. pt. Ā. *having grown*, x. 14, 3 [**vṛdh** *grow*].
vā́śī, f. *axe*, viii. 29, 3.
vāsar-á, a. *vernal*, viii. 48, 7 [***vasar** *spring* ; Gk. ἔαρ, Lith. *vasarà*].
vā́s-tu, n. *abode*, i. 154, 6 [**vas** *dwell* : Gk. ϝάστυ].
ví, m. *bird*, i. 85, 7 ; viii. 29, 8 ; pl. N. váyas, x. 127, 4 [Av. *vi-*, Lat. *avi-s*].
vi-krámaṇa, n. *wide stride*, i. 154, 2 ; x. 15, 3.
vi-cakramāṇá, pf. pt. Ā. *having strode out*, i. 154, 1 [**kram** *stride*].
ví-carṣaṇi, a. *active*, i. 35, 9.
víj, pl. *stake* at play, ii. 12, 5.
ví-tata, pp. *extended*, x. 129, 5 [**tan** *stretch*].
vi-tarám, adv. *far away*, ii. 33. 2 [cpv. of prp. **ví** *away*].
vit-tá, n. *property*, x. 34, 13 [pp. of **vid** *find*, *acquire* : *acquisition*].
1. **vid** *know*, II. P. **vétti** ; pr. sb. *know of* (gen.), ii. 35, 2 ; ipv. **viddhi**, viii. 48, 8 ; pf. **véda**, viii. 29, 6 ; s. 2. **véttha**, x. 15, 13 ; 3. **véda**, x. 129, 6². 7² ; pl. 1. **vidmá**, x. 15, 13 [Gk. οἶδα, ἴδμεν ; AS. *ic wāt*, *wē witon* ; Eng. *I wot* ; Lat. *vid-ēre* 'see'].
prá- *know*, x. 15, 13.
2. **vid** *find*, VI. **vindá**, vi. 54, 4 ; x. 34, 3² ; pf. **viveda**, x. 14, 2 ; a ao., v. 83, 10 ; viii. 48, 3.
ánu- *find out*, ii. 12, 11 ; v. 11, 6.
á-, s ao. *win hither*, x. 15, 3.
nís- *find out*, x. 129, 4.
vid-átha, m. *divine worship*, i. 85, 1 ; ii. 12, 15 ; 33, 15 ; 35, 15 ; viii. 48, 14 [**vidh** *worship*].
vi-dyút, f. *lightning*, ii. 35, 9 ; v. 83, 4 [**ví** *afar* + **dyut** *shine*].
vid-vā́ṃs, unred. pf. pt. *knowing*, vi. 54, 1 [Gk. ϝειδώς].
vidh *worship*. VI. **vidhá**, ii. 35, 12 ; iv. 50, 6 ; vi. 54, 4 ; viii. 48, 12. 13 ; x. 168, 4.
práti- *pay worship to*, vii. 63, 5.
vidh-ánt, pr. pt. m. *worshipper*, ii. 35, 7.
vi-dhā́na, n. *task*, iv. 51, 6 [*dis-position* : **ví** prp. + **dhā́na** from **dhā** *put*].
vi-pṛ́ch-am, acc. inf. *to ask*, vii. 86, 3.
víp-ra, a. *wise*, iv. 50, 1 ; m. *sage*, i. 85, 11 ; vii. 61, 2 ; x. 135, 4 [*inspired* : **vip** *tremble with emotion*].
vi-bhāt-ī́, pr. pt. f. *shining forth*, iv. 51, 1. 10. 11 [**bhā** *shine*].
vi-bhī́daka, m. a nut used as a die for gambling, vii. 86, 6 ; x. 34, 1 [probably from **ví-bhid** *split asunder*, but the meaning here applied is obscure].
vi-bhrā́ja-māna, pr. pt. Ā. *shining forth*, vii. 63, 3 [**bhrāj** *shine* ; Av. *brāzaiti* 'beams', Gk. φλέγω 'flame'].
ví-madhya, m. *middle*, iv. 51, 3.
vi-rapśá, m. *abundance*, iv. 50, 3 [**ví** + **rapś** *be full*].
Vi-rā́j, m. name of a divine being identified with Puruṣa, x. 90, 5² [*far-ruling*].
virā-ṣā́h, a. *overcoming men*, i. 35, 6 [= **vīra-ṣā́h** for **vīra-sā́h**].
vi-rúk-mant, m. *shining weapon*, i. 85, 3 [**ruc** *shine*].
ví-rūpa, a. *having different colours*, vii. 103, 6 [**rūpá**, n. *form*].
Vivás-vant, m. name of a divine being, v. 11, 3 ; x. 14, 5 [**ví** + **vas** *shine afar*].
víś, f. *settlement*, x. 15, 2 ; *abode*, vii. 61, 3 ; *settler*, i. 35, 5 ; *subject*, iv. 50, 8.
viś *enter*, VI. **viśá**.
á- *enter*, iv. 50, 10 ; viii. 48, 12. 15.
ní- *come home*, *go to rest*, x. 34, 14 ; 168, 3 ; s ao., **avikṣmahi**, x. 127, 4 ; cs **veśáya** *cause to rest*, i. 35, 2.
viś-páti, m. *master of the house*, x. 135, 1.
víśva, prn. a. *all*, i. 35, 3. 5 ; 85, 3. 8 ; 154, 2. 4 ; ii. 12, 4. 7. 9 ; 33, 3. 10 ; 35, 2. 15 ; iii. 59, 8 ; iv. 50, 7 ; v. 83, 2. 4.

9; vii. 61, 1. 5. 7; 63, 1. 6; x. 15, 6; 90, 3; 127, 1; 168, 2.
viśvá-tas, adv *on every side*, i. 1, 4; viii. 48, 15; x. 90, 1; *in all directions*, x. 135, 3.
viśva-dā́nīm, adv. *always*, iv. 50, 8.
viśvá-deva, a. [Bv.] *belonging to all the gods*, iv. 50, 6.
viśvá-psnya, a. *laden with all food*, vii. 71, 4 [psnya from psā *eat*].
viśvá-rūpa, a. (Bv.) *omniform*, i. 35, 4; ii. 33, 10; v. 83, 5.
viśvá-śambhū, a. *beneficial to all*, i. 160, 1. 4 [śám *prosperity* + bhū *being for, conducing to*].
viśvá-ha, adv. *always*, ii. 12, 15; viii. 48, 14; -hā, *id.*, i. 160, 5; *for ever*, ii. 35, 14.
viśvā́hā, adv. *always*, i. 160, 3 [víśvā áhā *all days*].
víśve devā́s, m. pl. *the all-gods*, vii. 49, 4; viii. 48, 1.
viṣ *work*, III. víveṣṭi: pf. vivéṣa, ii. 35, 13.
ví-ṣita, pp. *unfastened*, v. 83, 7. 8 [ví + si *bind*].
víṣu-ṇa, a. *varied in form*, viii. 29, 1.
víṣūcī, a. f. *turned in various directions*, ii. 33, 2 [f. of víṣv-añc].
vi-ṣṭhā́ *host* (?), x. 168, 2.
Víṣ-ṇu, m. a solar deity, i. 85, 7; 154, 1. 2. 3. 5; x. 15, 3 [viṣ *be active*].
víṣv-añc, a. *turned in all directions*, x. 90, 4.
vi-sargá, m. *release*, vii. 103, 9 [ví + sṛj *let go*].
vi-sárjana, n. *creation*, x. 129, 6 [vi + sṛj *let go*].
ví-sṛṣṭi, f. *creation*, x. 129, 6. 7 [ví + sṛj *let go*].
vi-srásas, ab. inf. *from breaking*, viii. 48, 5 [vi + sras *fall*].
ví-hāyas, a. *mighty*, viii. 48, 11.
vī *guide*, II. véti, i. 35, 9.
úpa- *come to* (acc.), v. 11, 4.
vī-rá, m. *hero*, i. 85, 1; ii. 33, 1; 35, 4 [Av. vīra, Lat. vir, OI. fer, Go. wair, Lith. výra, 'man'].
vīrá-vat-tama, spv. a. *most abounding in heroes*, i. 1, 3.
vīrá-vant, a. *possessed of heroes*, iv. 50, 6.
vīrúdh, f. *plant*, ii. 35, 8 [ví *asunder* + rudh *grow*].
vīr-yà, n. *heroic deed*, i. 154, 1. 2; *heroism*, iv. 50, 7 [vīrá *hero*].
1. vṛ *cover*, V. vṛṇóti, vṛṇute.
ā́-, int. ipf. ā́-varīvar *contain*, x. 129, 1.
ví- *unclose*, rt. ao. avran, iv. 51, 2.
2. vṛ *choose*, IX. Ā. vṛṇīte, ii. 33, 13; v. 11, 4; x. 127, 8.
vṛ́k-a, m. *wolf*, x. 127, 6 [Gk. λύκο-ς, Lat. lupu-s, Lith. vilka-s, Eng. wolf].
vṛk-ī́, f. *she-wolf*, x. 127, 6.
vṛktá-barhis, a. (Bv.) *whose sacrificial grass is spread*, iii. 59, 9 [vṛktá, pp. of vṛj + barhís, q. v.].
vṛk-ṣá, m. *tree*, v. 83, 2; x. 127, 4; 135, 1 [vṛk simpler form of vraśc *cut, fell*].
vṛj *twist*, VII. vṛnákti, vṛṅkté.
pári- *pass by*, ii. 33, 14.
vṛj-ána, n. *circle* (= family, sons), vii. 61, 4 [*enclosure* = vṛj].
vṛṇāná, pr. pt. Ā. *choosing*, v. 11, 4 [vṛ *choose*].
vṛt *turn*, I. Ā. vártate *roll*, x. 34, 9; cs. vartáya *turn*, i. 85, 9.
ā́-, cs. *whirl hither*, vii. 71, 3.
nís-, cs. *roll out*, x. 135, 5.
prá-, cs. *set rolling*, x. 135, 4.
ánu prá- *roll forth after*, x. 135, 4.
sám- *be evolved*, x. 90, 14.
ádhi sám- *come upon*, x. 129, 4.
Vṛ-trá, m. name of a demon, i. 85, 9; n. *foe* (pl.), viii. 29, 4 [*encompasser*: vṛ *cover*].
vṛ-tvā́, gd., *having covered*, x. 90, 1.
vṛdh *grow*, I. várdha, i. 85, 7; ii. 35, 11; *cause to prosper*, iv. 50, 11; *increase*, pf. vāvṛdhúr, x. 14, 3; cs. vardháya *strengthen*, v. 11, 3. 5.
vṛdh-é, dat. inf. *to increase*, i. 85, 1.
vṛṣ *rain*, I. várṣa *rain*: iṣ ao. ávarṣīs, v. 83, 10.
abhí- *rain upon*, ao. vii. 103, 3.
vṛ́ṣaṇ-vasu, a. (Bv.) *of mighty wealth*, iv. 50, 10 [vṛ́ṣan *bull*].
vṛ́ṣ-an, m. *bull*, i. 85, 7. 12; 154, 3. 6; ii. 33, 13; 35, 13; iv. 50. 6; v. 83, 6 (with áśva = *stallion*); vii. 61, 5; 71, 6; *stallion*, vii. 71, 3 [Av. aršan, Gk. ἔρσην].
vṛṣa-bhá, m. *bull*, i. 160, 3; ii. 12, 12; 33, 4. 6-8. 15; v. 83, 1; vii. 49, 1.
vṛṣa-lá, m. *beggar*, x. 34, 11 [*little man*].
vṛ́ṣa-vrāta, a. (Bv.) *having mighty hosts*, i. 85, 4 [vṛ́ṣan *bull, stallion*].
vṛṣ-ṭí, f. *rain*, v. 83. 6 [vṛṣ *rain*].
vṛ́ṣṇyā-vant, a. *mighty*, v. 83, 2 [vṛ́ṣṇya *manly strength*, from vṛ́ṣan *bull*].

véd-ana, n. *possession*, x. 34, 4 [vid *find, acquire*].
vedh-ás, m. *disposer*, iii. 59, 4 [vidh *worship, be gracious*].
ven *long*, I. P. **vénati**.
ánu- *seek the friendship of*, x. 135, 1.
voḷhṛ́, n. *vehicle*, vii. 71, 4 [vah *draw* + tṛ; Av. *vaštar* 'draught animal' Lat. *vector*].
vái, pcl., ii. 33, 9. 10 [180].
Vairūpá, m. *son of Virūpa*, x. 14, 5.
Vaivasvatá, m. *son of Vivasvant*, x. 14, 1.
váiśya, m. *man of the third caste*, x. 90, 12 [*belonging to the settlement* = **víś**].
vaiśvānará, a. *belonging to all men*, epithet of Agni, vii. 49, 4 [**viśvá-nara**].
vy-àkta, pp. *distinguished by* (inst.), x. 14, 9; *palpable*, x. 127, 7 [ví + añj *adorn*].
vyac *extend*, III. P. **vivyakti**.
sám- *roll up*, ipf. **ávivyak**, vii. 63, 1.
vyath *waver*, I. **vyátha**, vi. 54, 3.
vyátha-māna, pr. pt. Ā. *quaking*, ii. 12, 2.
vyúṣṭ, f. *daybreak*, vii. 71, 3 [ví + vas *shine*].
vy-oman, n. *heaven*, iv. 50, 4; x. 14, 8; 129, 1. 7 [ví + oman of doubtful etymology].
vraj-á, m. *pen, fold*, iv. 51, 2 [vṛj *enclose*].
vra-tá, n. *will, ordinance*, iii. 59, 2. 3; v. 83, 5; viii. 48, 9; *service*, vi. 54, 9 [vṛ *choose*].
vrata-cārin, a. *practising a vow*, vii. 103, 1 [cār-ín, from car *go, practise*].
vrā́ta, m. *troop, host*, x. 34, 8. 12.

Śaṃs *praise*, I. **śáṃsa**, vii. 61, 4 [Lat. *censeo*].
śáṃs-ant, pr. pt. *praising*, ii. 12, 14; iv. 51, 7.
śatá, n. *hundred*, ii. 33, 2; vii. 103, 10 [Gk. ἑκατό-ν, Lat. *centum*, Go. *hund*].
śám-tama, spv. a. *most beneficent*, ii. 33, 2. 13; x. 15, 4 [**śám**, n. *healing*].
śaphá-vant, a. *having hoofs*, v. 83, 5.
śabála, a. *brindled*, x. 14, 10.
śám, n. *healing*, ii. 33, 13; *comfort*, v. 11, 5; viii. 48, 4; *health*, x. 15, 4; *prosperity*, viii. 86, 8[3].
Śámbara, m. name of a demon, ii. 12, 11.
śáy-āna, pr. pt. Ā. *lying*, ii. 12, 11; vii. 103, 2 [**śī** *lie*].

śarád, f. *autumn*, ii. 12, 11; vii. 61, 2; x. 90, 6.
śár-u, f. *arrow*, ii. 12, 10; vii. 71, 1 [Go. *hairu-s*].
śárdh-ant, pr. pt. *arrogant*, ii. 12, 10 [śṛdh *be defiant*].
śár-man, n. *shelter*, i. 85, 12; v. 83, 5; x. 129, 1 [Lith. *szálma-s* 'helmet', OG. *helm* 'helmet'].
śáv-as, n. *power*, v. 11, 5 [**śū** *swell*].
śaśam-āná, pf. pt. Ā. *having prepared* (the sacrifice), i. 85, 12; ii. 12, 14; *strenuous*, iv. 51, 7 [**śam** *toil*].
śaśay-āná, pf. pt. Ā. *lying*, vii. 103, 1 [**śī** *lie*].
śáś-vant, a. *ever repeating itself, many*, ii. 12, 10; -vat, adv. *for ever*, i. 35, 5 [for **sá** + **śvant**, orig. pt. of **śū** *swell*, Gk. ἅ-παντ-].
śāktá, m. *teacher*, vii. 103, 5 [**śak** *be able*].
śās *order*, II. **śā́sti**, **śā́ste**.
ánu- *instruct*, vi. 54, 1.
abhí- *guide to* (acc.), vi. 54, 2.
śík-van *flame* (?), ii. 35, 4.
śikṣ *be helpful, pay obeisance*, I. **śíkṣa**, iii. 59, 2 [ds. of **śak** *be able*].
śíkṣa-māṇa (pr. pt. Ā.), m. *learner*, vii. 103, 5.
śiti-pád, a. (Bv.) *white-footed*, i. 35, 5.
śithirá, a. *loose*; n. *freedom*, vii. 71, 5 [Gk. καθαρό-ς 'free, pure'].
śivá, a. *kind*, x. 34, 2.
śíśu, m. *child*, ii. 33, 13 [**śū** *swell*, cp. Gk. κυέω].
śiśriy-āṇá, pf. pt. Ā. *abiding*, v. 11, 6 [**śri** *resort*].
śī-tá, a. *cold*, x. 34, 9 [old pp. of **śyā** *coagulate*].
śirṣ-án, n. *head*, x. 90, 14 [**śir(a)s** *head* + an; cp. Gk. κόρσ-η 'head'].
śuk-rá, a. *shining*, i. 160, 3; *bright*, ii. 33, 9; iv. 51, 9; *clear*, ii. 35, 4 [**śuc** *be bright*, Av. *sux-ra* 'flaming'].
śúc-i, a. *bright*, i. 160, 1; *bright*, ii. 35, 8; iv. 51, 2. 9; v. 11, 1. 3; viii. 29, 5; *clear*, vii. 49, 2. 3; *pure*, ii. 33, 13; 35, 3[2] [**śuc** *shine*].
śúbh, f. *brilliance*; = *shining path* (cog. acc.), iv. 51, 6.
śubh-áya, Ā. *adorn oneself*, i. 85, 3.
śubh-rá, a. *bright*, i. 35, 3; 85, 3; iv. 51, 6 [**śubh** *adorn*].
śumbh, *adorn*, I. Ā. **śúmbhate**.
prá- *adorn oneself*, i. 85, 1.

śúṣ-ka, a. *dry*, vii. 103, 2 [for **suṣ-ka**, Av. *huš-ka*].
śúṣ-ma, m. *vehemence*, ii. 12, 1. 13; *impulse*, iv. 50, 7; *force*, vii. 61, 4 [**śvas** *blow, snort*].
śū́-ra, m. *hero*, i. 85, 8 [Av. *sūra* 'strong', Gk. *ἄ-κυρο-ς* 'in-valid'].
śūdrá, m. *man of the servile caste*, x. 90, 12.
śū́śuj-ána, pf. pt. A. *trembling* (?), x. 34, 6.
śūṣ-á, a. *inspiring*, i. 154, 3 [**śvas** *breathe*].
śṛṇv-ánt, pr. pt. *hearing*, vi. 54, 8 [**śru** *hear*].
śṛdh-yā́, f. *arrogance*, ii. 12, 10 [**śṛdh** *be arrogant*].
śṝ *crush*, IX. **śṛṇā́ti.**
sám- *be crushed*: ps. ao. **śāri**, vi. 54, 7.
ścut *drip*, I. **ścóta**, iv. 50, 3.
śyā-vá, a. *dusky*, i. 35, 5 [OSl. *si-vŭ* 'grey'].
śyená, m. *eagle*, vii. 63, 5; m. *hawk*, x. 127, 5.
śrád *heart* only with dhā = *put faith in, believe in* (dat.), ii. 12, 5 [Lat. *cord-*, Gk. *καρδ-ίη* 'heart'].
śráv-as, n. *fame*, i. 160, 5; iii. 59, 7 [**śru** *hear*; Gk. *κλέϝος* 'fame', OSl. *slovo* 'word'].
śravas-yú, a. *fame-seeking*, i. 85, 8.
śri-tá, pp. *reaching to* (lc.), v. 11, 3.
śrī́, f. *glory*, i. 85, 2; iv. 33, 3; x. 127, 1.
śru, V. **śṛṇóti**, *hear*, ii. 33, 4; x. 15, 5; pl. 3. **śṛṇvire** = ps., x. 168, 4.
śru-tá, pp. *heard; famous*, ii. 33, 11 [**śru** *hear*, Gk. *κλυ-τό-ς* 'famous', Lat. *in-clu-tu-s* 'famous'].
śré-ṣṭha, spv. a. *best*, ii. 33, 3.
śró-tra, n. *ear*, x. 90, 14 [**śru** *hear*].
śráuṣ-ṭī, f. *obedient mare*, viii, 48, 2 [**śruṣ** *hear*, extension of **śru**].
śva-ghn-ín, m. *gambler*, ii. 12, 4.
śván, m. *dog*, x. 14, 10. 11 [Av. *span*, Gk. *κύων*].
śva-śrū́, f. *mother-in-law*, x. 34, 3 [OSl. *svekry, svekrŭve*].
śvity-áñc, a. *whitish*, ii. 33, 8 [**śviti** (akin to **śvetá**, Go. *hweits*, Eng. *white*) + **añc**].

Ṣáṣ, nm. *six*, x. 14, 16 [Av. *xšvaš*, Gk. *ἕξ*, Lat. *sex*, OI. *sē*, Go. *saihs*, Eng. *six*].

Sá, dem. prn. N. s. m. *that, he*, i. 1, 2. 4. 9; 154, 5; 160, 3; ii. 12. 1–14; ii. 33, 13[3]; 35, 1. 4. 5. 8. 10; iii. 59, 2. 8; iv. 50, 5[2]. 7. 8; 51, 4; v. 11, 2. 6; 83, 5; vii. 61, 1. 2; 86, 6; x. 14, 14; 34, 11; 90, 1. 5; 129, 7; *as such* = *thus*, ii. 12, 15; viii. 48, 9 [Av. *hō*, Gk. *ὁ*, Go. *sa*].
saṃ-yánt, pr. pt. *going together*, ii. 12, 8 [**sám** + **i** *go*].
saṃ-rarāṇá, pf. pt. Ā. *sharing gifts*, x. 15, 8 [**sám** + **rā** *give*].
saṃ-vatsará, m. *year*, vii. 103, 1. 7. 9.
saṃ-vid-āná, pr. pt. Ā. *uniting, with* (inst.), viii. 48, 13; x. 14, 4 [**vid** *find*].
saṃ-vṛ́j, a. *conquering*, ii. 12, 3.
sákh-i, m. *friend*, ii. 35, 12; vii. 86, 4; viii. 48, 4[2]. 10; x. 34, 2. 5; 168, 3.
sakh-yá, n. *friendship*, viii. 48, 2.
saṃ-gámana, m. *assembler*, x. 14, 1.
sac *accompany*, I. Ā. **sácate**, i. 1, 9; vii. 61, 5; *associate with*, viii. 48, 10; *reach*, x. 90, 16 [Gk. *ἕπεται*, Lat. *sequitur*, Lith. *sekù*].
sác-ā, adv. prp. *with* (lc.), iv. 50, 11 [**sac** *accompany*].
sájan-ya, a. *belonging to his own people*, iv 50, 9 [**sa-jana**, *kinsman*].
sa-jóṣas, a. *acting in harmony with* (inst.), viii. 48, 15 [**jóṣas**, n. *pleasure*].
sat, n. *the existent*, x. 129, 1 [pr. pt. of **as** *be*].
sát-pati, m. *true* (?) *lord*, ii. 33, 12.
sat-yá, a. *true*, i. 1, 5. 6: ii. 12, 15; x. 15, 9. 10 [**sat**, n. *truth* + **ya**].
satyá-dharman, a. (Bv.) *whose ordinances are true*, x. 34, 8.
satyānṛtá, n. Dv. cd. *truth and falsehood*, vii. 49, 3 [**satyá** + **ánṛta**].
sad *sit down*, I. P. **sī́dati**, i. 85, 7; *sit down on* (acc.). a ao. **sadata**, x. 15, 11 [Lat. *sīdo*].
ā́- *seat oneself on* (acc.), i. 85, 6; *occupy*: pf. **sasāda**, viii. 29, 2.
ní- *sit down*, pf. (**ní**)**ṣedur**, iv. 50, 3; inj. **sīdat**, v. 11, 2; *settle*: pf. s. 2. **sasáttha**, viii. 48, 9.
sád-as, n. *seat*, iv. 51, 8; viii. 29, 9; *abode*, i. 85, 2. 6. 7 [Gk. *ἕδος*].
sádas-sadas, acc. itv. cd. *on each seat*, x. 15, 11.
sá-dā, adv. *always*, vii. 61, 7; 63, 6; 71, 6; 86, 8.
sa-dṛ́ś, a., f. -ī, *alike*, iv. 51, 6 [*having a similar appearance*].
sa-dyás, adv. *in one day*, iv. 51, 5; *at once*, iv. 51, 7.

sadha-máda, m. *joint feast*, x. 14, 10 [*co-revelry* ; sadhá = sahá *together*].
sadhá-stha, n. *gathering place*, i. 154, 1. 3.
san *gain*, VIII. P. sanóti, vi. 54, 5.
sanáya, a. *old*, iv. 51, 4 [from sána ; Gk. ἕνο-ς, OI. *sen*, Lith. *sĕnas* 'old'].
sánt, pr. pt. *being*, x. 34, 9 [as *be* ; Lat. (*prae*)-*sent*-].
saṃ-dṛ́ś, f. *sight*, ii. 33, 1.
saptá, nm. *seven*, i. 35, 8 ; ii. 12, 3. 12 ; x. 90, 15² [Gk. ἑπτά, Lat. *septem*, Eng. *seven*].
saptá-raśmi, a. (Bv.) *seven-reined*, ii. 12, 12 ; *seven-rayed*, iv. 50, 4.
saptā́sya, a. (Bv.) *seven-mouthed*, iv. 50, 4 ; 51, 4 [saptá + āsyà, n. *mouth*].
sáp-ti, m. *racer*, i. 85, 1. 6.
sa-práthas, a. (Bv.) *renowned*, iii. 59, 7 [*accompanied by* práthas, n. *fame*].
sa-bā́dha, a. *zealous*, vii. 61, 6 [bādhá, m. *stress*].
sabhā́, f. *assembly hall*, x. 34, 6 [OG. *sippa* 'kinship', AS. *sib*].
samá, a. *level*, v. 83, 7 [Av. *hama* 'equal', Gk. ὁμό-ς, Eng. *same*, cp. Lat. *sim-i-li-s*].
sam-ád, f. *battle*, ii. 12, 3.
sám-ana, n. *festival*, x. 168, 2 [*coming together*].
samanā́, adv. *in the same way*, iv. 51, 8² [inst., with shift of accent, from sámana *being together*].
samānā́, a., f. ī, *same*, ii. 12, 8 ; iv. 51, 9 ; vii. 86, 3 ; *uniform*, vii. 63, 2 ; *common*, ii. 35, 3 ; vii. 63, 3 ; 103, 6.
samānā́-tas, adv. *from the same place*, iv. 51, 8.
sam-ídh, f. *faggot*, x. 90, 15 [sám + idh *kindle*].
samudrá-jyeṣṭha, a. (Bv.) *having the ocean as their chief*, vii. 49, 1 [samudrá, m. *collection of waters* + jyeṣṭha, spv. *chief*].
samudrā́rtha, a. (Bv.) *having the ocean as their goal*, vii. 49, 2 [ártha, m. *goal*].
sam-ṛ́dh, f. *unison*, vii. 103, 5 [sám + ṛdh *thrive*].
sáṃ-pṛkta, pp. *mixed with* (inst.), x. 34, 7 [pṛc *mix*].
saṃ-pṛ́cas, ab. inf. *from mingling with*, ii. 35, 6 [pṛc *mix*].
sáṃ-bhṛta, pp. *collected*, x. 90, 8 [bhṛ *bear*].
sam-rā́j, m. *sovereign king*, viii. 29, 9.
sa-yúj, a. *united with* (inst.), x. 168, 2.
sa-rátham, adv. (cog. acc.) *on the same car*, *with* (inst.), v. 11, 2 ; x. 15, 10 ; 168, 2.
sár-as, n. *lake*, vii. 103, 7 [sṛ *run*].
saras-í, f. *lake*, vii. 103, 2.
sárg-a, m. *herd*, iv. 51, 8 [sṛj *let loose*].
sárt-ave, dat. inf. *to flow*, ii. 12, 12 [sṛ *flow*].
sṛp *creep*, I. P. sárpati.
ví- *slink off*, x. 14, 9.
sarpir-āsuti, a. (Bv.) *having melted butter as their draught*, viii. 29, 9 [sarpís (from sṛp *run* = *melt*) + ā-sutí *brew* from su *press*].
sárva, a. *all*, vii. 103, 5 ; x. 14, 16 ; 90, 2 ; 129, 3 [Gk. ὅλο-ς = ὅλ-ϝο-ς, Lat. *salvu-s* 'whole'].
sárva-vīra, a. *consisting entirely of sons*, iv. 50, 10 ; x. 15, 11.
sarva-hút, a. (Tp.) *completely offering*, x. 90, 8. 9 [hu-t : hu *sacrifice* + determinative t].
sal-ilá, n. *water*, x. 129, 3 ; *sea*, vii. 49, 1 [sal = sṛ *flow*].
Sav-i-tṛ́, m. a solar god, i. 35, 1–6. 8–10 ; vii. 63, 3 ; x. 34, 8. 13 [*Stimulator* from sū *stimulate*].
sas *sleep*, II. P. sásti, iv. 51, 3.
sas-ánt, pr. pt. *sleeping*, iv. 51, 5.
sah *overcome*, I. sáha, x. 34, 9 [Gk. ἔχω, ao. ἔσ(ε)χ-ον].
sáh-as, n. *might*, iv. 50, 1 ; v. 11, 6³ [sah *overcome*].
sa-hásra, nm. *a thousand*, x. 15, 10 [Gk. χίλιοι, Lesbian χέλλιοι from χέσλο].
sahásra-pād, a. (Bv.) *thousand-footed*, x. 90, 1 [pad *foot*].
sahásra-bhṛṣṭi, a. (Bv.) *thousand-edged*, i. 85, 9 [bhṛṣ-ṭí from bhṛṣ = hṛṣ *stick up*].
sahásra-śīrṣan, a. *thousand-headed*, x. 34, 14.
sahasra-sāvá, m. *thousandfold Soma-pressing*, vii. 103, 10 [sāvá, m. *pressing* from su *press*].
sahasrākṣá, a. (Bv.) *thousand-eyed*, x. 90, 1 [akṣá *eye* = ákṣi].
sá-hūti, f. *joint praise*, ii. 33, 4 [hūti *invocation* from hū *call*].
sā *bind*, VI. syáti.
ví- *discharge*, i. 85, 5.
sā́, dem. prn. N. s. f. *that*, iv. 50, 11 ; vii. 86, 6 ; *as such* = *so*, x. 127, 4.
sā́d-ana, n. *seat*, x. 135, 7 [sad *sit*].

sā́dhāraṇa, a. *belonging jointly, common*, vii. 63, 1 [sa-ādhāraṇa *having the same support*].
sādh-ú, a. *good*, x. 14, 10.
sādhu-yā́, adv. *straightway*, v. 11, 4.
Sādh-yá, m. pl. a group of divine beings, x. 90, 7. 16.
sān-as-í, a. *bringing gain*, iii. 59, 6 [san *gain*].
sā́n-u, n. m. *back*, ii. 35, 12.
sā́-man, n. *chant*, viii. 29, 10; x. 90, 9; 135, 4.
sā́ya-ka, n. *arrow*, ii. 33, 10 [*suitable for hurling*: si *hurl*].
sārameyá, m. *son of Saramā*, x. 14, 10.
sāśanānaśaná, n. (Dv.) *eating and non-eating things*, x. 90, 4 [sa-aśana + anaśana].
siṃhá, m. *lion*, v. 83, 3.
sic *pour*, VI. **siñcá**, i. 85, 11 [OG. *sīg-u* 'drip', Lettic *sik-u* 'fall' of water].
 ní- *pour down*, v. 83, 8.
sidh *repel*, I. P. **sédhati**.
 ápa- *chase away*, i. 35, 10.
síndh-u, m. *river*, i. 35, 8; ii. 12, 3. 12; *Indus*, v. 11, 5 [Av. *hind-u-s*].
sisvid-āná, pf. pt. Ā. *sweating*, vii. 103, 8 [svid *perspire*: Eng. *sweat*].
sim, enc. prn. pcl. *him* &c., i. 160, 2.
su *press*, V. **sunóti, sunuté**, V. 14, 13 [Av. *hu*].
sú, adv. *well*, ii. 35, 2; v. 83, 7; vii. 86, 8 [Av. *hu-*, OI. *su-*].
sú-kṛta, pp. *well-made*, i. 35, 11; 85, 9; *well prepared*, x. 15, 13; 34, 11.
su-krátu, a. (Bv.) *very wise*, v. 11, 2; vii. 61, 2 [krátu *wisdom*].
sukratū-yā́, f. *insight*, i. 160, 4.
su-kṣatrá, a. (Bv.) *wielding fair sway*, iii. 59, 4.
su-kṣití, f. *safe dwelling*, ii. 35, 15.
su-gá, a. *easy to traverse*, i. 35, 11; vii. 63, 6.
su-jánman, a. (Bv.) *producing fair creations*, i. 160, 1.
su-tá, pp. *pressed*, viii. 48, 7; x. 15, 8.
sú-taṣṭa, pp. *well-fashioned*, ii. 35, 2 [takṣ *fashion*].
sutá-soma, (Bv.) m. *Soma-presser*, ii. 12, 6.
su-tára, a. *easy to pass*, x. 127, 6.
su-dáṃsas, a. (Bv.) *wondrous*, i. 85, 1 [dáṃsas *wonder*].
su-dákṣa, a. (Bv.) *most skilful*, v. 11, 1.
su-dā́nu, a. *bountiful*, i. 85, 10; vii. 61, 3.
su-dúgha, a. (Bv.) *yielding good milk*, ii. 35, 7 [dúgha *milking*: dugh = duh].
sú-dhita, pp. *well established*, iv. 50, 8 [dhita, pp. of dhā *put*].
su-dhṛ́ṣ-ṭama, spv. a. *very proud*, i. 160, 2.
su-nīthá, a. (Bv.) *giving good guidance*, i. 35, 7. 10.
sunv-ánt, pr. pt. *pressing Soma*, ii. 12, 14. 15; vi. 54, 6 [su *press*].
su-pátha, n. *fair path*, vii. 63, 6.
su-parṇá, a. (Bv.) *having beautiful wings*; m. *bird*, i. 35, 7.
su-palāśá, a. *fair-leaved*, x. 135, 1.
su-péśas, a. (Bv.) *well-adorned*, ii. 35, 1 [péśas, n. *ornament*].
su-praketá, a. *conspicuous*, iv. 50, 2 [praketá, m. *token*].
su-prajá́, a. (Bv.) *having good offspring*, iv. 50, 6 [prajā́].
su-prátīka, a. (Bv.) *lovely*, vii. 61, 1 [*having a fair countenance*: prátīka, n.].
su-práṇīti, a. (Bv.) *giving good guidance*, x. 15, 11.
su-prapāṇá, a. (Bv.) *giving good drink*; n. *good drinking place*, v. 83, 8.
su-bhága, a. *having a good share, opulent*; *genial*, vii. 63, 1.
su-bhú, a. *excellent*, ii. 35, 7 [sú *well* + bhu *being*].
sú-bhṛta, pp. *well cherished*, iv. 50, 7.
sú-makha, m. *great warrior*, i. 85, 4.
su-matí, f. *good-will*, iii. 59, 3. 4; iv. 50, 11; viii. 48, 12; x. 14, 6.
su-mánas, a. (Bv.) *cheerful*, vii. 86, 2 [Av. *hu-manah-* 'well-disposed'; cp. second part of *εὐ-μενής*].
sv-mṛḷīka, a. (Bv.) *very gracious*, i. 35, 10 [mṛḷīká, n. *mercy*].
su-medhás, a. (Bv.) *having a good understanding, wise*, viii. 48, 1.
su-mná, n. *good-will*, ii. 33, 1. 6.
sumnā-yú, a. *kindly*, vii. 71, 3.
su-rabhí, a. *fragrant*, x. 15, 12.
súrā, f. *liquor*, vii. 86, 6 [Av. *hura*].
su-rétas, a. (Bv.) *abounding in seed*, 160, 3.
su-várcas, a. (Bv.) *full of vigour*, x. 14, 8.
su-vā́c, a. (Bv.) *eloquent*, vii. 103, 5.
suv-itá, n. *welfare*, v. 11, 1 [su *well* + itá, pp. of i *go*: opposite of dur-itá].

su-vidátra, a. *bountiful*, x. 14, 10; 15, 3. 9.
su-vī́ra, a. (Bv.) *having good champions* = *strong sons*, i. 85, 12; ii. 12, 15; 33, 15; 35, 15; viii. 48, 14.
su-vī́rya, n. *host of good champions*, iv. 51, 10.
su-vṛktí, f. *song of praise*, ii. 35, 15; vii. 71, 6 [sú + ṛk-ti from arc *praise*, cp. ṛc].
su-vṛjána, a. (Bv.) *having fair abodes*, x. 15, 2.
su-śípra, a. (Bv.) *fair-lipped*, ii. 12, 6; 33, 5.
su-śéva, a. *most propitious*, iii. 59, 4. 5; viii. 48, 4.
su-ṣakhí, m. *good friend*, viii. 48, 9 [sákhi *friend*].
su-ṣṭutí, f. *eulogy*, ii. 33, 8 [stutí *praise*].
su-ṣṭúbh, a. *well-praising*, iv. 50, 5 [stubh *praise*].
su-háva, a. (Bv.) *easy to invoke*, ii. 33, 5 [háva *invocation*].
sū́, adv. *well*, v. 83, 10 [= sú *well*].
sū-nára, a. *bountiful*, viii. 29, 1 [Av. *hunara*].
sū-nú, m. *son*, i. 1, 9; 85, 1; viii. 48, 4 [Av. *hunu*, OG. *sunu*, Lith. *sūnù*, Eng. *son*].
sūpāyaná, a. (Bv.) *giving easy access*, *easily accessible*, i. 1, 9 [sú + upā́yana].
sū́r-a, m. *sun*, vii. 63, 5 [svàr *light*].
sūrí, m. *patron*, ii. 35, 6.
sū́r-ya, m. *sun*, i. 35, 7. 9; 160, 1; ii. 12, 7; 33, 1; vii. 61, 1; 63, 1. 2. 4; viii. 29, 10; x. 14, 12; 90, 13 [svàr *light*].
sṛ *flow*, III. sísarti.
úpa prá- *stretch forth to*, int. 3. s. sarsṛ-e, ii. 35, 5.
sṛj *emit*, VI. sṛjáti [Av. *herᵉzaiti*].
áva- *discharge downward*, ii. 12, 12; *cast off*, vii. 86, 5.
úpa- *send forth to* (acc.), ii. 35, 1.
sṛp-rá, a. *extensive*, iv. 50, 2 [sṛp *creep*].
sé-nā, f. *missile*, ii. 33, 11 [si *discharge*].
senā-nī́, m. *leader of an army*, *general*, x. 34, 12.
só-ma, m. *juice of the Soma plant*, i. 85, 10; ii. 12, 14; iv. 50, 10; vii. 49, 4; viii. 48, 3. 4². 7-15; x. 14, 13; 34, 1; *Soma sacrifice*, vii. 103, 7 [su *press*: Av. *haoma*].
soma-pā́, m. *Soma drinker*, ii. 12, 13.
soma-pīthá, m. *Soma draught*, x. 15, 8 [pīthá from pā *drink*].
som-ín, a. *soma-pressing*, vii. 103, 8.
som-yá, a. *Soma-loving*, x. 14, 6; 15, 1. 5. 8.
saumanas-á, n. *good graces*, iii. 59, 4; x. 14, 6 [su-mánas].
skand *leap*, I. P. skándati, int. inj. kániṣkan, vii. 103, 4.
skabhāya, den. *prop*, *establish*, i. 154, 1 [from skabh, IX. skabhnāti].
skámbh-ana, n. *prop*, *support*, i. 160, 4.
stan *thunder*, II. P.; cs. stanáyati, *id.*, v. 83, 7. 8 [Gk. στένω 'lament'].
stan-átha, m. *thunder*, v. 83, 3.
stanáyant, pr. pt. *thundering*, v. 83, 2; x. 168, 1.
stanayi-tnú, m. *thunder*, v. 83, 6.
stabh or **stambh** *prop*, *support*, IX. stabhnā́ti, ii. 12, 2.
ví- *prop asunder*, pf. tastambha, iv. 50, 1; vii. 86, 1.
stáv-āna, pr. pt. Ā. = ps. *being praised*, ii. 33, 11 [stu *praise*].
sthi-rá, a. *firm*, ii. 33, 9. 14 [sthā *stand*].
stu *praise*, II. stáuti, ii. 33, 11; v. 83, 1.
prá- *praise aloud*, i. 154, 2.
stu-tá, pp. *praised*, ii. 33, 12.
stuv-ánt, pr. pt. *praising*, iv. 51, 7; vi. 54, 6.
ste-ná, m. *thief*, x. 127, 6 [stā *be stealthy*].
sto-tṛ́, m. *praiser*, vi. 54, 9; vii. 86, 4 [stu *praise*].
stó-ma, m. *song of praise*, ii. 33, 5; vii. 86, 8; x. 127, 8 [stu *praise*].
stóma-taṣṭa, a. (Tp.) *fashioned into* (= being the subject of) *praise*, x. 15, 9.
strī́, f. *woman*, x. 34, 11 [Av. *strī*].
sthā *stand*, I. tiṣṭha; pf. tasthur, i. 35, 5; rt. ao. s. 3. ásthāt, i. 35, 10; iv. 51, 1; pl. 3. ásthur, iv. 51, 2 [Av. *hištaiti*, Gk. ἵστημι, Lat. *sisto*].
áti- *extend beyond*, x. 90, 1.
ádhi- *ascend*, x. 135, 3; *stand upon*, i. 35, 6.
ápa- *start off*, viii. 48, 11.
abhí- *overcome*, iv. 50, 7.
ā́- *mount*, i. 35, 4; *mount to* (acc.), i. 85, 7; *occupy*, ii. 35, 9.
úd- *arise*, v. 11, 3.
úpa- *approach*, rt. ao. asthita, x 127, 7.
pári- *surround*, pf. tasthur, ii. 35, 3.

prá- *step forth*, x. 14, 14.
spáś, m. *spy*, vii. 61, 3 [Av. *spas*; cp. Lat. *au-spex*, Gk. σκώψ 'owl'].
spṛ *win*, V. **spṛṇóti**.
nís- *rescue*, rt. ao. 2. du. spartam, vii. 71, 5.
spṛh, cs. **spṛháya** *long for*, x. 135, 2 [Av. *sperᵉzaite*].
sphúr *spurn*, VI. **sphurá**, ii. 12, 12; *spring*, x. 34, 9 [Av. *sparaiti*, Gk. σπαίρω 'quiver', Lat. *sperno*, Lith. *spiriù* 'kick', OG. *spurnu* 'kick'].
sma, enc. pcl. *just*, *indeed*, ii. 12, 5 [180].
syá, dem. prn. *that*, ii. 33, 7 [OP. *hya*, f. *hyā*; OG. f. *siu*].
syand *flow*, I. Ā. **syándate**, v. 83, 8.
syū́ma-gabhasti, a. (Bv.) *drawn with thongs*, vii. 71, 3 [**syū́-man** *band*; Gk. ὑ-μήν 'sinew'].
syoná, n. *soft couch*, iv. 51, 10.
srāma, m. *disease*, viii. 48, 5.
sru *flow*, I. **sráva**, vii. 49, 1 [Gk. ῥέϝει 'flows'].
svá, poss. prn. *own*, i. 1, 8; ii. 35, 7; iv. 50, 8; vii. 86, 2. 6; x. 14, 2 [Av. *hva*, Gk. σό-ς, ὅ-ς, Lat. *suu-s*].
svá-tavas, a. (Bv.) *self-strong*, i. 85, 7.
1. **svadhā́**, f. *funeral offering*, x. 14, 3. 7; 15, 3. 12–14.
2. **sva-dhā́**, f. *own power*, x. 129, 2; *energy*, x. 129, 5; *vital force*, ii. 35, 7; *bliss*, i. 154, 4 [**svá** *own* and **dhā** *put*; cp. Gk. ἔ-θο-ς 'custom'].
svadhā́-vant, a. *self-dependent*, vii. 86, 4. 8.
sv-ápas, a. (Bv.) *skilful*, i. 85, 9 [**sú** + **ápas** '*doing good work*'].
sváp-na, m. *sleep*, vii. 86, 6 [Gk. ὕπνο-ς, Lat. *somnu-s*, Lith. *sãpna-s*].
svayam-já, a. *rising spontaneously*, vii. 49, 2.
sva-y-ám, ref. prn. *self*, ii. 35, 14; *of their own accord*, iv. 50, 8 [115 *a*].
svàr, n. *light*; *heaven*, ii. 35. 6; v. 83, 4.
sva-rā́j, m. *sovereign ruler*, x. 15, 14.
sváru, m. *sacrificial post*, iv. 51, 2.
svar-víd, m. *finder of light*, viii. 48, 15.
svá-vant, a. *bountiful*, i. 35, 10 [*possessing property*: **svá**, n.].
svásṛ, f. *sister*, vii. 71, 1; x. 127, 3 [Lat. *soror*, OSl. *sestra*, Go. *swistar*, Eng. *sister*].
sv-astí, f. n. *well-being*, i. 1, 9; 35, 1; ii. 33, 3; vii. 71, 6; 86, 8; x. 14, 11; inst. s. **svastí** *for welfare*, viii. 48, 8; pl. *blessings*, vii. 61, 7; 63, 6 [**sú** *well* + **asti** *being*].
svād-ú, a. *sweet*, viii. 48, 1 [Gk. ἡδύ-ς, Lat. *svāvi-s*, Eng. *sweet*].
sv-ādhī́, a. (Bv.) *stirring good thoughts*, viii. 48, 1.
sv-ābhú, a. *invigorating*, iv. 50, 10.
svā́hā, ij. *hail*, as a sacrificial call, x. 14, 3.
svid, enc. emph. pcl., iv. 51, 6; x. 34, 10; 129, 5²; 135, 5; 168, 3.

Ha, enc. emph. pcl., i. 85, 7; vii. 86, 3; x. 14, 13; 90, 10. 16; 129, 2 [later form of **gha**].
ha-tvā́, gd. *having slain*, ii. 12, 3 [**han** *strike*].
han *slay*, II. **hánti**, i. 85, 9; ii. 33, 15; *smite*, v. 83, 2³. 9: I. **jíghna** *slay*, viii. 29, 4; pf. **jaghā́na**, ii. 12, 10. 11; ps. **hanyáte**, iii. 59, 2; ds. **jíghāṃsa**, vii. 86, 4.
han-tṛ́, m. *slayer*, ii. 12. 10.
hár-as, n. *wrath*, viii. 48, 2 [*heat*; from **hṛ** *be hot*: Gk. θέρ-ος 'summer'].
hár-i, m. *bay steed*, i. 35, 3 [Av. *zairi-* 'yellowish'; Lat. *helu-s*, Lith. *żelù*, OG. *gëlo*].
hár-ita, a. *yellow*, vii. 103, 4. 6. 10 [Av. *zairita* 'yellowish'].
háry-aśva, a. (Bv.) *drawn by bay steeds*, viii. 48, 10.
háv-a, m. *invocation*, x. 15, 1 [**hū** *call*].
havana-śrút, a. (Tp.) *listening to invocations*, ii. 33, 15 [**hávana** (from **hū** *call*) + **śrú-t** *hearing* from **śru** *hear* with determinative **t**].
havir-ád, a. (Tp.) *eating the oblation*, x. 15, 10 [**havís** + **ad**].
haviṣ-pā́, a. *drinking the oblation*, x. 15, 10 [**havís** + **pā**].
hav-is, n. *oblation*, ii. 33. 5; 35, 12; iii. 59, 5; iv. 50, 6; vi. 54, 4; viii. 48 12. 13; x. 14, 1. 4. 13. 14; 15, 8. 11. 12; 90, 6²; 168, 4 [**hu** *sacrifice*].
háv-ī-man, n. *invocation*, ii. 33, 5 [**hū** *call*].
hav-yá, (gdv.) n. *what is to be offered*, *oblation*, iii. 59, 1; vii. 63, 5; 86, 2; x. 14, 15; 15, 4 [**hu** *sacrifice*].
havya-vā́hana, m. *carrier of oblations*, v. 11, 4 [**vā́hana** from **vah** *carry*].
havya-sū́d, a. (Tp.) *sweetening the oblation*, iv. 50, 5 [**sūd** = **svād** *sweeten*].
hásta, m. *hand*, ii. 33, 7; vi. 54, 10; viii. 29, 3–5.

hásta-vant, a. *having hands*, x. 34, 9.
1. **hā** *leave*, III. P. **jahāti**.
áva-, ps. **hīyate**, *be left behind*, x. 34, 5.
2. **hā** *go away*, III. Ā. **jihīte**.
ápa- *depart*, vii. 71, 1 : 3. s. sb. s. ao. hāsate, x. 127, 3.
úd- *spring up*, v. 83, 4.
hí, cj. *for*, i. 85, 1 ; 154. 5 ; 160, 1 ; ii. 35, 1. 5. 9 ; iv. 51, 5 ; viii. 48, 6 ; *since*, viii. 48, 9 ; x. 34, 11 ; *pray*, x. 14, 4.
hiṃs, *injure*, VII. **hinásti** *injure* ; iṣ ao. inj., x. 15, 6 [probably a ds. of han *strike*].
hi-tá, pp. *placed*, v. 11, 6 [later form of dhita from dhā *put* ; Gk. θετό-ς *set*].
hi-tvā́ya, gd. *leaving behind*, x. 14, 8 [1. hā *leave*].
himá, m. *winter*, ii. 33, 2 [Av. *zima*, OSl. *zima* 'winter'; Gk. δύσ-χιμο-ς 'subject to bad storms', 'horrid'].
híraṇ-ya, n. *gold ornament*, ii. 33, 9.
hiraṇya-dā́, a. (Tp.) *giver of gold*, ii. 35, 10.
híraṇya-pāṇi, a. (Bv.) *golden-handed*, i. 35, 9.
hiraṇya-praüga, a. (Bv.) *having a golden pole*, i. 35, 5.
hiraṇyá-ya, a. *golden*, i. 35, 2 ; 85, 9 ; ii. 35, 10 ; viii. 29, 1.
híraṇya-rūpa, a. (Bv.) *having a golden form*, ii. 35, 10.
híraṇya-varṇa, a. (Bv.) *golden-coloured*, ii. 35, 9–11.
híraṇya-śamī, a. (Bv.) *having golden pins*, i. 35, 4.
híraṇya-saṃdṛ́ś, a. (Bv.) *having a golden aspect*, ii. 35, 10.
híraṇya-hasta, a. (Bv.) *golden-handed*, i. 35, 10.
hiraṇyākṣá, a. (Bv.) *golden-eyed*, i. 35, 8 [akṣá = akṣí *eye*].
hīḍ *be angry*, I. **héḍa** : pf. **jihīḷa**, x. 34, 2.
hī-ná, pp. *forsaken*, x. 34, 10 [hā *leave*].
hu *sacrifice, offer*, III. **juhóti**, iii. 59, 1 ; x. 14, 13–15.
á- *offer*, iii. 59, 5.
hū *call*, I. Ā. **hávate**, ii. 12, 8. 9 ; 33, 5 ; VI. Ā. **huvé**, vii. 61, 6 ; 71, 1 ; x. 14, 5.
hṛ *be angry*, IX. Ā. **hṛṇīte**, ii. 33, 15 ; *with* (dat.), vii. 86, 3.
hṛ́d, n. *heart*, ii. 35, 2 ; v. 11, 5 ; vii. 86, 8 ; viii. 48, 4. 12 ; x. 129, 4 [Av. *zard*].
hṛ́d-aya, n. *heart*, x. 34, 9.
he-tí, f. *dart*, ii. 33, 14 [hi *impel*].
he-tú, m. *cause* : ab. hetós *for the sake of*, x. 34, 2 [*impulse* : hi *impel*].
hó-tṛ, m. *invoker*, i. 1, 1. 5 ; v. 11, 2 [hū *call*].
hotrā-víd, a. (Tp.) *knowing oblations*, x. 15, 9 [hó-trā, Av. *zao-thra* ; cp. Gk. χύ-τρᾱ 'pot'].
hvā *call*, IV. **hváya**, i. 35, 1[4].
ví- *call divergently*, ii. 12, 8.

GENERAL INDEX

The letters a, b, c, d following the references to hymns indicate the first, second, third, and fourth Pāda respectively of the stanza.

Accent, in Sandhi: **kóśó 'va**, vi. 54, 3; **sūnávé 'gne**, i. 1, 9; **brāhmaṇò 'sya**, x. 90, 12 a; Svarita followed by Udātta: **nv àntár**, vii. 86, 2; **kvèdā́nīm**, i. 35, 7 c; **tanvā̀ śúśujānaḥ**, x. 34, 6 b; **vapuṣyè ná**, i. 160, 2 c; Udātta changed to Svarita: **tè 'vardhanta**, i. 85, 7 a; in compounds: Dvandvas, **dyā́vā-pṛthiví́**, i. 35, 9 b; 160, 2; Karmadhārayas, **su-ávān**, i. 85, 10 b; **ásaścant**, i. 160, 2; **súmakhāsas**, i. 85, 4 a; **á-kṣīyamāṇā**, i. 154, 4 b; **sútaṣṭam**, ii. 35, 2 a; **á-hitam**, viii. 29, 4; Tatpuruṣas, **Parjánya-jinvitām**, vii. 103, 1 c; **devá-hitim**, vii. 103, 9 a; **kavi-śastā́s**, x. 14, 4 c; **Ágni-ṣvāttās**, x. 15, 11 a; **ekaparásya**, x. 34, 2 c; Bahuvrīhis, **su-parṇás**, **su-nīthás**, i. 35, 7 a b; **a-reṇávas**, i. 35, 11 b; **su-dáṃsasas**, i. 85, 1 b; **hiraṇyākṣás**, i. 35, 8 c; **uru-vyácasā**, i. 160, 2 a; **āśu-hémā**, **su-péśasas**, ii. 35, 1 c d; **án-āgās**, v. 83, 2 c; **viśvá-cakṣās**, **uru-cákṣās**, vii. 63, 1; **tri-vandhurás**, vii. 71, 4 b; **su-ṣakhā́**, viii. 48, 9 d; governing compounds, **yāvayáj-janas**, iii. 59, 5 b; in declension, **nadyàs**, ii. 35, 3 b; **dádhat**, i. 35, 8 d; **gṛṇaté**, iii. 59, 5 b; **nidhīnā́m**, viii. 29, 6; **bahūnā́m**, ii. 35, 12; **pṛthivyā́s**, i. 35, 8 a; 160, 1 a; in syntax: at beginning of sentence, ii. 35, 12 c; iv. 50, 2 d. 11 c; v. 83, 4 a b. 7 a; vii. 63, 4 d; 71, 2 d (irr.); 86, 1 d; viii. 48, 6 b. 8 a; x. 15, 4 b; 34, 4 d. 14 a; with **kuvít**, ii. 35, 1 c. 2 b; iv. 51, 4 a; of cd. verb, i. 35, 9 c; v. 83, 4 a b; shift of, **júṣṭam**, iii. 59, 5 c; **didṛ́kṣu**, vii. 86, 3 a; **viśvá-**, i. 160, 1 a. 5 c; **cátur-**, iv. 51, 5 d; **amuyā́**, x. 135, 2 b.

Accusative, double, ii. 33, 4; 35, 1; iv. 51, 11 b; of goal, x. 14, 13 c; of time, vii. 103, 1 a; x. 168, 3 b.

Agni, description of, pp. 1–2; viii. 29, 2.

Ahura = Asura, meaning of, i. 35, 7; in Avesta, pp. 119, 124.

Alliteration, x. 14, 7 a b. 9.

Ambiguity, intentional, vii. 103, 8 c. 9 d.

Ambiguous form: **śáṃsā**, 2. s. ipv. or 1. s. sb.; vii. 61, 4 a.

Āmreḍita compounds: **divé-dive**, i. 1, 3. 7; **gṛhé-gṛhe**, v. 11, 4 b; **váne-vane**, v. 11, 6 b; **gā́tre-gātre**, viii. 48, 9 b; **píba-piba**, see note on x. 14, 7.

Anaphoric repetition: **Agnís**, v. 11, 4; **árhan**, ii. 33, 10; **ayāṃsam**, ii. 35, 15 a b; **iyám**, vii. 71, 6; **áva**, vii. 86, 5; **u**, x. 127, 3; **kás**, x. 135, 5; **túbhyam**, v. 11, 5; **tvám**, viii. 48, 15; **té**, x. 15, 5; **ní**, x. 127, 5; **Pūṣā́**, vi. 54, 5; **Mitrás**, iii. 59, 1; **mā́**, ii. 33, 4; x. 135, 2. 3 (**yā́m kumāra**); **yás**, ii. 12, 1–4 &c.; **yásya vraté**, v. 83, 5; **yā́su**, vii. 49, 4; **yé**, x. 15, 2; **ví**, ii. 33, 2; **sám**, x. 14, 8; **hváyāmi**, i. 35, 1; use of **sá**, i. 1, 9; v. 11, 6; of **té**, x. 15, 7 d.

Aṅgirases, description of, viii. 29, 10.

Antithesis: **pracyāváyanto acyutā**, i. 85, 4 b; **éko tribhís**, i. 154, 3 d; **éko víśvā**, i. 154, 4 d; **páre ávare**, ii. 12, 8 b; **samānám nā́nā**, ii. 12, 8 c d; **sám úpa**, ii. 35, 3 a; **jihmā́nām ūrdhváḥ**, ii. 35, 9 b; **jigṛtám jajastám**, iv. 50, 11; **ásammṛṣṭaḥ śúciḥ**, v. 11, 3 a; **ánāgās duṣkṛ́taḥ**, v. 83, 2 c d; **áyajvanām yajñámanmā**, vii. 61, 4 c d; **kṛṣṇír aruṣā́ya**, vii. 71, 1 b; **ácetayad acítaḥ**, vii. 86, 7 c; **samānám vírūpāḥ**, vii. 103, 6 c;

15, 4 d. 11 d; 127, 6 a; 129, 6 d (átbā); 15, 4 b; vii. 86, 5 b (cakr̥mā); x. 34, 4 d (nayatā). 8 c (nā́). 14 a (mr̥ḷatā); 90, 3 b (Pū́ruṣas); 127, 6 a (yāvayā); 129, 1 b (vyòmā); 135, 1 c (átrā); in cds. and derivatives: i. 35, 4 (abhí-vr̥tam); 160, 1 b (r̥tā́-varī); ii. 12, 4 c (jigīvā́n); vii. 71, 3 b (sumnāyávas); 63. 2 a (prasavitā́); x. 34, 10 c (r̥ṇā-vā́); 14, 12 (urū-ṇasau); 168, 3 c (r̥tā́vā).

Locative, absolute, vii. 63, 5 c; 103, 3 b; of the goal, i. 1, 4; v. 11, 3 d; of time, vii. 103, 9 c. 10 d.

Long reduplicative vowel, i. 154, 4 d; iii. 59, 1 b (dādhāra); ii. 33, 12 (nānāma); 35, 3 c (dīdivā́ṃsam); 4 d (dīdāya). 7 b; viii. 29, 6 a (pīpāya).

Loss of accent, ii. 35, 1 a b (asmai, asya); vi. 54, 4 a (asmai); vii. 63, 5 a (asmai); viii. 29, 6 (yathā).

Maruts, description of, pp. 21–2.

Metre, irregular, i. 35, 9 d; iii. 59, 2 d. 7 c. 8 c; iv. 12, 4 c; 35, 11 b; 50, 2 c; viii. 29, 5; x. 90, 2 b. 4 a; mentioned in the RV., p. 175.

Anuṣṭubh: v. 83, 9; vii. 103, 1; x. 14, 13. 14. 16; 90, 1–15; 135, 1–7; Pāda redundant by one syllable, x. 90, 4 a; 135, 7 c.

Gāyatrī: i. 1, 1–9; iii. 59, 6–9; vi. 54, 1–10; x. 127, 1–8.

Jagatī: i. 35, 1–4. 6–11; 160, 1–5; iv. 50, 10; v. 11, 1–6; 83, 2–4; viii. 48, 5; x. 15, 11; 34, 7; Pāda in Triṣṭubh stanza, i. 35, 3 a; v. 83, 10 c; vii. 103, 8; x. 14, 1 a. 10 b. 11 b; 34, 5 c; 129, 3 b; Pāda with Triṣṭubh cadence, i. 35, 9 d; stanzas in Triṣṭubh hymn, iv. 50, 10; v. 83, 2–4.

Triṣṭubh, i. 35, 1–11; 85, 5. 12; 154, 1–6; ii. 12, 1–15; 33, 1–15; 35, 1–15; iii. 59, 1–5; iv. 50, 1–9. 11; 51, 1–11; v. 83, 1. 5–8. 10; vii. 49, 1–4; 61, 1–7; 63, 1–6; 71, 1–6; 86, 1–8; 103, 2–10; viii. 48, 1–4. 6–15; x. 14, 1–12; 15, 1–10. 12–14; 34, 1–6. 8–14; 90, 16; 129, 1–7; 168, 1–4; Pāda in Jagatī stanza, viii. 48, 5 c; Pāda defective by one syllable, x. 14, 5 c. 8 d, by two syllables, x. 129, 7 b, redundant by one syllable, x. 129, 6 b.

Dvipadā (Jagatī + Gāyatrī Pāda), viii. 29, 1–10.

Br̥hatī, x. 14, 15.

Metronymic, irregular, ii. 12, 11 (Dānu).

Middle in passive sense, i. 35, 10 d; 154, 2 a; 160, 4 d. 5 a; ii. 33, 5. 11 c; vii. 61, 5 b.

Mithra in the Avesta, p. 119.

Mitra, description of, pp. 78–9.

Mitra-Varuṇa, description of, pp. 118–19; viii. 29, 9.

Naighaṇṭuka, ii. 12, 14. 15; 35, 9.

Nasalization of a final vowel at the end of an internal Pāda, i. 35, 6 a (upásthām̐ ékā); viii. 29, 6 (yathām̐ eṣá); x. 34, 5 c (ákratam̐ émíd).

Natural philosophy, starting point of, p. 207 (x. 129).

Nirukta, ii. 12, 3. 14.

Nominative for vocative, iv. 50, 10 a.

Numerals, syntax of, ii. 33, 2; x. 15, 10 c.

Objective genitive, x. 34, 3 d. 7 d.

Pada text, its treatment of the pcl. u, vi. 54, 2; of vocatives in o, ii. 33, 3 b (vajrabāho). 15 a (babhro); viii. 48, 2 c. 15 c (indo); of Pragr̥hya vowels, i. 35, 9 b (e, ī); i. 160, 1 b (ī); iv. 50, 10 b (ū); x. 168, 1 d (utó); of final etymological r, i. 35, 11 a (Savitar íti); ii. 12, 4 b (ákar íti); vii. 86, 2 b (antáḥ); viii. 48, 2 a (antár íti); of internal s before k, vii. 103, 4 c (kániṣkan); of suffixes: i. 1, 1 c; 160, 2 c; iii. 59, 6 c (-tama); viii. 48, 1 b (-tara); vii. 103, 6 d; x. 15, 9 a (-trā); vii. 103, 8 c (gd. -tyā); ii. 35, 4 c; iv. 51, 9 c d (-bhis); iv. 50, 7 d (den. -ya); x. 15, 6 a; 129, 4 d (gd. -yā); of certain long Saṃhitā vowels: i. 35, 8 b (cyāvaya); 85, 4 b (pracyāváyantas). 10 b (dādr̥hāṇám); x. 135, 7 (sádanam); i. 160, 1 b (r̥tāvarī); ii. 12, 4 (jigīvā́n); iii. 59, 6 a (carṣaṇīdhŕ̥tas); vii. 63, 2 a (prasavītā́); x. 15, 9 a (tātr̥ṣur); x. 34, 10 (r̥ṇāvā); its restoration of lost aspirate, i. 160, 3 d (dukṣata); its removal of Sandhi in cds., i. 154, 2 (giri-ṣṭhā́s); x. 15, 11 b (supraṇītayas); its treatment of dual compounds, i. 35, 1 b (mitrā́váruṇau); 160, 1 a (dyā́vā-pr̥thivī́); x. 14, 3 b

between Pādas, resolved : a a, ii. 33, 7 c. 10 a ; iii. 59, 4 c ; v. 83, 10 a ; viii. 29, 1 a. 3 a ; x. 14, 4 a ; 15, 4 c ; 34, 11 a ; 90, 13 c ; 129, 6 c ; a ā, i. 35, 2 c ; ii. 33, 6 c ; a i, x. 14, 8 a ; 15, 6 a ; a u, i. 35, 5 c ; a ṛ, vii. 103, 9 a ; ā a, i. 85, 11 a ; 160, 4 c ; v. 11, 4 a ; viii. 29, 1 a ; x. 90, 1 c. 3 a ; ā ā, i. 85, 7 a ; ā ṛ, i. 160, 1 a ; ā u, iv. 51, 2 c ; Pāda initial a restored : e a, i. 1, 9 b ; 85, 9 d ; iv. 50, 10 b ; x. 14, 5 c ; 129, 3 b ; 168, 2 d ; o a, i. 35, 11 b ; ii. 35, 13 d ; iii. 59, 6 b ; iv. 50, 10 d ; v. 11, 4 d ; vii. 86, 4 d. 5 b ; 103, 3 d ; viii. 29, 2 b ; 48, 12 b. 13 b ; x. 14, 9 b ; 15, 8 b. 12 b ; 34, 10 d.

2. of semivowels : at the end of a Pāda resolved before vowels : y a, i. 154, 4 a ; v. 83, 6 c ; vii. 86, 7 a ; viii. 48, 2 a ; y u, x. 14, 13 c ; 15, 8 c. 11 c ; v a, i. 154, 2 c ; iv. 51, 3 c ; x. 15, 5 c ; v e, x. 14, 4 c ; v ṛ, vii. 61, 3 c.

3. of consonants : r before r, i. 35, 11 c ; ii. 33, 2 a. 14 a ; 35, 4 c ; v. 83, 1 c ; Visarjanīya before k, i. 85, 6 c ; ii. 35, 1 d : s before k, i. 85, 6 c ; ii. 35, 1 d ; v. 83, 2 d ; vii. 103, 4 c ; s before p, v. 11, 6 d ; x. 135, 4 b ; t before ś, i. 85, 3 ; n before t, vi. 54, 9 a (Pū́ṣan táva) ; x. 90, 8 c (paśū́n t-) ; n before c, x. 90, 8 c (tā́ṃś cakre) ; n before ś, i. 35, 5 ; ii. 12, 10 b ; iv. 51, 2 d. 7 d ; v. 11, 6 b ; ān before y, i. 35, 10 b ; before l, ii. 12, 4 c ; ān before vowels becomes ām̐, ii. 33, 4 &c., irregularly remains, x. 90, 3 a (etā́vān asya) ; ān at the end of a Pāda before vowels remains, i. 35, 10 c ; ii. 12, 10 a. 12 a ; x. 90, 8 c ; before t at the end of a Pāda remains, ii. 33, 6 a.

Savitṛ, description of, pp. 10–11.

Sāyaṇa, i. 154, 2. 3. 6 ; 160, 3. 4 ; ii. 12, 1. 3. 8. 12. 14 ; 33, 5. 6. 8. 9. 10. 12 ; 35, 9 ; iii. 59, 1 ; iv. 51, 1. 3. 8 ; v. 83, 6 ; vi. 54, 3 ; vii. 86, 1 ; viii. 29, 10 ; x. 14, 8 ; x. 15, 3. 12.

Secondary root, i. 160, 5 d (inv.).

'Self' expressed by tmán in RV., vii. 63, 6 b ; by tanū́, vii. 86, 2 a. 5 b.

Separation of members of Devatādvandvas, ii. 12, 13.

Shortening, of e and o before a : i. 35, 5 a. 11 c ; 85, 3 a 6 d ; 154, 1 c ; 160, 3 d. 5 d ; ii. 12, 3 c. 7 d. 8 b. 9 d. 11 c ; 33, 5 c. 11 d ; 35, 8 a ; iii. 59, 2 a ; iv. 50, 1 a ; 51, 2 b. 3 c. 4 b ; vi. 54, 1 b. 3 b c. 4 a ; vii. 63, 4 b. 6 a ; 86, 6 b. 7 c. 8 c ; 103, 3 d. 4 a ; viii. 48, 8 d. 11 c. 12 d ; x. 14, 3 a ; 15, 1 d. 2 a. 5 d. 12 c. 14 a ; 34, 6 c. 11 c–d ; 90, 5 b c. 6 c ; 127, 4 a. 5 a ; 129, 6 a. 7 c d ; 135, 6 b ; of ā before ṛ, i. 160, 1 a ; of ī before a, x. 34, 4 b ; 127, 1 b, before u, 2 b, before ā, 3 b ; of radical vowel, ii. 35, 3 c ; iv. 50, 5 d ; of dual ā, vii. 61, 1 a (Varuṇa). 7 a (deva) ; of inst. ī, viii. 48, 8 a (svastí).

Slurred pronunciation of long vowel, i. 154, 3 a (śū́ṣám). 1 d (trédhā́) ; vii. 63, 6 a (nū́).

Singing, characteristic of the Aṅgirases, viii. 29, 10.

Singular, for plur. noun, i. 85, 10 c (vāṇám) ; ii. 33, 1 (árvati) ; change from — to plur., iv. 51, 11 c.

Six earths, p. 175.

Sociative sense of inst., x. 14, 3 a b. 5 a b. 10 d ; 15, 8 c. 10 c d. 14 c ; 34, 5 a.

Soma, description of, pp. 152–5 ; viii. 29, 1.

Soma sacrifice, vii. 103, 7. 10 d.

Stanzas syntactically connected, i. 1, 7. 8 ; 85, 4. 5.

Steed, ruddy — of heaven, i. 85, 5 c ; of the Sun, vii. 63, 2 d.

Steeds of the Maruts, i. 85, 4 d.

Strong form for weak, i. 85, 12 c (yanta) ; ii. 33, 1 b (yuyothās). 3 d (yuyodhi) ; iii. 59, 1 d (juhota) ; vii. 71, 1 d (yuyotam) ; x. 14, 14 b (juhota). 15 b (juhotana) ; 15, 7 d (dadhāta). 11 d (dadhātana).

Subjunctive and injunctive, when identical in form, distinguished by mā́, ii. 33, 4 a.

Suffixes treated like second member of a cd., i. 160, 1 b (ṛtā́varī). 3 a (pavítravān), &c.

Supplied, word to be, iii. 59, 7 c ; v. 11, 1 c ; vi. 54, 7 c ; vii. 61, 5 a. 7 d ; viii. 29, 5 a ; x. 14, 2 d. 5 c ; 15, 13 a ; 34, 10 b ; 127, 4 a c ; 168, 1 a. 4 c.

Sūrya, description of, p. 124.

Sūtras, viii. 29, 3.

Svarabhakti vowel, ii. 33, 1–3. 5–7. 9–11 (Rudᵃra) ; iv. 50, 11 a (Indᵃra) ; v. 11, 3 a (mātᵃrós).

Svarita, independent, ii. 33, 3 (abhìti) ;